The Pentateuch

The Pentateuch

FORTRESS COMMENTARY ON THE BIBLE STUDY EDITION

Gale A. Yee
Hugh R. Page Jr.
Matthew J. M. Coomber
Editors

Fortress Press
Minneapolis

THE PENTATEUCH
Fortress Commentary on the Bible Study Edition

Excerpted from the *Fortress Commentary on the Bible: The Old Testament and Apocrypha*
(Minneapolis: Fortress Press, 2014); Gale A. Yee, Hugh R. Page Jr., and Matthew J. M. Coomber, volume editors.

Fortress Press Publication Staff:
Neil Elliott and Scott Tunseth, Project Editors
Marissa Wold, Production Manager
Laurie Ingram, Cover Design.

Copyeditor: Jeffrey A. Reimer

Typesetter: PerfecType, Nashville, TN

Proofreader: David Cottingham

Library of Congress Cataloging-in-Publication data is available

ISBN: 978-1-5064-1442-3

eISBN: 978-1-5064-1443-0

The paper used in this publication meets the minimum requirements of American National Standard for Information Sciences—Permanence of Paper for Printed Library Materials, ANSI Z329, 48-1984. Manufactured in the U.S.A.

CONTENTS

PUBLISHER'S NOTE

About the Fortress Commentary on the Bible Study Editions

In 2014 Fortress Press released the two-volume *Fortress Commentary on the Bible.* See the Series Introduction (pp. 1–3) for a look inside the creation and design of the Old Testament/Apocrypha and New Testament volumes. While each comprehensive commentary volume can easily be used in classroom settings, we also recognized that dividing the larger commentaries into smaller volumes featuring key sections of Scripture may be especially helpful for use in corresponding biblical studies courses. To help facilitate such classroom use, we have broken the two-volume commentary into eight study editions.

Please note that in this study edition the page numbers match the page numbers of the larger Fortress Commentary on the Bible volume in which it first appeared. We have intentionally retained the same page numbering to facilitate use of the study editions and larger volumes side by side.

The Pentateuch was first published in Fortress Commentary on the Bible: The Old Testament and Apocrypha.

ABBREVIATIONS

General

AT	Alpha Text (of the Greek text of Esther)
BOI	Book of Isaiah
Chr	Chronicler
DH	Deuteronomistic History
DI	Deutero-Isaiah
Dtr	Deuteronomist
Gk.	Greek
H	Holiness Code
Heb.	Hebrew
JPS	Jewish Publication Society
LXX	The Septuagint
LXX B	Vaticanus Text of the Septuagint
MP	Mode of production
MT	Masoretic Text
NIV	New International Version
NRSV	New Revised Standard Version
OAN	Oracles against Nations (in Jeremiah)
P.	papyrus/papyri
P	Priestly source
PE	Pastoral Epistles
RSV	Revised Standard Version
TI	Trito-Isaiah

Books of the Bible (NT, OT, Apocrypha)

Old Testament/Hebrew Bible

Gen.	Genesis
Exod.	Exodus
Lev.	Leviticus
Num.	Numbers
Deut.	Deuteronomy

Josh.	Joshua
Judg.	Judges
Ruth	Ruth
1 Sam.	1 Samuel
2 Sam.	2 Samuel
1 Kgs.	1 Kings
2 Kgs.	2 Kings
1 Chron.	1 Chronicles
2 Chron.	2 Chronicles
Ezra	Ezra
Neh.	Nehemiah
Esther	Esther
Job	Job
Ps. (Pss.)	Psalms
Prov.	Proverbs
Eccles.	Ecclesiastes
Song.	Song of Songs
Isa.	Isaiah
Jer.	Jeremiah
Lam.	Lamentations
Ezek.	Ezekiel
Dan.	Daniel
Hosea	Hosea
Joel	Joel
Amos	Amos
Obad.	Obadiah
Jon.	Jonah
Mic.	Micah
Nah.	Nahum
Hab.	Habakkuk
Zeph.	Zephaniah
Hag.	Haggai
Zech.	Zechariah
Mal.	Malachi

Apocrypha

Tob.	Tobit
Jth.	Judith
Gk. Esther	Greek Additions to Esther
Sir.	Sirach (Ecclesiasticus)

Bar.	Baruch
Let. Jer.	Letter of Jeremiah
Add Dan.	Additions to Daniel
Pr. Azar.	Prayer of Azariah
Sg. Three.	Song of the Three Young Men (or Three Jews)
Sus.	Susanna
Bel	Bel and the Dragon
1 Macc.	1 Maccabees
2 Macc.	2 Maccabees
1 Esd.	1 Esdras
Pr. of Man.	Prayer of Manasseh
2 Esd.	2 Esdras
Wis.	Wisdom of Solomon
3 Macc.	3 Maccabees
4 Macc.	4 Maccabees

New Testament

Matt.	Matthew
Mark	Mark
Luke	Luke
John	John
Acts	Acts of the Apostles
Rom.	Romans
1 Cor.	1 Corinthians
2 Cor.	2 Corinthians
Gal.	Galatians
Eph.	Ephesians
Phil.	Philippians
Col.	Colossians
1 Thess.	1 Thessalonians
2 Thess.	2 Thessalonians
1 Tim.	1 Timothy
2 Tim.	2 Timothy
Titus	Titus
Philem.	Philemon
Heb.	Hebrews
James	James
1 Pet.	1 Peter
2 Pet.	2 Peter
1 John	1 John

2 John	2 John
3 John	3 John
Jude	Jude
Rev.	Revelation (Apocalypse)

Journals, Series, Reference Works

ABD	*Anchor Bible Dictionary*. Edited by David Noel Freedman. 6 vols. New York: Doubleday, 1992.
ACNT	Augsburg Commentaries on the New Testament
AJA	*American Journal of Archaeology*
AJT	*Asia Journal of Theology*
ANET	*Ancient Near Eastern Texts Relating to the Old Testament.* Edited by J. B. Pritchard. 3rd ed. Princeton: Princeton University Press, 1969.
ANF	*The Ante-Nicene Fathers.* Edited by Alexander Roberts and James Donaldson. 1885–1887. 10 vols. Repr., Peabody, MA: Hendrickson, 1994.
ANRW	*Aufstieg und Niedergang der römischen Welt: Geschichte und Kultur Roms im Spiegel der neueren Forschung*. Edited by Hildegard Temporini and Wolfgang Haase. Berlin: de Gruyter, 1972–.
ANTC	Abingdon New Testament Commentaries
AOAT	Alter Orient und Altes Testament
AbOTC	Abingdon Old Testament Commentary
AOTC	Apollos Old Testament Commentary
A(Y)B	Anchor (Yale) Bible
BA	*Biblical Archaeologist*
BAR	*Biblical Archaeology Review*
BDAG	Bauer, W., F. W. Danker, W. F. Arndt, and F. W. Gingrich. *Greek-English Lexicon of the New Testament and Other Early Christian Literature.* 3rd ed. Chicago: University of Chicago Press, 1999.
BEATAJ	Beiträge zur Erforschung des Alten Testaments und des Antiken Judentum
Bib	*Biblica*
BibInt	*Biblical Interpretation*
BJRL	*Bulletin of the John Rylands University Library of Manchester*
BJS	Brown Judaic Studies
BNTC	Black's New Testament Commentaries
BR	*Biblical Research*
BRev	*Bible Review*
BSac	*Bibliotheca sacra*
BTB	*Biblical Theology Bulletin*
BZAW	Beihefte zur Zeitschrift für die alttestamentliche Wissenschaft
CAT	Commentaire de l'Ancien Testament

CBC	Cambridge Bible Commentary
CBQMS	Catholic Biblical Quarterly Monograph Series
CC	Continental Commentaries
CH	*Church History*
CHJ	*Cambridge History of Judaism*. Edited by W. D. Davies and Louis Finkelstein. Cambridge: Cambridge University Press, 1984–.
ConBNT	Coniectanea biblica: New Testament Series
ConBOT	Coniectanea biblica: Old Testament Series
CS	Cistercian Studies
CTAED	*Canaanite Toponyms in Ancient Egyptian Documents*. S. Ahituv. Jerusalem: Magnes, 1984.
CTQ	*Concordia Theological Quarterly*
CurTM	*Currents in Theology and Mission*
ExpTim	*Expository Times*
ETL	*Ephemerides Theologicae Lovanienses*
ExAud	*Ex auditu*
FAT	Forschungen zum Alten Testament
FC	Fathers of the Church
FRLANT	Forschungen zur Religion und Literatur des Alten und Neuen Testaments
HAT	Handbuch zum Alten Testament
HBT	*Horizons in Biblical Theology*
HNTC	Harper's New Testament Commentaries
HR	*History of Religions*
HSM	Harvard Semitic Monographs
HTKAT	Herders Theologischer Kommentar zum Alten Testament
HTR	*Harvard Theological Review*
HTS	Harvard Theological Studies
HUCA	*Hebrew Union College Annual*
HUCM	Monographs of the Hebrew Union College
HUT	Hermeneutische Untersuchungen zur Theologie
IBC	Interpretation: A Bible Commentary for Teaching and Preaching
ICC	International Critical Commentary
Int	*Interpretation*
JAAR	*Journal of the American Academy of Religion*
JAOS	*Journal of the American Oriental Society*
JBL	*Journal of Biblical Literature*
JBQ	*Jewish Bible Quarterly*
JECS	*Journal of Early Christian Studies*
JJS	*Journal of Jewish Studies*
JNES	*Journal of Near Eastern Studies*

JNSL	*Journal of Northwest Semitic Languages*
JQR	*Jewish Quarterly Review*
JRS	*Journal of Roman Studies*
JSem	*Journal of Semitics*
JSJ	*Journal for the Study of Judaism in the Persian, Hellenistic, and Roman Periods*
JSNT	*Journal for the Study of the New Testament*
JSOT	*Journal for the Study of the Old Testament*
JSOTSup	Journal for the Study of the Old Testament Supplement Series
JSQ	*Jewish Studies Quarterly*
JSS	*Journal of Semitic Studies*
JTI	*Journal of Theological Interpretation*
JTS	*Journal of Theological Studies*
JTSA	*Journal of Theology for Southern Africa*
KTU	*Die keilalphabetischen Texte aus Ugarit*. Edited by M. Dietrich, O. Loretz, and J. Sanmartín. AOAT 24/1. Neukirchen-Vluyn: Neukirchener, 1976.
LCC	Loeb Classical Library
LEC	Library of Early Christianity
LHB/OTS	Library of the Hebrew Bible/Old Testament Studies
LW	*Luther's Works*. Edited by Jaroslav Pelikan and Helmut T. Lehmann. 55 vols. St. Louis: Concordia; Philadelphia: Fortress Press, 1958–1986.
NAC	New American Commentary
NCB	New Century Bible
NCBC	New Cambridge Bible Commentary
NedTT	*Nederlands theologisch tijdschrift*
Neot	*Neotestamentica*
NICNT	New International Commentary on the New Testament
NICOT	New International Commentary on the Old Testament
NIGTC	New International Greek Testament Commentary
NovT	*Novum Testamentum*
NPNF[1]	*The Nicene and Post-Nicene Fathers*, Series 1. Edited by Philip Schaff. 14 vols. 1886–1889. Repr., Grand Rapids: Eerdmans, 1956.
NTL	New Testament Library
NTS	*New Testament Studies*
OBT	Overtures to Biblical Theology
OTE	*Old Testament Essays*
OTG	Old Testament Guides
OTL	Old Testament Library
OTM	Old Testament Message
PEQ	*Palestine Exploration Quarterly*
PG	Patrologia graeca [= Patrologiae cursus completus: Series graeca]. Edited by J.-P. Migne. 162 vols. Paris, 1857–1886.

PL	John Milton, *Paradise Lost*
PL	Patrologia latina [= Patrologiae cursus completus: Series latina]. Edited by J.-P. Migne. 217 vols. Paris, 1844–1864.
PRSt	*Perspectives in Religious Studies*
QR	*Quarterly Review*
RevExp	*Review and Expositor*
RevQ	*Revue de Qumran*
SBLABS	Society of Biblical Literature Archaeology and Biblical Studies
SBLAIL	Society of Biblical Literature Ancient Israel and Its Literature
SBLDS	Society of Biblical Literature Dissertation Series
SBLEJL	Society of Biblical Literature Early Judaism and Its Literature
SBLMS	Society of Biblical Literature Monograph Series
SBLRBS	Society of Biblical Literature Resources for Biblical Study
SBLSCS	Society of Biblical Literature Septuagint and Cognate Studies
SBLSP	*Society of Biblical Literature Seminar Papers*
SBLSymS	Society of Biblical Literature Symposium Series
SBLWAW	SBL Writings from the Ancient World
SemeiaSt	Semeia Studies
SJT	*Scottish Journal of Theology*
SNTSMS	Society for New Testament Studies Monograph Series
SO	Symbolae osloenses
SR	*Studies in Religion*
ST	*Studia Theologica*
StABH	Studies in American Biblical Hermeneutics
TD	*Theology Digest*
TAD	*Textbook of Aramaic Documents from Ancient Egypt.* Vol. 1: *Letters.* Bezalel Porten and Ada Yardeni. Winona Lake, IN: Eisenbrauns, 1986.
TDOT	*Theological Dictionary of the Old Testament.* 15 vols. Edited by G. Johannes Botterweck, Helmer Ringgren, and Heinz-Josef Fabry. Translated by David E. Green and Douglas W. Stott. Grand Rapids: Eerdmans, 1974–1995.
TJT	*Toronto Journal of Theology*
TNTC	Tyndale New Testament Commentaries
TOTC	Tyndale Old Testament Commentaries
TS	*Theological Studies*
TZ	*Theologische Zeitschrift*
VE	*Vox evangelica*
VT	*Vetus Testamentum*
VTSup	Supplements to Vetus Testamentum
WBC	Word Biblical Commentary
WSA	Works of St. Augustine: A Translation for the Twenty-First Century
WUANT	Wissenschaftliche Untersuchungen zum Alten und Neuen Testament

WUNT Wissenschaftliche Untersuchungen zum Neuen Testament
WW *Word and World*
ZAW *Zeitschrift für die alttestamentliche Wissenschaft*
ZBK Zürcher Bibelkommentare
ZNW *Zeitschrift für die neutestamentliche Wissenschaft und die Kunde der älteren Kirche*

Ancient Authors and Texts

1 Clem. *1 Clement*
2 Clem. *2 Clement*
1 En. *1 Enoch*
2 Bar. *2 Baruch*
Abot R. Nat. *Abot de Rabbi Nathan*
Ambrose
  Paen. *De paenitentia*
Aristotle
  Ath. Pol. *Athēnaīn politeia*
  Nic. Eth. *Nicomachean Ethics*
  Pol. *Politics*
  Rhet. *Rhetoric*
Augustine
  FC 79 *Tractates on the Gospel of John, 11–27.* Translated by John W. Rettig. Fathers of the Church 79. Washington, DC: Catholic University of America Press, 1988.
  Tract. Ev. Jo. *In Evangelium Johannis tractatus*
Bede, Venerable
  CS 117 *Commentary on the Acts of the Apostles.* Translated by Lawrence T. Martin. Cistercian Studies 117. Kalamazoo, MI: Cistercian Publications, 1989.
Barn. *Barnabas*
CD Cairo Genizah copy of the Damascus Document
Cicero
  De or. *De oratore*
  Tusc. *Tusculanae disputationes*
Clement of Alexandria
  Paed. *Paedogogus*
  Strom. *Stromata*
Cyril of Jerusalem
  Cat. Lect. *Catechetical Lectures*
Dio Cassius
  Hist. *Roman History*

Dio Chrysostom
Or. *Orations*
Diog. *Diognetus*
Dionysius of Halicarnassus
Thuc. *De Thucydide*
Epictetus
Diatr. *Diatribai (Dissertationes)*
Ench. *Enchiridion*
Epiphanius
Pan. *Panarion (Adversus Haereses)*
Eusebius of Caesarea
Hist. eccl. *Historia ecclesiastica*
Gos. Thom. *Gospel of Thomas*
Herodotus
Hist. *Historiae*
Hermas, *Shepherd*
Mand. *Mandates*
Sim. *Similitudes*
Homer
Il. *Iliad*
Od. *Odyssey*
Ignatius of Antioch
Eph. *To the Ephesians*
Smyr. *To the Smyrnaeans*
Irenaeus
Adv. haer. *Adversus haereses*
Jerome
Vir. ill. *De viris illustribus*
John Chrysostom
Hom. 1 Cor. *Homiliae in epistulam i ad Corinthios*
Hom. Act. *Homiliae in Acta apostolorum*
Hom. Heb. *Homiliae in epistulam ad Hebraeos*
Josephus
Ant. *Jewish Antiquities*
Ag. Ap. *Against Apion*
J.W. *Jewish War*
Jub. *Jubilees*
Justin Martyr
Dial. *Dialogue with Trypho*
1 Apol. *First Apology*

L.A.E.	*Life of Adam and Eve*
Liv. Pro.	*Lives of the Prophets*
Lucian	
Alex.	*Alexander (Pseudomantis)*
Phal.	*Phalaris*
Mart. Pol.	*Martyrdom of Polycarp*
Novatian	
Trin.	*De trinitate*
Origen	
C. Cels.	*Contra Celsum*
Comm. Jo.	*Commentarii in evangelium Joannis*
De princ.	*De principiis*
Hom. Exod.	*Homiliae in Exodum*
Hom. Jer.	*Homiliae in Jeremiam*
Hom. Josh.	*Homilies on Joshua*
Pausanias	
Descr.	*Description of Greece*
Philo	
Cher.	*De cherubim*
Decal.	*De decalogo*
Dreams	*On Dreams*
Embassy	*On the Embassy to Gaius (= Legat.)*
Fug.	*De fuga et inventione*
Leg.	*Legum allegoriae*
Legat.	*Legatio ad Gaium*
Migr.	*De migratione Abrahami*
Mos.	*De vita Mosis*
Opif.	*De opificio mundi*
Post.	*De posteritate Caini*
Prob.	*Quod omnis probus liber sit*
QE	*Quaestiones et solutiones in Exodum*
QG	*Quaestiones et solutiones in Genesin*
Spec. Laws	*On the Special Laws*
Plato	
Gorg.	*Gorgias*
Plutarch	
Mor.	*Moralia*
Mulier. virt.	*Mulierum virtutes*
Polycarp	
Phil.	*To the Philippians*

Ps.-Clem. Rec.	*Pseudo-Clementine Recognitions*
Pss. Sol.	*Psalms of Solomon*
Pseudo-Philo	
L.A.B.	*Liber antiquitatum biblicarum*
Seneca	
Ben.	*De beneficiis*
Strabo	
Geog.	*Geographica*
Tatian	
Ad gr.	*Oratio ad Graecos*
Tertullian	
Praescr.	*De praescriptione haereticorum*
Prax.	*Adversus Praxean*
Bapt.	*De baptismo*
De an.	*De anima*
Pud.	*De pudicitia*
Virg.	*De virginibus velandis*
Virgil	
Aen.	*Aeneid*
Xenophon	
Oec.	*Oeconomicus*

Mishnah, Talmud, Targum

b. B. Bat.	*Babylonian Talmudic tractate Baba Batra*
b. Ber.	*Babylonian Talmudic tractate Berakhot*
b Erub.	*Babylonian Talmudic tractate Erubim*
b. Ketub.	*Babylonian Talmudic tractate Ketubbot*
b. Mak.	*Babylonian Talmudic tractate Makkot*
b. Meg.	*Babylonian Talmudic tractate Megillah*
b. Ned.	*Babylonian Talmudic tractate Nedarim*
b. Naz.	*Babylonian Talmudic tractate Nazir*
b. Sanh.	*Babylonian Talmudic tractate Sanhedrin*
b. Shab.	*Babylonian Talmudic tractate Shabbat*
b. Sotah	*Babylonian Talmudic tractate Sotah*
b. Ta'an.	*Babylonian Talmudic tractate Ta'anit*
b. Yev.	*Babylonian Talmudic tractate Yevamot*
b. Yoma	*Babylonian Talmudic tractate Yoma*
Eccl. Rab.	*Ecclesiastes Rabbah*
Exod. Rab.	*Exodus Rabbah*
Gen. Rab.	*Genesis Rabbah*

Lam. Rab.	*Lamentations Rabbah*
Lev. R(ab).	*Leviticus Rabbah*
m. Abot	*Mishnah tractate Abot*
m. Bik.	*Mishnah tractate Bikkurim*
m. Demai	*Mishnah tractate Demai*
m. 'Ed.	*Mishnah tractate 'Eduyyot*
m. Git.	*Mishnah tractate Gittin*
m. Pesaḥ	*Mishnah tractate Pesaḥim*
m. Šeqal.	*Mishnah tractate Šeqalim (Shekalim)*
m. Shab.	*Mishnah tractate Shabbat*
m. Sotah	*Mishnah tractate Sotah*
m. Ta'an.	*Mishnah tractate Ta'anit*
m. Tamid	*Mishnah tractate Tamid*
m. Yad.	*Mishnah tractate Yadayim*
m. Yebam.	*Mishnah tractate Yebamot*
m. Yoma	*Mishnah tractate Yoma*
Num. Rab.	*Numbers Rabbah*
Pesiq. Rab.	*Pesiqta Rabbati*
Pesiq. Rab Kah.	*Pesiqta Rab Kahana*
S. 'Olam Rab.	*Seder 'Olam Rabbah*
Song Rab.	*Song of Songs Rabbah*
t. Hul.	*Tosefta tractate Hullin*
Tg. Onq.	*Targum Onqelos*
Tg. Jer.	*Targum Jeremiah*
y. Hag.	*Jerusalem Talmudic tractate Hagiga*
y. Pesaḥ	*Jerusalem Talmudic tractate Pesaḥim*
y. Sanh.	*Jerusalem Talmudic tractate Sanhedrin*

Dead Sea Scrolls

1QapGen	*Genesis apocryphon* (Excavated frags. from cave)
1QM	*War Scroll*
1QpHab	*Pesher Habakkuk*
1QS	*Rule of the Community*
1QSb	*Rule of the Blessings* (Appendix b to 1QS)
1Q21	*T. Levi*, aramaic
4Q184	Wiles of the Wicked Woman
4Q214	Levi^{d} ar (*olim* part of Levi^{b})
4Q214b	Levi^{f} ar (*olim* part of Levi^{b})
4Q226	psJub^{b} (4Q *pseudo-Jubilees*)
4Q274	Tohorot A

4Q277	Tohorot B[b] (*olim* B[c])
4Q525	*Beatitudes*
4QMMT	*Miqṣat Maʿaśê ha-Torah*
4QpNah/4Q169	4Q Pesher Nahum
4Q82	*The Greek Minor Prophets Scroll*

Old Testament Pseudepigrapha

1 En.	*1 Enoch*
2 En.	*2 Enoch*
Odes Sol.	*Odes of Solomon*
Syr. Men.	*Sentences of the Syriac Menander*
T. Levi	*Testament of Levi*
T. Mos.	*Testament of Moses*
T. Sim.	*Testament of Simeon*

INTRODUCTION

The *Fortress Commentary on the Bible*, presented in two volumes, seeks to invite study and conversation about an ancient text that is both complex and compelling. As biblical scholars, we wish students of the Bible to gain a respect for the antiquity and cultural remoteness of the biblical texts and to grapple for themselves with the variety of their possible meanings; to fathom a long history of interpretation in which the Bible has been wielded for causes both beneficial and harmful; and to develop their own skills and voices as responsible interpreters, aware of their own social locations in relationships of privilege and power. With this in mind, the *Fortress Commentary on the Bible* offers general readers an informed and accessible resource for understanding the biblical writings in their ancient contexts; for recognizing how the texts have come down to us through the mediation of different interpretive traditions; and for engaging current discussion of the Bible's sometimes perplexing, sometimes ambivalent, but always influential legacy in the contemporary world. The commentary is designed not only to inform but also to invite and empower readers as active interpreters of the Bible in their own right.

The editors and contributors to these volumes are scholars and teachers who are committed to helping students engage the Bible in the classroom. Many also work as leaders, both lay and ordained, in religious communities, and wish this commentary to prove useful for informing congregational life in clear, meaningful, and respectful ways. We also understand the work of biblical interpretation as a responsibility far wider than the bounds of any religious community. In this regard, we participate in many and diverse identities and social locations, yet we all are conscious of reading, studying, and hearing the Bible today as citizens of a complex and interconnected world. We recognize in the Bible one of the most important legacies of human culture; its historical and literary interpretation is of profound interest to religious and nonreligious peoples alike.

Often, the academic interpretation of the Bible has moved from close study of the remote ancient world to the rarefied controversy of scholarly debate, with only occasional attention to the ways biblical texts are actually heard and lived out in the world around us. The commentary seeks to provide students with diverse materials on the ways in which these texts have been interpreted through the course of history, as well as helping students understand the texts' relevance for today's globalized world. It recognizes the complexities that are involved with being an engaged reader of the Bible, providing a powerful tool for exploring the Bible's multilayered meanings in both their ancient and modern contexts. The commentary seeks to address contemporary issues that are raised by biblical passages. It aspires to be keenly aware of how the contemporary world and its issues and perspectives influence the interpretation of the Bible. Many of the most important insights of contemporary biblical scholarship not only have come from expertise in the world of antiquity but have also been forged in modern struggles for dignity, for equality, for sheer survival, and out of respect for those who have died without seeing justice done. Gaining familiarity with the original contexts in which the biblical writings were produced is essential, but not sufficient, for encouraging competent and discerning interpretation of the Bible's themes today.

Inside the Commentary

Both volumes of *The Fortress Commentary on the Bible* are organized in a similar way. In the beginning of each volume, **Topical Articles** set the stage on which interpretation takes place, naming the issues and concerns that have shaped historical and theological scholarship down to the present. Articles in the *Fortress Commentary on the Old Testament* attend, for example, to the issues that arise when two different religious communities claim the same body of writings as their Scripture, though interpreting those writings quite differently. Articles in the *Fortress Commentary on the New Testament* address the consequences of Christianity's historic claim to appropriate Jewish Scripture and to supplement it with a second collection of writings, the experience of rootlessness and diaspora, and the legacy of apocalypticism. Articles in both volumes reflect on the historical intertwining of Christianity with imperial and colonial power and with indexes of racial and socioeconomic privilege.

Section Introductions in the Old Testament volume provide background to the writings included in the Torah, Historical Writings, Wisdom, Prophetic Writings, and a general introduction to the Apocrypha. The New Testament volume includes articles introducing the Gospels, Acts, the letters associated with Paul, and Hebrews, the General Epistles and Revelation. These articles will address the literary and historical matters, as well as theological themes, that the books in these collections hold in common.

Commentary Entries present accessible and judicious discussion of each biblical book, beginning with an introduction to current thinking regarding the writing's original context and its significance in different reading communities down to the present day. A three-level commentary then follows for each sense division of the book. In some cases, these follow the chapter divisions of a biblical book, but more often, contributors have discerned other outlines, depending on matters of genre, movement, or argument.

The three levels of commentary are the most distinctive organizational feature of these volumes. The first level, "The Text in Its Ancient Context," addresses relevant lexical, exegetical, and literary aspects of the text, along with cultural and archaeological information that may provide additional insight into the historical context. This level of the commentary describes consensus views where these exist in current scholarship and introduces issues of debate clearly and fairly. Our intent here is to convey some sense of the historical and cultural distance between the text's original context and the contemporary reader.

The second level, "The Text in the Interpretive Tradition," discusses themes including Jewish and Christian tradition as well as other religious, literary, and artistic traditions where the biblical texts have attracted interest. This level is shaped by our conviction that we do not apprehend these texts immediately or innocently; rather, even the plain meaning we may regard as self-evident may have been shaped by centuries of appropriation and argument to which we are heirs.

The third level, "The Text in Contemporary Discussion," follows the history of interpretation into the present, drawing brief attention to a range of issues. Our aim here is not to deliver a single answer—"what the text means"—to the contemporary reader, but to highlight unique challenges and interpretive questions. We pay special attention to occasions of dissonance: aspects of the text or of its interpretation that have become questionable, injurious, or even intolerable to some readers today. Our goal is not to provoke a referendum on the value of the text but to stimulate reflection and discussion and, in this way, to empower the reader to reach his or her own judgments about the text.

The approach of this commentary articulates a particular understanding of the work of responsible biblical interpretation. We seek through this commentary to promote intelligent and mature engagement with the Bible, in religious communities and in academic classrooms alike, among pastors, theologians, and ethicists, but also and especially among nonspecialists. Our work together has given us a new appreciation for the vocation of the biblical scholar, as custodians of a treasure of accumulated wisdom from our predecessors; as stewards at a table to which an ever-expanding circle is invited; as neighbors and fellow citizens called to common cause, regardless of our different professions of faith. If the result of our work here is increased curiosity about the Bible, new questions about its import, and new occasions for mutual understanding among its readers, our work will be a success.

Fortress Commentary on the Old Testament

Gale A. Yee
Episcopal Divinity School

Hugh R. Page Jr.
University of Notre Dame

Matthew J. M. Coomber
St. Ambrose University

Fortress Commentary on the New Testament

Margaret Aymer
Interdenominational Theological Center

Cynthia Briggs Kittredge
Seminary of the Southwest

David A. Sánchez
Loyola Marymount University

Reading the Old Testament in Ancient and Contemporary Contexts

Matthew J. M. Coomber

As students file into their desks on the first day of my "Introduction to the Old Testament" course, they are greeted with a PowerPoint slide that simply states, in bold red letters, "Caution: Dangerous Texts Ahead!" The students often respond with the mixture of chuckles and uneasy looks that I intend to provoke. To some extent, the slide is offered tongue in cheek, but not entirely. As with any wry statement, the cautionary slide holds an element of truth. The Old Testament contains powerful teachings and radical ideas that have moved the hearts and minds of both adherents and skeptics for millennia.

While the texts of the Old Testament have had a profound effect on societies and cultures for a long span of time, their texts often take a back seat to the Gospels and the Pauline Letters in popular Christian religion. Even though they constitute well over half of the content of Christian Bibles, very few of my students claim to have read much—if any—of the Old Testament or Apocrypha, despite the fact that I teach at a Roman Catholic university in which the vast majority of the students are Christian. In fact, only a handful of my students claim to have been exposed to the stories of the Old Testament outside of either Sunday school or in episodes of the popular cartoon series *Veggie Tales*. Due to this lack of exposure to the Old Testament, I feel compelled to give them fair warning about what they have gotten themselves into by signing up for what may seem like an innocuous required course. I take it as a professional responsibility to alert them to the fact that a keen examination of the ancient Near Eastern library that sits on their desks has the power to change their lives and forever alter the ways in which they experience the world.

Any collection of books containing calls to wage wars of conquest, to resist the temptation to fight while under threat, thoughts on God's role in governance, and meditations on what it means to live *the good life* has the potential to change lives and even inspire revolutions. To assume that the Bible is harmless is both foolish and irresponsible. After all, the Old Testament's contents have been used by some to support slavery and genocide while inspiring others to engage in such dangerous pursuits as enduring imprisonment, torture, and death in attempts to liberate the oppressed. And just as with using any powerful instrument, be it a car or a surgical blade, reading the Old Testament demands care, responsibility, and substantial consideration from those who put it to use.

Books that promote powerful ideas are complex tools that often belong to the readers as much as—if not more than—their authors. The level of consideration required to read, interpret, and actualize such books is magnified when approaching ancient texts such as those found in the Old Testament. These biblical books bridge multiple theological, cultural, and linguistic worlds, which demand multiple levels of understanding and interpretation. Readers must inhabit three worlds (contexts) when reading any of the books of the Old Testament or Apocrypha, from Genesis to 4 Maccabees: (1) the ancient contexts in which they were written, (2) the modern contexts into which the text is being received, and (3) all of those contexts in between wherein interpreters in each generation have shaped the reading of the texts for their own time and place. *The Fortress Commentary on the Bible: The Old Testament and Apocrypha* approaches these ancient texts with due reverence to this complexity. The purpose of this introduction is to explore a few of the many considerations that are required in reading this ancient Near Eastern scriptural library in its ancient and modern contexts.

A Few Considerations on Receiving Ancient Texts with Modern Minds

The word *context*, whether pertaining to events or a book, looks deceptively singular. A student trying to uncover the context of the US civil rights movement will find many contextual viewing points: those of African Americans who rose up against institutionalized oppression, those of segregationists who tried to maintain the status quo, those within the Johnson administration who worked to find a way forward without losing the Democrats' white voters in the South, and the list goes on.

Challenge of Finding an Ancient or Modern Context

The words *ancient context* and *modern context*, when applied to the Old Testament, also need to be considered in the plural. Considering the ancient context, the books of the Old Testament contain the theologies of diverse communities who lived, wrote, argued, and worked to understand their relationship with the divine under a wide variety of circumstances. An attempt to find a single context for the book of Isaiah, for example, is as complex as finding a single sociohistorical setting of the United States, from the colonial period to the present; it cannot be done. The same is true with the modern context. As these religious texts are received in Chicago or Mumbai, on Wall Street or on skid row, they flow into and take on very different meanings and contexts.

Differing Expectations and Intents of Ancient and Modern Histories

Readers in the age of science have certain expectations when reading a history, and these expectations inform how histories—whether written before or after this age—are received. Modern readers want to know, with scientific precision, when, why, and where events happened. Great value is placed on reconstructions of events that are backed up by reliable sources and with as little interpretive bias as possible. A *good* history of the Battle of the Bulge should include not only dates and locations but also eyewitness accounts of allied forces, Wehrmacht and SS divisions, and civilians. Expectations of accuracy and value in objectivity are a service both to the study of the past and to understanding how these events helped to shape the present. However, when dealing with the Old Testament it is easy to project our appreciation for accuracy and disdain for bias onto the ancient texts, which ultimately is not a fair way to approach these ancient texts.

Long before there was even a concept of "Bible," many of the texts of the Old Testament were passed down through oral tradition, only to be written down and finally canonized centuries later; this is evidenced in the repetitive Torah narratives, such as the creation refrain in Gen. 1:1—2:4a and the lyrical hymn of Deborah in Judges 5. To imagine the original texts as printed, bound, copyrighted, and collected works, as we hold them today, is both inaccurate and misleading. Moreover, assuming the intents and expectations of the oral historian to be akin to those of modern historians is misleading, and focusing on accuracy can limit the scope of a passage's message when the intent of the passage rests in the ideas it promotes. Cultures that employ oral tradition do not make dates, places, or accuracy a priority; rather, they are interested in the telling and retelling of a story to develop an understanding or identity that can answer the questions of the times into which they are received. Take the account of King Solomon's wealth in 2 Chron. 9:22-24, for example.

> King Solomon surpassed all the kings of the earth in wealth and wisdom. All the kings of the earth came to pay homage to Solomon and to listen to the wisdom with which God had endowed him. Each brought his tribute—silver and gold objects, robes, weapons, and spices, horses and mules—in the amount due each year (JPS).

Such an account served a purpose to the ancient author and his audience, but the account was certainly not accurate. Putting aside the issue of transoceanic travel for contemporary rulers in the Americas or the South Pacific, Israel held no such wealth in the tenth century BCE, and such superpowers as Egypt and Assyria would never have been compelled to offer tribute. While questions surrounding the reality of Solomon's wealth are not a center of contentious debate in the public sphere, questions pertaining to the creation of the universe are highly controversial; the front lines of this debate can be seen at the doors of the Creation Museum in Petersburg, Kentucky.

Founded by Ken Ham and Answers in Genesis (AiG), a Christian apologetics organization, the Creation Museum is a prime example of how scientific-age expectations are frequently placed on the ancient texts of the Old Testament. With the motto "Prepare to Believe," the museum promotes Gen. 1:1—2:4a as a scientific explanation for the creation of the cosmos, an event that is said to have occurred around 4,000 BCE, as determined through James Ussher's seventeenth-century-CE biblically based calculations. It is important to consider that the questions the Creation Museum seeks to answer do not likely match the agenda of the authors of Gen. 1:1—2:4a, which is connected to the Babylonian myth the *Enuma Elish* and/or the battle between the Canaanite god Baal and Yam, each of which centers on order's conquest of chaos. It also does not take into consideration that those who canonized the Torah followed this story with another creation story (Gen. 2:4b-25), which is juxtaposed with the first, making it unlikely that the ancient intent was to give a *scientific* account of our origins. Furthermore, the authors of the texts believed that the sky was a firmament that held back a great sky-ocean (Gen. 1:6-8), from which precipitation came when its doors were opened, and that the moon was self-illuminating (Gen. 1:14-18). A key danger in treating Old Testament books with modern historical and scientific expectations is not only receiving inaccurate messages about our past but also failing to realize the intent of the authors and the depth of meaning behind the messages they conveyed.

Projecting Modern Contexts onto the Ancient Past

The oft-repeated notion that only the winners write history is not entirely true, for readers rewrite the histories they receive by projecting their own personal and cultural perspectives onto them. The medievalist Norman Cantor stresses how individuals tend to project their own worldviews and experiences onto the past, thereby reinventing the past in their own image (156–58). Whereas Cantor dealt with issues of secular history, biblical history appears to follow suit, as found in such art pieces as Dutch painter Gerard van Honthorst's piece *King David Playing the Harp*. In the painting van Honthorst depicts the king with European-style attire and instrument. In contextually ambiguous passages, such as the land seizures in Mic. 2:1-4, we find scholars filling in the blanks with characters that make more sense in our time than in the ancient past, such as the mafia (Alfaro, 25). It is difficult for a reader not to project his or her own time and culture onto the text, for that is the reader's primary reference point; to escape doing so is likely not possible. But just as complete objectivity is not attainable, an awareness of its hazards can help readers exercise some degree of control regarding how much they project their present onto the past.

Bringing One's Ideology to the Text

Just as readers bring their notions of history to the Old Testament, so also they bring their ideologies. While attempts to view Old Testament texts through the biblical authors' eyes may be made, one's perceptions can never be entirely freed from one's own experiences, which help shape how a particular idea or story is read. This challenge is a double-edged sword. On one side of the sword, the ideology and experiences of the reader may cloud the text's original meaning and intent, causing unintended—and sometimes intentional—misreadings of a passage. When this occurs, the resulting interpretation often tells us more about the social or ideological location of the reader than the biblical characters who are being interpreted. Albert Schweitzer found that nineteenth-century biographies on the life of the "historical Jesus" turned out to be autobiographies of their authors; romantics uncovered an idealist Jesus, political radicals found a revolutionary, and so on (Schweitzer). On the other side of the sword, one finds an advantage shared by oral tradition. Reading a text through one's own experiences can breathe new life into the text and allow it to speak to current circumstances, as found in postcolonial, feminist, and queer interpretations. Since readers cannot fully remove themselves from their own ideological locations, it is important to acknowledge that a reader's ideas and biases are brought to the text and that much is to be learned by considering various interpretations.

Because ideology plays a role in interpretation, it should be noted that history—and biblical histories, in particular—do not exist in the past, but are very much alive and active in the present. YHWH's granting of land to Abraham's dependents, for example, plays a prominent role in the Israel-Palestine conflict. This is addressed by Keith Whitelam and James Crossley, who find the biblical text shaping modern perceptions of land via cartography. A post-1967 war edition of *The Macmillan Bible Atlas* contains a map of Israel with borders that look remarkably similar to the modern-day border with Gaza—despite great uncertainty surrounding ancient Israel's borders—and that is inscribed with Gen. 13:14-15: "The Lord said to Abram . . . 'Lift up your eyes, and look from the place where you are, northward and southward and eastward and westward; for all the land which you see I will give to you and to your descendants forever'" (RSV; see Whitelam 61–62; Crossley 176). Whether one sees this connection in a positive or negative light, clear political implications of the biblical past can be seen.

Differing Views on the Old Testament's History

Another factor to be considered, which is also highly political, is the lack of consensus pertaining to the historicity of biblical narratives and the state of ancient Israel, ranging from the exodus narrative to the Davidic monarchy. The degree to which these events and histories are *real histories* or *cultural memory* has been the subject of much debate and polemic within the academy. Many scholars agree that the story of the Hebrew exodus out of Egypt is cultural memory, with varying degrees of historical truth, ranging from seeing the Hebrews as an invading force to an indigenous movement within Canaan that rose up against exploitative rulers. But one of the most heated debates in the history of ancient Israel has revolved around the dating of the monarchy and the rise of Judah as a powerful state.

The traditional view, often referred to as the *maximalist* perspective, gives greater credence to the Bible's account of the monarchy's history. Scholars of this persuasion accept, to varying degrees, the Old Testament's stories of the rise of Israel beginning with King Saul and continuing on through the destruction of Israel and Judah. So-called *minimalists* give less credence to biblical accounts, relying more on archaeological and extrabiblical sources to develop their views of the monarchy and the presence of a powerful state, for which they find little evidence. While largely unnoticed outside the academy, the debate has caused great animosity within. Maximalist scholars have been accused of burdening archaeology with the task of upholding the biblical narratives (Davies), while minimalists have been accused of attempting to erase ancient Israel from world history (Halpern).

The purpose of addressing the maximalist/minimalist debate in this introduction is to emphasize that biblical scholarship contains diverse voices and points of view on the Bible's history, which will be seen in the commentaries of this volume. It is good that these different perspectives are aired. When approaching an area of history that is of such great importance to so many, yet with so little definitive information available, it is important to articulate and compare different ideas so as to produce and refine the historical possibilities of the Bible's contexts. In this way we see how differing views of biblical interpretation can work as a dance, where partners can complement each other's work, even if tempers can flare sometimes when partners step on one another's toes.

Reading the Old Testament in Its Ancient Context

It is apparent that contemplating the ancient contexts of the Old Testament requires several areas of consideration. While there is no end to the complexities involved with pursuing a greater understating of the world(s) out of which the books of the Old Testament developed, this section is intended to draw the reader's attention to some of the Old Testament's physical environments, political climates, and theological diversity.

Physical Environments of the Old Testament

The geography and ecology of ancient Palestine can easily be overlooked, but their value for understanding the Old Testament should not be underestimated. While the Old Testament represents diverse social settings that span hundreds of years, all of its authors lived in agrarian societies where land, climate, economics, and religion are inseparable. Due to agrarian societies' dire need to ensure successful and regular harvests—whether for survival or with the additional aspiration of building empire—farming practices become incorporated into religious rituals that end up dictating planting, harvesting, and land management. This strong connection between faith and farming led to rituals that served as an interface between spirituality and socioeconomic activities, effectively erasing the lines between religious and economic practice (Coomber 2013). In the end, the ritualization of agrarian economics helps shape perceptions of the deity or deities to which the rituals are connected: the Feast of Unleavened Bread (Exod. 23:14-17), the barley harvest festival incorporated in the Passover feast (Exodus 12; cf. John 19:29, the wheat-harvest Feast of Weeks, also known as Pentecost (Lev. 23:15-21; cf. Acts 2:1), and the fruit-harvest Feast of Booths (Lev. 23:33-36). Thus geography and ecology affected not only the way ancient Hebrews farmed but also how they came to understand God. Moreover, the geographical regions in which many of them farmed influenced these understandings.

Regions of Ancient Israel

Ancient Israel can be divided into a number of geographical areas, each of which presents its own unique environment. Furthest to the west is the *coastal plain*, which held great economic importance in the way of trade. This is especially visible in the development of manufacturing and shipping cities such as Ekron and Ashkelon. Due to the region's trade potential, it was usually controlled by foreign powers and is not frequently mentioned in the Old Testament (e.g., Judges 16; 2 Kings 16; Jer. 25:20; Amos 1:8; Zeph. 2:4).

The lowland *Shephelah* and the *highlands* are just east of the coastal plain, forming an important region of Israel, which is at the center of most of the Old Testament's stories. This fertile land, composed of low hills and valleys, is good for animal husbandry and the cultivation of grains, cereals, nuts, olives, and grapes. These areas were valuable for both subsistence farming and the production of trade goods, in which surrounding empires could engage. The agrarian potential of this area also made Shephelah and the highlands a target for foreign invasion. This region's political influence was heightened by the cities of Jerusalem, Samaria, and Lachish.

The *Jordan Valley*, east of the highlands, contains the lowest natural surface in the world and is part of a fault that extends into Africa. The valley follows the Jordan River from the city of Dan through the city of Hazor and the Sea of Galilee before flowing into the Dead Sea. Aside from the important role that the Jordan Valley plays in Ezekiel's vision of water flowing out of the temple to bring life to the Dead Sea (Ezekiel 47), the region is rarely mentioned.

To the east of the Jordan Valley is the *Transjordan highlands*, which is often referred to as "beyond the Jordan" (e.g., Josh. 12:1). Extending from the Dead Sea's altitude of 650-feet below sea level to the 9,230-foot peak of Mt. Hermon, this region contains a diverse range of topography and climates that allow for the cultivation of diverse agricultural goods, including grains, fruits, timber, and livestock. The agrarian potential of the area attracted a number of peoples, including the Moabites, the Ammonites, and the Edomites.

Whether valued for their sustaining, trade, or defensive capabilities, the topography of ancient Israel and its surrounding lands influenced its inhabitants' ability or inability to find sustenance and pursue their own interests. When empires such as Assyria and Babylon were on the rise, this region attracted their rulers who sought the earning potential of the land, and these events—or the cultural memories they inspired—influenced the Old Testament authors' stories of defeat and are reflected in their perceptions of God's attitudes toward them.

Climatic Challenges

While the land in and around Israel was some of the most sought after in the ancient Near East, its inhabitants endured serious meteorological challenges. The ancient Israelites lived at the crossroads of subtropical and temperate atmospheric patterns—producing rainy winter seasons and dry summers—and the effects of these patterns shaped the ways in which the Hebrews lived: the resulting erratic precipitation patterns result in a 30 percent chance of insufficient rainfall (Karmon, 27). The unpredictability of each growing season's weather pattern meant that the rainfall of a given season could play out in any number of ways, each demanding specific farming strategies for which farmers had little foresight or room for error. Subsequent failed seasons that diminished surpluses could lead to debt and the selling of family members into slavery or even the extinction of a family line.

Everything in society—from the interests of the poorest farmer to the king—depended on successful harvests and access to their crops, and the strong desire for divine assistance is reflected in Old Testament narratives that emphasize fidelity to YHWH. The seriousness placed on securing favorable rainfall and accessing harvests is clear in warnings against following other deities, such as the weather god Baal (e.g., Judg. 2:11; 2 Kings 3:2; Ps. 106:28; Hosea 9:10), God-given visions that foretell rainfall (Genesis 41), and the granting and withholding of rain as reward or punishment (Deut. 11:11-14; cf. 1 Kings 17–18). Additionally, there are strict rules to protect land access (Leviticus 25) and condemnation against abuses (1 Kings 21; Isa. 5:8-10; Mic. 2:1-4).

The physical environments of the Old Testament authors are an important consideration, because they not only affected the way the authors lived but also helped to shape their views of God and the world around them. From the development of the ancient Hebrews' religious rituals to finding either God's favor or wrath in agrarian events (see Zech. 10:1; 1 Kings 17–18), the topography and climatic environments that affected cultivation played key roles in how the biblical authors perceived and interacted with the divine.

Sociopolitical Contexts of the Old Testament

In addition to the challenges presented by Israel's geographic and climatic setting, its strategic location between the empires of Mesopotamia and northern Africa presented a recurring threat. As these empires invaded the lands of ancient Israel for military and economic reasons, the biblical authors and redactors received and transmitted these events into their religious narratives: foreign invasion was often perceived as divine punishment—with the notable exception of the Persians—and the defeat of foreign forces was perceived as a result of divine favor. Before addressing foreign influences on the Old Testament's ancient contexts, a brief overview of Israel's domestic structures should be considered.

Israel's Domestic Sociopolitical Contexts

While ancient Palestine's Mesopotamian neighbors developed cities and urban economies in the Early Bronze Age (3300–2100 BCE), Palestine largely remained a patchwork of scattered settlements that functioned as a peripheral economy, engaging in trade activity as neighboring empires made it lucrative, and receding into highland agriculture when those powers waned (Coomber 2010, 81–92). Adapting to the demands of waxing and waning empires—rather than taking significant steps toward powerful urban economies of its own—resulted in a marked reliance on subsistence strategies on into the seventh century BCE (Coote and Whitelam).

Biblical accounts of Hebrew societal structures present a patronage system that had its roots in small family units called the *bet av* ("father's house"), which together formed a *mishpahah* ("family" or "clan"), which expanded up to the tribe, or *shevet.* When the monarchy was established, the *malkut* ("kingdom") became the top rung. While the *malkut* and *shevet* held the top two tiers, the phrase "all politics is local" applies to ancient Israel: loyalty structures were strongest at the bottom.

Philip Davies and John Rogerson note that the *bet av*, "father's house," likely had a double meaning (32). While it indicated a family unit that included extended lineage and slaves—excluding daughters who left the family at marriage—it likely also denoted the descendants of a common ancestor, who may not have lived under a single roof (e.g., Gen. 24:38). While the *bet avim* grew through the births of sons and the accumulation of wives and slaves, the danger of collapse due to disease, war, and a lack of birth of sons presented a constant threat. Debt was also a threat to a *bet av*, inspiring legal texts that protected its access to arable land (Leviticus 25; Deut. 25:5). It was the patriarch's responsibility to care for the family's economic well-being, as well as to pass on traditions, the history of the nation, and the laws of God (Deut. 6:7; 11:8-9; 32:46-47). The *bet av* also had power over such judicial matters as those of marriage and slave ownership.

Mishpahah denotes a level of organization based on a recognizable kinship (Numbers 1; 26). It had territorial significance, as seen in tribal border lists of Joshua 13–19, and was responsible for dividing the land. While *mishpahah* is difficult to translate, Norman Gottwald offers the useful definition, "protective association of extended families" (Gottwald 1999, 257). If the immediate or extended families of a citizen who had to sell himself to an alien could not redeem him, the *mishpahah* became the last line of protection from perpetual servitude (Lev. 25:48-49).

Shevet refers to the largest group and unit of territorial organization, which was primarily bound together by residence. Military allegiances appear to have belonged to this level, against both foreign and domestic threats—as seen in the Benjamite battles of Judges 12 and 20–21. Gottwald sees the *shevet* as more of a geographic designation pertaining to clusters of villages and/or clans that gathered for protective purposes rather than as representative bodies within a political system (Gottwald 2001, 35).

The *malkut*, or kingdom, is a source of continued contention in the so-called minimalist/maximalist debate mentioned above. The Old Testament account claims that the kingdom of Israel was founded when Saul became king over the Israelite tribes (1 Samuel 9) and continued through the line of David, after Saul fell out of favor with God. Israel's united monarchy is reported to have spanned 1030 to 930 BCE, when King Rehoboam was rejected by the northern Israelites (1 Kgs. 12:1-20; 2 Chron. 10:1-19), leading to the period of the divided monarchy, with Israel in the north and Judah in the south. These two kingdoms existed side by side until Israel was destroyed by Assyria (734–721 BCE). Judah entered into Assyrian vassalage in the 720s and was destroyed by the Babylonians around 586 BCE. Those who give less credence to the biblical account take note that there is little extrabiblical evidence of a monarchy prior to King Omri, aside from the Tel Dan Stele, which refers to "the House of David," which may refer to a king.

While Israel's domestic organizational landscape played a major role in the development of biblical law and narrative, the biblical authors' interactions with surrounding peoples had profound effects on the stories they told. The main imperial influences, from the premonarchical period to the fall of the Hasmonean Dynasty, were Egypt, Philistine, Assyria, Babylon, Persia, the Greeks, and the Romans.

Israel's Foreign Sociopolitical Contexts

The Egyptian Empire played an important role in the development of the Torah, as seen in the stories of Abram and Sarai (Genesis 12), Joseph (Genesis 37–50), and throughout the entire exodus narrative, interwoven into many areas of the Old Testament. The authors of Exodus used the backdrop of Egypt's powerful *New Kingdom* (1549–1069 BCE) to display their faith in YHWH's power, and other books draw on this narrative as a recurring reminder of the Israelites' debt and obligations toward their god (e.g. Deut. 5:15, 24:17-22, 23:7-8; Ps. 106:21; Ezekiel 20; Amos 2:10; Mic. 6:4), and as a vehicle of praise (Psalms 78; 81; 135; 136). The Jewish holiday of Passover, which is referred to throughout the Old Testament, has its roots in this anti-Egyptian epic. A later and weaker Egypt returns to play a role in the story of Judah's lengthy downfall: King Hezekiah (d. 680s) enters into a failed anti-Assyrian alliance with Egypt (Isaiah 30–31; 36:6-9), and King Zedekiah (d. 580s) enters into a failed anti-Babylonian alliance with Pharaoh Hophra (Ezek. 17:15; Jer. 2:36).

While their point of origins are in dispute (Amos 9:7 puts their origin at Caphtor), the Philistines tried to invade Egypt in 1190 BCE, but were repelled by Ramses III, who settled them in the coastal towns of Gaza, Ashkelon, and Ashdod (Deut. 2:23). From there, they continued their incursions along the coastal plain and perhaps even drove out their Egyptian rulers, under the reign of Ramses IV (d. 1149 BCE). They play a key adversarial role in the book of Judges, as found in the stories of Shamgar (Judg. 3:31) and Samson (Judges 13–16). Their military competencies are reflected in the story of their capture of the ark of the covenant in 1 Sam. 4:1—7:2. Fear of the Philistine threat helped influence the people's decision to choose a king to unite the tribes (1 Sam. 8–9). The biblical authors continued to portray the Philistines as a threat to the Israelites, but Philistine influence in the highlands faded as the power of Assyria grew.

Assyria's fearsome power and influence in the region gave them a villain's role in the Old Testament. The biblical authors perceived Assyria's incursions into Israel and Judah as YHWH's punishment for such transgressions as idolatry and social injustice. While archaeological evidence of Philistine-Israelite interaction is scant, there is plenty of archaeological and extrabiblical evidence of Assyria's impact on Israel and Judah.

From the start of its ninth-century conquests, Assyria was feared for its ruthless force. The psychological impact of Assyria's powerful conscripted forces, iron chariots, siege engines, and public mutilations surface in the writings of the Old Testament authors. The Assyrians enforced submission through power and fear, deporting conquered rulers to prevent uprisings (2 Kings 17:6, 24, 28; 18:11). When uprisings occurred, Assyrian troops were deployed from strategically positioned garrisons to flay, impale, and burn the perpetrators, as portrayed in Assyrian palace-reliefs.

In the late eighth century, both Israel and Judah felt the full weight of Assyria's might. The northern kingdom of Israel was destroyed in 721 BCE after joining an alliance of vassals that stopped paying tribute to Assyria. At the end of the century, King Hezekiah entered Judah into a similar alliance with Egypt (Isaiah 30–31), which resulted in the invasion of his kingdom and the siege of Jerusalem. According to 2 Kgs. 18:13-16, the siege was broken when Hezekiah sent a message of repentance to the Assyrian king, Sennacherib, at Lachish, promising to resume his tribute obligations. Other texts in 2 Kings suggest that Sennacherib abandoned the siege to deal with political unrest at home (19:7, 37) or a plague (19:35-36). Despite his efforts to subvert Sennacherib's dominance of Judah, Hezekiah and his successors continued to rule as vassals.

Under the rule of King Nebuchadnezzar, the Babylonian Empire captured Nineveh in 612, destroyed the Egyptians at the battle of Carchemish in 605, and captured Jerusalem in 597, deporting many inhabitants. After a rebellion by King Zedekiah in 586, the Babylonians destroyed Jerusalem and the temple and deported a significant portion of Judah's population (2 Kings 24; 2 Chronicles 36). The prophets Ezekiel, Jeremiah, and Habakkuk saw Nebuchadnezzar's conquest as YHWH's punishment for the sins of the Judean state (Ezekiel 8–11; Jer. 25:1-14; Hab. 1:6-10). The events of the Babylonian conquest are largely supported by archaeology and extrabiblical literature (Grabbe, 210–13).

Biblical claims of the removal of all Judeans but the poorest "people of the land" (2 Kgs. 24:14-16; 25:12; Jer. 52:16, 28-30) are reflected in the archaeological record, which indicates that inhabited sites decreased by two-thirds, from 116 to 41, and surviving sites shrank from 4.4 to 1.4 hectares, suggesting a population collapse of 85 to 90 percent (Liverani, 195). Such a massive exile plays a formidable role in the Old Testament, as described in the stories of significant characters such as Ezekiel and Daniel. Rage associated with this event is found in Psalm 137, which recounts the horrors of the exile and ends with the chilling words "a blessing on him who seizes your [Babylonian] babies and dashes them against the rocks!" (137:9 JPS). The exiled Hebrews who returned to Palestine after the Persians conquered the Babylonians returned to a destroyed Jerusalem that no longer enjoyed the security of a defensive wall. Some of the returnees helped to reshape Judaism with a flourishing priesthood and the composition of scholarly works and biblical texts. While exile is portrayed in negative terms, many Jews remained in the lands to which they had been deported; this had the effect of spreading Judaism outside the confines of Palestine.

After overthrowing his grandfather King Astyages of the Medes in 553 BCE, Cyrus of Persia (d. 530) rapidly expanded his empire, moving westward into Armenia and Asia Minor and east toward India, and defeated Babylon in 539. But unlike previous conquests, the Old Testament treats Persian dominance as a time of hope. As successor to the Babylonian Empire, King Cyrus instituted a policy of allowing victims of Babylonian exile to return to their homelands, where he sponsored their local religions. To the biblical authors, this policy was met with celebration and as a sign of YHWH's love for his people. The authors of 2 Chron. 36:23 and Ezra 1:2 portray King Cyrus as crediting YHWH with his victories and with the mandate to rebuild the temple in Jerusalem; Ezra 1:7 even portrays the Persian king personally returning the vessels that Nebuchadnezzar had seized from the temple four decades before. While the Bible treats Cyrus's policy of return as inspired by YHWH, Davies and Rogerson note that the practice was neither new nor disinterested, as it served to restore the national culture of a large and culturally varied empire (59). It is important to note the great shift in how the biblical authors treated King Cyrus of Persia, as opposed to the kings of the Assyrians and Babylonians, whom they disdained. In Isaiah 40–50, Cyrus is championed as the great savior of the Judean deportees and of the rebuilding of Jerusalem. In fact, while oracles against foreign nations are a key theme in prophetic oracles, none are directed against Persia. Even when their rulers are compliant with the murder of Jews, they are portrayed as either acting against their own desires or out of ignorance (Daniel 6; Esther).

Like the exile, itself, the return from exile plays an important role in the politics and religion of the Old Testament. Accounts of these events are found in the books of Ezra and Nehemiah. While the Bible presents the return as a blessing from God and a time of joy, it does not seem to have been without its hardships. It can be deduced from Ezra and Nehemiah that resettlement involved various tensions; in Ezra 3:3, those who had remained in Judah during the exile, along with other neighboring peoples, take the Canaanites' role in the book of Joshua: "an evil influence which will, unless strenuously rejected, corrupt the 'people of God'" (Davies and Rogerson, 88). It was during the Persian period that the Jerusalem temple was rebuilt and the priesthood gained power and influence.

The long march of succeeding empires continued with the rise of Alexander the Great, who seized control of the Greek city-states in 336 BCE and conquered the Persian Empire before his death in 323. Unlike previous empires that might make their subjects worship a particular deity or relocate to a different region, the Greek ideal of *Hellenism* posed a particular cultural threat. Hellenism promoted a view in which people were not citizens of a particular region, but of the world, enabling the integration of Greek and regional cultures, thus breaking down barriers that separated local peoples from their foreign rulers. Within a hundred years, Koine Greek had become the lingua franca, and Greek philosophy, educational systems, art and attire, politics, and religion permeated the empire. The consequences of Hellenization had profound linguistic, political, and theological effects on the biblical authors who lived and wrote during this period. Jews who lived outside of Israel became more familiar with the Greek language than Hebrew. By the second century CE, Greek had become so widely spoken among the Jewish community in Alexandria, Egypt, that the Hebrew Bible was translated into Koine Greek, which came to be called the Septuagint.

Greek rule eventually led to the severe oppression of the Jewish people at the hands of the usurper king Antiochus IV (d. 164 BCE), who sought to weed out cultural diversity in the Seleucid Empire. King Antiochus, who called himself *Epiphanes* ("god made manifest"), was known for his erratic character, which manifested itself in his brutal hatred of the Jews. Even his allies referred to him by the nickname *Epimanes*—a play on Epiphanes—meaning "the crazy one." He is known for looting the Jerusalem temple to fund his battles against the Ptolemies and for forbidding the Jewish rite of circumcision and sacred dietary laws.

King Antiochus was also known for instigating treachery among the Jewish leadership, giving Jason—of the pro-Greek Onias family—the high priesthood in return for complying with Antiochus's plans to Hellenize Jerusalem by building a gymnasium and enrolling its people as citizens of Antioch (2 Macc. 4:7). Further strife erupted when Menelaus, another aspirant for the high priesthood, offered Antiochus even greater gifts for the office. The rivalry of Jason and Menelaus led to the sacking of Jerusalem, slaughtering of its citizens, and the looting of its temple (2 Macc. 5:11-23; Josephus 12.5.3 §§246–47). The horrors of life under King Antiochus IV are reflected in the horn that emerges from the fourth beast in the apocalyptic vision of Dan. 7:7-8, and is then slain by the "Ancient One" (7:11).

From stripping the temple to pay for his wars to setting up an altar for Zeus in the temple, King Antiochus IV's brutality against the Jews led to a revolt that started in the Judean village of Modein in 167 BCE and spread rapidly throughout the region—as chronicled in 1 and 2 Maccabees and in Josephus's *Antiquities of the Jews* (c. 100 CE). A guerrilla warfare campaign that was led by Judas Maccabeus eventually liberated and purified the temple—an event celebrated today in the Jewish festival of Hanukkah. The Maccabean revolt drove out the Greeks and expanded the borders to include Galilee. While the revolt was successful in ushering in a period of self-rule, the resulting Hasmonean Dynasty fell prey to the lust for power. As civil conflict broke out between two rival claims to the throne, the Roman general Pompey invaded Judea in 63 BCE, seizing control of the region for his empire. In 40 BCE, the Roman Senate appointed an Edomite convert to Judaism, *Herod the Great*, as king of Judea. Despised by his people, the puppet king had to take Jerusalem by force, from where he ruled harshly.

Each of these empires, vying for control over the Southern Levant, brought with them challenges that helped to shape the Hebrew people by influencing the ways they viewed themselves, their God, and their religious practices.

Religious Contexts of the Old Testament

Despite common perceptions of the Bible as a univocal work, the Old Testament represents diverse theologies of communities that spanned centuries and were influenced by the religious systems of their contemporaries. Babylonian and Canaanite musings over the power of order over chaos, as found in the *Enuma Elish* and Baal narratives, are present in Gen. 1:1—2:4a and referenced in Ps. 74:12-17. The authors of the Bible's Wisdom literature exchanged ideas with their foreign neighbors, as found in parallels between the Babylonian story I Will Praise the Lord of Wisdom and the book of Job, and passages from Proverbs that mirror the words of the Egyptian thinkers Ptah-Hotep and Amen-em-opet (e.g., Prov. 22:4; 22:17—24:22). Understanding the diversity of theological perspectives in the Old Testament can aid both exegesis and hermeneutics by giving the reader greater insight into the biblical authors' ideas of God and uncovering layers of meaning that might otherwise go unnoticed.

Monotheism and Henotheism

It should not be assumed that all Old Testament authors were monotheists: many were *henotheists*. Henotheism promotes a multi-god/dess universe in which the adherent gives allegiance to a supreme primary deity. Elements of this outlook appear to be found in God's decision to create humanity "in our image, after our likeness" (Gen. 1:26 RSV), and in YHWH's anxiety over the man that he created becoming "like one of us" in Gen. 3:22. YHWH also expresses his disgust in that the *sons of God* mated with human women, resulting in the birth of the nephilim (Gen. 6:2-4). In the *Song of Moses*, Moses poses the rhetorical question, "who is like you, O Lord, among the gods?" (Exod. 15:11). The writer of Ps. 95:3 proclaims, "YHWH is a great God, the king of all divine beings," while 97:9 asserts that YHWH is "exalted high above all divine beings." These examples pose a number of questions about the biblical authors' views on the divine. Two that will be briefly addressed here concern the identity of God and the role of the other deities being inferred. The supreme deity of the ancient Hebrews is given several names and titles, representing different personality traits and theological views.

Elohim

The name or title *Elohim*, which is usually translated from the Hebrew into English as "God," makes its first appearance in Genesis 1. The name Elohim is used to identify the Hebrews' supreme deity in several Old Testament texts, including those found in the books of Genesis, Exodus, Psalms, and Job. As in the Bible's priestly creation story (Gen. 1:1—2:4a), Elohim is portrayed as an all-powerful, confident, commanding, and somewhat distant deity, whose supremacy and majesty are emphasized.

YHWH

YHWH is an anthropomorphic god who exhibits tendencies toward both kindness and severity and is self-described as a jealous god who, unlike other ancient Near Eastern gods, demands the exclusive allegiance of his followers. The name YHWH, which is often translated into English as "the LORD"—from the Hebrew *adonay*—makes its first appearance in the second creation story (Gen. 2:4b). The name YHWH carries a sense of mystery. Derived from the Hebrew verb *hawah*, meaning "to be," YHWH is difficult to translate, but means something like "he who is" or "he who causes what is." Some believe that YHWH's origins can be traced to the god YHW, who was worshiped in the northwestern region of the Arabian Peninsula known as Midian: this is where Moses first encounters YHWH (Exodus 3).

YHWH has strong associations with Canaanite culture, which highlights discrepancies between biblical directions for the deity's worship and how the deity was worshiped in popular religion. Whereas the biblical authors convey strict messages that YHWH should be worshiped alone, the remains of Israelite homes reveal that other gods and goddesses, such as Asherah—whom the author(s) of Jeremiah refers to as *the queen of heaven*—were worshiped alongside YHWH (Dever, 176–89). Jeremiah 44 appears to give a glimpse into the popular polytheistic or henotheistic religion of sixth-century-BCE Judah. After YHWH threatens the people for worshiping other gods, the women say that they will not listen but will continue the traditions of their ancestors and give offerings to the queen of heaven, who protected them well (Jer. 44:16-17). Further biblical evidence of Asherah's popularity is found in the biblical authors' continual condemnation of her worship, often symbolized through the presence of pillars and poles, as they worked to direct the people toward monotheism (Deut. 7:5; Judg. 3:7-8; 1 Kgs. 14:15, 23; Jer. 17:17-18).

El

The name or title *El* appears around two hundred times in the Old Testament, with frequent use in the ancestor stories of Genesis and surfacing throughout the Old Testament. Its presence poses some interesting questions.

On one level, El is a common Semitic title for "divine being," and can be read as an appellative for "divinity," often compounded with other words such as *el-shadday* ("God Almighty" [Gen. 17:1; Exod. 6:3; Ezek. 10:5]) and *el-elyon* ("God Most High" [Gen. 14:22; Deut. 32:8-9; Ps. 78:35]). In addition to a title referring to God, El is also the name of the chief god of the Canaanite pantheon. Often portrayed as a bearded king on his throne, and referred to as the "Ancient One," El was worshiped in Canaan and Syria both before and after the emergence of Israel. The frequent use of El for God—and the Canaanite god's prominence in Israel—has led many to conclude that El developed into YHWH. Mark Smith asserts, "The original god of Israel was El. . . . Isra*el* is not a Yahwistic name with the divine element of Yahweh, but an El name" (Smith, 32; emphasis on *el* in "Israel" is mine). A cross-pollination of Canaanite and Hebrew religion is found in the use of Canaanite El imagery to describe the "Ancient One" in Dan. 7:9-10 who sits on a throne with white garments and hair as pure as wool. Furthermore, the description of "one like a human being coming with the clouds of heaven," who "came to the Ancient One and was presented before him" (Dan. 7:13), dovetails with images of the Canaanite god Baal coming before El. Whether or not the authors of Daniel 7 envisioned El, the imprint of Canaanite religion appears to have been stamped on ideas of God and passed down through the generations. While not accepted by biblical authors, popular religion in ancient Israel appears to have had a complex network of deities that fulfilled various roles in daily life. (For a helpful overview on differences between "popular" and "official" religion in ancient Israel, see Stavrakopoulou.)

The idea that El was absorbed into YHWH is also supported by the fact that the chief god of the Canaanite pantheon is never condemned in the Old Testament, but his son Baal, consort Asherah, and other gods face vicious condemnation (Num. 25:2; Deut. 4:3; Judg. 6:30; 1 Kgs. 16:31—18:40). Why would the biblical authors attack lesser Canaanite deities but leave the head god unscathed? One possible answer is that El had become synonymous with YHWH; both share a compassionate disposition toward humanity (Exod. 34:6; Ps. 86:15), use dreams to communicate (Gen. 31:24; 37:5; 1 Kgs. 3:5-15), and have healing powers (cf. *KTU* 1:16.v–vi with Gen. 20:17; Num. 12:13; Ps. 107:20 [Smith, 39]).

The Divine Council

As El served as chief of the Canaanite pantheon, YHWH was head of the *divine council*, whose members were often referred to as "the sons of gods." In Gen. 28:12; 33:1-2; Pss. 29:1 and 89:6-9, we find YHWH at the head of subordinate divine beings who are collectively referred to as the "council of Lord" (Jer. 23:18 and the "congregation of El" (Ps. 82:1). In Psalm 82, God attacks the congregants for their oppressive acts against humanity, for which they are doomed to die like mortals (vv. 5-7). In Job 1:6-7, Job's troubles begin when the divine council convenes with YHWH, and God asks "the satan" where he has been. The satan also appears on the divine council in Zechariah, where YHWH delivers judgment between two members of his entourage. The clearest depiction of the divine council's function is in 1 Kgs. 22:19-22, where YHWH seeks guidance and direction from the council, the members of which confer in open discussion before one spirit approaches YHWH with a proposal. Following a common motif in ancient Mediterranean literature, humans are sometimes transported before God and the divine council, as found in a party feasting with Elohim in Exod. 24:9-11 and Isaiah's commission as prophet in Isaiah 6 (Niditch 2010, 14–17).

Concluding Words on the Complexities of the Ancient Context

Reading the Old Testament in its ancient contexts requires a variety of considerations and an understanding that there are divergent views on these contexts. But this complexity should not discourage readers of the Bible from contemplating the origins of the Old Testament books, because a better understanding of their origins results in a broader understanding of their meanings and potential applications to our modern contexts. The authors of this volume's commentaries have worked to give the reader the best possible overview of the sociohistorical contexts that underlie the books of the Old Testament, opening its texts in new ways so that new meanings can be derived. While this section has highlighted some of the many considerations that need to be addressed when reading the "Very Dangerous Texts Ahead," the variety of contexts out of which the Old

Testament's books emerged is paralleled by the diversity of cultures, faiths, and societies into which they have been received.

Reading the Old Testament in Its Contemporary Contexts

Actively engaging the Old Testament in both its ancient and modern contexts enables readers to discover new levels of meaning that would otherwise go unnoticed. Through acknowledging an Old Testament text's historical setting, exploring how it has been interpreted through the millennia, and noticing the questions and challenges that it raises for our contemporary settings, engaged readers are better able to receive multiple levels of meaning that aid the reader in better understanding the biblical authors' intentions and discerning the passage's potential relevance to conversations that are unfolding today.

The Challenge of Bringing Ancient Context in Line with Modern Contexts

To participate in this process, however, is not a simple task. Beyond working to discern the various levels of meaning within the Old Testament, it is of paramount importance for readers to also acknowledge the preconceptions and biases they bring with them as they work to connect the ancient writings to their own world—an issue that is explored at length below.

As humorously demonstrated in A. J. Jacobs's book *The Year of Living Biblically*, it is important to remember that the texts of the Old Testament were not written for twenty-first-century audiences, but for citizens of the ancient world. As he recounts in his book, Jacobs tried to live as literally as possible according to the laws of the Hebrew Bible for one year. His experiment revealed that to live by the rules of the Hebrew Bible is to live as an outlaw in much of the modern world, whether because the Hebrew Bible calls for the execution of people who wear mixed fibers or because it mandates sacrificing animals in urban centers. This clash of ancient and modern cultures occurred in a very serious way in the tragic murder of Murray Seidman. Mr. Seidman's killer referenced Lev. 20:13 as his motivation for stoning the elderly and mentally disabled man (Masterson).

Conversely, some people, like Charlie Fuqua, assert that engaging with the Old Testament's historical contexts is not required. During the 2012 United States election, Fuqua ran for a seat on the Arkansas state legislature and released a book titled *God's Law: The Only Political Solution*. In his book, Fuqua calls for the creation of legal channels that will facilitate the execution of disobedient children, as commanded in Deut. 21:18-21 (2012, 179). While Fuqua's views represent a fringe group of theomonists that include such Christian reconstructionists as Cornelius Van Til and Rousas John Rushdoony, his example illustrates the importance of contemplating the important differences that exist between the biblical authors' societies and those into which their writings are received today. One must ask questions such as, Did the authors of Deut. 21:18-21 actually seek the execution of disobedient children, or did they pose an extreme example to illustrate a point on child rearing? Another important question to consider is, Did Deut. 21:18-21 originate at a time when resources were so scarce and the production of food so difficult that a child who didn't contribute to—but rather threatened—the common good posed a threat to the community's survival? Growing and cultivating food could certainly be a matter of life and death. Fuqua's failure to engage Deut. 21:18-21, choosing instead to blindly subscribe to the text at face value, is a very serious and dangerous matter, especially considering his aspirations for political office. But while vast differences separate the cultures and societies of the Old Testament authors and the world that we inhabit today, a surprising number of connections do exist.

Whether a Judean farmer or an American physician, we all share such aspects of the universal human experience as love, hate, trust, betrayal, fear, and hope—all of which are reflected both in the Old Testament and in our daily lives. Such themes as women working to find justice in societies that offer little, the quest for love along with its dangers and rewards, and people's struggle to understand their relationships with power, whether personal or political, are all found in the stories of the Old Testament and are still highly relevant to us today.

It should be pointed out, however, that earnestly engaging the Old Testament in its ancient and modern contexts is difficult, even hazardous. Several key considerations that help in an engaged reading of the books of the Old Testament are included here, including issues of biblical ownership, methods of interpretation, and approaches to the reception of its texts.

Whose Bible Is It, Anyway?

While the texts of the Old Testament are commonly used with an air of authority and ownership, their ownership is open to question. So, to whom do they belong? Now that their authors are long dead—and their works have passed through generations and around the world—who is the heir of these works? To which community would they turn and say, "The keys are yours"? One problem with answering this question is that the Old Testament's authors and editors did not represent a unified tradition through which a unified voice could be offered. Furthermore, the faiths and cultures of the twenty-first century CE are so far removed from the ancient authors' that they would most likely be utterly unrecognizable to them. On one level, it is a moot question. Those authors are dead, and they do not get a say regarding who uses their works, or how. Be that as it may, it is an important question to consider, for recognizing that the Old Testament has a number of spiritual heirs with divergent views of the divine underscores the vast interpretive possibilities these texts contain. While many faith traditions draw on the books of the Old Testament, the three largest—in order of appearance—are Judaism, Christianity, and Islam.

The Hebrew Bible (the *Tanakh*) of Judaism is composed of twenty-four books, which are divided into the Torah (Law), the Nebiim (Prophets), and the Ketubim (Writings). The Torah gives accounts of the creation, the establishment of the Hebrew people, and their movement out of captivity in Egypt toward the land that was promised to their ancestors. The public reading of the Torah is a religious ritual that culminates with the annual holiday of *Simchat Torah*, which celebrates its completion. Although the Tanakh forms the whole of Jewish biblical literature, it is supplemented by other interpretive collections.

The Christian *Old Testament*, sometimes referred to as the *First Testament*, sets the books of the Tanakh in a different order and serves as the first section of the *Christian Bible*, as a whole. Canonization of the Old Testament varies among different Christian traditions. Roman Catholicism,

Eastern Orthodoxy, and some Protestant groups include the seven additional books in their canon, as well as additions to the books of Esther and Daniel; these additions are called the *deuterocanon* ("second canon") or *Apocrypha* ("hidden"). Many of the books of the Old Testament are popularly seen as a precursor to the coming of Jesus and his perceived fulfillment of the law.

Islam incorporates many of the figures of the Old Testament into its sacred writings, the Holy Qur'an. Giving particular reverence to the Torah and the Psalms, the Qur'an honors Abraham, Isaac, and Moses as prophetic predecessors to the faith's final and greatest prophet, Muhammad (d. 632 CE).

While each of these traditions draws deep meaning and conviction from the Hebrew Scriptures, they also use them in different ways to reflect their own unique spiritual paths and theologies. The question of which group is the rightful heir of the biblical authors is impossible to answer definitively, since each claims to be in fact the rightful heir. The fact that such a diverse pool of people turns to these texts as sacred Scripture amplifies the many possibilities for Old Testament interpretation.

Evolving Views of the Old Testament and Its Interpretation

Whether or not it is done consciously, all readers of the Old Testament are engaged in some level of interpretation; there are no passive readers of the Bible. When people read the books of the Old Testament, they do so actively, bringing their own presuppositions, experiences, and cultural norms to a text. In essence, readers of the Old Testament bridge the ancient to the modern by way of exegesis and hermeneutics.

Exegesis looks at the texts in their ancient contexts, while hermeneutics works to discern how they relate to a modern reader's situation. Biblical scholars and readers have developed a number of methods for bringing the ancient and the modern together, often with specific objectives and theological motives in mind.

Biblical Literalism

Biblical literalism—which asserts that the Bible is the inerrant word of God, unaltered and untainted by human agency during its transmission from God to humanity—is a prevalent form of interpretation in the United States, practiced commonly within fundamentalist and some evangelical communities. The literal meanings of individual biblical texts were long considered alongside allegorical, moral, and mystical interpretations; it was not until the Reformation's second wave, in the seventeenth century, that literalism became a way to approach the Bible as a whole.

Protestant Christians who broke from the authority of Roman Catholicism found a strong sense of liberation in the idea of gaining access to God's direct word through the Scriptures. If an adherent could access God directly through a Bible, what need did they have for such individual or institutional arbitrators as priests, popes, or the Roman Church? Whereas early Reformers like Martin Luther and John Calvin viewed Scripture as being inspired by God with human involvement in its transmission, some of the second wave of Reformers, such as Amandus Polanus (d. 1610) and Abraham Calov (d. 1686), placed even greater emphasis on the Bible's inerrancy. The movement known as Protestant Scholasticism promoted the idea that any human involvement in the creation of the Bible was strictly mechanical; those who wrote the words were merely tools used by God. This was the first time that the idea of the inerrancy of Scripture as a literal interpretive approach was applied to the Bible—as a whole.

Despite the many developments in biblical interpretation that have occurred between the seventeenth and twenty-first centuries CE, many North American Christians still self-identify as biblical literalists. However, almost nobody practices biblical literalism in the strictest sense, for it would be an almost untenable position. The various contributions by the different religious communities that went into the writing of our biblical texts have resulted in contradicting versions of similar content (cf. Exod. 21:2-8 with Deut. 15:12-13). Given these challenges, how could A. J. Jacobs's experiment in living in strict accord with biblical law have any hope of being tenable, or even legal?

Historical Criticism

The influence of the Enlightenment—with its emphases on reason and searching for facts—gave rise to *the historical-critical movement*, which works to reconstruct the ancient contexts of the Bible. Baruch Spinoza (d. 1677) argued that the same scientific principles that were being applied to other areas of knowledge should be applied to the Bible as well. The results, which are still highly influential on how biblical scholarship is conducted today, have challenged such traditionally held Old Testament notions as the Genesis account(s) of the creation, Moses' composition of the Torah, and the historical validity of the Hebrew exodus out of Egypt, to name a few. Scrutinizing a particular text's origins through asking such questions as, Who wrote the text? For what purpose? and, Under what circumstances? Historical critics work to better understand what lies beneath the text.

Historical criticism's influence on biblical scholarship has shaped the way that many theologians read the Bible by adding to our understanding of the ancient contexts behind biblical texts. *Religionsgeschichte* ("history of religions") is a tool of historical criticism that reads biblical texts in their ancient religious contexts. Another historical-critical tool is *form criticism*, which has gleaned new meaning from such passages as the Song of Deborah (Judges 5) by considering their oral prehistory, reconstructing the *Sitz im Leben* ("original setting"), and analyzing their literary genres.

Social-Scientific Criticism

In the late 1970s—with the publication of Norman Gottwald's *The Tribes of Yahweh*—biblical scholars began to look at the books of the Old Testament through the lens of their sociological settings. Since then, numerous scholars have used societal patterns both to fill in many of the hidden contexts that are simply not addressed in the texts themselves and to better understand the societal motivations behind the Old Testament authors' messages.

One advantage to the social-scientific method of interpretation is its ability to inform hermeneutics (again, the application of biblical texts to modern circumstances). Social-scientific models have proven to be of particular use in shedding light on the contexts and motivations behind biblical texts while opening new ways of understanding how those texts might relate to the modern world (Chaney; Coomber 2011). A tempting misuse of social-scientific models of interpretation, however, is to treat the findings gained through social-scientific models as hard evidence that can stand on its own. Social-scientific models that deal with tribalism, urban development, religious-political interactions, or economic cycles can provide insight into how humans—and their systems—are expected to behave; they do not, however, prove how humans and systems did behave. It is for this reason that social-scientific approaches should be used in tandem with all available data, be it archaeological or literary.

Commenting on the great value of using social-scientific models in the interpretation of biblical texts, Philip Esler writes that their use "fires the social-scientific imagination to ask new questions of data, to which only the data can provide the answers" (Esler, 3). In other words, these models are useful for the interpretation of evidence, not as evidence in and of themselves. Social-scientific criticism has proven especially useful in the development of contextual readings of the Old Testament, which address issues ranging from political interpretations of the Bible to interpretations within such minority groups as LGBT (lesbian, gay, bisexual, and transgender) and disabled communities.

Contextual and Reception Readings and Criticisms

Contextual readings of the Old Testament provide excellent examples of how the ancient stories and ideas of the Old Testament can speak to the modern contexts of diverse communities. These forms of criticism, like social-scientific or literary criticism, often take on an interdisciplinary nature. While a plethora of contextual topics have been covered biblically, those that address issues of empire, gender, and race are briefly covered here.

Empire

Just as issues of empire were integral in the formation of the Old Testament, as addressed in the "Reading the Old Testament in Its Ancient Contexts" section above, Old Testament texts continue to influence the ways people approach issues of empire today. On the one hand, the imagery that celebrates conquest in the invasion of Canaan (Joshua) and the glory of Solomon's kingdom (e.g., 1 Kings 4) could be used to support the building of empire. On the other hand, those who challenge the rise or expansion of empires can draw on anti-imperial readings that condemn the conduct of royals and their exploitation of the citizenry (e.g., Micah 3), and legislation against economic injustice in the Torah, Writings, and Prophets.

Pro-imperial readings of the Old Testament can be seen in the building and expansion of US influence, such as the idea of *Manifest Destiny*, which portrays the Christian European settlement of the United States as God's divine will. Manifest destiny involved a reimagining of the Pilgrims—and later European settlers—as the new Hebrews, pushing aside the Native American peoples—who took on the role of Canaanites—in order to create a new Israel. The Rev. Josiah Strong's publication *Our Country* echoes this sentiment in its assertion that God was charging European Christianity "to dispossess the many weaker races, assimilate others, and mold the remainder" (Strong, 178). Reverberations of the Old Testament–rooted Manifest Destiny still surface in aspects of American exceptionalism, which influences the US political spectrum and can be seen in such approaches to foreign policy as "the Bush Doctrine," which works to spread American-style democracy as a path to lasting peace.

Just as the Old Testament has been used for empire building, it has also been used to challenge empire and its institutions. While the exodus narrative helped to shape the idea of Manifest Destiny, it also became a powerful abolitionist force in attacking the institutions of slavery and segregation. During the abolitionist movement, the powerful imagery of the exodus story gave hope and power to free African Americans and slaves alike. The power of the story was harnessed again in the mid-twentieth century, giving strength to those who struggled for racial equality (Coomber 2012, 123–36). Recent biblical scholarship has also turned to the Old Testament to address various issues of modern-day economic exploitation and neoimperialism (e.g., Gottwald 2011; Boer, ed.; West 2010).

A highly influential outcome of the crossing of Bible and empire has been *postcolonial interpretation*. As European empires spread throughout the world, they brought the Bible and Christianity with them. With the twentieth-century waning of European imperialism, colonized and previously colonized peoples have found their own voices in the Bible, resulting in a variety of new interpretations and new approaches to major Old Testament themes. Postcolonial interpretation has enriched the field from Mercedes García Bachmann's use of Isaiah 58 to address issues of "unwanted fasting" (105–12) to raising questions about whether the Christian canon should be reopened to include the folk stories and traditions of colonized Christian communities that feel unrepresented by the current Bible (Pui Lan).

Gender

Studies in gender have also revealed a wide range of interpretive possibilities and have come to the forefront of biblical scholarship during the past four decades. While often treated as the sex of the body, the word *gender* is a complicated term that addresses a variety of factors of embodiment, including mental and behavioral characteristics. *Masculinity* and *femininity*, for example, take on different attributes and expectations depending on the society or culture in which they exist. While gender is an area of study that is continually developing into various branches, both within and outside of biblical studies, one of its most predominant manifestations in biblical studies is found in *feminist criticism*.

Women have been longtime readers and commentators on biblical texts, even though their work has rarely been given the same consideration as their male counterparts, who have long served as the vanguard of the academy. Hildegard of Bingen (d. 1179) authored a commentary on Genesis 1–2 (Young, 262); R. Roberts (d. 1788) composed numerous sermons on a range of texts for a clergyman acquaintance (Knowles, 418–19); and abolitionist Elizabeth Cady Stanton (d. 1902) helped to publish *The Woman's Bible*. These three women serve as but a few examples of women who have made important contributions to biblical studies, though their work is unknown to many.

Feminist criticism continues to be a very effective mode for recovering women's insights, perspectives, knowledge, and the feminine principle in biblical texts, often rescuing those voices and interpretations from centuries of marginalization by patriarchal and even misogynistic interpretation. Elisabeth Schüssler Fiorenza claims that, unlike many other forms of biblical criticism, feminist biblical studies does not owe its existence to the academy but to social movements for change, and also to a desire for the ongoing pursuit of equal participation and equal rights, which have in practice been restricted to a small group of elite men (Schüssler Fiorenza, 8–9). Schüssler Fiorenza argues that since the Bible has most often been used in these struggles for either "legitimating the status quo of the kyriarchal order of domination *or* for challenging dehumanization, feminist biblical interpretation is best articulated as an integral part of wo/men's struggles for authority and self-determination" (9). Like so many forms of contextual and received readings, feminist criticism can serve as a liberating force by revealing perspectives within the Bible's texts that have otherwise gone unnoticed.

An example of recovering the woman's perspective in the Old Testament is found in feminist commentaries on such texts as Isa. 42:14, in which God says,

> For a long time I have held my peace,
> I have kept still and restrained myself;
> now I will cry out like a woman in labor,
> I will gasp and pant.

Patricia Tull has highlighted the way in which YHWH adopts the power of a woman in labor to emphasize God's own divine power of creation (Tull, 263). Another example of uncovering women's voices to find justice in patriarchal cultures—which work to subvert women's voices and rights—is found in Sharon Pace Jeansonne's treatment of Tamar as a woman who seizes power to find justice in a society that is set up to stop her from doing so (Jeansonne, 98–106).

Feminist criticism—as with most any other form of biblical criticism—is polyvocal, with a broad spectrum of biblical views, including those who have argued that the Bible might be best left alone (Bal, 14). Male scholars have also engaged with feminist-focused readings of Old Testament texts. Daniel Cohen's midrash on Genesis 3, for example, addresses misogynistic interpretations of the Garden of Eden story (Cohen 141–48).

Similar to some of feminist criticism's attempts to reclaim the women's voice in the Bible and address misogynistic interpretation, *queer criticism* works to uncover LGBT perspectives in the Old Testament and messages that are of importance to LGBT communities. Queer interpretation has addressed a number of such topics, including K. Renato Lings's work on homophobic critiques of the destruction of Sodom in Genesis 19—a text often used to condemn homosexuality—in which he argues that attaching homosexuality to the sin of Sodom was a later interpretive development, unrecognized by biblical authors (Lings, 183–207). Others have shed new light on the ways in which biblical texts are interpreted to affect modern-day political decisions, such as the issue of same-sex marriage (see Stahlberg).

Conclusion

To be an engaged reader of the Old Testament involves simultaneously navigating the worlds of the biblical authors and redactors, as well as all those who have interpreted its texts. It is through approaching a biblical text or idea through these multiple angles that the multilayered meanings of the Old Testament books can be unlocked, not only in regard to the authors' intentions, but also in ways that the biblical writers may have never been able to foresee. These multiple intersections with the biblical text help people to have meaningful conversation and debate on topics ranging from climate change, to same-sex marriage, to the international banking crisis, and more. Naturally, being an engaged reader requires considerable effort, but it is through deliberating on biblical texts in all of their complexity that deeper meaning can be found, and more honest—or at least informed—readings of the Bible's contents can be gleaned.

In this volume, the contributors' commentaries provide a tool through which people can develop their engagement with the books of the Old Testament and Apocrypha. Whether approaching this volume as a researcher, educator, member of the clergy, or student, it is the intent of the *Fortress Commentary on the Old Testament* to inform readers about the Old Testament books' historical contexts, interpretive histories, and the modern contexts with which they engage, while also serving as an opening through which the conversation can be expanded.

Works Cited

Alfaro, Juan I. 1989. *Justice and Loyalty: A Commentary on the Book of Micah*. Grand Rapids: Eerdmans.

Bachmann, Mercedes L. García. 2009. "True Fasting and Unwilling Hunger (Isaiah 58)." In *The Bible and the Hermeneutics of Liberation*, edited by A. F. Botta and P. R. Andiñach, 113–31. Atlanta: SBL.

Bal, Mieke. 1989. *Anti-Covenant: Counter-Reading Women's Lives in the Hebrew Bible*. Sheffield: Almond.

Boer, Roland, ed. 2013. *Postcolonialism and the Hebrew Bible: The Next Step*. SemeiaSt 70. Atlanta: SBL.

Cantor, Norman F. 1992. *Inventing the Middle Ages: The Lives, Works, and Ideas of the Great Medievalists of the Twentieth Century*. Cambridge: Lutterworth.

Chaney, Marvin L. 1999. "Whose Sour Grapes? The Addressees of Isaiah 5:1–7 in the Light of Political Economy." In *The Social World of the Hebrew Bible: Twenty-Five Years of the Social Sciences in the Academy*, edited by Ronald A. Simkins and Stephen L. Cook. *Semeia* 87:105–22.

Cohen, Daniel. 2007. "Taste and See: A Midrash on Genesis 3:6 and 3:12." In *Patriarchs, Prophets and Other Villains*, edited by Lisa Isherwood, 141–48. London: Equinox Publishing.

Coomber, Matthew J. M. 2010. *Re-Reading the Prophets through Corporate Globalization: A Cultural-Evolutionary Approach to Understanding Economic Injustice in the Hebrew Bible*. Piscataway, NJ: Gorgias.

———. 2011. "Caught in the Crossfire? Economic Injustice and Prophetic Motivation in Eighth-Century Judah." *BibInt* 19, nos. 4–5:396–432.

———. 2012. "Before Crossing the Jordan: The Telling and Retelling of the Exodus Narrative in African American History." In *Exodus and Deuteronomy: Texts @ Contexts*, edited by Athalya Brenner and Gale A. Yee, 123–36. Minneapolis: Fortress Press.

———. 2013. "Debt as Weapon: Manufacturing Poverty from Judah to Today." *Diaconia: Journal for the Study of Christian Social Practice* 4, no. 2:141–55.

Coote, Robert B., and Keith W. Whitelam. 1987. *The Emergence of Early Israel in Historical Perspective*. Sheffield: Almond.

Crossley, James G. 2008. *Jesus in an Age of Terror: Scholarly Projects for a New American Century*. London: Equinox.

Davies, Philip. 2000. "What Separates a Minimalist from a Maximalist? Not Much." *BAR* 26, no. 2:24–27, 72–73.

Davies, Philip, and John Rogerson. 2005. *The Old Testament World.* 2nd ed. Louisville: Westminster John Knox.

Dever, William G. 2008. *Did God Have a Wife? Archaeology and Folk Religion in Ancient Israel.* Grand Rapids: Eerdmans.

Esler, Philip F. 2005. "Social-Scientific Models in Biblical Interpretation." In *Ancient Israel: The Old Testament in Its Social Context*, edited by Philip Esler, 3–14. London: SCM.

Fuqua, Charles R. 2012. *God's Law: The Only Political Solution.* Salt Lake City: American Book Publishing.

Gottwald, Norman. 1999. *The Tribes of Yahweh: A Sociology of the Religion of Liberated Israel, 1250–1050* BCE. Sheffield: Sheffield Academic Press.

———. 2001. *The Politics of Ancient Israel.* Louisville: Westminster John Knox.

Grabbe, Lester L. 2007. *Ancient Israel: What Do We Know and How Do We Know It?* London: T&T Clark.

Halpern, Baruch. 1995. "Erasing History: The Minimalist Assault on Ancient Israel." *BRev* 11: 26–35, 47.

Jacobs, A. J. 2007. *The Year of Living Biblically: One Man's Humble Quest to Follow the Bible as Literally as Possible.* New York: Simon & Schuster.

Jeansonne, Sharon Pace. 1990. *The Women of Genesis: From Sarah to Potiphar's Wife.* Minneapolis: Fortress Press.

Josephus, Flavius. 1854. *The Works of Flavius Josephus: Comprising the Antiquities of the Jews, a History of the Jewish Wars, and Life of Flavius Josephus, Written by Himself.* Translated by William Whiston. Philadelphia: Jas. B. Smith.

Karmon, Yehuda. 1971. *Israel: A Regional Geography.* London: Wiley-Interscience.

Knapp, A. Bernard. 1988. "Copper Production and Eastern Mediterranean Trade: The Rise of Complex Society in Cyprus." In *State and Society: The Emergence and Development of Social Hierarchy and Political Centralization*, edited by J. Gledhill, B. Bender, and M. T. Larsen, 149–72. London: Unwin Hyman.

Knowles, Michael P. 2012. "Roberts, R. (ca. 1728–88)." In *Handbook of Women Biblical Interpreters*, edited by M. A. Taylor and A. Choi, 418–20. Grand Rapids: Baker Academic.

Kwok Pui-lan. 2003. "Discovering the Bible in the Non-Biblical World." In *Searching the Scriptures: A Feminist Introduction*, edited by Elisabeth Schüssler Fiorenza, 276–88. New York: Crossroad.

Lings, K. Renato. 2007. "Culture Clash in Sodom: Patriarchal Tales of Heroes, Villains, and Manipulation." In *Patriarchs, Prophets and Other Villains*, edited by Lisa Isherwood, 183–207. London: Equinox.

Liverani, Mario. 2007. *Israel's History and the History of Israel.* Translated by Chiara Peri and Philip Davies. London: Equinox.

Masterson, Teresa. 2011. "Man, 70, Stoned to Death for Being Gay." *NBC10 Philadelphia.* Accessed October 14, 2013. http://www.nbcphiladelphia.com/news/local/Man-70-Stoned-to-Death-for-Homosexuality-Police-118243719.html.

Niditch, Susan. 2010. "Experiencing the Divine: Heavenly Visits, Earthly Encounters and the Land of the Dead." In *Religious Diversity in Ancient Israel and Judah*, edited by Francesca Stavrakopoulou and John Barton, 11–22. London: T&T Clark.

Schüssler Fiorenza, Elisabeth. 2013. *Changing Horizons: Explorations in Feminist Interpretation.* Minneapolis: Fortress Press.

Schweitzer, Albert. 1968. *The Quest of the Historical Jesus: A Critical Study of Its Progress from Reimarus to Wrede.* New York: Macmillan.

Smith, Mark S. 2002. *The Early History of God: Yahweh and the Other Deities in Ancient Israel.* Grand Rapids: Eerdmans.

Stahlberg, Lesleigh Cushing. 2008. "Modern Day Moabites: The Bible and the Debate About Same-Sex Marriage." *BibInt* 16:422–75.

Stavrakopoulou, Francesca. 2010. "'Popular' Religion and 'Official' Religion: Practice, Perception, Portrayal." In *Religious Diversity in Ancient Israel and Judah*, edited by Francesca Stavrakopoulou and John Barton, 37–58. New York: T&T Clark.

Strong, Josiah. 1885. *Our Country: Its Possible Future and Its Present Crisis*. New York: The American Home Missionary Society.

Tull, Patricia K. 2012. "Isaiah." In *Women's Bible Commentary: Twentieth-Anniversary Edition*, edited by C. A. Newsom, S. H. Ringe, and J. E. Lapsley, 255–66. Louisville: Westminster John Knox.

West, Gerald. 2010. "The Legacy of Liberation Theologies in South Africa, with an Emphasis on Biblical Hermeneutics." *Studia Historiae Ecclesiasticae* 36, Supplement: 157–83.

Whitelam, Keith W. 2007. "Lines of Power: Mapping Ancient Israel." In *To Break Every Yoke: Essays in Honour of Marvin L. Chaney*, edited by R. B. Coote and N. K. Gottwald, 40–79. Sheffield: Sheffield Phoenix Press.

Young, Abigail. 2012. "Hildegard of Bingen (1098–1179)." In *Handbook of Women Biblical Interpreters*, edited by M. A. Taylor and A. Choi, 259–64. Grand Rapids: Baker Academic.

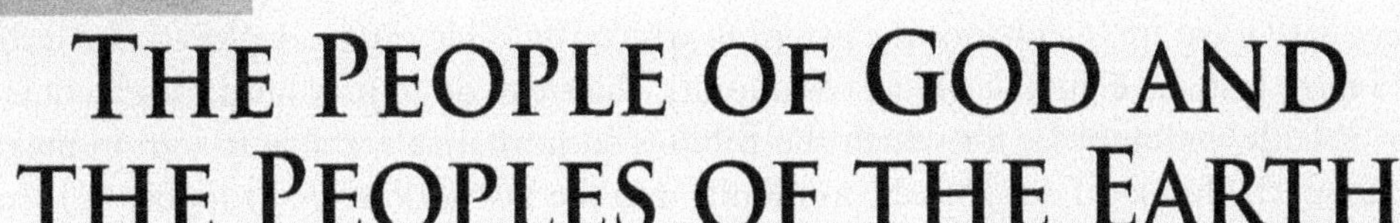

The People of God and the Peoples of the Earth

Hugh R. Page Jr.

The Bible Is Just the Beginning

The Bible is preeminently a book about people. That may strike some as a rather odd assertion given the stature enjoyed by the Bible as sacred text containing, in many faith traditions, everything one needs to know about God and salvation. Nonetheless, some of the more important foci of the Old and New Testaments have to do with the saga of the human family and the women and men that are dramatis personae in this unfolding drama. In the twenty-first century CE, our appreciation of how Scripture narrates that story is much more nuanced than it was perhaps a generation or two ago. We are much more aware of the processes by which traditions are shaped and preserved. We have a deeper understanding of the myriad stages through which the inspired words of prophets, poets, and sages proceed before being canonized: as well as of the place the Bible occupies in the global ecology of sacred texts. Moreover, we recognize that many of the world's sacred texts have important things to say about the human condition. Thus perspectives on what it means to be "people of God," women and men in a special relationship with a transcendent being, or members of a large and diverse human family sharing a common terrestrial abode vary widely. Moreover, in today's world, scholarship in fields such as genetics and anthropology is changing the way we think about human origins and notions of personhood.

It is because of new ideas about humanity and its origins that responsible readers of the Bible must, therefore, examine biblical conceptions of personhood, while keeping in mind the ways in which both the human family in general and those individuals called into special relationship with the God of Israel are construed. In so doing, they must also look at how such ideas have shaped, and continue to influence, notions about the world and its inhabitants today; are related to comparable ideas about personhood in other faith traditions; relate to what scientific evidence reveals about the human family; have been complicit in the exploitation of colonized peoples; and stand in relationship to those ideas about the human family articulated in documents such as the United Nations Declaration of Human Rights and the Declaration on the Rights of Indigenous Peoples. Such a task is necessary if we are to enhance the extent to which the Bible can be deployed as a resource in building a more just and equitable global community. Failure to do so may limit the extent to which members of faith communities for which the Bible is authoritative are able to join in meaningful dialogue about the future of our global community and the institutions that support it. It may also inadvertently lend credence to the idea that religious texts and traditions have no place in conversations about those ideals on which a cosmopolitan global community should be based in the future.

The Earth and Its Peoples—A View from the Ethnographic Record

Science has revealed that modern human beings are the result of a remarkable evolutionary process. We share common African ancestry, and our diversity at this point in time bears witness to an array of migratory, climatic, and genetic adaptations that span hundreds of thousands of years. Our cultural landscape is vast and remarkable in its variation. For example, the comprehensive cultural database maintained by Human Relations Area Files at Yale University (see http://www.yale.edu/hraf/collections.htm) contains information on several hundred cultures.

The *Ethnographic Atlas*, a massive project undertaken by George Peter Murdock (1969) and ultimately brought to full fruition in the 1970s, contains information on more than one thousand distinct groups. As an ethnologist, Murdock was particularly interested in both the comparative study of cultures and the identification of behavioral traits that manifest locally, regionally, and internationally (see especially Murdock 1981, 3). His work calls attention to the breadth of lifeways characteristic of peoples around the world. Scholarship continuing in the vein of Murdock's has led to the identification of some 3,500 cultures on which published data are readily available (see, e.g., Price, 10). Such studies have also resulted in the development of templates for comparing social organization, religious beliefs, and other information about the world's disparate peoples (see Ember and Ember; and Murdock et al.). Needless to say, the vision of the human family derived from this research is remarkable. Social scientists see this diverse collage of languages, customs, and religious traditions as the end result of developmental forces that have been operational for *aeons*. It is also for them a mystery to be probed using the critical tools at their disposal. Ethnographic investigations and theory testing have laid bare and will continue to reveal its undiscovered truths. However, humankind has not revealed, and is not likely to yield, the sum total of its secrets to even the most dogged of investigators. Like the stories of primordial reality we encounter in the biblical book of Genesis, such research offers a place from which to begin pondering what it means to be human.

Human life is, of course, dynamic. New social and religious groups are born constantly. The first two decades of the current millennium have even witnessed the dissolution of geopolitical boundaries, the creation of new nation states, and the birth of new religious movements. Thus notions of culture and personhood in our era are anything but static. Our human family continues to grow and with each passing day becomes more diverse and increasingly complex. Research in the social sciences has increased our understanding of how culture and identity evolve. We know more today than ever before about the ways language, physical environment, and other factors contribute to ideas about what it means to be a fully actualized self and to be in relationship with those other selves that are one's family members, friends, and neighbors. It has also shed light on the role that the collection and preservation of religious lore play in this process. Sacred traditions and texts serve as the repositories for stories about how people and the groups in which they are embedded came to be. They also function as points of reference for the nurture of persons and the communities in which they live.

The challenge we face in an era when such traditions are often read narrowly or uncritically—without an eye toward their implicit limitations—is to create charitable and inclusive approaches that allow us to engage and appropriate them. Such strategies necessitate that we become well versed in the ways that stories, both ancient and modern, shape our identities, beliefs, and relationships with one another. Whether one has in mind venerable tales such as the Babylonian *Enuma Elish* and the so-called Priestly account of creation (Gen. 1:1—2:4a), or modern cinematic myths like the *Matrix* or *Prometheus* sagas, narratives of one kind or another provide a context for understanding who we are and how we choose to live. Returning to the Bible itself, it is arguable that one of its central aims is to inform us of what it means to be finite beings that are threads in a sacred cosmic fabric woven, as it were, by a divine and ineffable artisan.

Ancient Near Eastern Lore and Conceptions of Personhood

In the late nineteenth and early twentieth centuries, scholars such as James Frazer and Stith Thompson began looking seriously at cultural practices and folklore from various parts of the world. The results were remarkable, though not without some degree of controversy. Frazer's efforts included his Victorian-era classic *The Golden Bough* (Frazer 1981) and an equally important, if less celebrated, three-volume work titled *Folk-Lore in the Old Testament* (Frazer 1918a; 1918b; 1918c); and Thompson's work on folklore motifs was pioneering insofar as it laid important groundwork for the comparison of tales from around the world. Although questions remain about the aims and theoretical presuppositions of these early works, their efforts, and those of the scholars following in their immediate footsteps, set the stage for much of the social-scientific research we have seen in the twentieth and twenty-first centuries, even in the field of biblical studies.

Among biblical scholars, the pioneers of form criticism and the so-called myth and ritual school found in this body of information—and other information gathered from ancient Near Eastern sources—a treasure trove useful for contextualizing and interpreting key portions of the Old Testament. Among form critics, Hermann Gunkel must be noted. His collection of essays in *What Remains of the Old Testament* and topical studies of literary *Gattungen* ("forms") as such pertain to the Bible in *The Legends of Genesis* and *The Folktale in the Old Testament* repay—even today—careful reading

(1928; 1964; 1987). Among myth and ritual adherents, Sigmund Mowinckel's work deserves pride of place, especially his *Psalmenstudien* (1966). These pioneers' use of ethnological resources in the study of Scripture were paralleled by those of Johannes Pedersen in his two-volume study of ancient Israelite culture (1926–1940) and extended in subsequent generations by Theodor Gaster's efforts to reclaim and expand the work of Frazer (1950; 1959; 1969); Mary Douglas's exploration of the body as social map (1966); Bruce Malina's use of a circum-Mediterranean paradigm to understand the roles of women and men in the Bible (1989); and others whose work has explored the intersections of Jewish, Christian, Mediterranean, and other cultural traditions both ancient and modern.

Several lessons can be gleaned from this body of research. The first is that people are in some ways "hardwired" to create and tell stories. These stories help in making sense of life crises such as birth, maturation, and death. They are also pivotal in defining the self and the social networks into which individual selves are embedded. A second lesson is that one particular genre, creation stories—whether they focus on the birth of deities (theogonies), the universe (cosmogonies), humanity, tribal confederations, monarchies, or all of the aforementioned—have a direct impact on the ways people understand their place in the world. Creation stories define social and ethnic boundaries, reify social and political hierarchies, and ascribe status based on age, gender, and other ontological and ascribed markers. These two factors should inform the ways information about individuals and groups embedded in poetry, rituals, royal inscriptions, and other texts is understood. A few examples from the ancient Near East are particularly illustrative.

The Mesopotamian flood tradition encountered in the Atrahasis myth has, among its more important purposes, articulation of a basic theological anthropology—one that is based on an understanding of the mutable and immutable dimensions of an, at times, capricious cosmos. Human beings are oddly situated in this power-filled and unstable environment. They are remarkable for three reasons. The first is because they are made of the flesh and blood of a divine insurgent and sacrificed because he led a rebellion against the harsh labor imposed on a subset of deities in the pantheon.

> When the gods themselves were men,
> They did the work. They endured the toil.
> The labor was onerous.
> Massive was the effort. The distress was exceedingly great. (Lambert and Millard, 42 [tablet 1.1.1–4], translation my own)

> Let them sacrifice the divine leader.
> Let the gods purify themselves by immersion.
> With his essence—flesh and blood—let Nintu mix the clay,
> So that divinity and humanity may be thoroughly
> Blended in the amalgam.
> For all time let us hear the drumbeat.
> In the flesh of the god let the ghost remain.
> Let her [Nintu] inform him [the slain god] of his token.
> So that there will be no forgetting,
> The spirit will remain. (Lambert and Millard, 58 [tablet 1.4.208–17], translation my own)

The human heartbeat is the "drum" reminding women and men for all time of the immortal lineage that is uniquely their own. The second reason that people are special is due to their being extended kin, as it were, of Atrahasis, the "exceedingly wise one," who managed to survive the great deluge by which all of humanity was destroyed. To them belongs the empowering, yet dangerous, model of this *liminal* ancestor. As William Moran noted more than four decades ago: "The Atrahasis Epic is an assertion of man's importance in the final order of things. It is also a strong criticism of the gods" (Moran, 59).

Humans are also special (see Moran, 60–61) for a third reason: because they are living proof of the imprudence of the gods and goddesses they serve. Created to assume the day-to-day labor deemed too difficult for immortals to bear, the din of their daily existence proved far too disruptive of their divine patrons' and matrons' sleep. Their death was decreed because they were, in a word, "noisy" (Lambert and Millard, 66 [tablet 1.7.354–59]). It is only through the quick-witted intervention of Enki, his personal god, that Atrahasis and his family are able to escape the inundation. Atrahasis is a powerful symbol of what can happen when human perseverance and divine subterfuge are allied.

The Atrahasis myth suggests that people are made of supernatural "stuff" and are heirs to a distinctive lineage. It also emphasizes that in a world filled with danger, the gods who are in control of the fates of women and men do not always have the best interest of the human family in mind. Although all mortals are in a sense beings belonging to and dependent on the gods, the implication of the sobering reality revealed in this myth is that in order to survive, women and men would do well to leverage their inner resources while at the same time relying, should all else fail, on timely divine intervention by those deities with whom they have a special relationship. Such assertions are, of course, in conversation with anthropologies articulated in other lore across a wide spectrum of genres. For example, Gilgamesh—particularly the Old Babylonian version of this Akkadian classic—focuses attention on the unique challenges confronted by one species of individual: monarchs. Of particular interest in this epic are their socialization, capacity to form friendships, quest for lasting renown, and insecurities about death. royal inscriptions, of which exemplars are too numerous to mention, continue in this vein and further define the traits of kings and those subject to their authority. Suzerainty treaties can be said to function in a comparable manner by defining the relationships of sociopolitical aggregates to one another. Sets of laws, like those found in the Code of Hammurabi, reify social status through taxonomies that identify insiders (e.g., king, free men, and those acquitted of offenses) and outsiders (e.g., criminals, widows, and orphans).

Another story, that of the travails of the god Ba'lu from the ancient city of Ugarit, offers a slightly different perspective on human life—this time from West Semitic lore. Unlike the story of Atrahasis, the Ba'lu myth is concerned primarily with how the enigmatic god of the fructifying rains—mainstays of human life—secures his place as head of the pantheon. Although the primary concern of this tale is Ba'lu's contest with rivals for ascendancy to the throne, it lifts the veil concealing the ongoing cosmic struggle between two such forces that inscribe the parameters for human existence: that is, life/fertility, represented by Ba'lu as numen of the storm, and Môtu, the embodiment of death and dissolution. At one point in this saga, he voluntarily submits himself to the authority and power of Môtu. His death, emblematic of nature's cyclic periods of aridity, leads his father 'Ilu, head of the pantheon, and his sister 'Anatu, to bewail its impact on the world. Both give voice to a lament intended, no doubt, to sum up the anguish of all affected by the storm god's departure.

> Ba'lu has died. What is to become of humanity?
> Dagan's child is no more. What will happen to earth's teeming masses? (CAT 1.5.6.23–24; 1.6.1.6–7)

The world and its inhabitants are part of the background landscape against which this divine drama unfolds. Nonetheless, as the narrative progresses, one realizes that each episode has a profound, if at times only partially articulated, impact on the peoples of the earth. Ba'lu returns to life, largely through the intervention of his sister 'Anatu. Eventually, he and Môtu have a fateful encounter that reveals, in no uncertain terms, that they are—and shall remain—in an interminable struggle.

> They fight each other like heroes
> Môtu is strong, as is Ba'lu
> Like raging bulls, they go head to head
> Môtu is strong, as is Ba'lu
> They bite one another like serpents
> Môtu is strong, as is Ba'lu
> Like animals, they beat each other to a pulp
> Môtu falls, Ba'lu collapses. (CAT 1.6.6.16–22)

The two battle to a virtual draw: an indication that the struggle between life and death is ongoing. The hope for "earth's teeming masses" is that the forces of life are able—at the very least—to withstand Death's furious and unrelenting onslaught. To be engaged nobly in the struggle is, therefore, to participate heroically in an age-old struggle that unites every member of the human family as kin. The warp and weft of day-to-day existence finds its ultimate significance in this ongoing cosmic battle. We see a stunning reflex of this mythology in the biblical Song of Songs, where the protagonists are anthropomorphized hypostases of Love (*'ahăbâ*) and Death (*māwet*).

> Seal me to your heart.
> Brand me on your arm.
> Love is equal to Death in its strength.
> Passion rivals Sheol in its ferocity.
> Its flames are a blazing fire.
> It is an eternal inferno. (Song of Songs 8:6, author's own translation)

Additional textual examples from Egypt and Anatolia could be cited, but the above suffice to show how implicit and explicit messaging about people—their nature, connection to one another, and relationship to the divine forces responsible for their creation and support—is conveyed in expressive culture.

The Hebrew Bible, Personhood, and Identity

Biblical references to the earth and its peoples are very much in conversation with these ancient Near Eastern traditions. The opening chapter of the Hebrew Bible contains a remarkable assertion in what scholars have traditionally designated the Priestly account of creation (Gen. 1:1—2:4a): that the world and everything in it is "good." It uses the Hebrew word *ṭôb* to describe its fundamental essence, a word whose semantic range connotes something sweet and pleasurable. Human beings are an important part of the created order. Made on the sixth day, they are distinguished only by gender: male and female. Neither ethnic nor regional markers are noted. All are made according to the divine "form" (*ṣelem*) and "pattern" (*dĕmût*)—that is, God's "image and likeness" according to the NRSV. Theirs are the tasks of reproducing and exercising control of the earth (1:26–28). The word used to describe what will be involved to reach this desired outcome (*kābaš*) connotes a process requiring forceful effort (Oswalt, 430). Also implied here is the idea that this is a laborious enterprise that is both collective and collaborative.

Following this masterful cosmogonic hymn, readers encounter in the remainder of Genesis a "mixed bag" of traditions about the earth's populace representing several sources: fragments of archaic poetry (2:23; 3:14-19; 4:23-24; 49); a descanting creation narrative (2:4b-24); etiological tales (11:1-9); ethnohistorical musings about the origins of particular peoples (4:17-22); an epic about the peregrinations of Israel's ancestors (11:31—36:43); and an extensive novella dealing with a key figure in the national saga: Joseph (37–50). While these materials can be read—as scholarly literature attests—from a variety of perspectives, one thing is very clear: together they tell the story of the God of Israel's relationship with the world and its peoples, some of whom—namely, Abraham, Sarah, and their descendants—are called to take on special responsibilities for the entirety of the human family (12:1-3). In fact, it could be argued that a significant portion of the Genesis tradition (1:1—11:32) has been intended as a creative "riff" on, or response to, Sumero-Akkadian lore (like that found in Atrahasis) about the origins of humanity.

One of the unifying threads holding together the narrative tapestry of Genesis and the remaining books of the Torah/Pentateuch is the story of how the world is affected by the shifting, strained, at times tumultuous, dynamic, and constantly evolving relationships among those who are the offspring of the primordial family. While highlighting theological themes such as *calling* (Exod. 3:1-15); *covenant* (Exod. 6:1-8; 20:1-17); *sin and redemption* (Exod. 32:1-35); *divine immanence and transcendence* (Exod. 25:1—31:18); *holiness* (Lev. 10:3; 20:26); *significant individuals* (Exod. 2:10; 15:20; 2:21; 3:1); *groups* (Exod. 3:8; 6:19); and *events* (Exodus 15; Num. 3:14-16; 9:15-16); these books also articulate a gestalt ("general sketch") for comprehending what it means to be part of a human family. This can entail struggling both to recognize its connectedness and to honor its diversity. It can also involve wrestling with the challenge of managing intergroup crises that influence the welfare of peoples living in proximity; competing for limited resources; and dealing with those changing geopolitical realities that generate population shifts, form new social movements, and give rise to diasporas. It is for this reason that one of the foci of these books, and the sources used therein, is the establishment of social, religious, and other boundaries that determine personhood, group affiliation, and status. For example, the Priestly creation story (Gen. 1—2:4a) can be said to inscribe broad and inclusive parameters for personhood. Since all human beings bear the imprint of the creator's "form" and "pattern," they can be said to belong to a single unified group, for which gender is the only subclassification (1:26-27). The implication of this is that everyone created *by* God belongs *to* God and is therefore part of the "people of God."

Genealogical tables, such as that found in Genesis 10, offer a more nuanced view of group identity based on location, language, and kin group (e.g., 10:5). The story of the Tower of Babel goes a step further in its linkage of linguistic heterogeneity to human hubris and a divine response to quell it (Gen. 11:5-7). Although it can be read simply as an entertaining etiology accounting for the diversity and spread of languages, it does contain a polemical strain resistant to linguistic solidarity, centralized government, and the conscription of resources needed to build monumental structures and to maintain the places—that is, cities—where they are most likely to be found in antiquity. Thus the story seems to be suggesting, on one level, that diversity and difference are preferable to a homogeneity whose consequences, intended or unintended, are to transgress the boundary separating mortals from God.

The block of material inclusive of the ancestral epic and the story of Joseph's rise to Egyptian prominence offers an even more complex picture of the "people of God." On the one hand, the "yes" given by Abram/Abraham to the call of YHWH (Gen. 12:1-3), and the covenant made with him (Gen. 15:18; 17:1-27) by YHWH, serve to distinguish him and his descendants among the "people of God"—that is, as a conduit of blessing to the entirety of the human family (Gen. 12:3). On the other hand, an inversion of status—from "temporary sojourner" to "inheritor" of Canaan (17:6-8)—is also promised, one that sets the stage for what is later described in Joshua and Judges. The story of Joseph's tensions with his brothers, as well as that of the peculiar circumstances leading Jacob and his kin to go to Egypt, set the stage for further musing on several issues. The first is how the kin group through whom all of the "people of God" are to be blessed understands its internal subdivisions (Genesis 49; Deuteronomy 32–33). The second has to do with how the kin group's liberation, covenant at Sinai, sojourn in the wilderness, and occupation of Canaan (Exod. 4:1—20:21; 32:1—35:29; Num. 1:1—36:13; Joshua; and Judges) are construed, particularly in terms of how these sources present Israel's relationship to its neighbors, both as stewards of a unique revelatory experience and part of a larger family of divine offspring. The third concerns the final book of the Pentateuch—Deuteronomy—that serves as the transitional bridge to the Former Prophets. From a literary standpoint, it is a rearticulation and expansion of core precepts first articulated in Exod. 20:1-17. It inscribes very narrow parameters for Israel's self-understanding and relationship to its neighbors. "When you come into the land that the Lord your God is giving you, you must not learn to imitate the abhorrent practices of those nations" (Deut. 18:9).

The book of Deuteronomy has very strict stipulations for the centralization of worship (12:1-28), prophetic practice (18:15-22), the conduct of war (20:1-20), and the care of those without material support (24:14-15, 17-18). All of these grow out of a particular self-understanding, stated most succinctly in what Gerhard von Rad long ago identified as a short creedal statement.

> A wandering Aramean was my ancestor; he went down into Egypt and lived there as an alien, few in number, and there he became a great nation, mighty and populous. When the Egyptians treated us harshly and afflicted us, by imposing hard labor on us, we cried to the LORD, the God of our ancestors; the LORD heard our voice and saw our affliction, our toil, and our oppression. The LORD brought us out of Egypt with a mighty hand and an outstretched arm, with a terrifying display of power, and with signs and wonders; and he brought us into this place and gave us this land, a land flowing with milk and honey. (Deut. 26:5-9)

Israel's identity as an "alien" subject to "hard labor" and "oppression," now liberated by YHWH, is the backdrop against which Deuteronomy's exclusive covenantal obligations are formulated. The jealousy of YHWH (Deut. 4:24) establishes impermeable cultural and ethical borders separating Israel from its neighbors. Deuteronomy and the historical narrative of the occupation of Canaan and the flowering of the monarchy are written in accordance with its principles. This so-called Deuteronomistic History (abbreviated Dtr by some scholars) consists of Joshua, Judges, the books of Samuel, and 1 and 2 Kings. It offers a far more complex, yet ultimately less inclusive, vision of the "people of God."

For example, we encounter the technical designation *'am yhwh* ("YHWH's people") in the Pentateuch's oldest strata (e.g., Judg. 5:11, 13—an ancient Hebrew poem; and Num. 11:29; 16:41). Here it refers to either the members of Israel's tribal confederation (Judges) or the Israelite community on the march through the wilderness following its flight from Egypt (Numbers). It is present much more frequently in Dtr, where it denotes those faithful bound by the Deuteronomic covenant (Deut. 27:9—*lĕ'am layhwh*); Israel before the establishment of the monarchy (1 Sam. 2:24); the fallen military contingent that supported Jonathan and Saul (2 Sam. 1:12); and as an *ethnonym* for those under the reign of David (2 Sam. 6:21), Jehu (2 Kgs. 9:6), and Jehoida (2 Kgs. 11:17). We also find the terms *'am hā'ĕlōhîm* or *'am 'ĕlōhîm* ("people of God") used in reference to the Israelite tribal contingent armed for battle (Judg. 20:2) and to those under David's sovereign rule (2 Sam. 14:13). Beyond these references, we encounter the term "YHWH's people" in 2 Chron. 23:16 (paralleling 2 Kgs. 11:17). Another enigmatic reference—to "the God of Abraham's people"—is found in Ps. 47:9, a poem asserting the universal kingship of *'ĕlōhîm* ("God").

Although references to "Yahweh's people" and "people of God" do not appear in the Latter Prophets (Isaiah, Jeremiah, Ezekiel, and the Book of the Twelve) or the Writings (outside of the Chronicler), we can certainly detect a keen interest in the world's peoples in many of these books. In some instances, the focus is decidedly polemical. The pointed critique of Israel's neighbors in prophetic oracles is an excellent example (e.g., Isaiah 14–19; Ezekiel 26–30). The bimodal subdivision of humanity in Proverbs (between those who heed Wisdom's voice and others who do not in Proverbs 8–9). A third case in point is the distinction made between "those who lead many to righteousness" in Dan. 12:3) and their opponents. In others, there is an affirmation of the God of Israel's keen interest in building an inclusive eschatological community (e.g., Isa. 66:18-21) and questioning a culture of entitlement and condemnatory rhetoric among Israelite prophets (Jon. 4:9-11). In Jewish apocryphal literature, we also see an interest expressed in the relationship among peoples. In the Greek Addition F to Esther, an editor has called attention to the different "lots" God has assigned to "the people of God" and to "all the nations" (10:10). The author of the Wisdom of Solomon takes a slightly different tack. While adopting a rhetoric that accentuates the difference between the "righteous" and the "ungodly" (Wisdom), it also calls attention to the common ancestry of humanity:

> there is for all one entrance into life, and one way out. (Wis. 18:9)

What we have, therefore, in the Hebrew Bible are multiple visions of what it means to be "people of God" and "peoples of the earth." Some are narrow. Others are selectively inclusive. All must be read with an eye toward genre, the setting in which the text was produced, and the social, political, and religious circumstances it seeks to address.

It goes almost without saying that biblical writers and their initial audiences were concerned with theological issues such as Israel's election and the implications such issues have on the community's holiness and distinctiveness when compared to its neighbors. In light of this special calling, as it were, boundaries—their creation, maintenance, and occasional erasure—take on particular significance. Maintenance is a sign of covenantal fidelity (Deut. 7:1-6) and purity (Lev. 10:1-3). Periodic transgression is, at least in some instances, a necessary survival strategy. Judges is an excellent case in point (see Page). We see evidence in this book of the crossing of bodily, cultural, and other borders as part of what characterizes Israelite life during that bittersweet epoch when "there was no king in Israel" and "people did what was right in their own eyes" (Judg. 21:25). Israel's identity as a people with a unique identity, mission, and teleological objective is, thus, variously articulated in the Hebrew Bible. These overlapping, competing, and complementary ideas of what it means to be a "people of God" among "the earth's peoples" require attentiveness to the religious objectives, political aims, and eschatological foci of the books in which they are found. Therefore, any attempt to fully reconcile all aspects of these disparate conceptions is likely to meet with frustration. Instead, it is perhaps better to recognize that the Hebrew Bible does not speak with a single voice on the issue of what it means to be part of the human family.

Looking beyond the Bible

One could argue that this absence of uniformity in the Hebrew Bible is an invitation not simply to read, but also to query and "talk back to" its books. Among the questions we should ask is what sources—in addition to Scripture—we ought to consult in making sense of who we are, what our relationship should be to one another, and what our place is in the universe. This process is far more involved than turning to Genesis or some other biblical book for a "proof text" (the practice of using a specific text as the final authoritative word on a given issue). Instead, it requires taking into consideration modern geopolitical realities such as globalization and what the pure, applied, and social sciences are telling us about our biological origins, diversity, and connectedness.

It also makes it incumbent on Bible readers to be aware of how documents such as the United Nations Declaration on Human Rights (1948) and the United Nations Declaration on the Rights of Indigenous Peoples (2007) influence how we think about our rights and responsibilities as people of faith and citizens of the world. For example, article 1 of the former states that "all human beings are born free and equal in dignity and rights. They are endowed with reason and conscience and should act towards one another in a spirit of brotherhood" (United Nations General Assembly 2000, 326). An affirmation of this kind shapes the way one thinks about religious texts and traditions that qualify human freedom, equality, dignity, or rights endowed at birth. Furthermore, according to article 18 of the Declaration, "Everyone has the right to freedom of thought, conscience, and religion; this right includes freedom to change his religion or belief, and freedom either alone or in community with others and in public or private, to manifest his religion or belief in teaching, practice, worship, and observance" (United Nations General Assembly 2000, 327). Such texts can't help but influence our reading and deployment of those parts of the Bible that affirm behaviors that affirm or disagree with these statements and the ideals they represent. In the case of those that run counter, a hermeneutic inclusive of exegesis and critical engagement is warranted. Article 7 section 2 of the United Nations Declaration on the Rights of Indigenous Peoples states that "indigenous peoples have the collective right to live in freedom, peace and security as distinct peoples and shall not be subjected to any act of genocide or any other act of violence, including forcibly removing children of the group to another group" (United Nations General Assembly 2007, 5). Moreover, article 8 section 1 affirms that "indigenous peoples and individuals have the right not to be subjected to forced assimilation or destruction of their culture" (United Nations General Assembly 2007, 5). The reading or deployment of biblical passages that appear to celebrate or support behaviors of this kind can be neither ignored nor interpreted in a way that treats lightly the ways they have been used to justify policies that abrogate the rights of indigenous peoples around the world.

Thus, in our current era, perhaps the Bible should be seen less as the single authoritative source from which the final word on what it means to be "people of God" and "people of the earth" is to be found, and more as one of several interlocutors—including lived experience—informing our consideration of what is an unfolding *mystery* about the larger human experience that we are invited to prayerfully ponder.

Works Cited

Douglas, Mary. 1966. *Purity and Danger*. London: ARK.

Eilberg-Schwartz, Howard. 1990. *The Savage in Judaism: Anthropology of Israelite Religion and Ancient Judaism*. Bloomington: Indiana University Press.

Ember, Melvin, and Carol R. Ember, eds. 1999. *Cultures of the World: Selections from the Ten-Volume Encyclopedia of World Cultures*. New York: Macmillan Library Reference USA.

Frazer, James. 1981. *The Golden Bough*. 1890. Reprint, New York: Grammercy.

———. 1918a. *Folk-Lore in the Old Testament*. Vol. 1. London: Macmillan.

———. 1918b. *Folk-Lore in the Old Testament*. Vol. 2. London: Macmillan.

———. 1918c. *Folk-Lore in the Old Testament*. Vol. 3. London: Macmillan.

Gaster, Theodor H. 1950. *Thespis: Ritual, Myth, and Drama in the Ancient Near East*. New York: Harper & Row.

———, ed. 1959. *The New Golden Bough*. New York: Criterion.

———. 1969. *Myth, Legend and Custom in the Old Testament.* New York: Harper & Row.

Gunkel, Hermann. 1928. *What Remains of the Old Testament and Other Essays.* Translated by A. K. Dallas. New York: Macmillan.

———. 1964. *The Legends of Genesis: The Biblical Saga and History.* Translated by W. H. Carruth. Reprint of the introduction to the author's 1901 *Commentary on Genesis.* New York: Schocken.

———. 1987. *The Folktale in the Old Testament.* Translated by M. D. Rutter. Translation of the 1917 ed. Sheffield: Almond.

Lambert, W. G., and A. R. Millard, eds. 1999. *Atra-Hasis: The Babylonian Story of the Flood.* 1969. Reprint, Winona Lake, IN: Eisenbrauns.

Malina, Bruce. 1989. "Dealing with Biblical (Mediterranean) Characters: A Guide for U.S. Consumers." *BTB* 19:127–41.

Moran, William L. 1971. "Atrahasis: The Babylonian Story of the Flood." *Bib* 52:51–61.

Mowinckel, Sigmund. 1966. *Psalmenstudien: 1921–1924.* Amsterdam: Grüner.

Murdock, George Peter. 1969. *Ethnographic Atlas.* 3rd ed. Pittsburgh: University of Pittsburgh Press.

———. 1981. *Atlas of World Cultures.* Pittsburgh: University of Pittsburgh Press.

Murdock, George Peter, C. S. Ford, A. E. Hudson, R. Kennedy, L. W. Simmons, and J. W. M. Whiting. 1987. *Outline of Cultural Materials.* 5th ed. New Haven: Human Relations Area Files.

Oswalt, J. N. 1980. "Kabash." In *Theological Wordbook of the Old Testament*, edited by R. Laird Harris, Gleason L. Archer, and Bruce K. Waltke, 1:430. Chicago: Moody Press.

Page, Hugh R., Jr. 1999. "The Marking of Social, Political, Religious, and Other Boundaries in Biblical Literature—A Case Study Using the Book of Judges." *Research in the Social Scientific Study of Religion* 10:37–55.

Pedersen, Johannes. 1926–1940. *Israel: Its Life and Culture.* 4 vols. London: Oxford University Press.

Price, David H. 2004. *Atlas of World Cultures: A Geographical Guide to Ethnographic Literature.* 1989. Reprint, Caldwell, NJ: Blackburn.

Rad, Gerhard von. 1966. *The Problem of the Hexateuch and Other Essays.* London: SCM.

Thompson, Stith. 2001. *Motif-index of Folk-Literature: A Classification of Narrative Elements in Folk-tales, Ballads, Myths, Fables, Mediaeval Romances, Exempla, Fabliaux, Jest-Books.* Rev. ed. 6 vols. Bloomington: University of Indiana Press.

United Nations General Assembly. 2000. "Universal Declaration of Human Rights (1948)." In *Sourcebook of the World's Religions: An Interfaith Guide to Religion and Spirituality*, edited by J. Beversluis, 325–28. Novato, CA: New World Library.

———. 2007. *United Nations Declaration on the Rights of Indigenous Peoples.* http://www.un.org/esa/socdev/unpfii/documents/DRIPS_en.pdf.

Reading the Christian Old Testament in the Contemporary World

Daniel L. Smith-Christopher

In nineteenth-century Charleston, South Carolina, the Old Testament seemed to assure Episcopal clergyman Frederick Dalcho that slavery was consistent with Christian faith. The same Old Testament, however, particularly Josh. 6:21, just as powerfully inspired fellow Charleston resident and former slave Denmark Vesey to plan a slave revolt. Those involved in the slave revolt felt assured that God would help them "utterly destroy all in the city, both men and women, young and old, with the edge of the sword" (Edgerton 1999, 101–25). In 2010, Steven Hayward, at that time F. K. Weyerhaeuser Fellow at the American Enterprise Institute, published an essay in which he read the story of Joseph in Egypt as a dire warning against government intervention, and suggested that his reading of these texts from Genesis served as a defense of a free-market, private-property economic system. Also in 2010, John Rogerson, professor of Scripture at Sheffield University, began his book on Old Testament theology, written because he, too, believed that the "Old Testament has something to say to today's world(s)," by stating that he wrote as "an Anglican priest . . . a humanist and a socialist" (Rogerson, 11). Dr. James Edwards, of the Center for Immigration Studies, reads some of the Mosaic laws of the Old Testament as defending firm national borders, low tolerance for immigration rights, and concerns for cultural corruption by outsiders (Edwards 2009 n.p., online), while Dr. Lai Ling Elizabeth Ngan of Baylor University, an Asian American scholar, finds that the Old Testament story about God's listening to the prayers of the "foreign woman," namely Hagar, "redefines boundaries that others have inscribed for her"; the story suggests that modern Christians should uphold the dignity of all peoples and resist denigrating people because of physical or racial differences (Ngan 2006, 83).

These are six Christians, all reading their Old Testament in the contemporary world. The fact that not all of these voices are biblical scholars, however, only serves to highlight the fact that reading the Christian Old Testament in the contemporary world is a complex mixture of the scholarly as well as the popular, stereotyped traditional views as well as innovative new insights, and that reading the Old Testament often strikingly divides readers into quite seriously opposing social and political views. Does this mean that reading the Christian Bible (Old or New Testament) in the modern world is a parade example of Cole Porter's 1934 song "Anything Goes"? Is it a matter of some disappointment that we can still agree with Leo Perdue's 1994 observation that "no commanding contemporary theology has yet appeared to form a consensus" (Perdue 1994, 8)?

I would argue that there is no cause for despair. Quite to the contrary! One of the most fascinating aspects of reading the Christian Old Testament in the contemporary world is not simply that there is unprecedented enthusiasm and diversity among scholars and viewpoints in the field but also that *this diversity itself is part of an ongoing debate and discussion*. At the outset, however, we should clarify that we are interested in thinking about serious readings of the Christian Old Testament, and not merely social or political propaganda that lightly seasons its rhetoric with a few Bible verses.

Marketplaces vs. Museums

Biblical scholarship is separated from religious propaganda not only by the fact that biblical scholarship presumes a basic orientation in the relevant historical contexts of the ancient world, familiarity with a diversity of texts both ancient and modern, and the ability to recognize a good argument supported by credible evidence or reasonable suggestions. These are all essential, of course. What really separates biblical scholarship from propaganda is the fact that biblical scholarship in the contemporary world is part of an ongoing discussion—a discussion that knows *and listens* to the challenges of others and seeks to contribute one's own insights *as part of the discussion*. As in all fields of discovery and intellectual endeavor, the success of biblical scholarship is not to be measured by the achievement of some dominant unanimity, but rather is judged by the quality and results of the participation in the scholarly tasks at hand and the *shared perception* that progress is taking place. We are seeing and understanding biblical texts in ever more profound and provocative ways. However, one of the most striking aspects of the rise of simplistic or propagandist use of the Bible is precisely its refusal to engage in dialogue, self-correction, or even acknowledgment of rival views, beyond the occasional ad hominem dismissal of arguments based solely on their association with groups identified by politicized generalizations—for example, "those liberals."

What we are suggesting is that there is an essential *dialogue* in modern, serious reading of the Bible. So, if this essay on reading the Christian Old Testament is not to be a rehearsal of some of the grand theories generally agreed on, now and forever (like a quiet museum tour of accomplishments), it is time for a new guiding image. I am intrigued by suggestions of the Cuban American New Testament scholar Fernando Segovia, who celebrates diversity in dialogue over the Scriptures. Segovia has famously suggested the "marketplace of ideas," rather like Wole Soyinka's discussion of the Silk Road market town Samarkand, as an image of modern sharing and exchanging of multicultural ideas and friendships (see Segovia and Tolbert; Segovia; Soyinka). An introduction to reading the Christian Old Testament in the contemporary world does not need to provide a historical survey of the "great ideas" that led to the present. Good surveys already exist, if European-dominated ideas are one's particular interest (e.g., Ollenburger; Rogerson 1984; Hayes and Prussner). Marketplaces can be elusive, however. They exist within the totality of the lives of people from everywhere, people who set up stalls and shop. Like the night markets of Auckland, New Zealand, or Darwin, Australia, they appear at designated places, at the designated hours, but otherwise there is only quiet. In short, the image of the marketplace suggests that we need a guidebook.

Laura Pulido, Laura Barraclough, and Wendy Cheng have recently published a marvelous, politically informed tour guide titled *A People's Guide to Los Angeles* (2012). The introduction itself is worth the price of admission. In these preliminary observations, the authors reflect on guidebooks and Los Angeles itself.

> *A People's Guide to Los Angeles* is a deliberate political disruption of the way Los Angeles is commonly known and experienced. . . . Guidebooks select sites, put them on a map, and interpret them in terms of their historical and contemporary significance. All such representations are political, because they highlight some perspectives while overlooking others. Struggles over who and what counts as "historic" and worthy of a visit involve decisions about who belongs and who doesn't, who is worth remembering and who can be forgotten, who we have been and who we are becoming.

They continue,

> Mainstream guidebooks typically describe and interpret their sites through the story of one person—almost always a man, and usually the capitalist who invested in a place, or its architect or designer. In doing so, they reinforce an individualized and masculinist way of thinking about history. Meanwhile, the collectives of people who actually created, built, or used the space remain nameless.

It would be difficult to think of a better series of thoughts to begin an essay on reading the Christian Old Testament in the contemporary world, because biblical analysis is rarely, if ever, written without some contemporary concerns in mind. Modern biblical theologies, for example, now usually identify the perspective of the author in the contemporary world (e.g., Brueggemann 1997; Rogerson 2010). Thus I am quite certain that part of the reason I agree with this need for a new image is that I write as a Christian who was born into, and very self-consciously remain informed by, the Quaker tradition. I also learned a great deal of biblical history, language, and theology from my fellow Christian sectarians the Mennonites, and I was first inspired to think seriously about biblical theology in high school by reading Vernard Eller, a theologian from yet another of my sister sectarian movements, the Church of the Brethren (informally known as the Dunkers). This means that I write as a Christian raised on "counterhistories" of the Christian movement—George Fox on Pendle Hill, Margaret Fell at Swarthmore, Conrad Grebel in Zurich, and Alexander Mack in Philadelphia—in addition to the canonical events of Christian history, such as the councils, the division between Rome and the Eastern Orthodox, Calvin, Luther, Wesley, and so on. I am thus well aware that texts, like towns, are susceptible to decisions about which locations are worthy of a visit, and which locations ought to be "memorialized" as deeply important. We could visit the old, established halls memorializing conquest or power—or we can find the marketplaces where we can encounter new ideas, argue with the "stall keepers" (the authors), make offers and listen to the counteroffers. In short, Christian biblical scholarship is tolerant of a variety of particular views of biblical texts, grammar, history, or theological interpretation. It is quite properly intolerant of the refusal to participate in dialogue with others. One of the hallmarks of propagandist abuses of the Bible in the modern world is the virtual absence of dialogue with other serious students of the Bible—a refusal to appear in the marketplace where ideas are examined and challenged.

It might seem that all this "marketplace" talk runs the risk of privileging process rather than results, and thus avoiding the hard work of evaluating whether ideas are good or bad, and then promoting the good. It is a uniquely contemporary heresy, however, to privilege solitary ideas or accomplishments while overlooking the long processes that often lead to any achievements worthy of celebration. Furthermore, to celebrate dialogue in the development of Christian thought about the Bible has sometimes been thought to be a uniquely modern phenomenon. That is already a mistake. What constitutes the "Old Testament," and even whether to have one, have both been matters of serious debate in Christian history.

The Christian Old Testament as a Product of Dialogue

Let us begin with a deceptively simple question: What constitutes the Old Testament? Christians do not even agree on this! Before the early Christian movement that historians now routinely refer to as "orthodox" arose victorious, the determination of what would be the authorized and foundational writings for Christian faith was a lively debate. The so-called *Festal Letter* 39 of Athanasius, which includes the earliest authoritative "list" of a canon of the Christian Bible, is dated to (a surprisingly late) 367 CE. Before then, debates about texts clearly ranged widely, and this does not even address the interesting continued use of noncanonical lore in popular, pre-Reformation medieval theater in the streets and churches of Europe (see Muir).

Furthermore, Athanasius's fourth-century declaration did not really settle the matter. Protestant, Catholic, and Orthodox Christians have each determined to authorize slightly different Old Testaments. Catholics, staying with the collection of Jewish writings that appeared in some of the old Greek translations known as the Septuagint (LXX), have included a series of books in the Old Testament that Protestants do not recognize, which Catholics call "deuterocanonical," and the Orthodox have chosen to include even a few more of these later Jewish (but still pre-Christian) writings. Protestants usually refer to these works as "the Apocrypha." Having said this, however, the difference between Christian canons has fewer implications for biblical scholarship than one might suspect at first. This is primarily because academic biblical studies, including biblical theological work, now tends to overlook specific church doctrines regarding the categories of "canonical," "deuterocanonical," and "noncanonical" writings. In the biblical studies marketplace, no text, artifact, ancient translation, or geographical context is "off limits" to research, comment, and consideration.

Canonical works obviously get the most attention—but it is hardly exclusive—and commentaries and critical analysis of *noncanonical* writing often make significant contributions to the further understanding of the canonical work as well. But we aren't finished with dialogue in relation to the existence of the Old Testament.

In fact, Christianity was marked by diversity in dialogue from the very beginning, as any sober reading of the arguments discussed in the book of Acts clearly reveals. One reason that dialogue is such an important context for thinking about the Old Testament is the fact that *the very existence of a "Christian Old Testament" was not a matter of widespread agreement in the earliest history of Christianity.* The early Christian convert Marcion (c. 85–160) famously proposed that true Christianity ought to discard any connection whatsoever to Judaism and the Jewish tradition; he embraced only a limited number of writings to represent this clean break between Jesus and the Jewish tradition (he proposed only a version of Luke, and ten Pauline epistles). However, the reaction was furious and widespread. W. H. C. Frend argues that Marcion holds the distinction of being "one of the very few opponents of orthodoxy whom Greek and Latin theologians united in damning. For nearly a century after his death . . . he was the arch-heretic" (212). Clearly, not every idea in the marketplace survives. We can stop cynically humming Porter's "Anything Goes" now.

The first Christian centuries, therefore, bequeath a task to all subsequent generations of readers of the "Christian Old Testament," namely, to take these writings into serious consideration when determining the nature of Christian faith. Furthermore, the vast majority of modern Christian communities (Protestant, Catholic, and Orthodox) have agreed with the church fathers and mothers of the first centuries that Christianity does indeed have a "canon," and that the Hebrew writings are part of it. Is this a settled issue, then? Hardly. Before we can speak of ways the Christian Old Testament is being read in the contemporary world, it is important to acknowledge, however briefly, that there are still ways it is *not* being read, and that it is even effectively ignored, in Christian faith and practice. Marcion still haunts us.

Tourism vs. Engagement: Ignoring the Marketplace?

As Aidan Nichols has recently acknowledged for the Catholic Church (2007), and as many others have suggested for other churches (Jenkins 2006, 42–47), a serious tendency remains among many Christian traditions in the modern world to overlook the larger part of their Bible before the Gospel of Matthew begins. Effectively ignoring the witness of the Old Testament for modern Christian faith and practice has sometimes been referred to as "Neo-Marcionism" (Nichols, 81). Even though few modern Christians would explicitly admit to it, the lack of effective education or preaching in Old Testament/Hebrew Bible studies is an alarming prospect for Christian faith and practice. A Christian theology cannot be true to the historic legacy of the faith tradition if it perpetuates such a neo-Marcionite subordination of these texts. This can happen in a number of ways, but it is more typical of popular and/or propagandist readings of the Bible than in biblical scholarship. In fact, some ways of "reading the Christian Old Testament" are simply ways to avoid it!

For example, there is a huge market for "Bible prophecy" books in the United States. One of the most significant criticisms of this popular literature is not only its total neglect of serious biblical scholarship on the prophetic books of the Old Testament but also its exclusive interest in how the books of the Bible may be "decoded" so that they can be understood to refer to contemporary events—as if the eighth-century-BCE book of Amos were actually speaking about twentieth-century Russia, or second-century-BCE portions of the book of Daniel were actually speaking about the twentieth-century ayatollahs of Iran. This "decoding" process usually neglects the historical content of the Old Testament book at hand in favor of what it is "understood" to be saying about modern times. In short, the actual content is merely a code. Its decoded meaning has nothing to do with what is actually written, when it was written, or who may have written it. One effective way of entirely ignoring a biblical book, then, is to completely reconstruct it without regard to its actual content as a historical work. This may not be Marcion's original idea, but he would clearly approve. This radical transformation of the work has little to do with actual study of it, nor is this part of the serious dialogue taking place about how the books of the Old Testament ought to inform contemporary Christian faith and practice.

This case of wildly popular literature on Bible prophecy in the modern world is particularly ironic. While some Christians frequently fault biblical scholars for not accepting the "plain sense" of the biblical text, it is astounding how carefully the various approaches to Bible prophecy omit any engagement with the most straightforward, or "plain," messages of the prophets of ancient Israel, namely, God's concern for the poor and the judgment threatened against the rich and powerful, those who, in the unforgettable images of Amos and Isaiah,

> trample the head of the poor into the dust of the earth,
> and push the afflicted out of the way (Amos 2:7)

or who

> join house to house,
> who add field to field,
> until there is room for no one but you,
> and you are left to live alone
> in the midst of the land! (Isa. 5:8)

No decoding seems necessary here. Radically altering the Old Testament texts beyond any credible historical or theological contexts in the process is clearly to do violence to those texts.

Another even more problematic way to virtually ignore the Old Testament in the Christian tradition is the Christian idea that the Old Testament is "old" and therefore largely replaced by the New Testament. Jesus is thus understood to have so reformed Jewish thought, very much as in Marcion's original proposal, that very little of the Old Testament is left of any real importance for Christian theology (save, perhaps, for the Ten Commandments). The dangers of such a "de-Semiticized" Jesus are legion, beginning with the problem of failing to understand Jesus' own faith tradition. For example, the event universally known as the "cleansing of the temple" is incomprehensible apart from recognizing that Jesus cites two Hebrew prophets in the act (Jer. 7:11 and Isa. 56:7). The reactions to Jesus' famous "reading" in his home synagogue in Luke 4 are equally incomprehensible apart from carefully noting the Old Testament references therein. Such examples can be multiplied throughout the New Testament.

Finally, the Hebrew tradition in both its historic and contemporary expressions is revered by a living people. Contemporary Christian scholarship is increasingly open to dialogue with Jewish biblical scholarship. Even though all Christians share most of the books of the Jewish canon with Judaism, there has been historically a significant difference in Jewish study of the Bible as opposed to Christian study (see summaries in Sommer 2012). One of the important characteristics of modern Christian readings of the Old Testament is that Jewish, Roman Catholic, Orthodox, and Protestant Scripture scholars are all in dialogue and discussion with each other in biblical studies on levels unprecedented before the twentieth century, and these dialogues continue in a variety of academic contexts in the twenty-first century.

Exorcising the ghost of Marcion from contemporary Christian scholarship of the Old Testament properly insists that taking the Old Testament seriously for Christian faith and practice involves a consideration of what Old Testament writings can say to the Christian tradition, not vice versa; Christian tradition should not use the Old Testament to buttress predetermined doctrinal ideas derived from the New Testament. Dictating terms to the Old Testament will never allow it to speak to Christian faith and practice in new and challenging ways. That isn't the way a marketplace works, after all, and trying to fix prices and control commodities only leads to other marketplaces.

The Role of Historical Events in the Old Testament for Christian Faith and Practice

We have already determined that the adjective *Christian* in our title means that we are interested in how the Old Testament speaks to Christian faith and practice, and therefore we are interested in discussing the role of "biblical theology." Here we encounter one of the loudest sectors of our marketplace. There are contemporary scholars (see Barr) who maintain an older tradition that suggests Old Testament scholarship should never be primarily "religious" or "theological," but rather historical, examining texts and other ancient evidence and then handing the results over to the theologians. Thus some scholars believe that biblical theology seeks to identify an exclusively *historical* expression of *past* belief (e.g., What did the ancient Israelites believe?). Indeed, the famous inaugural lecture of Johann Gabler in 1787, considered by some to be the "founding document" of this understanding of biblical theology (Gabler, 497), argued quite forcefully for maintaining a clear separation between biblical theology, defined as an exclusively historical enterprise, on the one hand, and systematic ("dogmatic") theology on the other.

It should be acknowledged that many modern biblical scholars would insist on this same separation between the historical and the theological approaches to Old Testament study and firmly place themselves in the "historical questions only" camp. Some scholars, again citing the late James Barr, have no objection to doing Christian theology based on biblical ideas, but believe that the formulation of these religious ideas ought to be a separate task from the exclusively historical task of Old Testament study. There are others who have doubts about religious belief in general or about the viability or validity of the specific religious traditions that make religious use of these writings. Some biblical scholars self-identify as atheists, for example, and there are even contemporary biblical scholars who openly condemn the very notion of a viable contemporary belief informed by the Bible (e.g., Avalos).

Both versions of the "historical analysis only" argument would maintain that it is not only possible but also necessary for a scholar of biblical texts to refrain from allowing contemporary interests or commitments (religious or otherwise) to "bias" or "interfere" with the task of historical analysis. This proposed form of historical analysis is represented as an activity that seeks to emulate scientific methodology as much as possible. The goal of this approach is thus described as "objective knowledge," or at least a close approximation of objective knowledge, even if these scholars were to acknowledge that certain influences or limitations of a time period certainly apply, such as the state of historical, archaeological, and textual studies at the time. In either case, the result is similar: a form of biblical studies that would be understood entirely as an aspect of historical investigation, no different in kind from determining what Shakespeare or Isaac Newton may have "believed," on religious (or any other) questions. Thus, while some may think or hope that their work could contribute to Christian faith and practice, they would carefully leave that task to others.

Interest-Free Biblical Analysis?

Recent debates, however, forcefully challenge many of the methodological assumptions that a bias-free analysis of historical texts is even a possible, much less laudable, goal. The term *postmodernism* is normally assigned to such challenges. Especially since the work of Thomas Kuhn (who gave us the concept of a "paradigm shift," 1996) and Paul Feyerabend (who calls for an "anarchist theory of knowledge," 2010), even the notion of an "objective" *scientific* analysis (science being the purported, even if largely self-appointed, model of objective analysis for all fields of inquiry) has been largely abandoned as both claim and goal. Motivations or interests do not necessarily poison results, but in the postmodern age, we are always vigilant about their influence, and thus the tendency in postmodernism is to declare such "interests" in the work itself. Does this preclude the possibility of doing biblical theology for modern Christian faith and practice? I contend that the postmodern criticism of a "bias-free" analysis of the Bible not only allows an enterprise of biblical theology but also positively encourages it.

The endless debates about the precise meaning of postmodernism need not distract us from a useful insight associated with this term: *all knowledge is contingent.* What we "know" usually depends on what we seek to know, and thus the questions we think to ask. Furthermore, what we investigate is influenced by own concerns, and we also sort out and determine which of our results are the most important. This is all part of the dialogue of diversity and, in twenty-first-century study of the Christian Old Testament, is now a widely acknowledged working assumption. Few would deny the importance of not only the identification of one's own working interests and assumptions in thinking about how the Christian Old Testament can speak to the modern age but also the retrospective work of placing older Old Testament theological writings in important social and historical contexts in ways that deepen our appreciation of their achievements and limitations (Rogerson 1984).

Is There a "Collapse of History" in Christian Old Testament Study?

There is an interesting debate going on in another sector of the marketplace. In his recent important monographs on the problems of Old Testament biblical theology, Leo Perdue refers to a "collapse of history" in recent biblical studies. One of the ways he formulates this point is to ask: Can these predominantly religious texts really help us reconstruct historical events in ancient Israel? If not, how can it be said that Israel's experience is important for contemporary readers who are seeking to read these texts as a guide to events that inform contemporary faith and practice? Perdue alludes to an important ongoing debate that began in the late twentieth century, a debate about our ability to know much actual history from what is available to us both in the Old Testament texts and in the relevant archaeological work (both ancient texts and artifacts) that supplements the study of biblical texts.

Especially after the publication of Thomas L. Thompson's widely cited monograph *The Historicity of the Patriarchal Narratives* (1974), fiery debates ensued between scholars who were divided (often unfairly) into "camps" called "minimalists" and "maximalists." These terms referred to those who despaired of the ability to be confident about historical events at all (thus "minimalists") and those who thought there was actually a great deal more evidence for biblical history than was often acknowledged (so Dever 2001; 2003). An interesting summary view of some of the historical debates is provided by Grabbe.

However, as some contemporary scholars have pointed out (see Brueggemann), these debates about historical events and biblical narratives mask the importance of answering a previous question, namely, whether *establishing that an event happened—or precisely how it happened—automatically dictates a corresponding religious significance to that event.* Clearly, it does not. Even if I can be convinced, for example, that the measurements of the temple provided in Ezekiel 40–48 are precise, accurate dimensions of the Jerusalem temple during the first millennium BCE, this does not strike me as having monumental importance for Christian faith and practice. It may have quite fascinating historical interest, but *theological* significance? This can also apply to less obscure issues. For example, determining that the texts in the opening chapters of the book of Exodus give us a more or less "historically reliable" report of the actual events of Israelites departing from Egypt does not thereby answer the question: Of what significance is the departure from Egypt *for contemporary Christian faith and practice*? Simply agreeing on the *historical* reliability of a biblical passage leaves considerable ground to cover on questions of *significance.* Simply agreeing on the historical details of the exodus, for example, does not thereby make one a liberation theologian. In fact, precious little of the powerful writings of liberation theology, beginning with the 1968 gathering of bishops in Medellín, Colombia (CELAM), actually debated the historical details of the book of Exodus. It is not that the historical story is insignificant; but rather its historical significance, if any, needs to be *part* of the theological argument, and not the entire task.

What happens when different perspectives can no longer be united on a particular reading of biblical events, especially on the accompanying significance of those events? Dominant and influential Old Testament theologies of the past depended on accepting an assigned weight to particular passages or biblical events that were considered central or guiding concepts, and thus critically important for modern theology. For example, Walter Eichrodt proposed that the idea of God's establishing agreements or "covenants" with God's people represents the central notion of the entire Hebrew Bible (Eichrodt 1961; 1967; the original German volumes were published in 1933 and 1935). Gerhard von Rad's equally influential Old Testament theology (Rad 1962; 1965; German 1957 and 1960) argued for the central importance of certain narratives of faith that Israelites allegedly repeated (he used the term "creeds") as indications of their faith, and thus suggested that Israelites were people who identified with such narratives. There is little doubt that such theological arguments, based on readings of the Old Testament, exerted a powerful influence on Christian theological education throughout the Western world in the twentieth century.

However, what if differing perspectives on the part of modern readers of the Bible—especially influenced by differing life situations (ethnicity, gender, etc.)—suggest to some modern readers that different biblical "events" in the Old Testament (whether unquestionably historical or not) are more important than others? Examples are not difficult to cite. On the one hand, after 1968, Latin American biblical scholars (especially Roman Catholic scholars) determined that the Moses and Exodus stories had a powerful message for them in their modern-day circumstances of economic poverty. On the other hand, Native American (Osage) professor of American studies Robert Allan Warrior famously challenged biblical theologians who celebrated the exodus and the entry to a "promised land" by noting that Native Americans frankly had more in common with the beleaguered Canaanites, reminding us that indigenous peoples continue to have an ambiguous relationship with the legacy of the book of Joshua (see Warrior). Nineteenth-century African American slaves also determined that the Jonah and Daniel stories had powerful messages for them in their circumstances of oppression and suppression (Levine; Cone 1992). Finally, recent suggestions view the conquest of Jerusalem in 587 and the subsequent exile of thousands of Judeans (Albertz; Ahn) as a biblical event with serious theological implications (Brueggemann; Smith-Christopher 2002). Nineteenth-century Maori Christians in New Zealand determined that the prophets were powerful examples of a new form of pantribal leadership that had new potential to unite previously fragmented tribal peoples in opposition to growing European settlement, and some even looked to the Davidic monarchy as a model for a new and culturally unprecedented Maori king, and thus an answer to the power and authority of the British Crown (Elsmore 1985; 1989). Is all this also a "collapse of history"? Or is it really the collapse of *dominant readings* of history in the face of alternative decisions about central ideas, events, and themes?

There is little doubt that some Christian biblical scholars and theologians lament the absence of the dominant Old Testament readings. Such a view arguably represents a kind of wistfulness for the "good old days" when a dominant perspective seemed to influence writing and doing (and teaching!) Old Testament theology in Christian institutions of higher learning. Not only does this "hoped-for dominant" perspective do violence to those who were never part of the "dominant perspective" (because they were either gender or cultural minorities, e.g., women, African American,

Asian American, Latino/Latina, or theological minorities such as Anabaptists, Quakers, or Pentecostals), but it is also arguably built on a largely discredited model of intellectual progress that mimics seventeenth- to twentieth-century Western imperial politics and social values—namely, the (intellectual) goal of domination and the vanquishing of opposition.

Surely an alternative to dominance or conquest is concord, dialogue, and cooperation in common causes. If we are to read the Christian Old Testament, and consider it theologically significant, then that theological significance will have to extend to the entire world. The *emerging* Christian world is now based in the Southern Hemisphere (Jenkins 2002). Reading the Christian Old Testament is thus by necessity a global enterprise. The modern marketplace is diverse indeed, and there are a number of ways to recognize this diversity.

Contemporary Worlds in Dialogue

We have seen that Segovia's "marketplace of ideas" does not so much despair of speaking of the past at all, much less signal a "collapse of history." The issue is not whether history can be written any longer. Rather, the issue is how different histories, and different texts, can be understood to matter in differing contexts. Marketplaces can resist organization. Nevertheless, there are perhaps two general ways of sorting the diversity in view. One way is to focus on the identities of the participants themselves, especially in those cases when they consciously and explicitly draw on these identities in their reading of the Bible. The other is to focus on challenges to the human enterprise in local or global contexts. Many of these challenges will require that we marshal our collective wisdom in order to survive as a species, and there are hardly more urgent reasons for biblical scholars to make their contribution to the ideological, spiritual, and political will of people to act in positive ways.

Text and Experience: The Feminist Pioneering of New Questions

New Testament scholar Elisabeth Schüssler Fiorenza points out that it was early feminist critical studies that largely opened up critical readings of both the New and Old Testaments from a perspective informed by particular "interests" (see Schüssler Fiorenza). One of first of these interests was reviewing the long-presumed subordination of women in the narratives of the Bible. It is interesting to see how this work progressed in a variety of different directions, all inspired by gender-related questions. For some feminist readers of the Bible, restating the often unacknowledged positive and powerful roles of women in the Bible is an important corrective to assumptions about the exclusive biblical focus on men (Gafney; Meyers 1988/2013). Phyllis Trible, on the other hand, pioneered the role of an unvarnished focus on destructive texts featuring violence against women, calling them "texts of terror" and thus highlighting dangerous tendencies within historical biblical cultures themselves (see Trible). Renita Weems, similarly, opened a line of investigation on the prophetic use of violent language associated with feminized subjects and objects that also betrayed violent attitudes (e.g., "Lady Jerusalem," Weems 1995). Kathleen O'Connor, Elizabeth Boase, and Carleen Mandolfo have taken this conversation further, suggesting that there is evidence of an ongoing dialogue with "Lady Jerusalem" that began with the violent imagery noted by

Weems in Hosea and Ezekiel, but then continued to Lamentations and Deutero-Isaiah, suggesting that there is acknowledgment of and even repentance for this violence (see O'Connor; Boase; Mandolfo). There are many other directions that studies can go, many of which explicitly identify as feminist, or gender-interested, analysis (see, e.g., Yee 2003).

The feminist approach, far from being a limiting perspective, has moved methodologically from an interest in one formulation of a "minority" perspective—namely, the role of women—to a comparative interest in how this critical approach relates to other issues of "gendering" and "embodiment" in the Bible (homosexuality, prostitution, especially the vexed question of temple prostitution, foreign wives of mixed marriages, gender in relation to slavery, etc.). This approach can also move beyond questions of gender. These early feminist perspectives quite logically moved toward an interest in those who are considered "marginalized" in Hebrew texts—for example, Edomites, Egyptians, Moabites, those lumped together as "aliens" in the Mosaic laws, foreign workers—for other reasons. Interesting work indeed. But what does it have to do with Christian faith and practice?

While not all feminist analysis of the Bible is done with the hope that it will contribute to a more equitable and egalitarian Christian movement in the contemporary world, a considerable amount is.

Cultural Identities and Social Situations in the Marketplace

Feminism is not the only "contemporary interest" that has driven new questions in Christian biblical analysis. Especially those who hope biblical analysis will affect Christian faith and practice have made significant contributions. Already in narratives of freed slaves in North America, African American readers of the Bible were reflecting on their own insights, especially as a countertheology to the European preachers who constantly preached obedience and subservience (see Raboteau; Hopkins and Cummings). In fact, it is possible to trace a twentieth-century flowering of these early readings, some of which began by reexamining the role of explicitly identified Africans in biblical history (see Felder) in a manner similar to those who reexamined the Old Testament stories explicitly about women. One clear goal was to highlight African presence in the Bible that had been neglected in the face of racial prejudice in the modern world against those of African descent. However, in the wake of important calls for a more assertive black theology in the twentieth century (Cone 1970), this project then expanded in different directions in ways very similar to the expansion of gender-related questions (and often intersecting with gender questions, e.g., in "womanist" analysis; see Weems 1991). In the African American context, the appearance of the groundbreaking work *Stony the Road We Trod* (Felder) was a major contribution to the maturing of contemporary, consciously African American biblical scholarship. Included in this collection were essays that dealt not only with historical-critical analysis of the Bible from an African American perspective, but with the use of the Bible in the history of African American interpretation. Further work on African American history of interpretation (Callahan; Wimbush) continues to make important contributions to unique insights into both the later use of Scripture, but also arguments contributing to historical understanding of the texts themselves. Not only is the role of the Bible in African American history itself the subject of important analysis, but African American biblical analysis is also interested in examining texts that have been used historically to suppress both those of explicitly African descent (for example, to defend slavery) and many non-European peoples. A convergence in methods, and sometimes goals, began to emerge that sought to forge alliances across explicitly named cultural or ethnic categories.

So, even though it has followed a different trajectory than African American scholarship, Latino/Latina literature now also holds an important place in the context of the United States. For example, Justo González, Jean-Paul Ruiz, and Miguel De La Torre (2002; 2007) have published monographs and commentaries on Old Testament themes. Interestingly, however, De La Torre has taken a somewhat pessimistic attitude as to whether cross-cultural analysis of the text will influence the general discipline. De La Torre is clear—Euro-Americans are largely not to be trusted for biblical analysis, because "Euroamerican Christians, either from the fundamentalist right or the far liberal left, probably have more in common with each other and understand each other better than they do Christians on the other side of the racial and ethnic divide" (De La Torre 2007, 125). Nevertheless, serious contributions continue to challenge biblical scholars to take seriously the contributions of those who write Old Testament analysis from an openly acknowledged perspective. Gregory Lee Cuéllar, for example, compares passages of Isaiah to the Mexican and Mexican American folk music style known as the *Corrido*, not only to suggest ways that the biblical texts can be understood in contemporary Mexican American communities, but also to propose potential new readings for the book of Isaiah itself (Cuéllar 2008).

While there have been a number of important works from Asian American biblical scholars in the late twentieth century that consciously draw on Asian themes and identity, a significant milestone was the publication in 2006 of the collected volume *Ways of Being, Ways of Reading*. This volume was comparable in many ways to the impact of the 1991 work *Stony the Road We Trod* in the African American scholarly context. It includes retrospective and survey essays, even very personal reflections on academic work (e.g., Yee 2006), as well as examples of contemporary work of some of the most prominent American scholars using cross-cultural approaches.

Finally, in terms of the American context, it is notable that Randall Bailey, Tat-siong Benny Liew, and Fernando Segovia have initiated a dialogue between Latino/a American, Asian American, and African American scholarship, hoping to find common ground in "minority" analysis of the Bible (Bailey, Liew, and Segovia), suggesting the possibilities of a convergence and maturing of methods of analysis, even as they reject any sort of false consensus on similarity of cultural contexts.

Although it is fair to say that readings explicitly related to specific cultural and ethnic identities and traditions continue in the century, attention has tended to turn toward social, political, and economic locations as another significant source of issues that influence the reading of Scripture. In the last quarter of the twentieth century, a number of Old Testament scholars consciously incorporated sociological and anthropological analysis in their ancient historiography of the Bible (Gottwald; Overholt 1992, 2003), and this dialogue with social sciences certainly continues (Chalcraft). Exegetical issues of the most recent writing in Old Testament studies soon converged on a series of questions closely associated with the influence of Edward Said's classic work *Orientalism*, which further built on the early social theories and the observations of the postcolonial theorists Frantz Fanon and Albert Memmi. Once this dialogue with Said's influence was articulated powerfully in the many works of R. S. Sugirtharajah, the rise of postcolonial approaches to Scripture became a significant movement in the early twenty-first century. Sugirtharajah's now classic compendium *Voices from the Margin* signaled a new energy in "interested perspectives" in the reading of the Bible.

The Rise of Postcolonial Biblical Analysis

We have already noted that Christianity—and its Bible—is seeing profound growth in the Southern Hemisphere in the twenty-first century. Twentieth-century Christians in developing societies, especially India, South America, and Africa, began to assert their own perspectives in the analysis of the Bible. After Said's influential work, they began to identify ways in which previous European scholarship contained certain social and cultural assumptions about Western superiority. They then began readings of the Bible within their past experiences of European colonial presence. In the process of reasserting a cultural and/or national identity, however, they soon realized that a reconstruction of cultural identity in the new world could never go back to a purified "precolonial" state, but must always be in dialogue with the social, political, and philosophical realities of having been deeply affected by Western thought and practice. Although in the context of religion and the Bible, one might better speak of "post-Western-missionaryism," the discussions in biblical studies borrowed a term from social and cultural theory to identify their new reviews of the Bible in their own contexts: *postcolonialism*. Postcolonial biblical exegesis provided special tools for Christians in formerly colonized states (or among indigenous peoples in Western European settled lands, North and South America, Australia, and New Zealand). The questions whether, and to what extent, largely imported biblical scholarship was (and is) tainted by imperial goals of control and economic expansion raised serious concerns about those readings of Scripture that seemed deeply involved in that imperial process (De le Torre 2002). A prime example of attempting to counter Western domination was the Latin American assertion that the exodus is the prime event of the Old Testament—and thus liberation is the prime theological theme. However, it is important to note that these questions were being raised largely by Christian Bible scholars. Not all criticism of colonial and missionary policies rejected Christianity and the Bible as an unwanted imposition (see Roberts); sometimes it rather engaged in the more creative task of rereading the texts.

If "postcolonial" contexts include minorities living in multicultural nations, then Fernando Segovia's "Diasporic" approach to reading Scripture becomes especially suggestive. In the American context, this obviously can include African American, Asian American, and Mexican American readings of particular texts that resonate with themes, motifs, or elements of minority existence such that they lead to expositions of Old Testament texts that are suggestive for all readers of the Bible—and not only to fellow members of particular ethnic or cultural groups.

Ethnic and culturally informed readings challenge the notion that European scholarship has a privileged position in biblical scholarship generally, and in the construction of Christian theologies built from Old Testament texts particularly. What we have learned about diversity in dialogue is that the Christian reading of the Old Testament in the contemporary world will be richer, more learned, and more convincing in both textual and historical analysis only if our marketplace grows in its resemblance to the actual diversity of our worlds. What new insights into particular Old

Testament texts await the future BA, MA, or PhD theses and papers written by young Tibetan, Chinese, Navajo, Roma, or Aboriginal Australian students and scholars? What will they see that the rest of us have too quickly dismissed or completely overlooked? In the twenty-first century, we are likely to benefit from an increase of book titles like that of Senegalese American biblical scholar Aliou Niang: *Faith and Freedom in Galatia and Senegal: The Apostle Paul, Colonies, and Sending Gods*.

Let us reaffirm that diversity ought always to lead to dialogue. Agreements, shared insights, and common convictions that we are all learning from the dialogue ought to deliver even the most cynical from the simplistic hope that we Bible scholars would just please get to "the bottom line." Marketplaces don't have a bottom line! Dialogue and haggling over texts is simply the reality. The invitation, therefore, is to listen and learn. Incidentally, lest Christians think that all this is somehow radically new, those familiar with classic rabbinic dialogue and argumentation over religious texts are aware that dialogue with God and with each other is at the heart of theology.

Issues Driving Contemporary Biblical Analysis

Questions from identities and cultural experiences are not, however, the only major and significant sources of urgency in reading and rereading the Christian Old Testament. A number of contemporary global crises have inspired a renewed examination of the ways in which the Bible can be reread. The modern interest in trauma as the psychosocial reality of a world in crisis has recently gained ground in biblical analysis (see O'Connor; Janzen; Kelle). The millions of humans who flee wars and crises as international refugees have also influenced biblical analysis on ancient exile and deportation (see Ahn). The potential list of pressing issues is depressingly long, of course, but it is possible to examine a few examples to illustrate how this section of the marketplace can be organized. In fact, we can move from an example that is already very old but critically ongoing, war and peace in the Old Testament; to an issue that arguably has its roots in the twentieth century, environmentalism; and finally note the signs of a rising issue so new that it has barely begun to generate serious thought among biblical scholars: evolutionary philosophy, transhumanism, and the nature of the person.

War, Peace, and Violence and the Old Testament

Since the fourth century CE, the Christian church has been faced with direct responsibility for violence. The monarchical descendants of the Roman emperor Constantine made Christianity the official religion of the empire, leading into the Byzantine Empire. Biblical study was now intimately connected to the foreign policy of a powerful military machine, and would continue to have foreign policy implications from that time to the present. The continued relevance of the Bible to issues of war and peace is not difficult to discern in the writings of the Christian warriors and their chaplains on the one hand, and the Christian peacemakers and their communities on the other, throughout Western history especially. A clear majority in this debate has supported more violent interpretations, however regretfully they are sometimes offered.

The Jesus who said, "Love your enemies and pray for those who persecute you" (Matt. 5:44), and the Paul who exhorted, "live peaceably with all" (Rom. 12:18), were effectively trumped in Christian faith and practice very early on by an uncritical admiration for the genocidal Joshua and the conquering David (see Davies). There have been a variety of ways in which Christians have responded to the use of the Old Testament as a moral trump over the pacifist Jesus. Once again, the similarities to the methods of feminist biblical analysis are instructive.

For example, especially since the churches in twentieth-century Europe began to mobilize an opposition to the Cold War threats in their own backyards, innumerable monographs have attempted to reexamine the actual practices of Old Testament violence and warfare, either with explicit admiration (so, famously, Yadin), or appropriate levels of horror (Craigie; Niditch; Collins). In modern Old Testament study, then, one is hopefully exposed to the potential dangers of a casual and unguarded use of biblical texts that are so clearly contrary to contemporary moral judgments and international standards of justice.

Finally, similar to those who sought to lift up exemplary moments previously overlooked, there are those who seek to highlight strongly peaceful passages in the Bible that may even have been in critical dialogue with more violent episodes in the canon and thus reveal an internal dialogue or debate that reveals stronger peace voices among the canonical choir (Enz; Smith-Christopher 2007). This approach articulates how a certain form of Hebrew nonviolence would have been a logical expression of theological tendencies that had their roots in the Servant Songs of Second Isaiah and the universalism of the book of Jonah, where we find openness to the repentance of national enemies like the Assyrians, who are portrayed as repenting ". . . of the violence of their hands." Further developments can affirm the wisdom ethic of peacefulness—an ethic that frequently contrasts self-control over against brute force and earnestly recommends a sober, wise consideration of counsel and diplomacy (Prov. 16:7, 32; 17:27; 24:5-6). In fact, the Wisdom tradition may itself represent precisely a staging place for international discussion, given that wisdom values are as universal in the ancient Near East as any literary themes can be. Ancient Egyptian wisdom, Mesopotamian wisdom, and Greek wisdom all compare quite favorably to ancient Israelite forms.

Texts that reflect an Israelite "exilic" lifestyle, lived in "active nonconformity to the world" (as the famous 1955 Mennonite Church statement puts it), would also build on biblical protests against narrow ethnocentrism (e.g., the book of Ruth, Jacob's apology to Esau, Isaiah 56 and 66, and the striking affirmation in Zechariah 9 of a mixed-race people of God). In fact, there is evidence of a rising protest against violence and narrow self-centeredness (e.g., Ezekiel 40–48) that can be seen to affirm the Deuteronomic critique of the monarchy, and especially the condemnation of the monarchy in the penitential prayers of Ezra 9, Nehemiah 9, and Daniel 9. Thus the fact that there are passages where God is alleged to have called for the massacre of foreign cities does not necessarily cancel out or trump the fact that there are more hopeful passages on this subject as well, texts that openly question whether the stance of the Hebrews toward foreign peoples should be hostile and that envision a different and more peaceful reality (Isaiah 2; 19; Micah 4).

Regrettably, offering a more peaceful reading of the Old Testament will not likely bring about world peace. But if the late Colonel Harry Summers of the Army War College is correct that "it is the passions of the people that are the engines of war" (Summers, 75–76), then perhaps careful biblical analysis will remove at least one major ideological prop and provocation that has certainly been used in the past to excuse quite reprehensible behavior among those who honor the Scriptures (see Trimm).

Environmentalism

Biblical analysis that is driven by ecological concerns can be clearly dated to responses to the famous 1967 article in *Science* by Lynn White, accusing Christianity for providing the "roots" of the ecological crisis in God's injunction to the first couple in Gen. 1:28 to "subdue" and "have dominion" over nature. The late twentieth century then saw an increase of literature that highlighted ways that the Hebrew Bible/Old Testament affirmed a spirituality of care and responsibility for the earth as God's creation. Much of this work owes a great deal to the early writings of Australian biblical scholar Norman Habel (see also Hallman; so now Craven and Kaska; Deane-Drummond). The often-cited "this-worldly" emphasis of much Old Testament ethical discussion, and even the imagery of deep fascination with and appreciation of the created world (Job 38–41; Psalm 147–48), however, continues to inspire further development in pioneering biblical theologies. Genesis portrays God involving Adam in the naming of other creatures (Gen. 2:19) and further records God's intention to "re-create" the world in the Hebrew version of the flood narrative, the basic outlines of which were clearly known to the Jewish people by the time of the Babylonian captivity, and most likely borrowed from Mesopotamian traditions.

A related development is in the direction of animal rights. Concern for animal welfare is not absent from Hebrew law or narrative (Deut. 25:4; Numbers 22). The flood story, of course, involves the considerable responsibility of Noah to preserve animals. The Old Testament strikingly expresses certain visions of peace by referring to changes in the animal kingdom (Isa. 11:6: the wolf living with the lamb) and even hinting that in their first created state, humans were vegetarian (before Gen. 9:4, where eating meat is first explicitly mentioned). Psalm 148 portrays the created animals of the world praising God, and Job famously portrays God's careful attention and knowledge of the details of the animal kingdom (Job 39; on animal rights work, see Linzey 1995; 2009; Miller).

Work in environmentalism more generally, and animal rights specifically, have been parts of a move to appreciate biblical themes that buttress a more responsible care for the earth (Toly and Block). There are, however, some serious economic and even political issues at stake here. On the issue of environmentalism particularly, there has been a serious backlash from those with business interests who see strong environmentalist movements as potential threats to their expansion of industry. Not unexpectedly, then, this reaction has motivated more conservative Christian scholars to reassert a strongly pragmatic and typically short-term ethic of consumption unmitigated by strong concerns for conserving resources in the long term. Christians in this tradition, rarely biblical scholars themselves, are clearly not impressed with nuanced arguments about responsibility for species and their survival. Nor are they likely to be impressed by arguments based largely on Old Testament passages, especially if that concern is perceived as requiring economic sacrifices. An interesting example of this reaction is the work of Steven Hayward, from the conservative think tank the American Enterprise Institute. In a published essay titled "Mere Environmentalism" (the title itself is an homage to evangelical hero C. S. Lewis) and subtitled "A Biblical Perspective on Humans and the Natural World," Hayward suggests that the Genesis narratives promote the hierarchy of creation with humanity at the top. He therefore construes a biblical mandate, not for preservation of the environment, but for a "stewardship" that promotes responsible use of resources and a free-market-driven effort to conquer the "untamed wilderness," and furthermore as free of government intervention as possible. Indeed, Hayward further argues that the story of Joseph in Pharaoh's household is a warning against centralized state control, because Joseph's centralization of resources for the Pharaoh leads directly to the enslavement of the Hebrews. Environmental degradation, therefore, may be a matter calling for repentance, but definitely not for government regulation (33). Finally, Noah offers sacrifice of animals after the flood, Hayward notes, so this story provides no basis for simple preservation, and certainly suggests that animals were to be used for human benefit.

The twenty-first century is likely to see more, rather than less, of this polemical exchange in biblical scholarship. Although more propagandistic approaches have tended to avoid participation in scholarly organizations like the Society of Biblical Literature, we are likely to see more direct engagement over the use, and abuse, of Scripture on various issues of social, and especially economic, importance.

The Nature of the Person: The Rise of Evolutionary Social Science and Philosophy

Finally, it is important in the context of this essay to speculate about issues that may well emerge more fully as the twenty-first century develops. In the wake of Daniel Dennett's polemical 1996 assertion of atheist scientism, titled "Darwin's Dangerous Idea," there is a rise of perspectives represented by the following: "If you believe in a traditional concept of the soul, you should know that there is little doubt that a fuller appreciation of the implications of evolutionary theory . . . is going to destroy that concept"; and, "we must openly acknowledge . . . the collapse of a worldview that has sustained human energies for centuries" (Stanovich, 3). Will biblical studies also be challenged by evolutionary thought? If so, in what way?

In Christian theology and biblical studies, the classic beginning point for discussion of the nature of the human person is the concept of the *imago Dei*, the creation of humanity in the image and likeness of God (Gen. 1:26-27). J. Richard Middleton, for example, seeks to rethink the *imago Dei* debates in a modern context, noting that older Christian theological uses of Genesis 1 were rather strained, and usually presumed that the significance of "the image" and "likeness" of God was precisely human *reason*. Recent discussion has emphasized the royal context of these terms, suggesting that humans are portrayed as royally deputized representations of divine authority and responsibility in the world. Middleton even suggests that the *imago Dei* is, in fact, a politically sophisticated as well as theologically loaded term in Genesis, because here we find the textual staging ground for a narrative culture war against Mesopotamian hegemonic narratives of conquest and subservience. These Mesopotamian narratives were weapons in a philosophical/ideological war that accompanied the invading and conquering armies that conquered both the northern kingdom (722 BCE) and Jerusalem and Judah (597/587).

While it is quite possible to celebrate the theological importance of all humanity from an explicitly evolutionary view of the emergence of *homo sapiens*, it is also clear that some interpretations of human evolution threaten to radically debase and reduce humanity to a mere "sack of genes," with little inherent worth, whose values, art, and faith are mere "spandrels" (that is, accidental and irrelevant by-products) that accompany the real work of genetic reproduction. The value of life is thus no longer inherent in creation, but purely instrumental, as some humans serve as sexual slaves, soldiers, and workers for the shrinking and increasingly ruthless elite. The masses are already once again being pacified by the modern equivalent of bread and circus: ever smaller and more inexpensive sources of digital pornography, graphic violence, and (contra Kant's imperative) the view of fellow humans as means rather than ends.

In this context, religious faith (including, of course, the Bible) is strongly dismissed as "nothing but" the result of evolutionary mechanisms for survival. We perceive deities only because of our ancient and genetically honed "agency detection devices" (instincts that perceive potential threats in the environment). Others suggest that religion was merely a part of a sophisticated social "mate selection" mechanism whereby mates with trustworthy values could be quickly identified. In short, religion is a neural response pattern.

The interesting question is no longer, "Can a biblical scholar believe in evolution and teach Genesis"? Of course they can, and do. What is new is the rising insistence of a form of evolutionary social thought that would dismiss all religious speculation as irrelevant. Such a radically reductionist anthropology seeks to replace the "Eden myth" with an equally implausible and comprehensive "African Savannah myth" that subsumes all humanity into categories of neural survival mechanisms driven by reproductive genes. Does the Old Testament have anything to say in this decidedly modern discussion?

The resources of Wisdom literature and its emphasis on sober assessments of God's moral patterns in the created world provide a foundation beyond Genesis for seeking dialogue with naturalists and biologists. But the issues will continue to press, and will no longer be simply the leisure-time, science-fiction reading of those whose day jobs are in biblical studies. Seeking biblical guidance on the nature of the human person will become increasingly pressing in this century in the light of (1) increased emphasis in the human sciences on "transhumanism," according to which humans can be enhanced by further evolutionary merging with technology; (2) manipulation of genetic information to favor certain human traits (already taking place passively by rejecting human eggs in artificial insemination processes that bear indications of undesired genetic traits); (3) progress in artificial intelligence such that ethical questions are becoming increasingly prominent (when does turning off a machine consist of killing a living being? etc.); (4) further work in cloning; and (5) the location and identification of personhood as directly (and some would say: *only*) a function of neural brain activity, thus raising the possibility of "downloading" human persons into hardware.

Are these exclusively theological issues? Do they have any implications for biblical analysis? Will a biblical analysis arise, for example, driven in part by the prescience of the science fiction writer Philip K. Dick, who anticipated many ethical issues dealing with modern technology? It is possible that biblical scholars will simply suggest that radically new technologies are not the business of textual analysis. However, when those technologies raise serious questions about the nature and value of the human person, it is hard to resist the notion that biblical analysis has something to say to this issue.

Return to the Beginning: Does the Marketplace Matter? Are There Any Real People There?

Finally, we can pick up on a discussion that was left aside at the very beginning of this essay. What about the clashes among various readings of the Old Testament? Is biblical studies hopelessly mired in disagreements such that, in the end, an individual must simply hum along with Porter's "Anything Goes"?

Appearances, especially in the contemporary world, can be deceiving. The reality of extensive and exciting discussion and debate in biblical studies does not mean that the field is wandering aimlessly. Furthermore, the impressive level of publication and discussion does not mean that there is no consensus of methods or results among biblical scholars. Biblical scholars, like professionals in other fields such as medicine, engineering, or astronomy, certainly stay in touch with each other's work, and through international organizations (the largest being the Society of Biblical Literature) continue to pursue common interests, projects, and even enjoy continued debates and disagreements. It is hardly the case, as philosopher Alvin Plantinga somewhat sourly suggests, that biblical scholars can never agree on anything, explaining (for Plantinga, presumably) why Christians usually do not take their work seriously.

Plantinga may be surprised, however. The influence of biblical scholarship on wider Christian practices might be slow in manifesting itself, but it is absolutely clear. Plantinga should be impressed with the articulate, profound, and serious assessment of the importance of biblical analysis in the 1994 document of the Pontifical Biblical Commission titled "The Interpretation of the Bible in the Church." Calling the historical-critical method of biblical analysis "indispensable for the scientific study of the meaning of ancient texts," the document critically assesses, both positively and negatively, many current approaches to biblical analysis common in universities and biblical scholarship, and recommends much of modern biblical scholarship to the Catholic world more widely. Furthermore, the document famously refers to fundamentalist readings of Scripture as "intellectual suicide." Unimpressed with official declarations by hierarchies? One need only examine the textbooks for Catholic *high school* students, including those explicitly recommended by the bishops, to see the profound impact of biblical scholarship on questions of multiple authorship, historicity, the dangers of literalism, and so on.

Only the most conservative Christians today believe that the only way to treasure the significance of the narratives of Genesis is to take them literally, or believe that Moses wrote every word of the Pentateuch. Only the most fundamentalist Christians today would think that the book of Jonah is about surviving in the gullet of a marine animal, or that nearly one-fifth of the entire population of ancient Egypt left with Moses in the thirteenth century BCE. Furthermore, what many Christians in the church pews and Sunday schools *do* know is that a profound Christian faith can be enriched by learning that an unnamed second prophet we call "Second Isaiah" likely reapplied some of the thought of the eighth-century Isaiah of Jerusalem, but also proclaimed radically new thoughts in the late sixth-century BCE when the Persian emperor Cyrus lived. Furthermore, Christians today know much more about the horrific tragedy of the destruction of Jerusalem in 587, and how Lamentations is a powerful poetic response to that tragedy, and how Psalms contains religious poetry from long after the time of David. None of these ideas are shocking to Christians in the churches any more, and none of them are destructive of anything but the most simplistic of readings of the Old Testament.

Finally, what Christians in the churches surely know is that the Bible invites—indeed nearly demands—the careful attention of many different cultures, genders, ages, and contexts who are brought into dialogue as they listen, read, discuss, and debate the meanings and importance of these texts of the Old Testament. There is important historical information we can know, but there is so much more to ask. For those who love only quiet museum tours of "certainties" enclosed in glass cases so that the masses can be enlightened, biblical studies in the contemporary world is not for them. The marketplace is teaming, ebullient, and alive.

Works Cited

Ahn, John. 2010. *Exile as Forced Migrations: A Sociological, Literary, and Theological Approach on the Displacement and Resettlement of the Southern Kingdom of Judah.* Berlin: de Gruyter.

Albertz, Rainer. 2003. *Israel in Exile: The History and Literature of the Sixth Century* B.C.E. Atlanta: Society of Biblical Literature.

Avalos, Hector. 2007. *The End of Biblical Studies.* New York: Prometheus.

Bailey, Randall, Tat-siong Benny Liew, and Fernando F. Segovia, eds. 2009. *They Were All Together in One Place? Toward Minority Biblical Criticism.* Atlanta: Society of Biblical Literature.

Barr, James. 2000. *History and Ideology in the Old Testament: Biblical Studies at the End of a Millennium.* Oxford: Oxford University Press.

Boase, Elizabeth. 2006. *The Fulfillment of Doom? The Dialogic Interaction between the Book of Lamentations and the Pre-Exilic/Early Exilic Prophetic Literature.* London: T&T Clark.

Brueggemann, Walter. 1997. *Theology of the Old Testament: Testimony, Dispute, Advocacy.* Minneapolis: Fortress Press.

Callahan, Allen Dwight. 2006. *The Talking Book: African Americans and the Bible.* New Haven: Yale University Press.

Chalcraft, David. 2006. *Social-Scientific Old Testament Criticism.* London: T&T Clark.

Collins, John J. 2004. *Does the Bible Justify Violence?* Minneapolis: Fortress Press.

Cone, James H. 1970. *A Black Theology of Liberation.* Maryknoll, NY: Orbis.

———. 1992. *The Spirituals and the Blues: An Interpretation.* Maryknoll, NY: Orbis Books.

Craigie, Peter. 1979. *The Problem of War in the Old Testament.* Grand Rapids: Eerdmans.

Craven, Toni, and Mary Jo Kaska. 2011. "The Legacy of Creation in the Hebrew Bible and Apocryphal/Deuterocanonical Books." In *Spirit and Nature: The Study of Christian Spirituality in a Time of Ecological Urgency*, edited by Timothy Hessel-Robinson and Ray Maria McNamara, RSM, 16–48. Eugene, OR: Pickwick.

Cuellar, Gregory L. 2008. *Voices of Marginality: Exile and Return in Second Isaiah 40-55 and the Mexican Immigrant Experience.* New York: Peter Lang.

Davies, Eryl. 2010. *The Immoral Bible: Approaches to Biblical Ethics*. London: T&T Clark.
Deane-Drummond, Celia. 2008. *Eco-Theology*. London: Darton, Longman & Todd.
De La Torre, Miguel. 2002. *Reading the Bible from the Margins*. Maryknoll, NY: Orbis.
———. 2007. *Liberating Jonah: Forming an Ethic of Reconciliation*. Maryknoll, NY: Orbis.
Dennett, Daniel. 1996. *Darwin's Dangerous Idea*. New York: Simon & Schuster.
Dever, William G. 2001. *What Did the Biblical Writers Know and When Did They Know It?* Grand Rapids: Eerdmans.
———. 2003. *Who Were the Early Israelites and Where Did They Come From?* Grand Rapids: Eerdmans.
Edwards, James. 2009. *A Biblical Perspective on Immigration Policy*. Washington, DC: Center for Immigration Studies. http://www.cis.org/ImmigrationBible
Egerton, Douglas R. 1999. *He shall go out free : The lives of Denmark Vesey*. Madison, WI: Madison House, 1999
Eichrodt, Walter. 1961. *Theology of the Old Testament*. Translated by J. A. Baker. Vol. 1. London: SCM.
———. 1967. *Theology of the Old Testament*. Translated by J. A. Baker. Vol. 2. London: SCM.
Elsmore, Bronwyn. 1985. *Like Them That Dream: The Maori and the Old Testament*. Wellington, New Zealand: Tauranga Moana Press.
———. 1989. *Mana from Heaven*. Auckland: Reed.
Enz, Jacob. 2001. *The Christian and Warfare: The Roots of Pacifism in the Old Testament*. Eugene, OR: Wipf & Stock (reprint).
Fanon, Frantz. 1963. *The Wretched of the Earth*. New York: Grove.
Felder, Cain Hope, ed. 1991. *Stony the Road We Trod*. Minneapolis: Fortress Press.
Feyerabend, Paul. 2010. *Against Method*. New York: Verso.
Foskett, Mary F., and Jeffrey Kah-jin Kuan, eds. 2006. *Ways of Being, Ways of Reading: Asian American Biblical Interpretation*. St. Louis: Chalice.
Frend, W. H. C. 1984. *The Rise of Christianity*. Minneapolis: Fortress Press.
Gabler, Johann P. "An Oration on the Proper Distinction between Biblical and Dogmatic Theology and the Specific Objectives of Each." In Ollenburger, *Old Testament Theology*, 497–506.
Gafney, Wilda C. 2008. *Daughters of Miriam: Women Prophets in Ancient Israel*. Minneapolis: Fortress Press.
González, Justo L. 1996. *Santa Biblia: The Bible through Hispanic Eyes*. Nashville: Abingdon.
Gottwald, Norman. 1979. *The Tribes of Yahweh*. Maryknoll, NY: Orbis.
Grabbe, Lester. 2007. *Ancient Israel: What Do We Know and How Do We Know It?* New York: T&T Clark.
Habel, Norman. 1993. *The Land Is Mine: Six Biblical Land Ideologies*. Minneapolis: Fortress Press.
Hallman, David G. 1994. *Ecotheology: Voices from South and North*. Maryknoll, NY: Orbis.
Hayes, John H., and Frederick Prussner. 1984. *Old Testament Theology: Its History and Development*. Atlanta: John Knox.
Hopkins, Dwight N., and George C. L. Cummings, eds. 2003. *Cut Loose Your Stammering Tongue: Black Theology in the Slave Narratives*. Louisville: Westminster John Knox.
Janzen, David. 2012. *The Violent Gift: Trauma's Subversion of the Deuteronomistic History's Narrative*. LHB/OTS 561. London: T&T Clark.
Jenkins, Philip. 2002. *The Next Christendom: The Coming of Global Christianity*. New York: Oxford University Press.
———. 2006. *The New Faces of Christianity: Believing the Bible in the Global South*. New York: Oxford University Press.
Kelle, Brad. 2013. *Ezekiel*. New Beacon Bible Commentary. Kansas City: Beacon Hill.
Kuhn, Thomas. 1996. *The Structure of Scientific Revolutions*. 3rd ed. Chicago: University of Chicago Press.

Levine, Lawrence. 1977. *Black Culture and Black Consciousness.* New York: Oxford University Press.
Linzey, Andrew. 1995. *Animal Theology.* Urbana: University of Illinois Press.
———. 2009. *Creatures of the Same God.* New York: Lantern.
Mandolfo, Carleen. 2007. *Daughter Zion Talks Back to the Prophets.* Atlanta: Society of Biblical Literature.
Meyers, Carol. 1988/2013. *Rediscovering Eve: Ancient Israelite Women in Context.* Oxford: Oxford University Press.
Middleton, J. Richard. 2005. *The Liberating Image: The Imago Dei in Genesis 1.* Grand Rapids: Brazos.
Miller, David. 2011. *Animal Ethics and Theology.* New York: Routledge.
Muir, Lynette R. 1995. *The Biblical Drama of Medieval Europe.* Cambridge: Cambridge University Press.
Niang, Aliou. 2009. *Faith and Freedom in Galatia and Senegal.* Leiden: Brill.
Nichols, Aiden. 2007. *Lovely Like Jerusalem: The Fulfillment of the Old Testament in Christ and the Church.* San Francisco: Ignatius.
Niditch, Susan. 1993. *War and the Hebrew Bible: A Study in the Ethics of Violence.* Oxford: Oxford University Press.
Ngan, Lai Ling Elizabeth. 2006. "Neither Here nor There: Boundary and Identity in the Hagar Story." In Foskett and Kuan, *Ways of Being*, 70–83.
O'Connor, Kathleen. 2002. *Lamentations and the Tears of the World.* Maryknoll, NY: Orbis.
Ollenburger, Ben, ed. 2004. *Old Testament Theology: Flowering and Future, Sources for Biblical and Theological Study.* Winona Lake, IN: Eisenbrauns.
Overholt, Thomas. 1992. *Cultural Anthropology and the Old Testament.* Minneapolis: Fortress Press.
———. 2003. *Channels of Prophecy: The Social Dynamics of Prophetic Activity.* Eugene, OR: Wipf and Stock.
Perdue, Leo. 1994. *The Collapse of History: Reconstructing Old Testament Theology.* Minneapolis: Fortress Press.
Plantinga, Alvin. 2009. "Two (or More) Kings of Scripture Scholarship." In *Oxford Readings in Philosophical Theology*, vol. 2, *Providence, Scripture, and Resurrection*, ed. Michael C. Rea, 266–301. Oxford: Oxford University Press.
Pulido, Laura, Laura Barraclough, and Wendy Cheng, eds. 2012. *A People's Guide to Los Angeles.* Berkeley: University of California Press.
Raboteau, Albert J. 1978. *Slave Religion: The Invisible Institution in the Antebellum South.* New York: Oxford University Press.
Rogerson, John. 1984. *Old Testament Criticism in the Nineteenth Century: England and Germany.* London: SPCK.
———. 2010. *A Theology of the Old Testament.* Minneapolis: Fortress Press.
Roberts, Nathaniel. 2012. "Is Conversion a 'Colonization of Consciousness'?" *Anthropological Theory* 12:271–94.
Ruiz, Jean-Pierre. 2011. *Readings from the Edges: The Bible and People on the Move.* Maryknoll, NY: Orbis.
Said, Edward W. 1979. *Orientalism.* New York: Vintage.
Schüssler Fiorenza, Elisabeth. 2009. *Democratizing Biblical Studies.* Louisville: Westminster John Knox.
Segovia, Fernando F. 2000. *Decolonizing Biblical Studies: A View from the Margins.* Maryknoll, NY: Orbis.
Segovia, Fernando F., and Mary Ann Tolbert, eds. 1985. *Reading from this Place*, vol. 1, *Social Location and Biblical Interpretation in the United States.* Minneapolis: Fortress Press.
Smith-Christopher, Daniel. 2002. *A Biblical Theology of Exile.* Minneapolis: Fortress Press.
———. 2007. *Jonah, Jesus, and Other Good Coyotes: Speaking Peace to Power in the Bible.* Nashville: Abingdon.
Sommer, Benjamin, ed. 2012. *Jewish Concepts of Scripture: A Comparative Introduction.* New York: New York University Press.

Soyinka, Wole. 2003. *Samarkand and Other Markets I Have Known.* New York: Methuen.

Stanovich, Keith. 2004. *The Robot's Rebellion.* Chicago: University of Chicago Press.

Sugirtharajah, R. S., ed. 2006. *Voices from the Margin: Interpreting the Bible in the Third World.* 3rd ed. Maryknoll, NY: Orbis.

Summers, Harry G. 1984. "What Is War?" *Harper's*, May, 75–78.

Toly, Noah J., and Daniel I. Block, eds. 2010. *Keeping God's Earth: The Global Environment in Biblical Perspective.* Downers Grove, IL: IVP Academic.

Thompson, Thomas L. 1974. *The Historicity of the Patriarchal Narratives: The Quest for the Historical Abraham.* Berlin: de Gruyter.

Trible, Phyllis. 1984. *Texts of Terror: Literary-Feminist Readings of Biblical Narratives.* Minneapolis: Fortress Press.

Trimm, Charles. 2012. "Recent Research on Warfare in the Old Testament." *Currents in Biblical Research* 10:171–216.

Rad, Gerhard von. 1962. *Theology of the Old Testament.* Vol. 1. New York: Harper & Row.

———. 1965. *Theology of the Old Testament.* Vol. 2. New York: Harper & Row.

Warrior, Robert Allen. 1996. "Canaanites, Cowboys, and Indians." In *Native and Christian: Indigenous Voices on Religious Identity in the United States and Canada*, edited by James Treat, 93–104. New York: Routledge.

Weems, Renita J. 1991. "Reading Her Way through the Struggle: African American Women and the Bible." In Felder, *Stony the Road We Trod*, 57–77.

———. 1995. *Battered Love: Marriage, Sex, and Violence in the Hebrew Prophets.* Minneapolis: Fortress Press.

White, Lynn, Jr. 1967. "The Historical Roots of Our Ecological Crisis." *Science* 155:1203–7.

Wimbush, Vincent L., ed. 2000. *African Americans and the Bible: Sacred Texts and Social Textures.* New York: Continuum.

Yadin, Yigael. 1963. *The Art of Warfare in Biblical Lands.* London: Weidenfield & Nicolson.

Yee, Gale A. 2003. *Poor Banished Children of Eve: Woman as Evil in the Hebrew Bible.* Minneapolis: Fortress Press.

———. 2006. "Yin/Yang Is Not Me: An Exploration into an Asian-American Biblical Hermeneutics." In Foskett and Kuan, *Ways of Being*, 152–63.

Themes and Perspectives in Torah: Creation, Kinship, and Covenant

Sarah Shectman

The first five books of the Hebrew Bible (the Christian Old Testament)—Genesis, Exodus, Leviticus, Numbers, and Deuteronomy—occupy a primary place in the biblical canon, not just because they come first, but also because they are likely the earliest part of the Bible to have been canonized. Sometimes these books are referred to as the Pentateuch, from the Greek *pente*, "five," and *teuchos*, "book." In Jewish tradition, the books are referred to as the *Torah*, a Hebrew word that literally means "teaching" or "instruction." The Torah itself uses the Hebrew term *torah* to refer specifically to the laws ("instructions") that YHWH (the proper name of the biblical deity) gives the Israelites through Moses (see, for example, Exod. 24:12; Deut. 4:44), not to the whole collection of five books. Outside of the Torah, the term may refer to YHWH's laws or to more general instruction or teaching, as from a parent (for example, Prov. 1:8); it also appears in phrases such as "the book of the teaching of Moses" (*sefer torat moshe*), which may have a broader meaning (see, for example, Neh. 8:1), perhaps encompassing the text of the Torah more or less as we know it. Thus though the biblical text says only that Moses wrote down the laws (*torot*; singular, *torah*) that YHWH instructed him at Sinai, later the term *torah* comes to encompass the whole collection of books, not only the laws, and the whole is understood as a larger written "Law."

Part 1: Perspectives on Reading the Torah

In the first part of this essay, we will consider two questions: First, What is the Torah? And second, Who wrote it?

What Is the Torah?

The material in the Torah falls into two main categories: narrative and law. The narrative begins in Genesis with the creation of the universe and the Garden of Eden. As humans proliferate after Adam and Eve's expulsion from the garden, their behavior deteriorates, prompting YHWH to obliterate them in the flood and start over with the lineage of Noah. Humans once again proliferate, this time culminating in the lineage of Abraham, who becomes the first ancestor of the Israelites when YHWH tells him to go to the land of Canaan and promises to make him a great nation there. YHWH then makes a covenant with Abraham, a central theme in the following narrative. The remainder of Genesis contains stories about the Israelite ancestors Abraham and Sarah; Isaac and Rebekah; Jacob, Leah, and Rachel; and Jacob's children, particularly Joseph. This family history is punctuated by the passing down of YHWH's promise and covenant to Abraham's descendants. Genesis ends with the descent of Joseph and then the rest of Jacob's family to Egypt.

The story in Exodus picks up sometime later, the Israelites having become numerous and been enslaved in Egypt. YHWH selects Moses to be the savior of the people, leading them out of Egypt after a great show of destructive and miraculous plagues. At Mount Sinai, YHWH renews the Abrahamic covenant with the Israelites, delivering numerous laws covering a wide variety of topics, not just religious but also civil, social, agricultural, and military. The Israelites are on their way to conquer Canaan, the land promised to Abraham and his descendants by YHWH, but the people immediately begin to question the leadership of both Moses and YHWH, prompting YHWH to punish them by keeping them in the wilderness for forty years, until the entire exodus generation has died. The Israelites move from place to place in the wilderness, fighting various battles and beginning the initial stages of their conquest of the promised land in the region across the Jordan River from Canaan. There, on the plains of Moab, Moses makes his farewell speech, recounted in the book of Deuteronomy, and then dies; with his death, the Torah comes to an end.

The law, as this narrative summary shows, is an integral part of the story: the connection of the law with the exodus event and with Sinai is deeply embedded in the narrative. But most of the legal sections also stand apart from the narrative flow, pausing events in order to recount the various stipulations that YHWH requires of the Israelites in order to maintain the covenant. The legal material thus stands on its own as a genre. But the whole of the Pentateuch, both narrative and law, has come to be understood as law (*torah*) in some sense—even the narrative material. Thus the narrative parts are often understood to be instructional as well and to provide a set of guiding principles.

This characterization reveals one of the primary issues in understanding the Torah, namely, the question of genre. The Torah presents itself as a history, in the sense that it provides a more-or-less continuous narrative recounting the origins and early events in the lives of the Israelite people. But it is not always clear that the Torah is meant to be understood in the way modern readers understand history. One obvious way in which it is unlike modern histories is in its inclusion of miracles and other supernatural events that do not withstand scientific scrutiny. Should the Torah thus be classified as fiction rather than history?

The question of whether these stories are purely fictional or whether they might have a historical kernel is a vexing one. There is no clear evidence for any of the people mentioned in the Torah in any outside sources or in the archaeological record, which are the primary means of testing the historicity of ancient texts. But does this mean that there is no history behind the Torah? It is difficult to say. Given the absence of evidence for this question, it is perhaps more useful to think in terms of the function of the text for an ancient Israelite audience. The narratives present a particular worldview (or worldviews), and thus they seem intended to be understood not exactly as history but as ancient Israel's understanding of its constitution as a nation and of YHWH's place in the national self-image. In this vein, scholars sometimes refer to the Torah as the "foundation document" of ancient Israel, the story of its creation and its relationship to its deity, YHWH. In such an analysis, rather than focusing on the issue of whether the story is myth or history, scholars choose to focus on the key themes of the Torah, in order to understand what those themes tell us about the Israelites' understanding of themselves and of their God.

Although the Torah stands on its own as one division of the Hebrew Bible, it is not clear that it was originally intended to be a self-standing unit. Though it forms a mostly continuous narrative, the storyline continues without interruption in the next book of the Bible, Joshua, with the conquest of the promised land and thus the fulfillment of the promise made to the ancestors in the Torah. However, Deuteronomy contains the last of the laws and ends with the death of Moses, which also suggests a strong break between the Torah and the following material. Complicating the matter further, Deuteronomy is in many ways different from the first four books of the Torah, giving a sort of retrospective view of the story so far and focusing in particular on certain theological issues such as idolatry and the centralization of worship at a single sanctuary. These themes feature prominently in the following books (Joshua, Judges, 1–2 Samuel, and 1–2 Kings) as well, prompting many scholars to refer to Deuteronomy–2 Kings as the Deuteronomistic History, a composition distinct from Genesis–Numbers. The book of Deuteronomy in particular, then, is a kind of "hinge" connecting the first four books with the following six.

Although the narrative of the Torah continues in Joshua–2 Kings, only certain episodes from the Torah are mentioned in those books. The exodus from Egypt, for example, is mentioned frequently, not just in the Deuteronomistic History but also in the prophets, Psalms, and many other books. Likewise, the subjects of Moses, covenant, and law appear often in other biblical books. But other episodes do not. Adam and Eve are not mentioned again outside of the first few chapters of Genesis; the Garden of Eden and Noah and the flood are mentioned only rarely, as are the ancestors who feature so prominently in Genesis. It seems, then, that the Torah contains a particular set of traditions that were not necessarily as important, or perhaps even known, to the authors of other books of the Hebrew Bible. Most of these authors also do not seem to have been aware of a book called the Torah (the Torah of Moses, see above)—though the author of the book of Nehemiah apparently did (see Neh. 8:1). By the time some of the later books of the Bible were written, a self-standing Torah may have existed and been known to those books' authors; but this was likely not the case for the majority of the books of the Bible.

The question of the Torah's original audience is a difficult one. Though the law is presented as having been related to the Israelites of the exodus generation directly by YHWH or indirectly through Moses, the rest of the material is told from a later vantage point and thus cannot have been initially composed for this generation. Furthermore, the historicity of these events has been seriously questioned and can no longer be taken for granted, and so we must judge the identity of the audience based on the content and themes of the Torah, or of its component parts. Large sections of Leviticus, for example, may have been intended as instructions for priests or for people bringing sacrifices to the temple. Other parts of the Torah, such as the stories about the ancestors in Genesis, may have been written for a more general Israelite audience, as they provide a national "foundation history" and emphasize themes relevant to ancient Israelite self-understanding, perhaps in the period of the monarchy or later (tenth century BCE and after). The laws about kingship in Deuteronomy 17, though addressed in the narrative to all Israel, were likely intended for the king specifically, as a check on his powers.

It is unlikely that the Torah was intended to be picked up and read by the average Israelite, not least because literacy was probably not very common in ancient Israel. Copies of written works would also have been available only to a few people, mainly those in larger cities with a political or religious establishment, or both. The Torah's contents may not have been known at all to most people for much of the biblical period. However, there is some evidence that the Torah or parts of it were meant to be read aloud to the Israelites on a regular basis. The book of Deuteronomy (Deut. 31:10-13; and see Deut. 6:7) instructs the Israelites to recite the *torah* (probably just law, but later meaning the whole five books) regularly, and Nehemiah 8–9 recounts one such public reading in a later period.

Over the centuries, though, especially with the rise of Christianity and its inclusion of the Hebrew Bible in its sacred Scriptures, the Torah became more widely known. With time, too, the Torah's audience changed, and different communities have derived different meanings from it. The Torah was translated into Greek in the second century BCE so that the community of Jews in Alexandria, Egypt, would have access to it, and we can imagine that the story of the Israelites' sojourn in Egypt would have resonated differently for that audience than it did for one remaining in Jerusalem. Similarly, the laws relating to sacrifice and the temple would have gained new meaning with the destruction of the temple by the Romans in 70 CE. In later periods, too, the Torah's stories would have taken on different significance in changing historical circumstances; thus, for example, slaves in antebellum America found deep meaning in the story of the Israelites' delivery from slavery, and modern women seeking equal rights saw an example of a female leader in the figure of Miriam, who challenges the authority of her brother as sole leader of the Israelites (Numbers 12).

Who Wrote the Torah?

Although tradition holds that Moses was the author of the whole Torah (hence the title "Torah of Moses"), the Torah itself does not say who wrote it. Moses is said to have written down certain parts of the law (Exod. 24:4; 34:28; Deut. 31:9, 24); YHWH is said to have written the Ten Commandments on the tablets of stone (Exod. 24:12; 31:18; Deut. 4:13; 5:22; 9:10). However, there are indications within the text itself that neither Moses nor any other single person wrote the whole thing. The first problem, noticed by scholars already in the medieval period, is that Moses dies just before the end of Deuteronomy—so he cannot have written the last few verses! And it hardly seems likely that Moses would have (or could have) boasted, "Never since has there arisen a prophet in Israel like Moses, whom the LORD knew face to face. He was unequaled for all the signs and wonders that the LORD sent him to perform in the land of Egypt" (Deut. 34:10–11).

But these are only minor problems, easily (if not convincingly) solved by the traditional suggestion that Joshua, Moses' successor, wrote the last few verses after the great leader's death. More problematic are the repetitions, contradictions, and gaps that appear throughout the Torah and that are much more difficult to reconcile with the idea of a single author composing a single, continuous narrative. For example, there are two creation stories, one appearing in Gen. 1:1—2:4a and the other in Gen. 2:4b—3:24. Moreover, these two stories differ about the order of creation, humans being created before the animals in the first story and after them in the second. The flood story in Genesis 6–9 also contains two narrative strands, which differ regarding such details as the length of the flood and the numbers of animals brought into the ark. Some parts of the Torah recognize a multiplicity of holy sites, whereas others insist that there can be only one. Some depict YHWH in human terms, but others insist on the deity's transcendence and incorporeality.

By the medieval period, scholars had begun to notice some of these issues and come up with alternatives to the hypothesis that Moses wrote the whole Torah. Beginning in the nineteenth century, a model that posited multiple authors, none of whom were Moses, began to take hold. This model holds that the Torah is composed of four main narrative strands, termed J, E, D, and P. E (Elohist), named for its use of the divine name *Elohim*, is the most fragmentary of the sources and is considered by some to be the oldest. J (Yahwist), so named for its exclusive use of the divine name YHWH, or *Jehovah*, in the German of the theory's originator, is generally thought to be a little later than E. D (Deuteronomist) appears mostly in the book of Deuteronomy, though some scholars see evidence of some D editing in other books of the Torah. P (Priestly) is the sparest narrative but contains the most extensive legal material, especially concerned with sacrificial and other cultic matters.

Early proponents of this source theory, called the Documentary Hypothesis, argued that an editor or editors, possibly also from a priestly school like P, were responsible for the combination of the material, which until that point had been independent written sources. Many scholars hold that J and E were combined first and separately, and then joined with P and then D. A growing number of scholars, especially in Europe, reject the distinction between J and E and instead see in this material a complex layering that accrued in stages over several centuries; often this material is referred to simply as "non-Priestly." Scholars have likewise continued to reevaluate the P and D material, and especially the nature of P as an independent source, though there is more agreement about what material belongs to the Priestly and Deuteronomic collections than there is about the non-Priestly material traditionally. The differences between these sources go beyond the use of divine names, which disappears as a distinction after Exodus 6, when all the sources start using the name YHWH. Some of these differences will be discussed below in the context of specific themes and theologies of the Torah.

Aspects of the sources' material suggest that they came from different times and places: E focuses on northern tribes and places, hinting at composition in the north in the period before the fall of the northern kingdom in 722 BCE. J's focus on the south suggests a time when the kingdom of

Judah was thriving, likely sometime in the seventh century BCE (as is indicated by the archaeological evidence). P's focus on the sacrificial cult suggests a time when the temple existed, either before or after the Babylonian exile. D's focus on centralization suggests a location in Jerusalem, which was the central locus of worship in the seventh century and also in the postexilic period.

Of course, the Torah is about a time much earlier than any of these proposed dates—the earliest of which is sometime during the period of the northern kingdom of Israel (ninth and eighth centuries BCE). According to the Bible's chronology, Moses lived well before this, sometime around 1400 BCE. The ancestors, Abraham and Sarah and their descendants, lived several centuries earlier. How do we know that the Torah, or at least parts of it, was not written in this period? The main reason is that the archaeological record provides no evidence that a people known as "Israel" existed before about 1200 BCE. There are no references to them in outside sources before the first mention in an Egyptian text known as the Merneptah Stela, dated to around 1200 BCE. In addition, the archaeology of the land of Israel does not indicate the appearance of a new people on the scene before this time. The culture that can be identified archaeologically as Israel only begins to emerge in the late second millennium BCE, and as it emerges, it shows remarkable continuity with the Canaanite culture that precedes it, indicating that the people called "Israel" were indigenous to the land of Canaan, not a group that conquered it from outside (Finkelstein and Silberman).

The production of a literary work as expansive as the Hebrew Bible would depend on the kind of social structures that only appear with urban culture and a strong central government (Schniedewind). But the need for such social structures relates only to the written work; it is likely that the Torah also contains some earlier oral traditions. A few texts bear the markers of oral composition; the existence of multiple versions of a story, such as the wife/sister stories in Genesis 12, 20, and 26, indicates that some traditions developed independently, in different times and places, before being brought together in the final written work. Likewise, the focus of traditions on certain geographical areas—especially where those traditions tend to be clustered into one or another of the sources identified in the Documentary Hypothesis—suggests the development of local traditions before the written composition of the Torah itself began. And evidence of archaic Hebrew indicates earlier composition for some texts as well.

The Torah also shows the influence of the literary traditions of the surrounding cultures: the treaties, laws, and myths of the Babylonians, Assyrians, Hittites, and Egyptians. Scholars debate when and how this influence happened, and as with the development of the sources and their traditions, it seems to have taken place over a lengthy span of time. All of these factors indicate that the composition of the Torah was a complex process. And though the Torah bears clear marks of its gradual composition, it works well together as a whole. It is unified not only by a fairly continuous plot arc but also by a number of narrative and theological themes. It is also important to keep in mind that, despite the fracturing in the text, someone did finally put the whole thing together, and this whole has been meaningful to numerous people for millennia. Though modern scholars have developed historical-critical methods of reading the Bible, using tools such as archaeology and source criticism, others have developed new ways of reading the final form of the text, seeking meaning from the fact that the whole exists as it does, contradictions and all (see, for example, Childs). In particular, the final form of the text serves as a striking narrative of the nation of Israel's birth and development, its special relationship with YHWH, and YHWH's powerful role in history. Its various themes are knit together in such a way that the story has continued to resonate with people of different religious faiths, ethnicities, and nationalities for over two millennia.

Part 2: Themes in the Torah

The key themes of the Torah can be grouped into three main categories: creation, kinship, and covenant. Each of these categories is established early in the Torah and is a focus of a particular part of the whole, but each also continues throughout the Torah. So, for example, creation is highlighted at the beginning of the Torah, in the story of the creation of the world in Genesis 1–3. However, the theme of creation repeats in the story of the creation of the nation of Israel through the ancestor Abraham and his descendants; this creation in turn is a twofold creation, beginning in the period of the ancestors and culminating in the period of the exodus generation.

Kinship likewise runs as a thread throughout the Torah. The stories of Genesis are focused on family history—on a particular kinship group, beginning with Abraham and continuing through his grandson Jacob's children, the ancestors of Israel's twelve tribes. Outside of Genesis, kinship concerns are manifest in stories about the roles and relationships of the tribes, and the narrative is punctuated throughout by genealogical lists that make clear the importance of kinship—and the close connections between various kinship groups in and around ancient Israel.

The Torah narrative is marked by three covenants: the covenant with Noah, the covenant with Abraham, and the covenant with all Israel. These covenants mirror the three periods of creation in the Torah, from the primeval period, to the ancestral period, and into the larger nation of Israel. It is the covenant that constitutes the creation of the people of Israel and illustrates their special relationship to YHWH. The covenant is passed down generationally, from father to son. A primary component of the covenant is the promise of land, progeny, and blessing first made to Abraham; this promise is left unfulfilled at the end of the Torah, however, as the Israelites have not yet entered the promised land.

Creation

The theme of creation figures in the Torah in a number of ways, not only in the most obvious, the creation of the world at the beginning of Genesis. The whole of the Torah is a much larger creation story, of the nation of Israel. The role of YHWH in the world and especially in the history of Israel is a key and related theme, as is the theme of divine presence and absence that goes along with it.

The well-known beginning of the book of Genesis details the creation of the world, land, water, sky, plants, and animals, including humans. Unlike the other animals, humans are created "in the image of God" and are the culmination of the creation account in Genesis 1. Their purpose is to exercise dominion over creation and to "be fruitful and multiply," setting the stage for the unfolding narrative in the rest of the Torah. Genesis 2–3, which provides a slightly different account of creation, also makes humans paramount, though in this case the focus is on the relationship of the humans to one another and to YHWH.

The story continues with a long genealogical list of the ensuing long-lived generations—the results of the humans' being fruitful and multiplying. Unhappy with the state of things, however, YHWH destroys this first attempt at creation, saving only Noah and his family and rebuilding from that line. Another genealogical list follows, this time outlining the numerous other nations and peoples that surrounded the ancient Israelites and were seen as descending from this common ancestor.

As noted above, there are two creation stories side by side at the beginning of Genesis; both emphasize the deity's role in creation, but in different ways. Both also focus on the creation of humans, but again they differ in how they do this. They also diverge in the divine name they use: the first employs Elohim ("God") and the second YHWH ("Lord"). The first story describes the creation of humans as "in the image of God," suggesting a close connection between deity and humanity. The question of just what "in the image of God" means, however, is a perplexing one with major implications. Is it a literal comparison, or figurative? Does it suggest that humans are literally godlike in some way? Does it apply only to men, or to both men and women? Historically, the verse has been used to justify numerous entitlements and obligations of the human race (see Jónsson).

The humans seem to be given dominion over all creation in a fashion parallel to God's power. But Genesis 1 also depicts a God who is quite separate from creation. Unlike the deity in Genesis 2–3, this one does not come down and walk around on the earth, forming humans by hand, nor does God in Genesis 1 speak directly with the humans as YHWH does in the second creation story. God in Genesis 1 is depicted as transcendent, existing above and acting on the world. Thus the "image of God" in Genesis 1 may not refer to human form. It may instead indicate the place of God in creation: above it and the master of it, as humans are in relation to their own environment, over which they are given dominion by God. Many interpreters have also taken "image of God" to mean something moral or ethical: humans are like God (and unlike the animals) in that they have an ethical sense, though this view is problematic because the Hebrew term for "image" usually means something more physical or concrete.

If Genesis 1 has been important for understanding the place of humans in the world, then Genesis 2–3 have had a major impact on the status of women in relationship to men. The creation of the woman after the man in this story has been taken to indicate that she is of inferior status to him. Despite the creation of the man and woman simultaneously as the final act of creation, and both "in the image of God," in Genesis 1, interpreters have seen in Genesis 2–3 a prescription for women's subordinate status to men. More than the derivative status of woman in Genesis 2, however, Genesis 3 has been used in various ways to justify women's secondary status. First, women are blamed for the "fall from grace," "original sin," and the expulsion from the garden. Yet, a closer look at the text shows that "fall" and "sin" are terms that never appear in this episode. True, the woman is punished for transgressing YHWH's edict, but the man is punished as well. And as modern scholars have shown, the woman is not "cursed" with subordination to man but rather is punished with difficult labor and childbirth and with hard toil—as is the man (see Meyers).

Women's subordinate status and sinful nature were thus seen as having been encoded in the natural order of things at the creation. These chapters of Genesis were therefore fundamental to the women's rights movement from its inception. Beginning in the medieval period, women recognized the role of these texts in their subordination and moved to reject the traditional interpretations.

In the late nineteenth century, the suffragist movement had to tackle these texts; and the feminist movement in the 1970s likewise required a rejection of sexist interpretations of the story. Many feminists moved toward a rejection of the Bible as a whole, seeing these texts as irredeemably patriarchal (see Daly); but other feminists offered alternative readings, seeing in Genesis 1 a depiction of equality between the sexes and in Genesis 2–3 an empowering depiction of an intellectually curious woman (see Trible).

These chapters have also been important for the understanding of humanity's place in creation. The command in Genesis 1 to humans to have "dominion" over the earth and to "subdue" it was taken as justification for human exploitation of the world and of all its resources. More recently, the text has been used instead as an argument for environmental stewardship and for people's responsibility toward the world and toward all people "in the image of God."

In addition to the creation of the world and everything in it, the Torah is also the story of the creation of the nation of Israel, YHWH's own covenant people. This story begins with the selection of Abraham, the first ancestor of the Israelites. YHWH tells Abraham (at first named Abram) to leave his home and go to Canaan, a land that YHWH promises to give to Abraham and his descendants, who will be as numerous as the stars of the sky. After Abraham's arrival in Canaan, YHWH makes a covenant (treaty) with him and reiterates the promise as the content of this covenant, which is predicated on Abraham and all the men of his household being circumcised. Thus the nation of Israel is born, though it is not until Abraham's grandson Jacob (also called Israel) that the nation gets its namesake. It is Jacob's twelve sons (and two of his grandsons) after whom the various tribes of the nation are known.

An important aspect of the theme of the creation of the nation of Israel is the threat to its existence that the nation continually faces. The ancestors and their wives are frequently threatened with death by those around them. All of the matriarchs are barren at one point or another, creating narrative tension about the ability of the fledgling nation to survive. Not only that, but the patriarchs repeatedly put their wives and children in questionable situations, risking their ability to have children and for those children to live to adulthood. In each case, though, with YHWH's help, the line of Abraham continues and even flourishes.

These narrative details probably reflect not only real aspects of life in ancient Israel, such as infertility and infant mortality, but also the precarious situation of the Israelites at many points during their history. Archaeological evidence reveals that the Israelites emerged as a subgroup from within an indigenous Canaanite population, rather than invading and conquering (as the biblical narrative itself depicts). So the early Israelites must have had to develop customs, habits, and other markers of identity to distinguish themselves from the nations, especially the Canaanites, around them (see Killebrew). Further, they were surrounded at nearly all times by great and expansionistic empires. The threat of assimilation and destruction would have been real throughout most of Israel's history.

Unlike the initial slate-wiping and re-creation with Noah, however, YHWH does not reject this chosen line, even when its members are disobedient. The role of YHWH in Israel's history is thus paramount. The message comes through clearly throughout the Torah: YHWH takes an active interest in the survival of the nation of Israel, ensuring that barren wives become fertile, that children survive, that wealth is accrued, that slaves are freed, and that enemies are vanquished. YHWH has power not only over Israel but over all people. Beginning the story with the creation of the entire world demonstrates the extent of YHWH's power. Other ancient Near Eastern creation stories also show that the gods (a whole pantheon of them) create the world, and they may occasionally take an interest in a special person. Likewise, ancient Near Eastern histories certainly mention gods as having enabled a king, for example, to perform various feats, and the gods are invoked as parties to treaties and oaths. But in no other contemporary texts is the activity of any deity—much less only one deity—incorporated in the same fashion that it is here in Israel's foundational story.

As a result, the theme of divine presence and absence is critical to the Torah. Israel owes its success to its special relationship with YHWH, which is manifested in the deity's presence among the people—either physically or metaphysically, depending on the text. The importance of YHWH's presence also has a flip side: YHWH's potential absence, which is seen as the abandonment of the people. This problem is especially evident in the Priestly material, particularly in the book of Leviticus. Leviticus is concerned with the sacrificial system and the ideas of purity and impurity, all of which are mentioned as safeguards for the purity of the Israelite encampment, where YHWH is understood to be present. Impurity will force YHWH to leave and thus to abandon and imperil Israel, inviting catastrophe. Such a catastrophe was realized with the Babylonian exile, which many Israelites understood as YHWH's abandonment of them—an understanding expressed, in retrospect by the postexilic Priestly author, as YHWH's threat at the beginning of the covenant relationship: "the land will vomit you out for defiling it, as it vomited out the nation that was before you" (Lev. 18:28; see also Ezekiel 8–10).

This theme also appears at the very beginning of the Torah: YHWH is initially present in the Garden of Eden, walking in it and interacting with the man and woman. They are in close relationship with one another. But after the humans disobey YHWH's command not to eat the fruit of the knowledge of good and evil, this relationship is severed. The humans are now fundamentally alienated from the divine; having "become like" YHWH by gaining knowledge, they are forever separated from YHWH, lest they also achieve immortality by eating the fruit of the tree of life and become, for all intents and purposes, divine themselves. Having become too much like YHWH, they are forever removed from YHWH's presence, and reentry is blocked. In the future, additional barriers will be set up to maintain the separation (but also the mutual coexistence) of the human (common) and the divine (holy) spheres, as in Leviticus. Thus the story of the Torah is one of alienation from the divine and the ongoing efforts of YHWH and the Israelites to maintain their special relationship.

The tensions between divine presence and absence differ somewhat in different parts of the Torah, however. In the earlier (non-Priestly) material, although human and divine are seen as fundamentally separated from one another, as recounted in the Garden of Eden story, YHWH moves about on the earth, interacting directly or through intermediaries with numerous people. Though the Israelites' frequent misbehavior threatens YHWH's allegiance to the people, YHWH's permanent abandonment of them seems to be less of a concern. In the Priestly and Deuteronomic material, in contrast, YHWH is seen as present in a less physical, though no less real, fashion. In P, YHWH is present among the people as the cloud of fire that descends on and dwells in the tabernacle (see

Num. 9:15-23). The elaborate Priestly cultic system is meant to ensure YHWH's presence there by maintaining the purity of the land. Deuteronomy also has some concern with the purity of the land (for example, Deut. 23:13-15), though YHWH's presence is linked more to the idea of covenant than to purity specifically. Deuteronomy also develops a theology linked to YHWH's *name* dwelling in the land, rather than YHWH being physically present in an embodied sense.

The ideas of divine presence and absence or alienation from the divine have continued to reverberate through the ages. In Judaism, alienation from the divine after creation is addressed through the concept of *tikkun olam*, or repairing the world. Jewish mystical belief holds that vessels containing divine light shattered after creation, and performing commandments (*mitzvot*) is a way of gathering the sparks and restoring the divine (Robinson, 383). According to this principle, right relationship with the divine is restored through positive action. In some modern Jewish denominations, this idea has been expanded to include social justice, environmentalism, and other movements, expressing the divine through common experience with all people.

Kinship

The Torah begins as a universal history, narrows its focus to become a family history, and ends as a national one. The theme of kinship is thus of primary importance, whether it is kinship among all peoples of the earth, among a single clan or tribe, or within an entire nation conceived of as descended from a common ancestor. Indeed, all of humanity is depicted as descended from a common ancestry—first from Adam and Eve and then from Noah and his wife. Large portions of Genesis and other books are genealogical lists, also emphasizing the genetic connection.

Immediately after the creation story, Genesis begins to describe history in terms of families, beginning with the family of Adam and Eve, thereby emphasizing the importance of this theme (Petersen, 8). After the primeval history, which focuses on the families from which all humanity is descended, the narrative moves to the family history of Abraham, tracing his descendants from Isaac to Jacob to Jacob's twelve sons, the eponymous ancestors of the tribes of Israel. A key feature of this narrative is the threefold promise by YHWH to Abraham of progeny, land, and blessing (Gen. 12:1-3). While Abraham is dwelling in Haran (in northern Mesopotamia), YHWH appears to him and tells him to leave his extended family and travel to a land that YHWH will show him, promising to give him that land on his arrival. Abraham takes his wife Sarah and his nephew Lot and sets out. When he arrives in Canaan, YHWH announces that this is the land he will receive and that will be passed down to his son. But though Abraham and his descendants live in this land (with minor forays to Egypt for Abraham and to Aram for Jacob), things take a turn with Jacob's sons, who all end up in Egypt. When Exodus picks up the story, the Israelites have been enslaved to the Egyptians. Moses appears and takes the descendants of Jacob, now called the Israelites, out of Egypt and slavery and back to the promised land, but the Torah ends before they actually get there. Thus this promise is unfulfilled at the end of the Torah, though the people are perched on the edge of the land, ready to move in and take it over.

Along with the promise of the land, Abraham receives a promise that he will be the forebear of numerous offspring. In the Priestly material, this promise is linked to the command made to

Adam at creation that he "be fruitful and multiply" (Gen. 1:28). This promise initially looks to be unfulfilled too, as Abraham's wife Sarah is barren. Abraham has a child, Ishmael, with Sarah's slave Hagar, but Ishmael is excluded from the promise by YHWH; it is only Sarah's son who will be the heir of the promise. Sarah finally conceives, with YHWH's aid, and bears Isaac. Isaac's wife Rebekah is also initially barren and requires divine assistance in order to have her two sons, the twins Jacob and Esau. Jacob, the heir, likewise has wives who are barren at various points, though between them and their two slaves they manage to bear twelve sons and a daughter. Barrenness and difficulty in childbirth thus serve in the Torah to emphasize both the power of YHWH and the special nature of the sons born out of such circumstances. And despite all these apparent setbacks, Genesis ends with the promise of progeny already well fulfilled; the overproliferation of the Israelites at the beginning of Exodus, to the extent that the Egyptian pharaoh is concerned that the Egyptians will be overrun, leaves the reader in no doubt about YHWH's power to fulfill the promise.

Though kinship is important in the Torah, it is only certain lineages in the larger Abrahamic kinship group that are deemed to be the "right" kinship lines. Abraham and Isaac both have two sons, but only one son is allowed to inherit the promise and with it the covenant, the formalization of the relationship between Abraham and YHWH that includes the promises (Genesis 17). Abraham's son Ishmael is excluded from becoming the heir, and thus from inheriting the promise, when Sarah objects to the son of her slave inheriting alongside her own son (or when YHWH informs Abraham that Ishmael will not inherit; compare Genesis 17 and 21). Likewise, Rebekah helps ensure that her favorite, Jacob, will inherit the promise and covenant, to the exclusion of his twin brother, Esau. Esau also seems to disqualify himself through his own actions, giving away his birthright and marrying the wrong women (Gen. 26:34); for this generation, as for the one before, a woman from Abraham's lineage in Aram is required for the "right" heir. With Jacob's sons, though, we move into a broader definition of the lineage; all of his sons inherit the promise and the land (and are no longer required to marry women from a specific family). The correct lineage having been identified, it can now proliferate and thus fulfill the progeny part of the promise.

This emphasis on lineage appears elsewhere in the Torah, too, though it does not receive quite the same emphasis elsewhere that it does in Genesis. It reappears as a theme especially in the genealogies interspersed throughout the Torah; these genealogies are manifestations of fulfillment of the command to "be fruitful and multiply" and the promise to Abraham of countless progeny (Exodus 6; Numbers 26). The genealogies primarily trace lines of male descent (from fathers to sons)—the tradition of matrilineal descent in Judaism developed much later. Women do figure into genealogies on occasion, especially where there is more than one wife and the author considers it important to note which woman is the mother of which child.

The third and final aspect of the promise, blessing, is a little harder to quantify. YHWH tells Abraham that he will be blessed and that "in you all the families of the earth shall be blessed" (Gen. 12:3). But just what does this mean? It has often been taken to refer to Abraham's role as a medium of blessing for all humanity, through his own relationship with YHWH. But it might simply mean that Abraham, owing to the fulfillment of the other aspects of the promise, will be invoked as a blessing by those who wish to achieve the same kinds of success. In either case, though, the Torah story seems to be a mixed bag as far as blessing is concerned. The Israelites do end up numerous and on the verge of possession of the land, but it is a long and rocky road that they take to get there.

YHWH's choice of Israel for the covenant, which involves the promise of numerous offspring, is closely connected to—even requires—the emphasis on lineage, as the covenant becomes a generational promise that is passed down within the line of a single son for two generations before being expanded to include all twelve of Jacob's sons. There is never an expansion of the genealogy to include non-Jacobite (non-Israelite) lineages in the covenant. In reality, other groups of people were absorbed into the Israelite nation, and the Torah does allow for the admission of others into the "community of Israel," but the concept of Israel as a separate and selected people remains one premised on the idea (if not the reality) of genealogical purity (see Cohen). It is for this reason that the Torah includes numerous genealogies; they detail the kinship between Israel and other peoples, but they also serve to delineate Israel's own genealogy specifically. The lists of member clans and families are carefully enumerated, not only for the purposes of census taking but also for outlining the roles of certain groups, especially in the tribe of Levi.

Genealogies are a special favorite of the Priestly author, who uses them to structure the narrative and divide it into portions. These genealogies are mostly concerned with men, but women are introduced into them from time to time; the inclusion of women in the genealogies is linked in particular to validating certain lineages (Exod. 6:14-25)—the pedigree of a lineage is indicated not only by the male line but also by the wives and mothers (see Shectman, 148–53).

Though these long lists of "begats" can seem tedious at first, the genealogies are an integral part of the narrative. They provide a framework for much of it, functioning as summaries at key junctures in the narrative (Genesis 10; 25; 36; Numbers 1–3). In addition to lists of general kinship or national groups (in the so-called Table of Nations in Genesis 10–11) and specifically Israelite tribes and clans, genealogical notices also appear for other, non-Israelite groups. The largest of these is a detailed genealogy of the descendants of Jacob's twin brother, Esau, who becomes the ancestor of the Edomites, one of ancient Israel's close neighbors. The inclusion of this list, the similar tribal structure of the Edomites, and the relationship between the characters of Esau and Jacob all suggest that these two groups had similar social structures and close affinities—and perhaps also that the biblical authors, through narratives and genealogies, wanted to differentiate the two (very similar) nations from one another.

The genealogies record births but also some marriages. As was noted above, marriages are important because they are one of the ways that a person establishes the "right" lineage: Isaac must marry a woman from Abraham's family (Genesis 24). Esau disqualifies himself from receiving his father's blessing and covenant by, among other things, repeatedly marrying the wrong women (Gen. 28:6-9). That one of his wives is an Ishmaelite—a descendant of Abraham's other son—further proves his inappropriateness as heir. Jacob, like Isaac, also marries women from his extended family (his cousins on his mother's side—a common phenomenon and not considered incest in many cultures, even today). Miriam and Aaron challenge Moses' authority by complaining that he has married a Cushite woman (Numbers 12).

Although we might expect the emphasis on Israelite lineage and inheritance to extend to a general prohibition on marriage with outsiders—or exogamy—this is not the case in the Torah. Though certain groups are prohibited—namely, Moabites and Edomites—there is no blanket prohibition on outside marriage. Wives from specific kinship groups are required only for certain figures: Isaac and Jacob in particular, figures from the early part of the narrative, when the nation is still being established and thus the need for self-differentiation is greater. Although in some instances the choice of a wife from a specific tribe or clan appears to help validate a particular lineage (see especially Aaron's line in Exodus 6), many major figures marry exogamously. Judah, the ancestor of one of the largest and most important tribes, marries a Canaanite woman—a member of a group that Israelites are elsewhere forbidden to marry (see Deut. 7:1-4). Joseph marries Asenath, the daughter of an Egyptian priest (Gen. 41:45). And Moses' Cushite wife is vindicated when Miriam is punished for challenging the marriage.

The most rigid marriage restrictions apply to the priests (Leviticus 21) and are related to cultic purity (see below) and to the purity of the priestly lineage. Priests are not allowed to marry prostitutes or divorced women; the high priest must marry a virgin "of his own people," probably meaning any Israelite woman, not only a woman from the priestly tribe of Levi. Marriage between members of different tribes seems not to have been a problem, though for logistical reasons it may not have been widespread. Especially in rural areas and in the earlier part of Israel's history, people are likely to have married fairly locally, from neighboring villages within their larger clan, but less likely from other tribes (Meyers, 142). There is only one case in which marriage within a close kinship group is required of any Israelites: the case of daughters of a man with no sons (Num. 27:1-11; 36:1-12), who hold temporary rights of inheritance when their father dies. In order to ensure that the land they temporarily inherit does not pass out of their clan's holdings, such women are required to marry within their clan (Shectman, 162–64).

Archaeological evidence indicates that the Israelites were very closely related to their Canaanite neighbors. Even though some biblical authors might have forbidden intermarriage with Canaanites in order to differentiate the Israelites from them, in reality it is likely that once the Israelites emerged as a distinct group around 1200 BCE, they intermarried with neighboring peoples frequently. We see remnants of these marriages in the text, despite the prohibitions against them. The marriages of early ancestors such as Judah and his son Simeon (Exod. 6:15) to Canaanite women, though likely not historical, may reflect a recognition by the biblical author that in the past the groups intermarried. There are also indications that the Israelites sought to make alliances with their neighbors through marriage. Jacob's objection to the episode involving his daughter Dinah and a Canaanite prince in Genesis 34 seems to focus not on her near-marriage to a Canaanite but to the souring of relations with the Canaanites when Dinah's brothers Simeon and Levi retaliate for what they see as an affront to their honor. Similarly, as the Israelites go from Egypt to the promised land, they attempt to move peacefully through the territories of some of their non-Canaanite neighbors (Num. 20:14-21; 21:21-32; but compare Deuteronomy 2), though they are not always granted these terms. It is only the Canaanites—the Israelites' closest neighbors—who are slated for complete annihilation even before the Israelites reach their territory, though again, both the biblical and the archaeological evidence suggests that such complete destruction did not take place (see Moore and Kelle).

In the early period of Israel's history, this creation of distinctions between the Israelites and Canaanites would have been quite important, as the nascent Israelite nation sought to establish its own independent identity. The archaeological evidence suggests that the early Israelites mostly lived in rural areas, and so they probably did not have frequent contact with non-Canaanite people. A broader prohibition on exogamy would therefore not have been necessary. It is not until the later period of Israelite history, with the Babylonian exile and afterward, that broader prohibitions on intermarriage appear in the biblical text. In this period, the Israelites in exile would have been in contact with an increasing number of people; without their own political structure and territorial autonomy, the threat of assimilation and intermarriage would have been greater. Thus, in later books such as Ezra and Nehemiah, we see broader prohibitions on exogamy, which are developed more fully in the rabbinic period (see Cohen). But most of the Torah seems to have been written before this view took hold.

A variety of types of marriage exist in the Torah, among them monogamy, polygyny (multiple wives), concubinage, and levirate marriage, the latter of which requires that a childless widowed woman's brother-in-law marry her and that their first son count as the deceased husband's heir (Deut. 25:5-10). There is thus no single concept of "biblical marriage," despite the frequent use of this phrase in modern society. Perhaps because Gen. 2:24 says, "Therefore a man leaves his father and his mother and clings to his wife, and they become one flesh," many people believe that a "biblical" marriage is a marriage between one woman and one man. But nowhere does the Torah say that a marriage *must* look like this, and the marriages of Abraham, Jacob, and perhaps even Moses (if Zipporah and the Cushite wife are indeed two different wives) do not conform to such a model.

Furthermore, the families modeled in the Torah, especially in Genesis, do not conform to our modern idea of a nuclear family. Including as they do multiple wives and their children, the families exist as small communities of their own. These families are filled with rivalries, younger sons usurping older ones, daughters seducing fathers, wives fighting over husbands, and sisters challenging brothers. These are not the kinds of "family values" that we often hear touted as the biblical model. Nevertheless, these stories do impart certain lessons. Beyond theological messages about faith in YHWH, the stories emphasize the importance of family and of hospitality to strangers, and they provide numerous models for nonviolent conflict resolutions (see Petersen).

Covenant

YHWH makes a series of covenants with various people over the course of the Torah's narrative. What is a covenant? It is an agreement between two parties, rather like a treaty. Indeed, the biblical covenant resembles the political treaties we know of from other ancient Near Eastern cultures, especially the Hittites and the Assyrians. These political treaties are typically between a sovereign and a vassal and outline the obligations of both parties. Various deities are invoked as "witnesses" to the treaties, and the documents conclude with long lists of punishments in the case that the vassal party breaks the treaty, much like the lists of blessings and curses in Leviticus 26 and Deuteronomy 27–28.

So, too, the covenants in the Torah are between a suzerain (YHWH) and a vassal (Israel), but the content of these treaties varies. The first treaty is between YHWH and Noah and "every living creature of all flesh"—that is, all the animals as well! YHWH prohibits eating meat with blood in it and shedding human blood (Gen. 9:4-6); Noah is also given dominion over all the animals and is commanded to "be fruitful and multiply," in terms reminiscent of the same command made to Adam in Genesis 1, though in that case the term *covenant* is not used. In return, YHWH promises never again to destroy the world with a flood and sets the rainbow in the sky as a sign of this covenant.

The second covenant is made with Abraham; there are actually two covenants with Abraham. The first is made in Genesis 15 and is often referred to as the "covenant between the pieces" as it involves the ritual killing and dismembering of animals to solemnize the pact. In this case, YHWH reiterates the promise to give Abraham and his offspring the land of Canaan. Nothing is required of Abraham in return according to this covenant's terms.

Two chapters later, YHWH makes another covenant with Abraham (Genesis 17). Genesis 15 and Genesis 17 are probably two originally independent versions of a single covenant, from two separate sources. This covenant too includes YHWH's promise to fulfill the original promise to Abraham of land and numerous progeny; YHWH also assures the still-childless Abraham that he will have a son through Sarah, his first wife; Ishmael, his son by the Egyptian slave Hagar, will not be the inheritor of this promise and covenant. In this covenant, unlike the one in Genesis 15, Abraham is required to do something in return: he and all the males of his household must be circumcised. This rule applies even to Ishmael and other members of the household who will not actually be part of the covenant—that is, they are not part of the lineage that ultimately becomes Israel and for whom the promise will be fulfilled. This covenant is also called an "everlasting covenant" (Gen. 17:19), which suggests that it can never be broken. Indeed, so far none of these covenants have involved any stipulations about what happens if one party or the other breaks the terms of the treaty. Thus these covenants are generally seen as eternal and unbreakable.

Abraham is often referred to as the "first Jew" because the covenant and circumcision are connected to the idea that the Israelites, and later the Jews, are YHWH's "chosen" people. Yet the term "chosen" (Hebrew *yivhar*) is never used in reference to Abraham. In fact, this idea does not appear in the Torah until near its end, in the book of Deuteronomy (Deut. 4:37; Seebass, 83). Nevertheless, the selection of Abraham and the inheritance of the covenant by his son Isaac and his grandson Jacob establishes a particular lineage with a special relationship to YHWH, a covenant that the deity has promised will be eternal. This proved to be a problem with the rise of Christianity, with its claims that a new covenant had been established. Very early Christianity was a movement within Judaism, so initially there was no theological problem. But as Christianity increasingly became a religion of gentiles, separating itself from other Jewish movements, Christian leaders like the apostle Paul began to reject the idea that they must follow all of the laws of the Torah (that is, the stipulations of the covenant; see below). Thus, in the letter to the Galatians, Paul offers a radical new reading of the promise to Abraham. The promise, Paul says, is passed down through faith, rather than being hereditary (see Galatians 3). Just as Abraham has faith in YHWH's promise (Gen. 15:6), so do Christians who have faith inherit the promise, and thus the covenant. Circumcision and other legal observances are not required. The blessing also becomes the key aspect of the promise, rather than the promises of progeny and land that are emphasized in the Torah: blessing (that is, salvation) is conveyed to Christians through faith, not through observance of the law. According to this interpretation, the new covenant (or "testament") in Christ supersedes the Jewish covenant initiated with Abraham.

The covenant with Abraham having been made and passed down through the generations to Jacob's sons, the new nation of Israel finds itself, at the beginning of the book of Exodus, enslaved to the Egyptians. Now quite numerous (the promise of numerous progeny being fulfilled), the Israelites pose a threat to the Egyptians, who use oppressive measures to arrest the population's growth. At this point, YHWH is notably absent from the narrative, apparently paying little attention to Israel in the centuries that pass between the end of Genesis and the beginning of Exodus and allowing the Israelites to become enslaved. Yet there is no indication in the text that YHWH has broken the covenant by allowing the Israelites' enslavement or that the Israelites are being punished for breaking their side of the agreement. Indeed, it is not until Exod. 2:24 that we read, "God remembered his covenant with Abraham, Isaac, and Jacob."

The Egyptians' attempts at oppression do not serve their intended purpose, but they do cause the Israelites to cry out. YHWH hears the Israelites' cries and determines to save the people, commissioning Moses to lead them to freedom. The Israelites escape to the Sinai wilderness, headed to the promised land and the fulfillment of the promise of the land. At Sinai, YHWH appears to the people and makes the third and final covenant of the Torah, this time with the entire nation of Israel. Now, though, the covenant takes on a very different form: it becomes a collection of laws, beginning with the Ten Commandments and expanding from there. The promises of land and progeny play less of a role in the making of this covenant in Exodus–Numbers, though they feature more prominently in the book of Deuteronomy, which is framed as a retrospective on the preceding narrative. Instead, the key features of this covenant are that the Israelites are to worship YHWH and only YHWH and that they are to observe all of the ritual, ethical, and social stipulations of the various collections of laws gathered together in the books of Exodus through Deuteronomy.

The new content of the covenant, the laws (Hebrew *torah*), occupy considerable space in the Torah. The bulk of the laws appear in Exodus and Leviticus, at the narrative point where the Israelites are encamped near Mount Sinai. YHWH appears and delivers most of the laws, some directly to the people and the rest to Moses, who ascends the mountain to receive them. A reiteration of many of these laws, as well as additional ones, also appears in the book of Deuteronomy. The laws cover a range of topics: religious laws governing various aspects of belief, worship, and sacrifice; criminal laws covering crimes such as murder and theft; and civil laws covering institutions such as marriage, inheritance, and slavery. The laws in Exodus include the Ten Commandments as well as numerous other social and religious precepts, along with instructions on how to build the tabernacle, the wilderness shrine that is a stand-in for the later Jerusalem temple. The laws of Leviticus are largely focused on the sacrificial cult and the system of purity and impurity that is the particular focus of the priesthood. The laws in these two books and in Deuteronomy appear as fairly coherent legal collections that have been inserted into the narrative. In Numbers, the interplay between law and narrative is more complex; the two are not always as clearly delineated from one another as they are in Exodus and Leviticus. In part, this may be due to the fact that in Numbers the Israelites depart from Mount Sinai, and thus the narrative loses its strong connection between place and lawgiving that allowed for the large sections of legal material to appear in the earlier narrative.

The covenant becomes explicitly conditional at this point: not only do many laws carry punishments, including the death penalty in some cases, for the person who breaks them, but if the Israelites do not obey the laws of the covenant, then YHWH will also abandon them to their enemies and they will be exiled from the promised land. It is noteworthy that exile from the land is the ultimate punishment for the people's breaking the covenant. The final curse in Deuteronomy for violation of the covenant speaks of a dispersed and miserable life for the people in places such as Egypt, where they will not even be able to sell themselves as slaves, so awful will their situation be (Deut. 28:64-68).

Despite the fact that the Israelites' foundational history included a period spent as slaves, the Torah's stance on slavery is mixed. As noted, the period of slavery in Egypt is not a punishment of the people, though the experience is certainly viewed as a terrible episode in their history, and YHWH's deliverance of the people from Egypt is one of the most frequently cited of the deity's miraculous and salvific acts. However, in the very same book, biblical laws condone slavery—and not only of foreign war captives or people perceived as Israel's enemies but also of other Israelites (Exod. 21:2-11). Thus the Torah has been used both as a justification for the institution of slavery and, in the past two centuries, as a source of liberation theology, which encourages freedom from political oppression.

Much of the legal material covers, broadly speaking, what is called the "cult"—that is, the system of Yahwistic religious observance. This includes broad stipulations such as the First Commandment (the First and Second Commandments in Jewish tradition): "I am the Lord your God, who brought you out of the land of Egypt, out of the house of slavery; you shall have no other gods before me" (Exod. 20:2-3). It also includes rules related to the priests and the temple. The biblical authors understood the sacrificial system to be a key part of Yahwism, beginning with Noah's first sacrifice after the flood. We read of ancestors setting up altars and making offerings in the book of Genesis (12:8; 26:25), even before the Israelites have been instructed in the specific details of the sacrificial system, which appear mostly in Leviticus. According to some biblical authors, then, the sacrificial system has more or less always been in operation. Even before the laws stipulating that sacrifices be performed only at certain places appeared, sacrifices could be performed almost anywhere. According to the Priestly author, however, sacrifice only begins with the revelation of the law at Sinai; before this time, the Priestly narrative does not depict anyone offering a sacrifice—they could not have done so, after all, without having yet been told how to do it! Similarly, the author of Deuteronomy insists that sacrifice can only be performed at a single location, which most scholars believe was likely Jerusalem; according to this view, Deuteronomy was written in Jerusalem in the later part of the Judean monarchy (eighth–seventh centuries BCE) as a means of centralizing worship at Jerusalem's temple. Other sources seem to assume that sacrifices continued to be offered in multiple locations even after the temple was built. Archaeological evidence also reveals that sacrifice was an Israelite practice even in the earliest history of the people—as it was for most ancient Near Eastern people—and that it continued at multiple Israelite sites even after the building of the Jerusalem temple.

Sacrifices were to be offered for a variety of reasons; there were a number of different types of them, some offered in the temple daily and others brought by individuals only on certain occasions.

The animals or other items for sacrifice were mostly brought by the people, but the process of sacrifice itself was officiated by the priests, who according to the Torah belonged to the lineage of Aaron, Moses' brother and a member of the tribe of Levi. They were assisted by Levites who were not from the Aaronide line. Only the Aaronide priests had access to the inside of the temple (analogized in the portable wilderness shrine—the tabernacle, or "tent of meeting"—in the Torah).

The purpose of sacrifice in many cultures is the feeding of the deity, and this aspect of sacrifice is retained at some level in the Torah, despite the attempts by some authors, especially P, to deanthropomorphize YHWH. Thus, in Gen. 8:21 (a non-Priestly text), YHWH smells the "pleasing odor" of Noah's offering, and Lev. 3:11 (a P text) says, "The priest shall turn these into smoke on the altar *as food*, an offering by fire to the Lord" (author's translation). However, sacrifices in the Torah have an additional and more important function as well: they are meant to absolve the people of culpability from their sins and to purify the temple. In the biblical view, the world was separated into two domains, holy and common, and two states, pure or impure. Purity had to do with abstract concepts rather than with physical characteristics such as dirtiness. Common things were allowed to be in either of these two states, though the pure state was preferred. But holy things, primarily meaning the temple and the things in it—including, in the innermost sacred area, YHWH—had to remain always in a state of cultic purity.

There were various causes of impurity, some of them physical (contact with a corpse, sexual intercourse, certain illnesses) and some of them moral (idolatry, bloodshed, and certain other ethical transgressions; see Klawans). Impurity was dangerous not only because it was incompatible with the holy but also because it was contagious and thus had to be stopped before it could spread too far. Ritual impurity was the more easily purged, generally through sacrifice and often through ritual bathing and the washing of clothes; moral impurity was harder to remedy, and its steady accrual would eventually cause the land to become so impure that YHWH would abandon the covenant, causing the nation to be exiled.

It is important to distinguish purity and impurity from *sin*, an idea that pertains to moral transgressions rather than cultic ones. Impurity is not inherently sinful—indeed, it can even result from obeying certain commandments—though a deliberate failure to rectify it is. The primary biblical root typically translated as "sin" does not always carry the same sense of moral transgression that the word has come to have in modern English, especially as a result of Christian theologies of "original sin" and a "fall from grace." In particular, the *hatta't* sacrifice, often translated "sin offering" (see Leviticus 4), is meant as a means of ritual purification and does not have an overt moral meaning. (And it should be noted that no biblical term for sin appears in Genesis 2–3, the story of so-called original sin; the idea that Adam and Eve "sinned" is based on later interpretations, both Jewish and Christian.) Though there is certainly a concept of sin in the Torah, cultic impurity and culpability are not necessarily dependent on sin—impurity accrues in the course of a normal life and would continue to do so even if everyone lived without sin.

Once YHWH has rescued the Israelites from slavery, delivered the laws to them, and renewed the covenant (all of which takes about a year), we might expect that things would go smoothly and the Israelites would move swiftly on to the conquest of the promised land. But of course, that is not what happens; instead, the Israelites wander in the desert for thirty-nine more years before entering the land of Canaan, occasionally engaging in battle but only beginning the process of conquest. When they finally do enter the land, Aaron, Miriam, and Moses have all died, and Moses' successor Joshua now leads the people. How does this happen? The remainder of the Torah narrative, in which the Israelites wander the wilderness, is peppered with episodes of complaint and conflict on the part of the Israelites. And this is not a new theme: Genesis and the early parts of Exodus, too, are littered with conflict between characters.

The conflicts in the Torah are of two main types: those between humans and those between humans and YHWH. Conflicts between humans include issues such as inheritance, water rights, the right to lead the people, and rivalries between wives. Those between humans and the divine appear especially in the wilderness narrative and tell of the Israelites' doubt that YHWH (and Moses) will in fact lead the people safely into the promised land. In perhaps the most egregious episode, the Israelites abandon YHWH altogether, making a molten calf to worship as a god instead (Exodus 32). It is only after Moses' intercession that YHWH relents from utterly destroying the people in punishment.

Though at one level such stories might make the Israelites look ungrateful and badly behaved in the face of divine benevolence, they also help to explain to an Israelite audience the frequent ups and downs in the course of Israel's history in the period of the monarchy, through the Babylonian exile, and afterward. They reveal an Israelite self-understanding that is based not only on YHWH's love of the people but also on the people's constant conflicts with the deity and with others. Indeed, the very name *Israel* is given an etymology based on struggle. In Gen. 32:28, Jacob struggles all night with a divine being; when Jacob prevails, the man says, "You shall no longer be called Jacob, but Israel, for you have striven [from the Hebrew root *srh*] with God and with humans, and have prevailed." Israel is a sort of permanent underdog, constantly striving, which may well reflect their status historically, in a region where they were continually dominated by larger and often oppressive powers. But this self-understanding also carries hope: YHWH has always looked out for the nation and has promised them continuing love, despite their misbehavior.

Through these themes—creation, kinship, and covenant—the Torah presents the foundational story of the Israelite nation. These themes are all connected to a larger idea of relationships: the relationship of humans to the world, of YHWH to the Israelites, and of the Israelites to one another. The narrative material details the history of these relationships, replete with conflict though they may be, and the laws supply the tools with which the covenant people are to maintain them. It is easy to see how this text resonated with and reassured an audience reading the Torah following the destruction of the Jerusalem temple by the Romans in 70 CE, and how it continues to resonate for Jews, Christians, and Muslims, all of whom trace their lineage, in one way or another, to Abraham. Though the text may have come together in stages from the hands of multiple authors with multiple worldviews, in the end the individual *torot* become a Torah that is greater than the sum of its parts.

Works Cited

Childs, Brevard S. 1979. *Introduction to the Old Testament as Scripture*. Philadelphia: Fortress Press.

Cohen, Shaye J. D. 1999. *The Beginnings of Jewishness: Boundaries, Varieties, Uncertainties*. Hellenistic Culture and Society 31. Berkeley: University of California Press.

Daly, Mary. 1973. *Beyond God the Father: Toward a Philosophy of Women's Liberation*. Boston: Beacon.

Finkelstein, Israel, and Neil Asher Silberman. 2001. *The Bible Unearthed: Archaeology's New Vision of Ancient Israel and the Origin of Its Sacred Texts*. New York: Free Press.

García López, F. 2006. "הרוֹת, *tôrâ*." *TDOT* 15:609–46.

Jónsson, Gunnlaugur A. 1988. *The Image of God: Genesis 1:26–28 in a Century of Old Testament Research*. ConBOT 26. Lund: Almqvist & Wiksell.

Killebrew, Ann E. 2005. *Biblical People and Ethnicity: An Archaeological Study of Egyptians, Canaanites, Philistines, and Early Israel 1300–1100* B.C.E. SBLABS 9. Atlanta: Society of Biblical Literature.

Klawans, Jonathan. 2004. "Concepts of Purity in the Bible." In *The Jewish Study Bible*, edited by Adele Berlin and Marc Zvi Brettler, 2041–47. New York: Oxford University Press.

Meyers, Carol. 2013. *Rediscovering Eve: Ancient Israelite Women in Context*. New York: Oxford University Press.

Moore, Megan Bishop, and Brad E. Kelle. 2011. *Biblical History and Israel's Past: The Changing Study of the Bible and History*. Grand Rapids: Eerdmans.

Nicholson, Ernest W. 1986. *God and His People: Covenant and Theology in the Old Testament*. Oxford: Clarendon.

Petersen, David L. 2005. "Genesis and Family Values." *JBL* 124, no. 1:5–23.

Robinson, George. 2000. *Essential Judaism: A Complete Guide to Beliefs, Customs, and Rituals*. New York: Pocket Books.

Schniedewind, William M. 2004. *How the Bible Became a Book*. New York: Cambridge University Press.

Seebass, Horst. 1975. "רחַבָ@f *bāchar*." *TDOT* 2:73–87.

Shectman, Sarah. 2009. *Women in the Pentateuch: A Feminist and Source-Critical Analysis*. Hebrew Bible Monographs 23. Sheffield: Sheffield Phoenix Press.

Trible, Phyllis. 1978. *God and the Rhetoric of Sexuality*. OBT. Philadelphia: Fortress Press.

Weinfeld, Moshe. 1975. "תירִבְ@; *b^erîth*." *TDOT* 2:253–79.

GENESIS

Rodney S. Sadler Jr.

Introduction

A division of Genesis into two major sections (1–11 and 12–50) represents well the major concerns of this book. The initial section (1–11), which may be discussed under the heading "The Founding of a World: The Genealogical Journey from Adam to Abram," introduces the reader to God, the world, and humanity and frames the relation among these three principal "characters" of the tale that will unfold throughout the rest of the Hebrew Bible and the Christian Testament. It can be subdivided as follows:

1:1—2:25	Providence Introduced: God's Creation of the World
3:1—5:32	Providence Thwarted: Fractures of the Initial Family
6:1—11:32	Providence Restored: Flood and New Creation

The second section, "The Founding of a Family: The Circuitous Journey from Haran to Egypt," focuses readers' attention on the development of one specific family, the family of Abram/Abraham and Sarai/Sarah, who descend from the line of Shem the son of Noah, and their circuitous trek to Egypt. It can be subdivided as follows:

12:1—25:18	Providence Heeded: Abram/Abraham the Faithful's Cycle
25:19—37:1	Providence Manipulated: Jacob/Israel the Trickster's Cycle
37:2—50:26	Providence Manifest: Joseph/Zaphenath-paneah and the Redemption Novella

Together, these two basic sections constitute the book we know as Genesis and are the appropriate introduction to Exodus inasmuch as they offer insight into the making of a world, the founding of a family, and the trek of that family from the northernmost regions of the Fertile Crescent to the two lands of Egypt, whence our story will continue.

In this exploration of Genesis, the concept of providence relates to the notion of God's gracious control of the cosmos and human destiny. This theme seems to be at the heart of the larger story in Genesis. Thus in this division, providence is revealed in two basic moves. Initially it is offered in relation to the cosmos and the first humans universally. Herein it is offered by YHWH/God, rejected by humanity, and then finally restored in a new creation by means of the divine reassertion of authority represented by the flood narratives. Subsequently, providence governs the lives of those in the Abramic/Abrahamic line and is revealed in the lives of three eponymous ancestors. First, Abram/Abraham, who lives faithfully under God's control, frequently seeks to realize the divine promises made to him through his own actions, but learns that it is only by God's hand that they will be manifest; second, Jacob, whose story reveals the consequences of human manipulation of God's providence in the fractures of his familial relationships; and third, Joseph, whose novella reveals the activity of God at work amid the seemingly random and often devastating events of his life. The concept of providence is quintessential in this account, since through his trials and tribulations and several nadirs, he is eventually exalted in a manner that only becomes evident in his own hindsight (50:20). Theologically, this book serves as an exemplar of the notion of providence as God's ultimate control over the cosmos, and human destiny rests at the heart of each of its narratives. As such, it would have served as a "primer on providence" to its initial audience, and in its present location in the canon, it continues to play that role in the lives of subsequent believers in the "God of Abraham."

Genesis 1-11: The Founding of a World: The Genealogical Journey from Adam to Abram

The founding of the world, or the primordial history (chaps. 1–11), introduces the reader to God, the world, and humanity. It is from this section of the larger book that we first encounter the chief protagonist in the biblical narratives, God. God, introduced by several names (e.g., Elohim, YHWH Elohim, YHWH, El Shaddai, El Elyon) and described with various character traits, is shown to be at the center of this book and, indeed, the entire created order. It is God who alone is able to create, the sole subject of the Hebrew verb *bārā'* ("create") in the Hebrew Bible. As Creator, God stands alone in authority, autonomy, and in awesomeness; this quality is used in numerous instances in Scripture to authenticate God's right to act in the world (see chaps. 37–40, where God's creative power serves to legitimate his ability to act unabated by human consideration).

In Genesis, we are introduced to God by a distinctive name as well. In 2:4b, for the first time, we encounter the name YHWH. This brief abbreviation, called the Tetragrammaton because it is often presented as four Hebrew letters *yôd*, *hê*, *wāw*, *hê*, identifies the particular deity of the Hebrew Bible. YHWH or YHWH God is not just a god; YHWH is presented as the one deity to whom allegiance is due; even when other deities are referenced, the distinctive attributes of YHWH set this deity apart as uniquely worthy of devotion and fealty. YHWH is the central character of the primordial history, and this collection of eleven chapters is our introduction to this transcendent being.

The primordial history also introduces us to the world in which the biblical narratives will unfold. It is a strange world, an alien world to those of us who live in the scientific, postmodern, Westernized world. It is a world that is covered with a *rāqîa'*, or "dome" (1:6) like a glass terrarium; where the sun, moon, and stars are pressed into the dome (1:16-17); where the great seas are gathered together in a single *miqwēh*, or "collecting vessel"; where dry grounds are watered by an ethereal *'ēd*, or "mist" (2:6). Yet it is our world, defined as essentially good, carefully crafted to meet the needs of all of its inhabitants, but most particularly its human inhabitants (1:28-30). It is our world that is repeatedly described in the first chapter as "good," the product of God's thoughtful, creative proclamation in Gen. 1:1—2:4a, the product of YHWH God's careful crafting and tactile manipulation in Gen. 2:4b-17. It is a world made ready for us to *kābaš*, or "tame," and *rādâ*, or "administer," as we are set as stewards of this YHWH's artistic masterpiece we call earth.

And the third member of this triumvirate of characters is, well, us. Humanity is also introduced in the primordial history. We are *'ādām*, or "earthlings," taken from the dust of the *'ădamâ*, or the "earth" (2:7). We are vested with a hint of divinity, in one instance described as reflecting the *ṣelem*, or "image," of God (1:26-27) and in another described as animated by the *nĕšāmâ*, or "breath," of YHWH God (2:7). We are special, set apart, singled out in creation for distinctive glory. It is only after we are created that God declares the world to be "very good" (1:31). Yet we are also found to be disobedient (Genesis 3), murderous (Genesis 4), and capable of total depravity (Genesis 6). Still, despite our shortcomings, which are legion, YHWH will continue to be gracious to us, forgiving us when we have fallen, protecting us when we have made ourselves vulnerable, and redeeming a righteous remnant when we seem to have all but lost our way.

In part, the primordial history is the beginning of a dramatic love story, a story that unfolds as a romance between YHWH and humanity, complete with instances of heartfelt commitment interspersed with instances of serial infidelity. It is a passionate affair that leads to violence, separation, reconciliation, and eventually forgiveness and restoration. At the end of this section in chapter 11 of Genesis, we will finally meet the human partner who will follow faithfully YHWH's call and who will eagerly assent to the providential covenantal relationship that YHWH has sought with humanity.

Genesis 1–2: Providence Introduced: God's Creation of the World

The Text in Its Ancient Context

Genesis 1–2 contains the two primary stories associated with the creation of the world and introduces the reader to God's providence by means of demonstrating God's authority over and care of creation. Historically, the two chapters have been taken as a single narrative, yet a closer investigation demonstrates that they are actually two distinct narratives composed for different reasons and likely at different times.

The initial Priestly (P) narrative, in Gen. 1:1—2:4a, is the most famous of the two stories and occurs as a formulaic description of the creation of the cosmos from an originally watery earth. In the space of six days, the story asserts that God (*'ĕlōhîm*) creates the heavens and the earth in a fairly methodical and extraordinarily orderly set of events. The formula of creation unfolds in a repetitive process that generally begins with God's statement "Let there be *x*," followed immediately by an assertion that *x* comes to be, that *x* is called by a name, that *x* is evaluated as "good," and then some sort of acknowledgment of the passing of time, "and there was evening and there was morning, day *y*." The formula recurs over the course of six days, with subtle alterations in each day. For example, there is no evaluation on day two, and the complexity of God's action tends to increase over each day; but the general flow of the formula persists until the sixth day.

On the sixth day, the earth is populated by living land creatures in complexity increasing beyond the birds of the fifth day. This process culminates with the creation of the *'ādām*, or "earthling," in 1:26. The earthling's creation violates the general pattern in several ways. First, it occurs after the daily evaluation of the creation of other living creatures in verse 25. Second, its creation is offered in conjunction with a divine self-reflection: "Let us make humankind [earthlings] in our image." This phrase alone could bear considerable analysis, for the nature of the *ṣelem*, or "image," held in common between the *'ĕlōhîm* and the earthling is never clearly explicated, nor is the suddenly plural quantification of the deity, who though represented by the theoretically plural term *'ĕlōhîm* is consistently associated with singular verbs in all other instances except in this verse. Because of the common image, however, the earthling is vested with considerable authority over creation to both "subdue" and exert "dominion" over it. Finally, in verse 31, God offers an assessment of the entire creation with the addition of the earthling, and only now does the assessment merit the evaluative statement "very good."

From this it is clear that this is not just a general statement about creation. It is an anthropocentric assessment that celebrates creation in a way that emphasizes our own role in it as God's crowning glory. The orderly and potent deity crafts a world that is only assessed to be "very good" (1:31) once we are included in it. Further, the overall narrative ends up as a metaphor focused on the comparison between God and humanity. Creation unfolds over six days, allowing God the opportunity to *šabbāt*, or "rest," on the seventh day, and thus, by analogy, human beings should also *šabbāt* on this day that God has "hallowed" (2:3).

At the end of this first creation story, the original audience could have seen the narrative's overall purposes. It has confirmed that God is orderly and morally "good," that the world is orderly and "good," and that with the inclusion of humanity the overall schema is "very good." This positive assessment of theology, cosmology, and anthropology marks this narrative in a way that would have been clear to its early audience. Perhaps finding its final form as an address to a community that experienced exile in the aftermath of the Babylonian captivity in the latter sixth to early fifth centuries BCE, this story was intended to contrast the creation narratives of the Babylonians (Brueggemann, 25), whose stories of creation posited that the world was the by-product of the slain corpse of Tiamat, the goddess of the sea, and that humans were crafted from the blood of Kingu, her illegitimate spouse, to be slaves to a host of spiteful deities. This narrative offers a distinct view of God, the world, and humanity that would have answered its initial audience's questions quite well. Further, by cohering with the seven-day paradigm for a week that culminates in Sabbath, which would have already been known to the original audience, this narrative would have validated the world as they knew it.

Here Brueggemann's caution that this is not a scientific description but a theological affirmation should be heard (Brueggemann, 25; cf. Sarna, 3–4). This is a story told to resolve distinctive concerns of a particular audience at a particular time and was not intended to bear the burden of being the final universal statement about the scientific creation of the world. If we remember that point, the narrative can speak to us with renewed pertinence as a theological statement about the nature of God, the world, and humanity.

The second, Yahwistic (J) creation narrative, in Gen. 2:4b-24, describes creation in an arid land, by a deity described in much more anthropomorphic terms, who is called *yhwh 'ĕlōhîm.* With the different moniker comes a deity who does not create by word in six days but who creates the world by manual manipulation in a single day (2:4b), who forms the earthling as the first act of creation (2:7) and intimately performs CPR on it to bring it to life, and who fashions the rest of creation in response to the needs of the earthling. Instead of creating by divine command, *yhwh 'ĕlōhîm* "planted a garden" (v. 8), "took" and "put" the earthling in it (v. 15), "formed" from the earth other living creatures (v. 19), and finally performs an elaborate surgical procedure wherein the deity bifurcates the earthling (vv. 21-23), taking its *ṣēla'*, best read not as a single "rib" but as its "side." From this "side," *yhwh 'ĕlōhîm* forms the earthling's appropriate counterpart. It is only then that the earthling is described with the gendered terms *'îš*, or "man," and *'iššâ*, or "woman," in the narrative (Meyers, 72–94; cf. Sadler 2010, 72).

This second narrative would have served the early audience not simply as a creation account but also as an elaborate etiology, or "origin story," for the institution of marriage, justifying this institution on the basis that the original earthling was split into two and can only become whole when united with its counterpart in a paired unit. And so this section ends with the statement, "Therefore a man leaves his father and his mother and he clings to his woman, and they become one flesh" (v. 24).

The Text in the Interpretive Tradition

These two narratives have been combined over the years of Christian interpretation to form a single narrative, often ignoring the definitive fissures in the accounts. In part, this has led to wonderful and poetic retellings like James Weldon Johnson's "Creation," wherein the poet weaves the two stories together masterfully, demonstrating the common understanding of the creation story. In part, this has contributed to the idea that there is just one story of creation and fueled the debates that pit the biblical creation narrative (read as singular) against scientific perceptions of the big bang and evolution.

Lost in such interpretive decisions is the fact that these accounts deftly address questions posed by the original audience about the nature of God, the world, and humanity; about the reason for a seven-day week and Sabbath rest; about the intimate relationship between the deity and the human creature; and about the reason human beings marry. Subsequent Judeo-Christian communities have often lost sight of these narratives' original concerns and replaced them with our own issues and our own concerns. In the process, we have lost sight of the rhetorical power wielded by these stories for their initial audiences.

The Text in Contemporary Discussion

There are a number of issues that these texts still present for contemporary communities. The concerns about the nature of God, the world, and humanity are still issues with which we wrestle today, and these texts provide incredibly useful insight into these questions, positing a careful and good Creator who developed a good world in which we are integral members. Today questions of ecology are also at the forefront of our concerns as we seek to determine whether the instructions from Gen. 1:28 to "subdue" and exercise "dominion" entitle us to do to creation whatever we will or if the narrative instead, in light of global climate change and the growing scarcity of our natural resources, charges us to be stewards of what God has granted to us.

Perhaps no issues are more pressing from the initial narrative than those that have to do with the importance of the "image of God." This compelling notion, revisited in Gen. 9:6 and offered as a reason for the valuation of human beings and the prohibition of taking human life, has served as the theological basis of many contemporary struggles for liberation and equality. What would this world be like if every human being truly began to appreciate what it means that we humans are all vested with the image of God? As Martin Luther King Jr. notes, "Man is a child of God made in His image, and therefore must be respected as such" (King, 255). May we all one day appreciate this core value and its implications for establishing interpersonal and social justice!

The second narrative continues to be relevant today as the concept of permanent-pair bonding is much less prevalent as a social institution than it has been in previous generations. That this was deemed a core concern of the ancestors of our faith traditions, significant enough to grant it a location at the outset of the biblical narratives, should not be lost on us. The notion of the attainment of wholeness through lifelong pair bonding should not be ignored as we consider these texts. To the contrary, these texts have also been used as "clobber texts" on the LGBT community, noting that they establish the basis of the relationship between "Adam and Eve, not Adam and Steve." As we appropriate these texts in the contemporary world, we will have to revisit anew how these texts continue to inform our relationships in the contemporary world.

Genesis 3–5: Providence Thwarted: Fractures of the Initial Family

The Text in Its Ancient Context

This section of Genesis introduces us to the individual personalities of the first family and suggests the initial instance of human rebellion against the providence of God. Starting in chapter 3, these flat characters begin to take shape as more rounded characters with depth and dimension. This chapter begins with the story of the "tempting" of the original pair. To the original audience, this story is more than simply a morality tale; it is also a joke. It begins in verse 1 by introducing us to a serpent that is described as being *'ārûm*, or "cunning" or "crafty," and climaxes in verse 7 with the first pair learning that they are *'êrummim*, or "naked." In their attempt to gain the power of the knowledge of everything, literally all that lies between the two extremes of good and evil, in their attempt to become wise and powerful like *yhwh 'ĕlōhîm*, who has forbidden them from eating from the fruit of the tree of the knowledge of good and evil (2:17), they have found themselves vulnerable; they have realized they are naked. The irony of the end of this action would not have been lost on the original audience, which may have both chuckled and sighed at the consequence of the protagonists' actions.

For this community, the serpent would have been understood to be a wise creature and would have served as a metaphor for wisdom; it was clearly a "beast of the field" as it is identified in the narrative, not a spiritual or angelic figure (i.e., Satan, a figure only evident by name in 1 Chronicles, Job, and Zechariah in the Hebrew Bible; see Brueggemann, 47; De La Torre, 66–68). Along the lines of the story of Gilgamesh, which contains in tablet 1 column 4 the account of the wild man Enkidu, who is taught by sexual relations with a wise female figure, Shamhat, to be a wise human (Dalley, 55–56), this narrative provides an etiology for the cognitive ability of human beings, distinguishing them from the other animals (cf. Eccles. 3:18-19). This is evident by the couple's realization of their nakedness in verse 7, a reversal of the prior assessment about their status in 2:25. Yet it is also a story of loss, as the consequence (3:14-24) for the actions of these previously oblivious creatures is that the females will bear children in pain, the males will live only by the sweat of their brows, that all of humanity will be forbidden from accessing the tree of life and the garden paradise, and that they will all eventually die (see Meyers, 72–94).

This loss is the result of their rebellion against YHWH's instruction. The stated penalty for the action of eating the fruit in 2:17 and 3:3 is death, making their choice to eat the fruit consequential. We should note, however, that this choice is nowhere in this passage deemed "sin." Hebrew equivalents for this term (*ḥaṭṭā't*) do not occur in the text until 4:7, when the concept is introduced in YHWH's warning to Cain about his feelings toward his brother Abel.

Subsequently, YHWH God not only utters curses but also lifts up the fallen human beings, fashions clothing for them, and makes provision for them to have not the death associated with rebellion but a life outside the Garden of Eden. As we end this story, our vision of God has expanded, for God is not only the powerful, careful Creator of Genesis 1 or the intimate, hands-on Creator of Genesis 2 but also the forgiving, gracious God who can see flawed humanity and find a way to redeem us in spite of our rebellion against God's providence.

It is important to recognize that the initial audience would not have thought the woman was "tempted" in ignorance. Inasmuch as she was part of the original earthling, she received the same instruction as her male counterpart when they were together as a combined entity. The woman was not "tempted" in isolation; she gave the fruit to her husband who was "with her" (3:6). We should also note that the fruit is never identified as an apple either.

Further, the original audience would probably have realized that there does not appear to be any attempt to hierarchically relate men and women until after the curses are ascribed here (3:16). In this regard, such a state of disordered relationships can be described as a product of YHWH God's response to human disobedience; it was not a part of YHWH God's intention for the created order.

As the story continues, the original earthlings give birth to the next generation. The story in Genesis 4 is probably best remembered because of the line "Am I my brother's keeper?" uttered by the antihero Cain in verse 9. This painful story begins as two brothers both try to please YHWH

God, and ends describing the further failings of humanity fostered by the first recorded instance of a human being competing for God's favor; in this brief narrative is the seed that will give rise to countless billions of deaths caused ostensibly by humanity's religious fervor. Ironically, the first murder is not over property rights, over sexual partners, over social status, over material goods, over a struggle for rights, over a struggle to survive; the first murder is predicated on an attempt to please God.

A few quick notes on this story might yield some insight into this brief but often misunderstood account:

- Though Abel the felled brother is often thought to be the key brother and the symbol of religious obedience and moral exemplar in this story, we should note that he never utters a word and is a fairly flat character. His name actually means "Vapor," suggesting his ephemeral nature in the narrative.
- His brother's name is "Cain," which in Hebrew would be similar to the English moniker "Smith" or "-smith," meaning one who crafts something from metal. In essence, it is the story of an agriculturalist that is cursed from the ground and then becomes a "craftsman" or "smith." It is an etiology or origin story for people who are neither shepherds nor farmers in an otherwise dimorphic society, but who live by the cunning of their hands.
- The well-known mark of Cain (4:15) is not a curse. It is actually the Lord's mark of protection on him so that he will not be killed (though the story is surprisingly silent about by whom he would have been killed). In essence, far from being a curse, the mark of Cain is a symbol of divine protection conferred by a caring God on an errant human character.

In the end, we are left with a further-developed picture of YHWH God, who again has forgiven humanity for its missteps, here even forgiving the capital offense of homicide (cf. 9:5-6). The narrative has also provided a means past the sinful nature (4:7) that human beings manifest. In part, this should serve as a reminder that the grace of God is not a "New Testament" innovation! No, God's grace, though not explicitly so named, is evident even in the earliest texts in the Old Testament.

The story in Genesis 5 merits less attention, but we should note that it is not insignificant. Many of the narratives in the first five books of the Bible relate to patronyms, or genealogical lists of male ancestors. This was significant for the people of ancient Israel/Judah because they wanted to be able to trace their familial roots back to the very beginning of the world. This continuity of the march of humanity is relevant to us as well, for in it we can see that the origins of human beings are said to be common; we are all ultimately related according to the Genesis narratives. Human beings all are described as being from one family emerging from one common ancestral lineage. There is no attempt to describe different origins of different racial types or different ethnic groups from different geneses. All of humanity comes from one source, and these genealogies affirm our ultimate kinship in the common origins of all human beings.

A final significant feature of chapter 5 is the introduction of Noah and his three sons, who will become key figures in the overall narrative in the next several chapters. Through them humanity will receive its second genesis.

The Text in the Interpretive Tradition

Genesis 3 has been historically understood as the "fall of humanity," an interpretive tradition that likely is fostered in the Christian tradition by Paul, who in Romans 5 and 1 Corinthians 15 brings together the notion of "sin" (*hamartia*) and this story of Adam. To this was added the instruction found in 2 Cor. 11:3 and 1 Tim. 2:13, both of which describe the deception of Eve. These texts give rise to the traditional interpretation that posits the fall of humanity into "sin" by means of the serpent's deception of the woman. In the traditional interpretation, the man has often been denied ultimate culpability because he is presumed to have been absent when the woman was "tempted" by the serpent. It goes without saying that the traditional reading has been employed to misogynistic ends.

In this interpretive tradition as well, the serpent is conflated with the devil and Satan, likely based on a reading of Rev. 12:9, where the great dragon is described in both tangible and transcendent ways (see Isa. 27:1). In this regard, the ancient Near Eastern account of the cunning serpent who was a "beast of the field" or a "wild animal" (3:1) who promises to make the humans wise has been reinterpreted as the story of the devil or Satan, a malevolent spiritual being in an antagonistic relationship with God whose goal is the destruction of humanity.

Thus the story of this initial act of human striving that leads to rebellion against YHWH God's providence has been recast as a story of the fall of humanity at the hands of God's great foe, Satan, and the subtle details of the extant narrative have been lost, obscured beneath strata of subsequent theological and ideological detritus. As the narratives continue to unfold over the next few chapters, human depravity will become a significant focus of the story, so the traditional interpretations are not without merit; still, interpreters must be careful not to conflate subsequent interpretive traditions that ascribe "sin," "Satan," and "the fall" to this etiological narrative that defines as realities of the world the earliest audiences would have known with its painful births, the need for human toil, growing patriarchy, and a healthy fear of serpents (see Sarna, 24–29; De La Torre, 66–68). More recent interpreters like Miguel De La Torre have offered a revised assessment of this text not as "the fall" but as an initial instance of "rebellion" (De La Torre, 72) as human beings exert their own autonomy in response to God's providence.

Traditional interpretations of chapter 4 tend to elevate Abel, who somehow becomes a moral exemplar in the narrative because of his offering of an appropriate sacrifice and his subsequent victimization at the hand of his own brother; he is even seen as a prefiguration of Jesus or the martyrs of the world (see Louth, 104–9). Historically, Genesis 4 has served as a narrative that epitomizes humanity's inhumanity, as it shows that the bitter resentments of those as close as two brothers can end in a homicidal rage with the shedding of innocent blood. This narrative has also been used to denote the rapid progression of sin in the world that quickly escalates from willful disobedience to God in chapter 3 to fratricide in chapter 4. This sets up the scenario we will encounter in chapter 6 as we discuss the nadir of human morality in preparation for the flood story.

The traditional interpretations of the account in chapter 5 focus on the saintly nature of Enoch and the extremely long lengths of human lives described herein (Louth, 118–22). The particularly long lifespan of Methuselah has become a well-known aspect of this story, and it has become a commonplace description for a person of advanced age to be deemed as "old as Methuselah."

The Text in Contemporary Discussion

Exploring these narratives in chapter 3, we should ponder the differences between the society for whom these narratives were initially composed and our own. How do those differences manifest differences in interpretive emphases? Does the interjection of early Christian interpretive traditions of "original sin" and the unifying metanarrative of the "Bible" complete with a theology describing sin's introduction in Adam and solution in Christ obscure the meanings that the initial audiences would have derived from these texts? How can we begin to appreciate these stories on their own merits without presuming a post-Pauline interpretive posture?

Looking at these narratives in chapters 4–5, how can we help but notice the prevalence of violence in our contemporary world? This narrative that describes the first murder as the result of sibling rivalry over religious fealty brings home the fact that we really are all related, we really are as human beings all siblings in an interdependent relationship with one another (Genesis 5). The passage of time has not lessened the poignancy of this account, nor have we yet learned to be each other's keepers over the millennia. The rhetorical question asked by Cain continues to resonate throughout the years and serves as a constant reminder that his presumed answer "no" was wholly antithetical to what should have been. As creatures of community who flock together in societies, we live in a symbiotic relationship with one another and our lives are dependent on the maintenance of our web of mutuality and on our efforts on behalf of each other. Our survival as a species depends on our recognizing the importance of each and every other human being and caring about their plight. In the end, may we all seek to answer Cain's question, "Am I my brother's keeper?" with a definitive yes!

Genesis 6:1—11:32: Providence Restored: Flood and New Creation

The Text in Its Ancient Context

After the initial manifestations of human rebellion in the prior section, God reasserts providence over a creation in disarray. The narratives in this section of Genesis present the path toward a new creation wherein YHWH God will definitively address human depravity and will reestablish order, manifesting particular affection for a distinctive line in Noah's progeny introduced at the end of chapter 11. Chapter 6 begins with a story most would categorize as a biblical mythology. Here, as in Greek mythology's stories of Heracles and Perseus, we find an account referring to sexual unions between human and divine beings. The offspring produced from these unions are, like those in Greek mythology, superhumans endowed with great ability, the "heroes of old" and "warriors of renown." The phrase *bĕnê hāʾĕlōhîm*, or "sons of God," in 6:2 seems to recall entities like those in Job 1:6 and to refer to undefined "heavenly beings." In this case, the "sons of God" are probably angelic creatures from the heavenly realm interacting with human beings and thereby producing semidivine progeny.

The Nephilim of 6:4 represent an interesting dimension in this narrative. They are thought to have been biblical giants who likely engaged in many miraculous tales known to the original audiences of this text, hence the reference to them being men of *hašēm*, "name" or "renown" (6:4). The term "Nephilim" may actually come from a Hebrew root, *npl*, that means "fallen," hence we could understand them to be the "fallen ones," which may have some bearing on the overall account of these great demigods fallen from the heavens who once ruled on earth. Though they do not appear to be present in the narratives that describe human wickedness (vv. 5-7, 11-12), the limitation of these figures to their brief appearance in the preflood narratives suggests that they too did not survive the flood.

Human life is limited here to 120 years. This is probably more of a general number than an actual time. This recalls the fact that human beings are said to have endured death in Genesis 3 and seems to expedite the period from the near thousand years of some of the characters mentioned in Genesis 5. It is odd that we see stories of such great longevity in these accounts since many speculate that contemporary people live longer than people in the ancient world may ever have lived. Perhaps the extraordinary lengths of these characters' lives served some function in the calculations of the calendars of ancient Israelite/Judahite peoples.

In verse 3, we note the potent concept of the *rûaḥ*, or "Spirit" of YHWH. Here we should recognize the obscure use of the Hebrew verb *dyn* used with *rûaḥ*, meaning likely "judge" or "contend" in relation to the Spirit of YHWH's action in human beings. The Septuagint's use of a form of the verb *katamenō* suggests that the Spirit's job was to animate human life; hence the reference to the limitation of the Spirit's presence leading to the reduction in the spans of life to 120 years. Though utilizing different terms than Gen. 2:7's *nišmat*, there does seem to be an allusion to this narrative in which human beings are vested with sacral significance by the "breath" of YHWH God. In this regard, the concept of God's indwelling spirit as the vivifying aspect of human life implies that because we bear the spirit (or wind/breath) of God, we live. It is this quality that animates and sanctifies otherwise lifeless flesh (see Eccles. 3:21).

The latter portion of Genesis 6 establishes the reasons for YHWH's eventual destruction of the world by flood. Verse 5 describes human beings as completely "evil." Actually, this verse emphasizes the extremity of this moral deficit by the use of the Hebrew terms *rab*, or "great," and *kōl*, or "every," to syntactically emphasize the extreme nature of humanity's evil. It is not just that they are evil, but their *great* evil is evidenced in that *every* thought framed in their mind is evil throughout *every* portion of the day.

And thus YHWH is sorry to have made them. The term *nāḥam* used here for "was sorry" suggests that God "repented" for having created humanity. The injection of pathos at the end is consistent with the anthropomorphism of the Yahwistic writer, who describes YHWH as either "grieved" or "vexed" to the heart. Here we have the first reason given for the destruction to come in the flood. This legitimating narrative suggests that humanity is wicked. It is difficult not to recognize the impact of the depravity on YHWH, who determines in 6:7 to destroy all categories of animal life and indeed all of creation because of it. The anthropocentric perspective of the author, who imagines that because of humanity's faults, all of creation must be undone, should not be lost on us. The world at large suffers due to humanity's wickedness. In the author's view, as we go, so goes the whole world; this is a message we should heed in an age of widespread oppression, corporate greed, gross income inequality, and global climate change.

Then in 6:8, with a suddenness intended to jar the reader, we are introduced to the sole exception to the rule of depravity. As in other instances in this book, at precisely the moment when the reader might expect to see YHWH's unbridled rage, we are introduced to a figure to whom YHWH will demonstrate compassion. Though it seems as if humanity has reached its fitting end, through Noah the "bearer of an alternative possibility" YHWH will offer humanity another chance (Brueggemann, 79). Over the course of the next three chapters, Noah will be revealed as a complex character who is both an exemplar of faithful behavior and a troubled father whose words will pit his sons against each other in 9:24-27.

If the reader attends carefully, there is a second legitimization for the flood given in 6:11. Now the title given to the deity is *ʾĕlōhîm*, or "God," and the narrator informs the reader that the earth was "corrupt . . . and . . . violen[t]." This different reasoning with a different vocabulary evidences a different source for this material. In essence, the flood story is one of the clearest examples in Genesis of its composite nature.

We see further evidence of this phenomenon as we explore chapters 7–8. The fissures in the story become apparent when the reader discerns the duplications and inconsistencies in the narrative. For example, there are two instances where the reason for God's destruction of the world are noted (vv. 5 and 11); there are multiple accounts of the number of animals taken on the ark (cf. 7:1-5 with 7:8-10); there are discrepancies about the length of time of the flood (cf. 7:12 with 7:24); there are even two different resolutions to the crisis (8:20-22; 9:11-17). To further accentuate the differences in the narratives, we can also distinguish different terms used to identify the deity in the different accounts. Suffice it to say that the actual narrative is far more complex than it appears to be at first reading.

"J" Source Flood Narrative	**"P" Source Flood Narrative**
• 6:5 **YHWH** saw that the inclination of hearts (minds) was evil. • 6:6 YHWH is sorry for creating humanity.	• 6:11 **God** notes that earth was filled with violence and flesh was corrupt (two justifications).
• 7:1-5 YHWH says take seven pairs of clean and one of unclean animals.	• 6:19 Two of every kind of animal. • 7:8-10 Two of every kind of animal (may be from an addition). • 7:11 Catastrophe caused by great deep bursting and windows of sky opening.
• 7:7 Noah and his family go into ark. • 7:12 Rains forty days and forty nights. • 7:17b Flood continues for forty days.	• 7:15 Noah and his family go into ark. • 7:24 Flood swells for 150 days.
• 8:2b-3a Rain from heaven restrained.	• 8:1-2a Fountains of deep and windows of heaven closed.
• 8:8-12 Noah opens window and sends forth birds. • 8:20-22 Noah offers a sacrifice.	• 8:14-19 Noah removes cover and sees earth dry and sends out family. • 9:6 Note the return to Priestly language from Gen. 1:27. Created in God's image. • 9:11-17 Covenant set between God and world not to cut off all flesh by waters of flood—sealed with a rainbow.

(Excerpted from Campbell and O'Brien, 211–13)

Despite the diverging details, we can discern an essential story line. The deity is enraged by the depraved behavior of human beings and for that determines to destroy the world by flood. One family will be saved from the impending disaster by means of an ark because of the deity's affection for the faultless character of its patriarch, Noah. The flood rages on the earth for a prescribed period of time, eliminating all manner of life save those beings in the ark. Once the flood subsides, the remaining humans and the deity are reconciled and a new creation begins from the redeemed remnant in the ark (8:16—9:17).

The extant combined story is a morality tale reminding human beings that our behavior matters to the deity and commending the upright and faithful behavior of Noah. It also serves to further the description of the deity, who though opposed to the deplorable actions of humans always remains ready to redeem and restore an otherwise flawed and fallen world. The act at the end of the flood account of the deity hanging the "rainbow" in the sky (9:13-16) would have been understood as the act of a warrior who hangs up his *qešet*, or "war bow," symbolizing the cessation of hostilities. Herein we find another etiology, for this serves as the origin of the rainbow in the sky.

The stories in Genesis 9:18-28 and 10 are two of the seemingly least relevant stories for contemporary Christians in all of Genesis, particularly when they are read apart. The first is the story of a familial curse that is incurred by Noah's grandson (Canaan) because one of his sons (Ham) sees his nakedness as he lies drunk and exposed in his tent and does nothing to remedy it. The problem for readers here is that the text appears to be somewhat corrupted; the one cursed is not the one who saw "the nakedness." Yet the narrative seems intent on producing a particular outcome, yielding a perpetual cursing of Canaan and his offspring. Genesis 10 presents a series of patronymics, or genealogies of generations exclusively through the paternal lines, of the three sons of Noah. On the surface, these appear to be ancient stories chronicling insignificant events that should have little relevance to contemporary audiences.

A close reading of the initial story about the cursing of Canaan with the second about the descendants of Noah's sons reveals that these narratives together provide a legitimating ideology for the ensuing biblical narratives. These two narratives together provide a biblical justification for the subsequent dispossession and oppression of the indigenous Canaanite population in Palestine by the people of Israel who, we will learn in Genesis 10, are the sons of Shem. Once this purpose is understood, these two passages take on a crucial significance in the larger biblical metanarrative, establishing the basis of relationships that will unfold between the "chosen" people and those who will be displaced.

Further exploration of Gen. 9:18-28 shows the tenuous nature of the curse. It is a curse uttered by a drunken father against the wrong offspring for an offense that is not clearly explicated, which really is void of God's sanction or any sense of moral standing. Yet the presence of the curse here offers a justification for Israel's taking of the land of Canaan from the Canaanites. Without such a story, the larger metanarrative of the Hebrew Bible would seem incomplete; this narrative offers, even if inadequately, a justification for the dislocation and oppression of the Canaanites and answers a question for the ancient audience that is as yet unasked but clearly anticipated (Sadler 2005, 26–27).

Genesis 10 has been called the "Table of Nations" and provides a series of patronymics of the sons of Noah in an order that demonstrates their increased significance in the subsequent biblical narratives. It begins with an account of the sons of Japheth, about whom little is known and who can be summed up neatly in five verses. The second son presented is Ham, who is described as the ancestor of all the great civilizations of old including the empires of Egypt, Cush (Nubia), Assyria, and Babylon among other nations of note. The descendants of these eponymous ancestors will resurface in the narrative in numerous instances in the Hebrew Bible, and this group is therefore the focus of verses 6-20. The final group presented in this chapter is the sons of Shem. Though his sons are presented in verses 21-32, this is only a precursor for another account, which will continue in 11:10-32, culminating in 11:26-32 with the introduction of Abram. Thus the genealogy of Shem becomes the dominant patronymic in the Table of Nations, establishing the familial line through which YHWH will choose to bless the world.

The narrative at the beginning of Genesis 11 represents an interpretive problem. Here, in the aftermath of the flood, we see the people of the world cooperating and working together on a major building project at Babylon. This unity is in remarkable contrast to the enmity and infighting that seem to govern other chapters (e.g., Genesis 4 and 6). Yet this unity does not seem to please YHWH. Genesis 11:6 suggests the "problem" represented in this passage. It is not sin or selfishness but the very unity and the possibility of human achievement evidenced in their common striving that drives the action in this narrative. It seems as if their actions, while not clearly "sinful," have violated YHWH's desire that they fill the earth, a desire hinted at in verses 4 and 8, or that they are getting "too big for their britches," as we might say in North Carolina. YHWH's subsequent action both protects the exclusive rights of YHWH to achieve great things and serves as a precursor for the spreading of human beings across the world. The story thus becomes a play on the name Babylon from Babel, juxtaposing it to the similar-sounding term for "confusion," *bālal.* It is also an etiology for the origins of multiple human languages and the initial Diaspora of humanity throughout the world.

In the aftermath of this story, Genesis 11 addresses the lineage of Shem with an extended patronymic that ends with the family of Abram. This narrative concludes the primordial history (Genesis 1–11) and introduces the reader to the family that will be the focal point of the subsequent narratives. With providence restored, the emphasis shifts from a general history of YHWH's interactions with all the peoples of the world to a narrative of YHWH's providence manifest in the lives of the members of a single family; from this point forward, Genesis becomes the story of YHWH's encounters with the descendants of Abram/Abraham.

The Text in the Interpretive Tradition

Genesis 6 presents a story that challenges our traditional assumptions about the nature of biblical material. Here we find details similar to texts we otherwise deem "mythological," thought to be part of the fictive imagination of a primitive pagan society. This caused considerable speculation among early interpreters (Louth, 12–126). The introduction of such unconventional mythological content has led many to dismiss the figures in 6:1-4 as having little significance "for the life of faith" (von Rad, 114). Further, Brueggemann suggests that the text itself "ill fits with the main flow of biblical faith" (Brueggemann, 71). Thus interpretation of this passage has focused on what to do with such stories.

The story of the flood has traditionally been understood as a unified narrative about God's punishment of fallen human beings for their propensity to sin. In the traditional understanding of the story, the details of the J account seem to rise to the fore, though aspects of the P account are also included. In this regard, the tradition takes from J the forty-day-and-forty-night flood caused by rain whose end is verified by the repetitive act of sending forth birds. Yet from P we note that the animals enter the ark two by two and the end of the flood is punctuated by God's rainbow, symbolizing God's promise not to destroy the world again by "the waters of a flood" (Gen. 9:11).

Why does Noah curse his son in Gen. 9:25-27? Answers to this question based on early attempts to explain this discrepancy have ranged from the act of Ham "seeing the nakedness" meaning that (1) Ham had sex with his father, uncovering the nakedness of his father; (2) Ham sexually mutilated his father; (3) Ham had sex with his mother, understood as the nakedness of his father, and produced the incestuous child Canaan; or (4) Ham simply saw his naked father and caused him shame by announcing it. These various answers are all based on potential readings that early interpreters could have had of this passage (see Sadler 2006, 390–92; McClenney-Sadler, 93–94).

What is less in dispute is the cursing of Canaan. In some respects, even if it is possible that the author's intent were to curse Ham to slavery, it is unlikely, since Ham is the ancestor of the Egyptians, the Cushites (modern Sudan), the Putim (modern Somalia), and the Libyans, as well as the great powers of Mesopotamia. The curse was likely intended for the Canaanites who, we will learn, will soon lose their land to the sons of Shem.

Perhaps one of the most significant traditions arising from this passage is the "Curse of Ham." This misappropriation combines aspects of the "Curse of Canaan" found in Gen. 9:25-27 and the Table of Nations in Genesis 10. In this regard, if Ham is cursed, then his descendants can also bear this shame. If those descendants are read to be the black Africans who descend from Ham (inasmuch as several prominent sons of Ham are indigenous to parts of northeastern Africa), then the curse can be read as a curse on Africans or "black" peoples. This is an interpretive move that originated in the 1820s and serves to undergird more than a century and a half of slavery, Jim Crow, racist, and racialist thought in the United States as it provided a theological basis for viewing black peoples (read sons of Ham) as hierarchically inferior to white peoples (read sons of Shem and Japheth) based on the Noahide curse (Haynes, 65–104).

Contrary to this interpretive move has been a tendency of Africana peoples to read the descendants of Ham in the Table of Nations as an attestation to the historic greatness of African peoples. In this regard, references to the people of Cush (Nubia), Egypt, Put (Somaliland), Libya, Babel (Babylon), and Assyria, among other great nation states in the lineage of Ham, were used to affirm that the ancestors of Africana peoples were empire-building kings. This interpretive move has fostered the notion of Africans' "stolen legacy" and served as the basis of a corrective history to the dominant Western notion of Africans as those from the "dark continent," void of history or civilization and worthy of domination by European colonial interests (Sadler 2005, 26–32; 2010, 73–74).

Traditional interpretations of Gen. 11:1-9 have suggested that the basis of YHWH's dispersion of the people was found in verse 4, in the sin of pride and their desire to build a city and make a name "for ourselves" (Heb. *lānû*). This is at best an implicit concern in the narrative, for nowhere in this passage is any clear offense explicitly stated. Yet the interpretive tradition has made this a narrative about human sin and God's punishment evidenced by the referenced peoples' subsequent inability to speak with one language.

Genesis 11:10-32 serves to clarify the lineage of Abram/Abraham, who is understood to be the "father of our faith" (see Rom. 4:16; Gal. 3:29). In this regard, this genealogy of the sons of Shem becomes more significant for interpretation than that found in Gen. 10:21-29, inasmuch as this list has immediate bearing on the origins of Abram/Abraham.

The Text in Contemporary Discussion

As we look at the story that begins in Genesis 6, we should note that verses 1-4 describe a very different world from the one we imagine in our scientific age, complete with encounters between heavenly beings and earthly women, which produced mythical hybrid creatures. Though these remarkable details should not distract us from the overall thrust of this narrative—and in fact the contents of these verses are probably overlooked by most readers, whose eyes hurry to the more familiar aspects of the Noah story—the initial few verses should make us suspicious about what precisely is going on in this story! Are these divine-human marriages between "sons of God" and human women the cause of the destruction of the world in the flood narrative (see v. 5)? How much attention should we pay to these aspects of the biblical canon? Should we discuss such narratives in Sunday school or biblical studies courses, and if not, why not? Does this alter our understanding of biblical material at all? We might even wonder how this material typically ascribed to Greek mythologies found its way into "the Word of God."

Further into the narrative, other concerns arise. What is the reason that the earth will be destroyed? How many times do these details occur (i.e., 6:5-7 vs. 6:11-13)? A cursory reading reveals that there do appear to be multiple accounts of certain aspects of this story. Why is this so? There are other discrepancies in this narrative too. How many animals are to go into the ark? Is the devastation caused by rain or some cosmic flooding? How long do periods of the devastation last? What are the names used for God? When we look closely, we can see a conflation of numerous details. What is the reason behind the retelling of the same narrative with slightly different details? Could this all be evidence of the composite nature of this text composed from distinct but generally compatible written sources?

In the midst of it all, we can still see a few familiar details. We see that the deity still cares for humanity, here expressed in the personhood of Noah. We also see that God continues to provide a means for redemption for God's people, here expressed in the ark. So even in the midst of the Lord's destruction of the world, we note God's persistent grace and love for humanity. If nothing else, this truly describes the nature of our God and is evident even at the outset of the first book of the Bible!

A closer examination of this tale makes readers acutely aware of the different voices that have been conflated to provide this one story. Perhaps this story, more than many others, provides a context for contemporary readers to discern the seams in the extant narrative and to understand that many biblical accounts are composed of disparate source material. As we look at such a narrative, we should wonder why the editor of this book did not do a better job of hiding its seams. We might also wonder if there were multiple flood stories that circulated among the people of ancient Israel/Judah. Further, for those aware of other flood accounts, like that found in the Gilgamesh Epic, it might be logical to consider whether that Mesopotamian narrative, fragments of which have been identified in Canaan at Megiddo, played a role in the composition history of this account.

Genesis 9:18-10 has had a distinct history of interpretation in the United States, serving as theological grounding for "racialist" thought. In this regard, the extensive use of the Curse of Ham and the Table of Nations as passages supporting slavery, segregation, and racialist thought in American political discourse should cause us to question whether the Bible is the source of racial thought. In this regard, did God intend to create three races of people corresponding to the three sons of Noah? If so, why is there no reference to differences in color, no value given to such color differences, no subsequent use of the names Shem, Ham, and Japheth to define racial groups, or any other such reference to race?

In my monograph, *Can a Cushite Change His Skin? An Examination of Race, Ethnicity, and Othering in the Hebrew Bible*, I argue that the Hebrew Bible is void of racial thought or racial hierarchies of any type. In fact, it appears that peoples whom we would identify in each of the three most commonly perceived racial types existed side by side, often functioning in alliances of mutual interdependence. Far from presenting a racialized vision of polygenesis (or differing origins) for those of different human subspecies groups, the Bible skillfully crafts its narratives of the origin of all humans. All peoples arise from a single family with a common genesis; there is no explicit attempt to define color differences as indicative of ontological differences in human types (Sadler 2005, 26–32). If there is no biblical basis for racial thought, how is it that we so often ascribe racial differences as God-given attributes?

This section ends with another interesting mythic-sounding narrative, about the Tower of Babel in Gen. 11:1-9. So, what is the sin of Babel? we might ask. Perhaps there is no sin in the way that we would perceive it. YHWH determines independent of explicit moral reasoning that the people should not achieve too much too soon. Could it be that the interjection of a moralistic reasoning into this text is alien to the original Yahwistic authors and the by-product of postbiblical theological appropriations of this text? Might the suggestion that the postflood population has actually "done something wrong" be endemic to us and absent from the original audience? More simply stated, *could we be reading moral justifications into stories where they are not present?* How do we justify such interpretive moves? Does this seem similar to the tension YHWH has with the original couple, who desire to increase in cunning by eating the forbidden fruit? Could it be that in that instance as well YHWH was keeping privileges that YHWH possessed from human beings? Could the anthropomorphic presentation of YHWH in this Yahwistic presentation of the narrative be jealously guarding certain benefits and refusing to have them manifest in humanity? What might this say about the deity that we meet in this passage and in other instances as perceived by the authors/editors of the J source?

Genesis 12–50: The Founding of a Family: The Circuitous Journey from Haran to Egypt

The ancestral saga of the people of Israel represents a significant narratological component of the larger story of Israel's origins. We should pay particular attention to the literary context in which these texts are located inasmuch as the redactors have employed them for specific purposes:

- They form a bridge between the primordial history and the exodus saga.
- They fill in the gap between where the historical credo (Deut. 26:5-9) began in Aramean territory and the arrival of the descendants of Abram/Abraham in Egypt.
- They demonstrate the surety of YHWH's word and the faithfulness of the ancestors. In spite of the passage of time, YHWH will bring to fruition the promises made to Abram/Abraham of a land populated by his descendants.
- They also demonstrate that the ancestors remain faithful to the promise, though it is never fully realized during their lives. They live as aliens in the land of promise, fully expecting that it will one day be theirs.

Theologically, the reader could determine that the way of believers in YHWH is not always an empirical account of promises realized; it is often a story of yet unfulfilled faith. An interesting dimension of the nature of the ancestors' relationship with God is that it is a relationship based on faith, for many of the promises God makes will not be fulfilled in their lifetimes. They will be left for future generations, who will have to be instructed in faith and taught about these promises so that they will know how they are to live in expectation of God's providence.

More troubling, there is a darker side to these narratives evident to contemporary audiences, who are separated from these stories by context and time. These stories serve to justify the Israelite acquisition of the land from their Canaanite (Amorite) predecessors, laying the groundwork for subsequent accounts when the descendants of Israel will appropriate "an other's" land. These texts will provide several "legitimating ideologies" justifying the taking of the land and the subsequent subjugation of the indigenous peoples. The constant promises made about the acquisition of the land tend to ignore the sentiments of the Canaanites and their interests.

As readers, we need to be critically aware of this dimension of the ancestral saga, particularly as we teach and preach from it. Perhaps we might even question as we read what such "promises" would sound like to those who will inevitably be "cursed" in order that chosen others will be "blessed." Though told from a particular perspective, how might that perspective have been deemed problematic to/by others? We might consider the role an uncritical reading of these texts has historically played in the dispossession of the Native American Indians, the Aboriginal Australians, or the black South Africans; in the enslavement of Africans in the Atlantic slave trade; and in the global colonialist activity of the Europeans in the post-Enlightenment era. Further, we might also consider the way these texts continue to undergird contemporary policies of Israel and the United States as the Israeli occupation and settlement of Palestinian lands persists in our contemporary era. Biblical interpretation is not innocuous; it is always consequential, affecting the outcomes of people in our world today, and thus interpretation should always be done with careful consideration of its impact and implications.

The following brief outline can serve to illustrate the overall structure of the ancestral saga:

12:1—25:18	Providence Heeded: Abram/Abraham the Faithful's Cycle
25:19—37:1	Providence Manipulated: Jacob/Israel the Trickster's Cycle
37:2—50:26	Providence Manifest: Joseph/Zaphenath-paneah and the Redemption Novella

Genesis 12:1—25:18: Providence Heeded: Abram/Abraham the Faithful's Cycle

The Text in Its Ancient Context

This narrative is one of the most significant in all of Scripture, for it serves as the basis of the relationship between Abram and YHWH. It begins where the last chapter left off with Abram in Haran. It is a narrative powerful for its simplicity. God tells Abram to go, offers no details, and Abram goes. The point of this narrative is likely to emphasize the fidelity of Abram, who will in most instances follow God's providence without pause, question, or imposition of his own will. God says do and Abram does. As we are told in verse 4, "Abram went as YHWH had spoken to him."

This call account is perhaps the exemplar for each of the call accounts that are to follow, for Abram offers neither resistance nor any hint of hesitation to the Lord's request (e.g., Exod. 3:11; Isa. 6:5; Jer. 1:6). Abram simply is said to have done what YHWH called him to do, and by so doing, the example of his fidelity is rehearsed throughout the Bible (see Romans 4; Gal. 3:6-7; James 2:21-23). Abram is called to go to a land YHWH will show him. This "land" becomes the dominant motif for blessing that will recur throughout the rest of Genesis and the majority of the Hebrew Scriptures.

This narrative is also rich because of what it shows about the nature of blessing. The Hebrew term for blessing (*brk*) occurs five times in the space of three verses, clarifying for the reader that blessing is at the heart of the narrative. Genesis 12:3 suggests that those who bless Abram will be blessed (plural) and the one who curses him will be cursed (singular). Though this interesting textual difference could be viewed as an error in the text, it may well be intentional, denoting the favor that Abram enjoys will confer greater blessing on others than cursing.

The structure of this narrative is instructive. Genesis 12:2 and 12:3 both begin by discussing the impact of the blessing on Abram and end by discussing blessings that attend to others. Abram is blessed by God, but he is not the end of this action; the end is a global blessing for "all the families of the earth." Walter Brueggemann says that "most likely the meaning of the phrase is not that Israel has a direct responsibility to do something for others, but that the life of Israel under the promise will energize and model a way for the other nations also to receive a blessing from this God" (Brueggemann, 120). Others have seen a much more active role for Abram and his descendants in God's blessing of others. For example, Gerhard von Rad suggests that "Abraham is assigned the role of a mediator of blessing in God's saving plan, for 'all the families of the earth'" (von Rad, 160). Still, others note the apparent shift in emphasis that seems a part of God's work here. So Terence Fretheim reads verse 3b as "an initially exclusive move for the sake of a maximally inclusive end. Election serves mission" (Fretheim, 424). This passage shows that God does not choose Abram to elevate him for his own sake, but to use him to be a blessing to others; though God may use an individual and even bless him, the ultimate goal involves a universal blessing that encompasses the whole world. The blessing of Abram will be the catalyst for others being blessed. The clear implication from this is that blessing is a *transitory* concept; it is intended to multiply and impact others.

We should be aware that throughout the ancestral saga, there will be several instances where the patriarchs will establish cult sites, places that were said to be sacred because a patriarch built an altar to YHWH there. This is important because the sites would likely have been known as places where people had worshiped YHWH or *'ēl*, and their affiliation with a patriarch would give greater credibility to those sites. Sites like Shechem and Bethel would have been known as significant cult sites affiliated with subsequent worship of YHWH, and thus these narratives serve to ground the origins of worship at such sites and their significance in the experiences of prominent faithful leaders.

The latter part of this story (vv. 9-20) includes the first of three wife-sister stories (cf. Genesis 20 and 26). In each example of this type (or form) of story, the patriarch claims that his wife is actually his sister to prevent foreigners from seeing her beauty, recognizing her as the patriarch's wife, and then killing him in order to take her (see von Rad, 270). In the first two instances (Genesis 12 and 20), Abram/Abraham and Sarai/Sarah are the protagonists, and in the third it is their son Isaac and his wife Rebecca. The first of these narratives is slightly different from the other two. Here the Yahwistic author of the J source seems to be less concerned about preserving the character of the protagonists. We are left unsure at the end why Abram apparently lies to Pharaoh, telling him that Sarai is his sister, and we are left unsure if Sarai has had sexual relations with Pharaoh. What we do know, however, is that YHWH eventually intervenes, rescues Sarai from this arrangement, and Abram leaves with much greater wealth than when he arrived (Gen. 12:16; 13:2). Apparently, in addition to this strategy's saving his life, it has also served to enrich him (see also Gen. 20:13-16).

Surprisingly, neither Pharaoh nor Abimelech nor any other foreign king attempts to take the life of Abraham or Isaac because of their desire for the patriarchs' beautiful wives. Perhaps the only parallel to this story where a king takes the beautiful wife of a foreign national is when David takes Bathsheba from Uriah (2 Samuel 11). In this regard, the narrative may well have been intended as a morality tale in response to David's grievous error with the wife of Uriah the Hittite.

Genesis 13 concerns the separation of Lot from Abram, and though an understated section of the overall narrative, it becomes particularly important for the overall story. This is a story about separation. According to the account, Abram and his nephew Lot both have accumulated considerable assets and become very wealthy men. Their wealth is apparently divided between the two of them, so they need to separate their flocks to prevent the comingling of their enslaved peoples and thus to prevent infighting. Because their possessions are so great, the land is not able to support them together. In essence, great wealth causes separation, and the bonds of familial unity are threatened by the burden of distinguishing between their possessions.

This accumulation of wealth and the need to differentiate it provides a context for the separation of Lot from Abram, which serves two main purposes in the overall narrative: (1) by the physical separation of these two characters, it emphasizes that Lot will not serve as heir to Abram's promises; and (2) by Lot's taking the fertile Jordan valley and then moving further to the east, it facilitates the subsequent apportionment of the region of Canaan for Abram (Gen. 13:14-17). In these few verses, the extent of the land that YHWH promises to Abram becomes clear. This narrative also subtly foreshadows in verse 13 the troubles Lot will have in his chosen space; here we learn that the indigenous people are both *ra'*, or "evil," and very *ḥaṭṭa'*, "sinful." His choice of what appears to his eyes to be the best land will prove consequential and costly, while YHWH chooses Canaan for Abram and promises to give it to him *'ad-'ōlām*, or "forever."

In Gen. 14:13, we have the first mention of Abram as a Hebrew. This is no familiar term with a long history of use prior to this point in the narrative, and it is most likely that there was no national or distinctively ethnic group called the "Hebrews" to which Abram belonged. Scholars have suggested that the word "Hebrew" might be related to terms like the Egyptian term *Apiru* found in the Amarna Letters or the term *Habiru* from the Cuneiform Mari Letters, which means a migrant, transient, or rebellious outsider. During the Late Bronze period (1500–1200 BCE, the period prior to the Iron-Israelite period), these groups were known to have been raiders that caused trouble for the Egyptians in Canaan (see Lemche, 95). If we accept this as the origin of the term "Hebrew," it gives us crucial insight into the way Abram was viewed by the established powers. He was a landless figure from the margins of society who threatened the current status quo and the indigenous systems of authority.

This becomes evident in the narrative, as once Lot is taken captive during a regional dispute (Gen. 14:12), Abram takes his *ḥanîkîm*, or "trained" men (Gen. 14:14), and raids those who have captured his nephew and rescues him, his allies, and his possessions. Abram has his own armed and trained militia of some 318 men; he is a clear threat to the established regional powers, supporting the notion that the designation "Hebrew" is a functional equivalent to the *Apiru* or *Habiru* interlopers.

Genesis 14:17-21 tells the tale of the aftermath of Abram's mission to rescue Lot. When he returns from his battle, he is said to have taken a tenth of what he captured and given it to a previously unmentioned character called King Melchizedek of Salem, identified as a Canaanite priest of *'ēl-'ēlyôn* ("God Most High," cf. Ps. 78:35). It is unclear why Abram, who has built his own altars heretofore (implying in Gen. 12:8 and 13:4 that he made his own sacrifices) and who otherwise avoids affiliation with Canaanite religious practices, here defers to a Canaanite priest. Yet this becomes the record of the first tithe offered in Scripture.

Perhaps this story has a deeper meaning reflecting a later cultic reality for the people of Judah. If we recognize that Salem is one of the towns Jerusalem comprises and that Melchizedek's name contains within it the root *ṣdk*, the basis of the name Zadok, the subsequent priest during the time of King Solomon, perhaps we can note an etiological purpose to this account, linking the giving of the tithe to the Zadokite priesthood of Jerusalem (a group later known in the New Testament as the Sadducees) in an early account of Abram's own faithful act (see also Fretheim, 439–40). This story will have subsequent messianic significance in Psalm 110, where David—and in Hebrews 5–7, where Jesus—will be deemed priests in the "order of Melchizedek" (Ps. 110:4; Heb. 6:20).

Genesis 15 opens with a concern for Abram's lack of an heir. This problem is acute, for the basis of YHWH's promise to Abram is that his ample descendants will perpetually possess the land that he inhabits as an alien. This concern continues until Isaac is born, serving both narratological and theological ends. Narratologically, it promotes the tension in the story as a number of persons seem poised to serve the role of potential heir (Eliezer, Lot, Ishmael); but each of them is subtly disqualified in the emerging narratives. Theologically, it provides a context in which YHWH proves able to do the impossible. YHWH is challenged to provide offspring like the "stars" (15:5) to one who has had no children. In this respect, the ancestral sagas, like the primordial history, introduce us to and teach us about the nature of YHWH.

The assurance given in Gen. 15:4 that "your very own issue shall be your heir" is the basis of the subsequent Hagar narratives, for Hagar provides Abram with a child of his own issue (Genesis 16). Yet this child is conceived by Sarai's ingenuity and not by YHWH's intentionality; hence, this attempt to facilitate providence is doomed at the outset. We should note, however, that in Gen. 15:6 Abram believes in YHWH and that it is reckoned to him as "righteousness."

In this passage, we learn the high costs associated with establishing covenants. Here, as YHWH affirms the covenantal relationship with Abram and the promises of land and offspring, God has the patriarch take several animals and bifurcate them. It is between these carcasses that the covenant is "cut" (Gen. 15:10), with YHWH symbolically passing between the pieces in the smoking pot and flaming torch (Gen. 15:17). We should note from this experience that the cutting of covenants comes with the shedding of blood and with death. It is serious business, punctuated by the sacrificial loss of blood and life, calculated to serve as a reminder of the obligations that attend to this promissory agreement. There is an implied threat in the covenant that, should one of the parties violate the covenant, that same fate may well befall him (Sarna, 114–15).

We should also note the extent of this land apportioned to Abram in this passage. Not only is he promised the land of Canaan, but all the land from the Nile to the Euphrates is to belong to his descendants. In essence, this represents the extent of the Fertile Crescent, which reached into lands controlled by the great powers of Egypt and Mesopotamia. It is unlikely that the realm of Israel ever extended that far, even under the united kingdoms of David and Solomon, at the peak of their international influence. Attend also to the foreshadowing of the Hebrews in captivity for four hundred years (v. 13) and how the liberative event foretold in verse 14 will figure into the schema presented here in the acquisition of foreign lands and in the dispossession of their inhabitants.

Christians should note the sacrificial nature of cutting covenants and the way in which this narrative serves as a precursor to the crucifixion and as an interpretive lens to make sense of the death of Jesus. To fully appreciate the Christ event requires Christians to have an understanding of the sacrificial nature of the Yahwistic cultus, for it was on this framework that the early Christian community began to ponder the meaning of the tragic event of the crucifixion. As this initial covenant with Abram was sealed by the loss of life and the shedding of blood, so too Jesus' own crucifixion could be viewed as the basis of a new covenant, or a New Testament in his blood.

The problem of Abram's inheritance is temporarily solved in Genesis 16 by the birth of Ishmael to a slave woman from Egypt named Hagar. This is a morally complex narrative filled with many matters of concern about the way that Hagar is used by the combination of this matriarch and this patriarch to "fulfill" YHWH's promise. In what can best be described as a "rape," Sarai gives Hagar to her husband Abram without consulting her. The subsequent act of Abram "going in" to her without her permission seems both to be brutal and to demonstrate the gross abuses of a system that allows for slavery and the commodification of this young woman's sexuality. Hagar's will, though of no real concern to Sarai and Abram, apparently is of some consideration to the narrator, who notes that when Hagar realizes that she has been impregnated, her mistress is "belittled in her eyes" (Gen. 16:4). In this far too subtle way, the narrator suggests disapprobation for the abuse Hagar has suffered at the hands of her enslavers (Bellis, 73, 74–79). Narratives of formerly enslaved Africans in

America often contain such scenes of epiphany when an enslaved woman recognizes that she has become a sexual surrogate for her enslaving mistress and breeder for her enslaving master.

We should also note that this account contains a legitimating ideology for the Israelites' negative assessment of Ishmael's offspring. He is deemed in verse 12 a "wild ass of a man" who has enmity with various peoples, including the members of his own family. This goes a long way to framing Israel's view of the descendants of Ishmael, foreshadowing subsequent animosity between the two ethnic groups that will call Isaac and Ishmael their fathers.

Genesis 18–19 forms an important literary complex in the midst of the Genesis narratives, uniting two stories that address the treatment of strangers. Both stories, which are often taken as separate accounts, feature divine figures that come as human visitors and resident hosts that respond to the visitors in distinctive ways. The resident hosts' responses facilitate the subsequent divine disposition that they receive as well. For Abraham's actions in Genesis 18, YHWH grants Abraham the promise of a son and similarly in Genesis 19 gives Lot his life and the lives of his family, while YHWH destroys Sodom and its inhabitants as a result of their actions. Though the details of the individual narratives differ, the overall framework is similar, and for that reason, the texts should be read together as a single unit.

In the first account, Abraham sees YHWH coming to him in the guise of three men. His initial response upon seeing these strangers is to run to them and offer them the hospitality of his home, literally asking that they not pass "your servant" by (v. 3). The care of the stranger is a crucial concern, inasmuch as an alien would be vulnerable in this realm, fully dependent on the indigenous population to sustain him or her; without the assistance of residents, strangers would be exposed to the elements, have no provisions, and be subject to those who would otherwise prey on them. In its original context, Genesis 18 establishes the appropriate way to receive the stranger and uses this as a context to contrast the behavior of the people of Sodom in Genesis 19.

In that chapter, the two men who enter the town are greeted similarly by Lot, who ushers them back to his home to protect them from the violence that will be done to them if they spend the night in the square of Sodom. After they arrive at Lot's home, they are confronted by the men of Sodom, portrayed as a complete group (from the youngest to the oldest) who are uniform in their desire to "know" these visitors. In Genesis 19, we note the clear contrast between the behavior of Lot and the behavior of the men of Sodom, whom YHWH will judge at the end of the narrative.

In the ancient world, the unit Genesis 18–19 would have served as a narrative that demonstrates God's concern for the way strangers are treated. Inasmuch as the visitors in both chapters 18 and 19 are divine figures, the narrative subtly suggests that the way we treat strangers should be as divine visitors. Mistreatment of such figures could have dire consequences. That this is a concern about justice more than sexuality (see Judg. 1:7) is evident in several subsequent biblical passages, such as Isa. 1:10, which refers to the abusive officials of Jerusalem; Matt. 10:14-15 and Luke 10:10-12, which addresses the issue of towns inhospitable to Jesus' apostles; and most significantly Ezek. 16:49, which explicitly declares the "iniquity of Sodom" to be that they in their prosperity did not aid the poor.

One of the strangest stories in Genesis follows the story of destruction of Sodom in Gen. 19:30-38. It is the story of the birth of two sons to the two daughters of Lot. The narrative in many respects resembles the story of the Curse of Canaan in Gen. 9:18-27. Both stories feature an inebriated father, offending offspring, the hint of sexual impropriety, and the denigration of a subsequent foreign people. While some interpreters have suggested that the Genesis 9 account implies the birth of an illegitimate offspring to Ham through his sexual violation of his mother (i.e., producing Canaan), the story in Gen. 19:30-38 explicitly describes the eponymous ancestors of the Ammonites and Moabites born through an incestuous union between a father and his daughters (see McClenney-Sadler, 94–96) as, in the words of Randall Bailey, "incestuous bastards" (Bailey, 121–38).

As we embark on the narrative in Genesis 20, we should attend to the fact that this story has an odd beginning: "From there Abraham journeyed to the land of the Negev" (Gen. 20:1). This introduction suggests that we are continuing a story about Abraham, and fails to recognize that the most recent stories have been those about Lot and his travails. Again, this suggests that we have transitioned between sources (see von Rad, 226). As we pick up with the Elohist (E) source and its description of what will be the second wife-sister story, Abraham tells King Abimelech that Sarah is his sister and Abimelech takes her for a wife. Unlike the initial wife-sister story, in Genesis 12, the Elohist's version attends with greater care to the integrity of his characters. We are told in 20:12 that Sarah really is Abraham's sister through his father, thereby he is shown to be morally upright, having not technically lied to Abimelech. Sarah's integrity is also preserved, as verse 6 declares that God kept her unsullied by Abimelech. While the integrity of the ancestors is much less of an issue in the Yahwistic account, the Elohist clearly is concerned with these details. The matter of Sarah's purity is of particular concern in the extant combined narrative, particularly because in the next chapter she will give birth to Isaac; it is imperative that the reader know he is not the child of Abimelech, but of Abraham.

It is also noteworthy that Abraham is called a *nābîʾ*, or "prophet," in Gen. 20:7 of the Elohist's narrative. This is the only time this term is used for Abraham and the first time this term is used for any figure in the Hebrew Bible. Subsequently, in verse 17, Abraham also serves as an intercessor and prays for the fertility of the women in Abimelech's house in light of the intermediary role ascribed to him in verse 7. It can be discerned that the term *nābîʾ* in the Elohist's account attends more to intercession than proclamation (von Rad, 228). Finally, we should also note that in verse 14 Abraham is again said to have benefited materially from his deception of a foreign leader and his unorthodox use of his wife. YHWH and the angel of YHWH were divine presences in the first story (Gen. 16:7-13), unlike this account, which favors the term *ʾĕlōhîm*. This is evidence again of the Elohist's version, as is the retelling of the driving away of Ishmael (Gen. 21:9-21).

Genesis 21:1-7 attends to the birth of Isaac. This all-too-brief account, which Brueggemann declares is "strangely anticlimactic" (Brueggemann, 180), describes a pivotal moment in the overall narrative, as the promise of offspring born of Abraham by Sarah is finally realized in Abraham's "old age." The attempts of Abraham and Sarah to resolve their dilemma of childlessness by their own activity have proven futile in the case of Lot (Gen. 12:5), Eliezer (Gen. 15:2), and Ishmael (Genesis 16). Now all that remains is to clear the way for Isaac to be the uncontested heir, thus the story of Sarah's demand that Abraham drive Hagar and Ishmael away (Gen. 21:9-21). We should recognize the composite nature of these texts at this point: in Gen. 21:14, Ishmael is put on his mother

Hagar's shoulders along with their provisions; this is offered even though in Gen. 17:25 we learned that Ishmael was circumcised at thirteen years old! Clearly, there is a discrepancy in the sources regarding the age of Ishmael; but what is not at issue is that Ishmael, like Isaac, will be blessed to be the father of a nation (Gen. 21:13, 18) because of his descent from Abraham. As we consider the stories of Ishmael and Isaac, we should also attend to the dispossession of the firstborn, as Isaac will assume the position usually reserved for the elder son (according to primogeniture); this theme will recur throughout Genesis.

A final concern from Genesis 21 is the anachronistic reference to Philistines in the story of Abraham (also see Genesis 26 and the story of Isaac). Twice in Genesis 21 (vv. 32 and 34) Abimelech is identified as a Philistine. The Philistines, a group of people who originated in the Aegean region and who entered into Canaan from the Mediterranean Sea in the Iron I period (Katzenstein, 326–28), would not have been in the region during Abraham's lifetime. The reference to Philistines in Canaan during the time of Abraham suggests that these texts were composed far later than the period in which most scholars would imagine Abraham to have lived.

The Aqedah, or "binding," of Isaac (Gen. 22:9) is perhaps one of the most significant stories in the overall account of Abraham's life thus far. Unlike Genesis 21, where the birth of Isaac is described in a cursory way, fulfilling an important aspect of the promises given in Genesis 12, Genesis 22 spends a great deal of time addressing the threat posed to those promises by none other than God. In the course of Gen. 22:1-19, we will learn a great deal about Abraham and about God. The narrative begins with God's charge to Abraham in Gen. 22:2 to "take your son, your only son Isaac, whom you love, and go to the land of Moriah, and offer him there as a burnt offering." This command takes the reader completely by surprise inasmuch as the anticipation that has been building since our initial encounter with Abram, and which has just been resolved in Genesis 21, is now undermined a chapter later. Now it appears that we are introduced to a new set of concerns: (1) Is God a deity who requires child sacrifice? (2) Has Abraham, who has been faithful heretofore, finally received the one thing he is not willing to relinquish? and (3) How will the promises made ever be realized if Isaac is sacrificed? Each of these concerns is resolved before the end of this narrative, which ultimately shows that the divine protagonist does not require child sacrifice, that Abraham remains faithful, and that the promise through Isaac, who is perhaps a bit disturbed by the experience, is intact.

The power of this narrative is in Abraham's faithfulness. Like the story of Abram's calling in Genesis 12, Abraham here responds in utter faithfulness to God's command. The linkage between the two texts can also be seen in that they represent the only instances of the imperative phrase *lek-lĕkā* (Gen. 12:1; 22:2) in the Hebrew Bible (Sarna, 150). From his faithful *hinnēnî*, or "Here I am," in verse 1, to his faithful action to go in response to God's word in verse 3, to his reaching out his hand to take the knife in verse 10, there is no hint of hesitation, resistance, or even a second thought to God's providence. If God has determined to *nissâ*, or "test," Abraham, Abraham has determined to demonstrate his worthiness by putting all he has on the line. Abraham successfully passes the test not by fulfilling the mandate to sacrifice his son; but by his "inward intention" to do so (Sarna, 153), he is thereby proven faithful. A final note is in order about the location where God tells Abraham to offer his son. He sends him to the land of Moriah (Gen. 22:2). This seems to refer to the same place that Solomon will eventually establish the temple of YHWH in 2 Chron. 3:1, linking the eventual cult site of the people of Israel to the mountain where their own existence nearly came to a sudden end. In this regard, the offering of animals atop the Moriah altar in Jerusalem may have represented symbolic rehearsal of the averted child sacrifice of Isaac (see von Rad, 243). The story of the potential sacrifice of the firstborn at Moriah both resonates with the instruction in Exod. 13:2 that the firstborn of humanity or animals be sanctified to YHWH and is an eerie foreshadowing of both the child sacrifices that will eventually be offered in the Valley of Ben Hinnom (2 Chron. 28:1-3; 33:1-6; Jer. 7:31-32; 19:1-6; 32:35) and the sacrificial death of Jesus (Rom. 3:21-26; Eph. 5:1-2; Heb. 2:17; 9:24-28; 10:12; 1 John 2:1-2; 4:10) in the Christian canon that will take place just beyond the slope of the Mountain of Moriah. But YHWH in this narrative is not like those deities who demand the sacrifice of children; instead, YHWH is shown to be *yhwh yir'eh* (Gen. 22:14), the LORD who provides, "seeing to" the needs of faithful adherents (Brueggemann, 191).

In Gen. 23:1—25:18, the last chapters of the Abraham cycle, Sarah dies (Gen. 23:2) having secured her lineage through her son Isaac. Sarah is shown to be a powerful figure whose actions significantly influence the unfolding story of YHWH's covenantal promises. In fact, without her agency and her participation in these narratives, the story of Israel may well have been compromised. After her death, Abraham buys a field from Ephron, a Hittite, in order to bury Sarah (Gen. 23:10-20). Even in death, Sarah figures prominently, here serving as the catalyst for Abraham's purchasing the only piece of land he would ever own in Canaan (23:17-20).

In Genesis 24, we have a significant novelette describing the story of the acquisition of Rebekah as a wife for Isaac. Herein Abraham adjures his servant to swear an oath to get a wife for his son Isaac from his kin people. The oath is sworn by the servant's placing his hand beneath Abraham's thigh, and concurring before YHWH that he will not take a wife for Isaac from the Canaanites. It is interesting to see that even in this text set in ancestral times, the prejudice against the Canaanites as marital partners (a theme that recurs in Gen. 27:46—28:2) is substantial, likely reflecting the context of postsettlement Israel or postexilic Judea.

This elaborate story recalls how YHWH guides this servant to Abraham's kinfolk in Aram-Naharaim, where he meets Rebekah, a niece of Abraham, at a well (Gen. 24:1-15). Wells, like contemporary bars, or "watering holes," will recur in several narratives as places where men will encounter women and begin significant unions (see Gen. 29:1-12; Exod. 2:15-21). This context likely adds tension to the narrative in John 4, where Jesus encounters a Samaritan woman at a well. The encounter is ultimately successful as the servant returns with Rebekah to Isaac. Isaac takes her into his mother Sarah's tent and is *yinnāḥēm*, or "comforted," after his mother's passing (Gen. 24:67). From this account, we see that YHWH remains faithful to the promises made to Abraham to raise up a nation and that Isaac has found an appropriate marriage partner, consistent with the will of his father.

In Genesis 25, we come to the end of the Abraham cycle. Abraham herein takes another wife, Keturah, introducing by way of their offspring the ancestral line of many of the peoples of the Arabian Peninsula who, though they are a fulfillment of the promises made to Abraham of numerous offspring, will not participate in the promise of the land of Canaan. Also, in Gen. 25:7-11, Abraham dies at 175 years old, having never seen the fullness of YHWH's promises to him but having faithfully ensured that his son would continue his pursuit of those promises. He is buried with Sarah on his little piece of the promised land purchased from Ephron. The end of this account comes in Gen. 25:18.

The Text in the Interpretive Tradition

The account of the first wife-sister story is a significant challenge to the general understanding of the character of Abram. In this first chapter of his narrative, just after he has shown himself to be faithful to YHWH's call, he has already attempted to manipulate the circumstances of his life by calling on Sarai to pose "less than the full truth" to the Egyptians who will encounter her. From this action, he benefits richly at his wife's expense and thus has been viewed by some interpreters as "cowardly and lacking in integrity" and "focus[ed] on self" in his engagements with Pharaoh. This account has also been viewed as a prefiguration of Israel's experience in Egypt due to details in common between the accounts as the famine, the migrations back and forth, the lead figures' intimacy with Pharaoh, and the plagues on the Egyptians, among other details (Fretheim, 428–29).

The relationship between Sarah and Hagar has been variously portrayed over the years. From the moral contrast between the spiritual Sarah as the mother of "promise" and the fleshly Hagar found in Paul's thought (Gal. 4:22-31) and in Augustine's work, to Pope Urban II's use of the contrast between the two as a basis for the Crusades, to Nachmanides' discussion of the abuse of Hagar by Sarah and Abraham, these figures have been viewed in disparate ways throughout time. Contemporary readings by feminists and womanists have been more careful to note the tenuous situation in which both women find themselves in the midst of a patriarchal world (James, 51–55).

The traditional interpretation of the Hagar stories portrays Hagar as an impertinent shrew who casts aspersions on her mistress because of Sarai's inability to conceive. Sarai and Abram are generally viewed as above reproach in their abuse of Hagar. If there is anything they have done wrong, it is that they have not waited on YHWH to act, but have tried to fulfill God's promise to them on their own. Scarcely is a word uttered about their abuse of power and violation of a seemingly unwilling young woman (see Sheridan, 41–45).

This story in Genesis 18–19 has been understood traditionally as two separate accounts, the first emphasizing YHWH's promise to Abraham and Sarah that they would bear a son (with the hint of that son's name, *yiṣḥāq*, occurring in this instance in Sarah's response to this promise). She laughs (*tiṣḥaq*), in one of several instances where etymologies for his name are offered (e.g., 17:17; 18:12-13; 21:6; 26:8). This sets the story neatly in the larger account of the unfulfilled promise of descendants to Abraham and provides a fourth potential means for an heir (first Lot, who moves away; second Eliezer, the enslaved man; and third, Ishmael, the son of the enslaved woman Hagar).

The second account, in 19:1-29, has traditionally been taken as one of the harshest indictments of homosexual behavior in Scripture. In this interpretive tradition, the homosexual urges of the men of Sodom condemn the city. The people are destroyed for this abominable behavior, which takes its name "sodomy" from this story, in a manner consistent with the expectations of Lev. 18:22 and 20:13, where such behavior is decried (Brueggemann, 163).

There have also be a considerable number of alternative readings of this passage, one most notably found in Walter Wink's short essay "Homosexuality and the Bible." Subsequent texts such as Alice Bellis and Terry Hufford's *Science, Scripture, and Homosexuality* argue that this passage is ambiguous at best as a prohibition against homosexuality and decries rape (Bellis and Hufford, 96–100). Choon-Leong Seow argues less ambiguously that the text is not about homosexuality, but about gang rape and a dangerous culture at Sodom (in Robert L. Brawley, *Biblical Ethics and Homosexuality*) as does Robert A. J. Gagnon in *The Bible and Homosexual Practice*. Each of these recent authors has given sustained attention to the essential concerns raised in this passage and considered how 19:1-29 continues to influence life in our world today.

Others have noted the interbiblical interpretive concern. For example, reading Ezek. 16:49, we note a description of the "guilt of Sodom" (cf. Isa. 1:10; 3:9; Jer. 23:14). There the actual offense has to do with the abuse of the "poor and needy," read the socially vulnerable in the midst of the community. In this regard, the actual sin of Sodomy may more fittingly be described not as homosexuality but as victimizing the socially vulnerable (Brueggemann, 165).

On the latter narrative in Gen. 19:30-38, though the tendency has been to see this account as an attempt to diminish the Moabites and the Ammonites as bastard nations from problematic unions, Brueggemann significantly notes that the authors/redactors of the text do maintain that these groups are of pure stock and that they are still deemed part of the Abrahamic family. This theological reading of the text, though unconvincing in light of the host of legitimating ideologies that denigrate "the other" in Genesis, does note the value of descent from Abram in a text so focused on this lineage (Brueggemann, 176). While not assuming that the overall perspective on the narrative is positive, Terence Fretheim notes that "even out of the worst of family situations, God can bring goodness, life, and blessing to the world" (Fretheim, 476).

Regarding the second wife-sister story, found in Genesis 20, Origen in his *Homilies on Genesis* 6.1 emphasizes that Abraham is called a "prophet" in this narrative and that he has prophetic authority to "heal" Abimelech's wife and female servants. He also allegorizes Sarah to be the personification of virtue, therefore not his wife to be held as his exclusive possession, but as his sister capable of being shared with others (Sheridan, 83–84). Brueggemann notes, following Calvin, that Abraham does not attend to God's providence as he should (178).

The binding of Isaac in Genesis 22 is a narrative with a rich history of interpretation. For example, Nahum Sarna, from a Jewish perspective, suggests that this is an opportunity for Abraham to demonstrate the fullness of his actualized faith (Sarna, 153). This notion is Christianized by Gerhard von Rad, who suggests that this is God's "temptation" of Abraham (von Rad, 239). Brueggemann notes, instead, the Christian tendency to address God's ironic "testing" and then "providing," noting the tension that resonates in the church's faith claims about crucifixion and resurrection (Brueggemann, 188–94). In each of these interpretive traditions, this striking narrative demonstrates a tension in the portrayal of God, who both makes promises and then puts them at risk. We should also note the extensive history of Christianizations of this account. Caesarius of Arles in his *Sermon* 84.2 suggests that this story is a prefiguration of the Christ event, even noting that the three days' journey is a trinitarian formula (Sheridan, 102–3). Clement of Alexandria follows a similar line of thought in his *Christ the Educator* 1.5.23 (Sheridan, 105).

The Text in Contemporary Discussion

As we look at these narratives in Genesis 12, we should question the perspective of the author of these texts, who never seems concerned about the fact that the giving of land to Abram means the taking of land from others. Does this suggest a bias in the authors of these texts that we should attend to as we interpret them for teaching and preaching? Whose voice is being silenced herein and to what effect? What is the lingering impact of this bias on human relations in our world today?

We might also attend to one of the subtle but not insignificant details of these stories. According to Gen. 12:5, we learn that Abram is a wealthy slaveholder who does not travel alone, but who takes an entourage with him on his journeys. What does this say about the perspective of the narrative? Who would the likely audience for such an account be? How have the voices of the impoverished, the enslaved, and the marginalized been acknowledged or ignored in these narratives? (See, e.g., Gen. 16:1-4 and note the response of Hagar to what Abram and Sarai do to her as a foreign enslaved woman in their caravansary.)

Exploring Genesis 14, we might ask why Melchizedek is recognized as such a prominent figure in subsequent narratives. Is this simply an attempt to associate Abram with conveying the tithe to the Zadokites, or does this also demonstrate the murky lines between ancient religious practices? Does Melchizedek the priest of *ʾēl-ʿēlyôn* in this account function like Jethro in Exodus 18 and Balaam in Numbers 22–23 as a foreign figure who serves as an intermediary for YHWH? If so, what does this say about the assumption of the sons of Israel being the exclusive worshipers of YHWH? Could there be others who worshiped this deity before Israel? What does this suggest about our own attempts to exercise exclusive privilege in our worship of God? Does the Lord transcend the boxes that our faith tries to impose on God?

In Genesis 16, who speaks for Hagar? In this narrative, Hagar has had her voice taken from her. She has no voice in Sarai's decision to use her as a breeding implement for her husband. She has no voice in his decision to "go into her" and impregnate her. She is a female character who seeks to ensure the future of her son and herself once her position in the household of Abram is imperiled. But how have we traditionally understood her character, particularly in relationship to Sarai? Is it fair to characterize her as an "uppity" slave who has forgotten her place? Does that reading do justice to the text? It is time that we reread this narrative from the vantage point of Hagar and note that even the most faithful characters in the biblical narrative like Abram and Sarai often possess character traits that are antithetical to contemporary ethical norms.

In more recent exegesis, it has been determined that there is much more going on in the Genesis 18–19 narratives than meets the eye. The linkage of chapters 18 and 19 has been restored, and the contrast between the behavior of Abraham and Lot and the men of Sodom has been explicated. Further, recent scholarship has sought to address several other crucial concerns as well. For example, when this narrative has been compared with the account in Judges 19, it is clear that the abhorrent action is not as much the homosexual behavior (which itself would have been problematic), but the act of communal rape of the vulnerable person who has come to the community for protection. In the Judges account, we note that though the initial victim of the rape was intended to be the Levite, the actual victim is his secondary wife (concubine) who is abused and discarded. It is the offense of her attack that leads the people of Israel to destroy the Benjamites of Gibeah. Thus, in both of these accounts, the ultimate horror is not homosexuality as much as it is gang rape.

Feminist scholars have also noted the treatment of women as problematic in both the Genesis 19 and Judges 19 accounts. In these readings, the ultimate concern seems to be about preserving men from the sexual violation by other men at the expense of the women. Lot offers his daughters, who are refused by the perverse men in favor of the male outsiders. The Levite and his host offer their women to save him as a male outsider from the abuse he may face. While I concur that there does seem to be a distinctive prioritization of protecting the males, I would still suggest that the message of this unit has less to do with homosexuality and more to do with preserving the "more valuable" men in a patriarchal system from the abuse and humiliation of the act of domination that the gang rape would suggest (see Scholz, 123–26).

Perhaps the most potent message to arise from this unit is that YHWH is a God who is both merciful, as described in the negotiations with Abraham (Gen. 18:16-33), and concerned for the abuse of the vulnerable as evidenced by Genesis 19. A careful reading will demonstrate that YHWH is not acting in a moralizing manner, but demonstrating the ultimate importance of the imperative to care for the socially vulnerable; it is the violation of their rights that is the actual crime of "sodomy." Inasmuch as the strangers here are all representatives of the divine realm, perhaps the subtle message is that we should treat the socially vulnerable as if they were God in our midst. Such a message resonates with Matt. 25:31-46 and calls for a greater sensitivity toward the "least of these."

The brief narrative at the end of Genesis 19 about the sexual violation of Lot by his daughters is intentionally crafted to denigrate subsequent people groups, in this instance the Moabites and the Ammonites. In this regard, both the Genesis 9 and 19 narratives can be described as legitimating ideologies serving rhetorically to diminish the foreign "other" in the eyes of the subsequent Israelite/Judahite audience, providing a justification for their subjugation and alienation. Again, these texts pose a danger when subsequent interpreters read them uncritically. Should we adopt the perspectives of the authors/redactors of such texts because they are found in Scripture, we risk having their oppressive *Tendenz* become normalized for us. More simply stated, we need to be aware when interpreting such texts that valorize the denigration of others, for they can justify our abuse of those deemed "other" in our contexts.

The second wife-sister story, in Genesis 20, provides striking differences from the initial narrative in Genesis 12. The reader should attend carefully to the differences between these narratives and note that it is not insignificant that there is additional information given in the second narrative about Abraham's legitimate sibling relationship with Sarah and the fact that Sarah was not violated sexually by Abimelech. Why are such details requisite in this account? Why, more importantly, do we see such similar accounts in the same book? Perhaps what is most troubling of all would be, Why does it not seem that Abraham has learned anything about God's providence in the first wife-sister incident that alters his behavior in this instance? Does this suggest an artificial quality to these duplicate narratives?

The birth account of Isaac in Genesis 21 has been so long in coming that it does appear to be anticlimactic when it finally comes to pass. Perhaps this says something about the editors of the

Genesis narrative, who are more concerned that Isaac is born than they are to expend effort to discuss the birth. The true consequentiality of Isaac's birth is evident in Genesis 22, however. If the reader was not given a sense of the importance of Isaac in the account of his nativity, it is inescapable in the next chapter, as his life is put at risk by the command of God.

Reading this, one might ponder what kind of God would test a faithful follower like this? How does this experience align itself with other key narratives, like that of Job, where YHWH tests a man faithful to a fault to determine the measure of his faith? These questions can introduce the notion of theodicy, or the justice of God, for they force us to attend to the fundamental question of why it is that "good" people endure "hardships" and whether there is some divine intentionality in such tests of endurance. For Christians, the question of the relationship between the sacrifice Abraham is called to make and God's own sacrifice of his Son Jesus is one that is inevitable and requisite. In what ways does the Aqedah prefigure the crucifixion?

Genesis 24 contains an elaborate mini-novella of its own in the description of Abraham's procuring a wife for his son Isaac. Among the many questions that this passage raises are: Why is there the need to seek a wife from the same familial line? What is it about indigenous women that is deemed so wholly problematic, particularly when Abraham himself seems to marry one in the next chapter (Genesis 25)? What is the thrust of this overall narrative? Is it the faithfulness of the servant or the providence associated with his finding of Rebekah? In any case, it seems as if God is again operating behind the scenes to ensure that God's will is done and narratologically to ensure that the lineage of the promised line is pure (Gen. 24:4).

In part, the apparent concern for the familial purity (see Brueggemann, 238–40, on familial purity and syncretism) of the Abrahamic family raised in the chapter prior seems to be less of a concern for Abraham, who in Genesis 25 marries Keturah, a woman whose connection to the familial line is not clearly delineated. Through her, Abraham bears a host of children that will serve as the eponymous ancestors of many of the peoples of the Arabian Peninsula. As we look at such narratives that recount the birth of Arabian peoples through Hagar (vv. 12-18) and Keturah (vv. 1-6), we have to note that they all are descendants of Abraham, hence the fulfillment of the promise made that he would have offspring like the "dust of the earth" (Gen. 13:16) and the stars of the heavens (Gen. 15:5).

In this regard, we may wish to question why they are not vested in the promise of that land deemed holy. This is particularly troubling in relation to the children of Esau in Genesis 36, for he too is a son of Isaac, through whom the blessing was conveyed. If the reason for their removal from the promise stems from the loss of Esau's birthright (Gen. 25:29-34) and blessing (Gen. 27:30-40), then the consequences of this act of dispossession are significant indeed. Further, the effort of the authors/editors of this text to eliminate through the machinations of this literary composition all potential claimants to the promised land save those directly descended from Jacob should arouse a hermeneutic of suspicion among readers; why, we might ask, are so few of Abraham's dustlike and starlike descendants able to participate in the fulfillment of the promise? What role did the authors/editors of the narratives play in crafting a tale that serves to their advantage, and disadvantages those considered "others" in the story? What are the lingering implications of those interpretive moves that persist in our contexts? How might our uncritical appropriation of the narrative contribute to perilous assessments of human valuation of "others" and dangerous social policies toward "others" today?

Genesis 25:19—37:1: Providence Manipulated: Jacob/Israel the Trickster's Cycle

The Text in Its Ancient Context

In this section, Jacob is introduced as a character who will seek to manipulate YHWH's providence by attempting to control his own destiny and to manifest his own fortune. This elaborately interwoven narrative will unfold, as Brueggemann notes, based on a chiastic structure of parallel events linking Jacob's conflict with Laban to his eventual covenant with Laban, his divine encounter at Bethel to his divine encounter at Penuel, and his conflict with his brother Esau to his reconciliation with Esau as the story unfolds (Brueggemann, 213). There is an intentional balance between breaking and mending of relationships in this account as Jacob, despite his seemingly manipulative ways, eventually realizes the power of God's providence at work in his life.

This account begins with another instance of barrenness overcome by YHWH's miraculous intervention (Gen. 25:21), culminating in the story of the birth of Isaac and Rebecca's twin sons, Esau and Jacob. Esau, the elder son, is described as wild; he is characteristically masculine, a great hunter, his father's favorite (Gen. 25:28a), with a hairy body. He becomes the father of the Edomites through his union with Hittite and Ishmaelite wives (Gen. 26:34-34; 28:6-9). His twin brother, Jacob, is described as refined; he is a shepherd and is more cunning and cerebral, his mother's favorite (Gen. 25:28b), and decidedly less hairy. He will be named Israel (Gen. 32:28) and serve as the ancestor of the nation that bears his name. This story, like the previous story of Isaac and the subsequent story of Joseph, will emphasize the displacement of the firstborn in favor of a younger brother.

In this instance, the displacement of the firstborn is predicted in Gen. 25:23 and comes about by way of deception. Though Jacob is traditionally described as the deceptive "trickster" brother who takes advantage of his pathos-driven older brother (see Hiebert, 20), the narrative is actually more complex. In Gen. 25:29-34, Jacob uses Esau's intense hunger against him to secure his birthright; instead of deceiving him, he exploits the wild passions of Esau, which become his own undoing. In the second instance (Genesis 27), the deception starts with his mother Rebekah (Gen. 27:5-17), who engineers Jacob's deceit of his father Isaac and displacement of his brother's blessing. As with Sarah, the powerful matriarch's will is determinative in the fulfillment of YHWH's objective. In this regard, though Jacob alone does live up to the designation "trickster," his family's actions facilitate much of the behavior for which he has been recognized. This character trait is evident throughout the better part of the narratives describing him.

Before considering subsequent chapters in the Jacob cycle, it is necessary to consider the intervening narratives in Genesis 26. This chapter contains the third wife-sister story (Gen. 26:1-11). In this story, unlike the first two wife-sister stories, in Genesis 12 and 20, Rebekah is not taken as a wife by Abimelech the anachronistic Philistine king (von Rad, 271; see also the note on Genesis 20 above), and Isaac is not enriched by the bride price as Abram/Abraham was. The same theme of the fear of the foreign ruler and his people persists (von Rad, 270), and in this instance it is resolved by an edict from Abimelech protecting Isaac and Rebekah from harm (Gen. 26:11).

As in the other two wife-sister stories, the movement of the ancestors is toward the south; it is almost as if these accounts provide an occasion for the ancestors to move toward the south, the ultimate goal of Genesis narratives being to bring the people that will be Israel to sojourn in Egypt. In this instance, YHWH specifically tells Isaac not to go to Egypt but to another land (Gen. 26:1-3). Hence, Isaac settles in Gerar. The extant form of the entire Genesis narrative, with its three wife-sister accounts, thrice brings the readers tantalizingly close to the book's Egyptian goal, while ultimately in each instance thwarting expectations as the ancestors eventually return to the north.

The stage again is set for brotherly conflict in chapter 27 in this story of the younger son taking the privileges of inheritance typically promised to the elder son. As a result, Jacob flees from Esau and is sent by Isaac to find a wife from his mother Rebekah's family. The relationship between the brothers in this narrative is more significant than might originally be presumed, suggesting the subsequent relationship between the two peoples who will trace their lineage from these siblings. According to the legitimating ideology in Gen. 27:39-40, Esau's descendants, the Edomites, will serve the children of Israel, a relationship that is consistent with what is known about the subsequent history of these nations (see Sarna, 178; Hiebert, 21).

On the way in Genesis 28, Jacob encounters YHWH in a dream, and YHWH makes to Jacob many of the same promises previously made to Abram/Abraham of innumerable offspring, of land, of YHWH's abiding presence, and that Jacob will be a blessing to all the families of the earth (cf. Gen. 12:1-3). In response, Jacob names the place Bethel (or "House of God"), sets up a *maṣēbâ*, or standing stone-pillar sanctifying the site, and makes a vow that if YHWH cares for him and brings him safely back home in peace, YHWH will be his God (Gen. 28:10-22). In addition, Jacob promises to offer to YHWH a tithe of everything he receives, a practice that will continue among the cultic rituals of settled Israel, echoing another Abramic practice inaugurating such activity in Gen. 14:20. This is Jacob's first real engagement with God, but the story is theologically compelling, for over the course of the next several chapters, we will learn that YHWH is faithful to do all Jacob has asked. This narrative, hence, is the inaugural story of YHWH's fellowship with the eponymous ancestor of the distinctive people deemed Israel.

One theologically troubling aspect of Jacob's vow is its conditional nature. Unlike the bold action in response to the divine encounters seen in Abraham's narratives, Jacob's fidelity to YHWH in Gen. 28:20-21 is predicated on a condition that *'im*, "if," God will act, then "YHWH will be my God." Sarna suggests that Jacob really is not really "bargaining" with God, because all that Jacob wants God has already promised (Sarna, 200). Brueggemann, however, notes that "Jacob will be Jacob. Even in the solemn moment, he still sounds like a bargain-hunter. He still adds an 'if'" (Brueggemann, 248). The conditional nature of Jacob's vow seems like a further attempt of this patriarch to manipulate divine providence.

Over the next several chapters, Jacob will meet Rachel at a well and be led to his uncle Laban's house (Gen. 29:1-14), fall in love with and arrange marriage to Rachel (Gen. 29:15-20), and be tricked by his uncle to marry the "lovely" in terms of her eyes (Gen. 29:17 NRSV) or "tender eyed" (Gen. 29:17 KJV) Leah. (There is considerable disagreement on the meaning of *rakkôt* among translators of Gen. 29:21-30; see von Rad, 291; Sarna, 204; Fretheim, 553). He will eventually marry both of Laban's daughters (an arrangement wisely prohibited in Lev. 18:18) and be given the enslaved women Zilpah and Bilhah, each of whom will bear children for him. This complex arrangement unfolding over Genesis 29–30 establishes a fierce sibling rivalry between Rachel and Leah (e.g., 30:15) that will extend to the offspring of Jacob in the next generation. As Brueggemann notes, the narrative "portrays the way to the next generation as a way of conflict. The sons are born in rivalry, envy, and dispute. Undoubtedly, this presentation of the sons is a mapping of the tribes of Israel. But in the narrative itself, they are simply children yearned for, given, yet given in the midst of anguish" (Brueggemann, 253).

In Gen. 30:1-24, Jacob has children by Leah, Zilpah, Bilhah, and finally the once-barren Rachel. Eventually he has twelve sons and one daughter, who generally serve as the eponymous ancestors of the twelve tribes. The trickster Jacob resurfaces inasmuch as he strikes up a deal with Laban to take his spotted and striped sheep through "genetic manipulation" (Gen. 30:37-43), breeds spotted and striped sheep, then becomes rich in another act of deception (Gen. 31:20), and flees from Laban, who himself had determined to deceive Jacob (Gen. 30:35-36). But as in all things, God prospers Jacob, and when confronted by Laban and accused of stealing his uncle's *teraphim*, or "household gods," he attests to God's faithfulness and protection (Gen. 31:42). It is as this chapter ends that Laban proclaims the classic parting blessing, the *mispâ*, which is oddly Yahwistic even though arising from the pagan Laban (Gen. 31:49).

Jacob's story is one of deceit, lies, and half-truths. He is often identified as the morally ambiguous trickster, a theme not uncommon in African folklore like that of the Yoruba figure Eshu Elegba. There are a number of instances of questionable integrity in this tale:

- Jacob sells his imprudent brother Esau soup at the price of his birthright.
- Jacob deceives his father to steal his brother's blessing.
- Laban deceives Jacob, leading him to marry Leah before Rachel.
- Laban coerces Jacob to stay with him for many additional years of service.
- Laban takes the flocks that he has promised as payment to Jacob.
- Jacob manipulates Laban's flocks to produce offspring he can acquire.
- Jacob secretly flees from Laban with all he has acquired.
- Rachel deceives her father while sitting on the household gods that she has stolen from him.

Despite the tendency for deception and duplicity in the Jacob story, the narrative does not seem to impose a moralistic judgment against Jacob; instead, it almost seems that like Abram/Abraham, who twice prospers by selling his wife (Genesis 12; 20); like Tamar (Genesis 38), who will benefit from deceiving (Niditch, 41) her erring father-in-law Judah (and Judah, who caused Tamar's deceptions by his deceitful retention of his third son in Gen. 38:11); like Joseph, who will deceive his brothers and father; and like Joseph's brothers, who sell Joseph and deceive their father (Genesis 37–50), what appear to be moral flaws are often the means used in providential ways to achieve YHWH's desired will in these narratives. The trickster dimension of Jacob, not unlike the cunning sought by the original woman and man in Genesis 3, seems to be a valuable asset to facilitate the survival of God's people and the realization of YHWH's will. Brueggemann offers a poignant assessment of Jacob that aptly describes the way such character flaws are considered in the Genesis narratives.

> It is the earthy man through whom the resilient purposes of God are being worked out. The purpose of God is somehow operative in the places of scandal and deception. . . . Precisely in this doubtful character, the promise of God is being fulfilled. . . . In the midst of the ambiguities, the promise is having its way. (Brueggemann, 252)

Thus, amid the manifold manipulations in this account, God's providence continues to govern the movement of the narrative.

The reunion of Jacob and Esau is prefaced in Gen. 32:3-21 with several decisive actions. Jacob, fearing his brother will kill him, makes arrangements to offer him a portion of his wealth to appease his anger. Further, he divides his goods so that Esau will not be able to defeat him and destroy the entirety of his family should he attack. He even entreats YHWH to protect him once he hears that Esau is coming to meet him with four hundred men. Undeniably, Jacob recognizes that he has wronged his brother and has legitimate reason for concern. In a confusing amalgam of sources in Gen. 32:22-23, he is said both to have crossed the Jabbok with his family (32:22) and to have remained on one side while sending his family and possessions to the other side (32:23). The latter version in verse 23, however, provides the requisite context for what occurs next.

Jacob is alone and has a mystical encounter in the night with a "man" whose identity remains undisclosed. Who is the man? The story seems to imply that it was God (Gen. 32:28-30). But could the one with whom he wrestled have been Esau and this event served as his struggle to make his peace with his brother? Why does the man only wrestle him at night and have to let go when "day is breaking"? Might it be so his familiar face won't be recognized? Also, the question, "Why is it that you ask my name?" in Gen. 32:29 suggests Jacob might have known who he was.

Further, there are several different references to the notion of "faces" in this narrative. The first occurs in Gen. 32:20 (v. 21 in Hebrew) in reference to the presents that Jacob sends to Esau to win favor; he says in Hebrew, "I will cover his face [appease him] with the present going in front of my face [before me] and after that I will see his face, perhaps then he will lift my face [accept me]." The second is in Gen. 32:30 (v. 31 in Hebrew) in reference to his nocturnal struggle, as he says that he has seen God "face-to-face" at the place he names Peniel, "The face of God." The third is in Gen. 33:10, where he declares to Esau, "I have seen your face, [it is] like seeing the face of God."

How might this have sounded to the original audiences of this story? Could it be that Esau was Jacob's nighttime foe who, seen in the daylight, manifests the face of "God" with whom he wrestled in the shadows? Suffice it to say that there may be no clear answer to this query, save to understand the complexity of the extant narrative and the ambiguity the redactors (intentionally?) allowed to remain in the conveyed accounts.

In the midst of this nighttime struggle, Jacob has his name changed. His opponent declares in Gen. 32:28 that he will no longer be called Jacob, but Israel because he has "struggled with God and with humans and has prevailed." Though he will continue to be called Jacob throughout his narrative, the name Israel will come to define his descendants as the distinct recipients of the blessings promised to Abraham at the beginning of the ancestral saga. It will also describe their ability to prevail and persevere amid the struggles that will attend to their collective existence.

This is the first reference to the name "Israel" in all of Scripture, as the ancestor of the focal people in the Bible is herein identified. It merits attention that the name Israel is not distinctly Yahwistic and designates this people as those who follow El. El taken as a generic term can simply mean God, but during the Canaanite period this figure would have been recognized as the head God of the Canaanite pantheon (Smith, 7–10). The reverence of the deity by this name is further evidenced at the end of Genesis 33, where Jacob settles on a plot of land that he purchases from the sons of Hamor near Shechem. There he builds an altar and calls it *'ēl 'ĕlōhê yiśrā'ēl*, or "El, the God of Israel" (Gen. 33:20). His settling in Shechem complicates his experience with Esau and adds a final instance of deceit to the end of the narrative. Though he says that he will return with his brother, he tells him he will soon follow him, and as his brother heads to Seir, he heads in the opposite direction, first to Succoth and then to Shechem.

The rape of Dinah in Genesis 34 is not the first abuse of women that we encounter in the Bible, nor is it the first rape that can be found on the pages of Scripture. The Genesis 16 story of Sarai's giving of her enslaved girl Hagar to Abram to serve as a surrogate womb for his offspring is reminiscent of the late-night encounters between slaveholders and enslaved women on American plantations. This sexual appropriation of an unwilling and perhaps unwitting woman as evidenced in Gen. 16:4 cannot be excused because the perpetrators are the beloved ancestors of our faith traditions. The offering of Lot's daughters in Gen. 19:8 is also an instance of abuse, as a father, based on an ethos perhaps more consistent with his era than one acceptable in our own, willingly offers his virgin daughters as sexual surrogates, alternative victims to be raped instead of YHWH's angels. Also, the account of Leah and Rachel offering Zilpah and Bilhah as spousal surrogates to Jacob should cause us to question the representation of women in these narratives. The story states that Shechem *yiqqaḥ* ("took"), *šekkab* ("laid with"), and *yĕ'annehā* ("oppressed/humiliated her"). Actions similar to those committed by the patriarchs and authorized by the matriarchs above are finally viewed through a disparaging lens. Here the offense seems to be a personal one, not just to Dinah, but also to the men in her life who appear to be violated by what was done to their daughter/sister. The narrator's conveying of the words and sentiments of the men while silencing Dinah betrays the focus of "his" concern. Though the abuse of a woman is finally decried, she remains silent in her suffering, and her will is unexamined as her fate rests in the hands of the men who circumscribe her life (Niditch, 40–41).

After violating Dinah, Hamor seeks to resolve the offense by marrying his son Shechem to Dinah (Gen. 34:3-4). This is a strategy of redemption that is found in the Torah. For example, Deut. 22:28-29 suggests that in such an instance of rape, the guilty man must pay a bride price, marry the woman he violated, and remain married to her for life with no possibility of divorce. In an act of deception that is reminiscent of their father, the sons of Jacob pretend to accept Shechem's offer of marriage, convince him that he and all the men of his city must be circumcised in order to intermarry with the offspring of Israel, and then slaughter the men of the city as they are recovering from their circumcisions. This act embarrasses Jacob and imperils his family, yet it seems to maintain what we will subsequently learn is YHWH's prohibition against intermarrying with Canaanites (e.g., Josh. 23:12-13, where the Israelites' possession of the land is predicated on adhering to this standard).

The final few chapters of the Jacob cycle are not uneventful. In Genesis 35, Jacob returns to Bethel, where he first encountered God when he initially fled from his father's house and his brother Esau. As part of his journey to Bethel, he ritually purifies those with him, having them rid themselves of their foreign "gods." This is perhaps the first time the verb *ṭāhar*, "purify," is used denoting a ritual purification since the flood narratives (Gen. 7:2, 8; 8:20), where the term is used in reference to ritually "clean" animals permissible for eating on the ark in the Yahwistic account, long before such practices will be put in place. Here the notion of purification is used in preparation for Jacob's reunion with God in fulfillment of his pledge to YHWH in Gen. 28:20-22 to worship and offer a tithe to this deity.

Once he arrives at Bethel (Gen. 35:6), he establishes an altar at *ʾēl bêt-ʾēl*, encounters *ʾēl-šadday*, who offers him the Priestly blessing "be fruitful and multiply" (Gen. 1:22), changes his name to Israel (again), and reiterates several of the promises to him that have previously been made to Abram of offspring and land (Gen. 35:7-12). In response, Jacob establishes another *maṣēbâ*, or standing stone-pillar, pours a libation and oil on it as an offering, and thereby consecrates the place (Gen. 35:14). At the end of this chapter, he suffers two significant losses. Genesis 35:16-21 describes the death of Rachel and her burial at Ephrath or Bethlehem, and Gen. 35:27-29 describes the death of Isaac at Hebron. Though not much is mentioned of the long-awaited reunion between father and son, the few verses at the end of Genesis 35 suggest a time when not only Jacob and Isaac were reconciled, but Jacob and Esau were as well, since these two sons of Isaac are said together to have buried their 180-year-old father.

Genesis 36, the final chapter of the Jacob cycle, turns to the descendants not of Israel (Jacob) but of Edom (Esau). Here more than in any other chapter, the relationship between the Israelites and Edomites is explicated, and the children, kings, and clans of Esau are explained in the careful, exacting style for which the Priestly writer is known. In the final chapter of this cycle, the fact that Esau is the elder brother can be correlated with the fact that Edom was known to have been settled in the region for a much longer period than Israel. This is attested by Gen. 36:31 declaring, "And these are the kings who ruled over the land of Edom before a king ruled the descendants of Israel." The relation between these two contentious peoples will unfold over the next thousand years as the offspring of each will rule side by side, will struggle against each other, and will even rule over each other. In fact, one of the final kings of Judea will be Herod the Idumean, a son of Esau (Hubner, 382–83).

Jacob as a character is one who has sought to manipulate his own destiny but who learns through trial and error to depend on YHWH's providence. In fact, God's providence works to bring both Jacob's acts of deceit and his acts of fidelity into submission to a plan he cannot hope fully to comprehend. In the end, despite the deception that characterizes Jacob's life, his fate remains firmly in YHWH's hands.

The Text in the Interpretive Tradition

The story of Jacob, beginning in Genesis 25, has been variously interpreted over the years. He has been considered to be a trickster, deceptive, manipulative, cunning, and so on. Brueggemann makes an interesting claim about the nature of the overall Jacob narrative, however: "One senses that while the deception attempts to turn the blessing, in fact, the deception is only a tool for the blessing to go a way already decided upon" (Brueggemann, 230). Should this line of reasoning be followed to its logical conclusion, the Jacob presented in the narrative is often a figure that benefits through guile and apparent deceit, but the overall narrative suggests that divine providence has shaped his life just so to achieve larger purposes. He will be of benefit in greater ways than are evident initially; his trickster character is only a "tool" to achieve a predetermined end.

Hiebert offers another bit of insight regarding the reversals of primogeniture like those we see in the stories of Isaac, Jacob, and Joseph. Those who benefit from the reversals are "secondary sons, that is, by those outside the positions of power in society held by fathers and their firstborn sons." In this regard, the reversals and the trickster quality of Jacob enable him to "gain access to powers denied" to him by this birth position. So these narratives can be read as the "quest by the disenfranchised to share in the power and benefits of the family and society" (Hiebert, 21).

The story of Jacob's nocturnal wrestling match at Peniel has been variously understood. While it seems simplest just to assume that the figure with whom Jacob wrestles is his brother Esau, early Christian authors tended to presume that the figure was actually God, often prefiguring the Christ narrative (Sheridan, 218–24). More recently, Sarna determines that the figure is not Esau himself but one who must "stand for Esau" as his "alter ego" and identifies the figure as his "celestial patron" (Sarna, 404). Brueggemann conflates his assumption that the nocturnal wrestler has been YHWH with the concerns of Esau, concluding that that the stranger is "Yahweh, with shadows of Esau present" (Brueggemann, 272). It is clear that there is no interpretive unanimity regarding this passage that clarifies all the issues it raises.

The account of the rape of Dinah in Genesis 34 poses the question of who is the actual party offended by such an infraction. In this account, where Dinah is completely objectified and is not able even to express her pain, it appears that the authors/editors are more concerned with the rape as a violation of the property rights of Jacob and a source of shame for her brothers than they were about the status and well-being of Dinah (Niditch, 41; De La Torre, 288). It is in this vein that De La Torre asks why God in the text is silent about Dinah's rape and why God does not act to intervene. In part, he suggests, it is because of the male perspective of the authors. Since they do not care, it appears that God, too, does not care about what happens to Dinah (De La Torre, 292).

The Text in Contemporary Discussion

As we consider the development of the stories of Abraham's offspring, it should be increasingly clear that the authors favor one familial line, while those of other lines continue to be portrayed in a less favorable light. This pattern holds true as we examine the relationship between Jacob, the father of the Israelites, and Esau, the father of the Edomites. While the theological purposes of such an act are evident, the implications for the way that subsequent readers of the narrative internalize these patterns of privileging favored groups and deprivileging "others" should be examined. While it is consistent with the goals of the author to have the reader identify with the Abrahamic, Isaacic, Jacobic protagonists and their familial lines, it is imperative that as we read we consider how these stories shape not only our understanding of the "biblical other" but also those we deem to be "other" in our own contexts today.

One cannot read the story of Jacob without considering the morally complicated portrayal of his behavior. How do we reconcile his taking advantage of his brother (Gen. 25:29-34), the deceit of his father to dispossess his brother (Gen. 27:1-29), and other such trickery with a key biblical figure on whom the unfolding narrative rests? Perhaps a more troubling issue is how to deal with the biblical perspective that God uses such human machinations to realize providential arrangements. This issue resurfaces throughout explorations of the trickster cycle.

As we explore the promises given by God to Jacob in Genesis 28, we cannot help but notice the distinctive conditional response he gives to YHWH in his vow. YHWH will be his God *if* YHWH fulfills certain conditions. This bargaining seems to run contrary to the faithful theological posture of Abraham. How is this portrayal resonant with his character in these narratives? In spite of our tendency to deem his character traits as suspect, does Jacob represent aspects of the human tendency to bargain and manipulate in our relationship with God and others?

The story of Jacob's time with Laban in Genesis 29–31 raises a plethora of questions, many of them in relation to women's concerns. How does the arrangement between Jacob and Laban serve to commodify both Rachel and Leah, thereby making them the payment for Jacob's labor (see Gen. 31:15)? To what extent are these women treated as "exploited and dispossessed slaves" by the men in the narrative (Niditch, 39). How do the sisters participate in the oppression of women by offering their enslaved women Bilhah and Zilpah as sexual surrogates and breeders for Jacob? How does the rivalry between these sisters contribute to unhealthy familial relationships among Jacob's offspring? How are readers to understand the actions of these matriarchs in light of contemporary sensibilities?

Genesis 32 presents one of the most puzzling narratives in Genesis. As Jacob has had his reunion with Laban in Genesis 31 and commemorated it with the pillar of Mizpah, he faces another conflict, that with his brother Esau. After sending flocks to appease his brother and sending his family ahead of him across the River Jabbok, Jacob wrestles with a "man" all night at Peniel, "the face of God." With whom did he wrestle? Was it with God? Was it with Esau, whose face he looks on in Genesis 33? Was it with his own conscience personified? The possibilities are rich, but ultimate clarity is elusive. Also, what role does this nocturnal encounter play in his life? If it is meant to be the moment of his transformation from trickster to faithful adherent, why then does he again deceive Esau at the period of their encounter (Gen. 33:15-17)? How does the retaliation for the rape of Dinah in Genesis 34 attest that his sons have adopted his trickster ways? Does he come to realize the consequences of deception in response to his sons' actions in Gen. 34:30?

We see these actions in Genesis 34, where in response to the rape of their sister Dinah, the sons of Jacob deceive the inhabitants of Shechem, tricking them into circumcising themselves to forge an alliance with the sons of Israel, and then slaughtering the men of the city as they lay incapacitated. Had these men lived, would their circumcisions have made them heirs of the covenant like the Idumeans conquered by John Hyrcanus (see Hubner, 383)? But far more significantly, how do we attend to a narrative that describes a brutal offense to a woman that does not allow that woman a voice in her own story? How do we respond to the proposition that the crime of rape could be atoned by having the rapist marry the woman raped? Are there advantages to such a system in an ancient context? If so, what might they be and what do they presume about the status of women in relation to men? Is this really, as Niditch notes, a dispute between two groups about the ownership of a woman and the status of men (Niditch, 41)?

Genesis 37:2-50: Providence Manifest: Joseph/Zaphenath-paneah and the Redemption Novella

The Text in Its Ancient Context

The final section of Genesis is the Joseph novella. This well-developed story of the life of Joseph is unlike the brief cycles that told only occasional events in lives of Abraham, Isaac, and Jacob. It is the story of a man who will suffer considerable hardship, who will be attacked and threatened with death by his brothers, who will be sold by Midianite raiders to Egyptian overlords, who will be sexually assaulted by his mistress, who will be falsely imprisoned by his master, yet who will be redeemed by God's providence in a miraculous account of divine intervention. The Joseph redemption novella unfolds in three movements:

Joseph's conflict with his brothers (Genesis 37)
Joseph gains favor in Egypt (Genesis 39–41)
Joseph reunited with his brothers (Genesis 42–50)

This is a complete narrative that unfolds over the final chapters of the book with only the single significant interruption found in Genesis 38, which chronicles the Judah and Tamar story. Joseph's account, like many of the other stories in Genesis, features a disruption of primogeniture, as a younger brother will be foretold to rise to prominence over his older brothers. It will also feature sibling rivalry, reversals of fortune, deceit, and divine providence, as each of these themes contributes to the drama that unfolds in this concluding narrative of the ancestral saga.

The stage is set for brotherly conflict in Genesis 37, when the precocious younger brother Joseph is surmised to be the favorite son of his father Jacob/Israel by his older brothers. Dreams figure prominently in the narrative that weaves together classic J material with the divine insight provided by dreams often associated with E. In two dreams (Gen. 37:5-8 and Gen. 37:9-11), Joseph is given a precognition that he will eventually rule over his brothers, information he decides to share with them. This dream disclosure angers the brothers, as does the *kĕtōnet passîm*, or special garment, that Israel gives to Joseph, the son he has with Rachel in his "old age" (v. 3). In a rage resembling that of Cain in Genesis 4, the brothers hate (vv. 4, 8) and are jealous of Joseph (v. 11). Instead of luring Joseph to a field, this narrative has Jacob send him to the pastures to find his brothers, who are shepherding their flocks. When he arrives, they develop a scheme for fratricide, but convinced by their brother Reuben (vv. 21-22), they decide instead to place Joseph in a pit. At this point, the narrative is uncertain. He is removed from the pit and sold either by his brothers (vv. 25-27) according to J, or by Midianites (v. 28) according to E, to passing Ishmaelite traders. Thus begins his journey to Egypt, where he will be sold to an Egyptian court official (v. 36), a journey that will end with the entire family of the descendants of Israel in Egypt. Meanwhile, the brothers deceive Jacob, convincing him that his favorite son has died by slaughtering a goat, dipping Joseph's garment in that blood, and bewailing his demise. It should not escape notice that the trickster Jacob, known for his deceit, is now being deceived by his own children (the pomegranate does not fall far from the tree).

It is at this point that we find an odd intervening story about levirate marriage in Genesis 38. Judah, one of the sons of Jacob, has three sons: Er, Onan, and Shelah. For his oldest, he takes Tamar for a wife. Because he is "wicked," Er dies prematurely, before he can raise up offspring by himself (vv. 6-7). This places Tamar in a precarious situation, for she is now a woman who, although she is not married, cannot return as a virgin to her clan. Furthermore, she is not a mother and thus has no real standing in the patriarchal order of her deceased husband's clan (Niditch, 41–43). She is a woman in need of a remedy for her social dislocation.

According to custom, the second son of Judah, Onan, is then tasked to raise up offspring for his brother Er. He instead "goes into" (has sexual relations with) his sister-in-law, then spills his seed on the ground, and because of this, YHWH puts him to death (vv. 8-10). Ordinarily this would mean that Tamar had access to the third son, but Judah deceptively withholds Shelah for fear that he will meet the same fate as his deceased brothers. When it becomes clear that Judah has no intention of giving Shelah to Tamar, and in the aftermath of the death of Judah's wife, Tamar pretends to be a *zōnā*, or "prostitute" (Gen. 38:15), and sits at the entrance to a town Judah will pass on his way to Timnah, and waits for him to come. When he arrives and they negotiate terms (he leaves his signet, cord, and staff with her to hold until he delivers a kid to her), he "went into her" and impregnates her unwittingly, and leaves. Later, after Judah finds out that Tamar is pregnant, he prepares to have her burned as an honor killing (v. 24) only to have her offer up the items that he gave her in pledge (v. 25). Convicted, he declares that she is "more righteous than" he because he violated the terms of levirate marriage and she has cunningly strategized to ensure his family line through an appropriate kinsman (v. 26).

Though this story seems to be completely disconnected from the larger narrative, we should note that it resonates with the larger theme of familial obligation. In this instance, Judah and his son have failed to perform their responsibility to their fallen kinsman's spouse and failed to *hāqēm zera'*, or "raise up seed," for Er. Unfulfilled obligation here creates a significant interfamilial crisis imperiling both the appropriate inheritance for Er's lineage and the life and social status of Tamar. The story also has remarkable resonances with the overall narrative in which it is placed; Joseph's and Tamar's experiences with Judah can be correlated, as they both are deceived by, request a youngest son from, hide their identities from, take objects from, and are eventually reconciled to Judah (see McClenney-Sadler, 98–102). Despite the sexual intrigue engaged by Tamar, she is deemed *ṣādĕqâ*, or "righteous" (v. 26), inasmuch as she preserves the family of Judah in ways reminiscent of other female figures such as Rahab (Joshua 2 and 6) and Ruth (Ruth 3), who use their sexuality in ways that preserve the chosen family line and YHWH's divine plan (Niditch, 24–26).

If Genesis 38 introduces a compelling use of feminine sexuality, Genesis 39 demonstrates an inappropriate application of it, as Joseph is seduced by the socially potent wife of Potiphar, the captain of Pharaoh's guard, for whom he works. In response to her attempts to entice him, Joseph offers a morally compelling argument in Gen. 39:9-10 to dissuade her, noting his obligations to both Potiphar and to God. Undeterred, she continues her pursuit of this attractive young protagonist (39:6), forcing him to flee from her, leaving his clothing in her grasping hands. Her act of sexual impropriety becomes the narrative's vehicle to land Joseph in prison. His incarceration becomes an occasion for the reintroduction of YHWH to the narrative (39:21-23) and a reminder of YHWH's favor and presence in his life, assuring the reader that God's providence is still at work even amid Joseph's hardships.

Genesis 40 has Joseph as a prisoner in favor with his jailers. While incarcerated, he interprets two dreams describing the destinies of two of Pharaoh's officials imprisoned with him (Gen. 40:9-15, 16-19) and is shown to have been an accurate diviner (Gen. 40:20-22). After two years, the official for whom Joseph interpreted a dream of restoration tells Pharaoh about Joseph (Gen. 41:9-13). Pharaoh brings Joseph out of prison, confides to him his dream, and learns the fate of his nation. Joseph interprets Pharaoh's dream as foreshadowing seven years of plenty prior to seven years of famine and (shrewdly) encourages Pharaoh to appoint a man who is *nābôn weḥākām*, or "understanding and wise" (Gen. 41:33), over the land to supervise a food conservancy project to prepare for the impending famine (Gen. 41:33-36). Pharaoh, appreciating Joseph's sage counsel, appoints him over "all the land of Egypt" (v. 41), gives him unassailable authority over its people (vv. 42-44), the name Zaphenath-paneah, and Asenath daughter of Potiphera, priest of On, for a wife (v. 45). This good fortune is all attributed to the providence of God, whom Joseph commemorates in the naming of his two sons in verses 51-52. Despite the unimaginable hardships Joseph has endured, God has redeemed him and given him a place second only to Pharaoh's in Egypt.

As would any good storyteller, the narrator brings Joseph's brothers back into the story in Genesis 42. Joseph, now empowered and well-positioned, will have to attend to the needs of his family, which has treated him with hatred and disdain. Famine again serves as a reason for the Abramic clan to venture south (cf. Gen. 12:10; 26:1), this time to Egypt itself to find food. Again, the trajectory of Genesis has been leading the children of Abraham to Egypt since chapter 12, for they have to be there in order to introduce the exodus narratives. Over the course of the next few chapters, Joseph will deceive his brothers, imprison them as spies, take two of them as prisoners, and otherwise test them (Genesis 42–43). This testing culminates when he ensnares his brother Benjamin and convinces his other brothers that Benjamin must remain in Egypt as his slave; this inspires Judah to offer himself in place of Benjamin (Genesis 44). Thus, in Genesis 45, Joseph reveals himself to his brothers and assures them that all that has happened has been done by God's hand in order to preserve their lives. The initial dreams of Joseph's rule from Genesis 37 have been fulfilled as God has lifted him above his family members; but the purpose of his elevation is also clarified. It has been a result of providence; he has been elevated not for his own sake but so that they all might find salvation in their moment of distress (Gen. 45:7-8).

So Israel heads to Egypt in Genesis 46. The eponymous ancestor of the people symbolically represents the nation as it goes to sojourn in Egypt. In verses 2-5, God authorizes Jacob's migration, assuring him that this was part of God's plan, that God would remain with him, and that God would bring his family up from Egypt in the future. The journeying of the descendants of Abram is all but complete, as God has led them to Egypt as seventy souls (a fitting number forecasting the eventual number of people involved in the Egyptian translation of the Hebrew Bible into Greek—the LXX). The family, reconciled finally as Jacob sees Joseph, settles in the land of Goshen (Gen. 47:27).

One of the most interesting but oft-overlooked parts of the Joseph novella occurs in Genesis 47. After Jacob has come into Egypt, blessed Pharaoh, and settled in "Rameses" (note the anachronistic mention of this pharaoh—Gen. 47:1-12), the narrator offers a detailed description of the impact of the famine. Because of the famine, wealth becomes centralized in the hands of Pharaoh's house as Joseph takes all of the Egyptians' money, their livestock, and then their lands and their very lives in exchange for food and seed (Gen. 47:13-19). The chapter climaxes with the revelation in verse 21, where the MT has the odd reading, "he caused the people to pass to the cities," while the LXX reads that he "enslaved them." This variance in witnesses is clarified by verse 25, where the people proclaim that they will be "slaves for Pharaoh." It seems that the concept of slavery in Egypt can be attributed to Joseph, who implements a system of government that sanctioned forced labor for the entire population of Egypt. This may reflect a practice that was prevalent in the land during the annual flooding of the Nile, when agrarian life would have been halted and the displaced population would have been conscripted to work on government building projects. However it is imaged, the participation of the great patriarch Joseph in the development of the system that would subsequently imperil his own people is a crucial irony that cannot be overlooked. It is a reminder that the oppressive systems that people foster may well become the very systems that compromise the freedom of their posterity. This serves as a foreshadowing of the situation in which the descendants of Jacob will find themselves at the beginning of Exodus.

As Genesis 47 concludes, Jacob nears the end of his life. In anticipation of his death in verses 29-31, he asks Joseph to make a promise like the one Abram compelled his eldest servant to do in Gen. 24:2-4, to put his hand under his thigh and swear an oath. His desire is to be carried out of Egypt to be buried with his ancestors in Canaan; this promise is echoed in Gen. 49:29-32. Joseph brings his sons Ephraim and Manasseh to meet his father and is told by Jacob of God Almighty's promise that his descendants would possess the land of Canaan (Gen. 48:1-7). Afterward, Jacob blesses the two sons of Joseph and, as has become a recurrent theme in Genesis, reverses the primogeniture by offering the blessing of the elder son to Ephraim and the blessing of the younger to Manasseh, symbolically conveying the promises that should have gone to Manasseh to the younger Ephraim (Gen. 48:8-22).

After blessing each of his sons in Gen. 49:1-28, with a particularly meaningful blessing conveyed to the messianic line of Judah in verses 9-12, Jacob repeats his charge that his sons bury him with his ancestors in Canaan (vv. 29-32). Joseph thus leads a caravan of his family and Pharaoh's servants to the cave at Machpelah on the piece of land that Abraham purchased, and he buries his father Jacob there once he has been "gathered to [his] people" (v. 29). On their return to Egypt, the brothers, afraid of Joseph without the protection of their father, seek to preserve their lives by deceiving Joseph with a false request from Jacob that Joseph forgive them. They even volunteer themselves to Joseph as slaves (Gen. 50:18), further foreshadowing the book of Exodus. Not needing to be chided, however, Joseph again repeats the theological moral to the overall novella reflected in Gen. 45:7-8: "Though you planned evil against me, God planned it for good" (Gen. 50:20). The entire ordeal Joseph has endured is viewed through the lens of God's providence and is deemed a requisite step in the fulfillment of God's overall plan of salvation for the descendants of Israel.

As the narratives of Genesis draw to a close, God's providence is now evident to all as the deity has been revealed as the controller of the destinies of even the forlorn and forsaken and the redeemer of those who have been cast off and cast aside. God gives a wanderer like Abram the promise of a home; barren women like Sarah, Rebekah, and Rachel children; a murderer like Cain a protective mark; castaways like Hagar and Ishmael a nation; a trickster like Jacob who deceives all whom he encounters a good name; an arrogant upstart like Joseph transformed by years of suffering and humiliation the ability to forgive; and each of them one another as family members. In Genesis, the human family through its various travails of deception, jealousy, hatred, and even murder has been demonstrated to be resilient, reliable, and despite manifold fractures and failures, redeemable. Through each of the zeniths and nadirs of human existence, God's hand has been at work using each and every success and failure as a requisite part of God's larger plan.

In this regard, the Joseph novella provides the basis of a theology of hope for those desperately groping for God's hand in the midst of the overwhelming darkness that often attends human experience in a world shaped by human rebellion. As the book draws to a close in Genesis 50, it concludes with Joseph's prophetic pronouncement that "God will surely come to you, and bring you up out of this land to the land that he swore to Abraham, to Isaac, and to Jacob" (Gen. 50:24). Joseph's promise that God will take the people "up" is remarkably similar to the words that end the Hebrew Bible in 1 Chron. 36:23, predicting a time when the people will "go up" to Jerusalem. Perhaps this is not by accident. It is this confident portrayal of God's imminent return and deliverance that reminds the people to trust that YHWH, who has brought the people "thus far on the way," will lead them faithfully to the promised land. The providence that has been at work from the dawning of the world at the outset of creation to this point of the redemption of Joseph and his reconciliation with his brothers will sustain the sons of Israel no matter what obstacles they may, and soon will, face.

The Text in the Interpretive Tradition

In his assessment of Genesis 37, De La Torre compares Joseph the dreamer to Dr. Martin Luther King Jr. and suggests that dreamers' goals are to bring in a utopian order, overcoming present oppressive paradigms and promoting a more just and equitable society (De La Torre, 302–3). Elsewhere, the author has noted the similarity between Joseph's enslavement by his brothers and the experiences of enslaved Africans, who like Venture Smith were sold by their African "brothers" (Sadler 2010, 77). Brueggemann has suggested that the narrative may be a call to the listening community to let the dream be at work, even when its outcome is less than clear (Brueggemann, 293).

The story of Tamar and Judah in Genesis 38 has been variously understood as a narrative of a woman's empowerment and cunning that secures her a place in the familial line (Niditch, 41–43); as "one of the strangest and most ethically troubling" stories in Scripture in part because Tamar in the course of her narrative is involved in "sexual intercourse with her brother-in-law (v. 8), in coitus interruptus (onanism, v. 9), in prostitution (vv. 15-16), and in sexual intercourse with her father-in-law (vv. 24-26)" (Hiebert, 23–24); and as a story meant to decry masturbation as onanism, or the sin of Onan, who spilled his semen on the ground in order to avoid impregnating his brother's wife (De La Torre, 263). This rich account describes a woman's attempt to exercise autonomy over her own life and to shape her own future when the masculine forces in society have failed her.

There is an interesting interpretative tradition to Genesis 47 in the discussion of Joseph's role in the development of slavery in Egypt. For example, Sarna reads Gen. 47:21 as though Joseph took the population from the cities, reading with a problematic MT. Other commentators, following the choice of the NIV and the NRSV favoring the witness of the Samaritan Pentateuch and the Septuagint, read verse 21 as though Joseph produced the slavery that will eventually affect his own people (see Fretheim, 655). Brueggemann notes that Joseph "played the royal game and forgot the promise" by fostering an oppressive system in Egypt that will eventually enslave his own people (Brueggemann, 358).

The stories of Joseph's reconciliation with his brothers are a fitting way to close these narratives. They are the stories that epitomize the troubled human relationships that characterize our own brokenness as people in this world. They offer the promise that even after humanity's grossest acts of injustice, threats of murder, and manifestations of hatred, forgiveness and reconciliation are still possible. Thus Hiebert concludes, "Throughout the book of Genesis, these stories of conflict and resolution hold up the values of courage and compassion over those of accusation and retaliation" (Hiebert, 23). In the end, there is the promise of restored relationships with both God and our human siblings as God's providence offers redemption to all who may have fallen on hard times along the way.

The Text in Contemporary Discussion

We begin this final section of Genesis in chapter 37 with an account of the elevation of Joseph over his brothers. How does this narrative continue the theme of the disruption of primogeniture and the elevation of the youngest? Is there a connection with such disruption and the elevation of the youngest in this narrative with the story of the anointing of David (1 Samuel 16)? If so, what might the message of this account be? Is there an arrogance associated with Joseph at the beginning of this narrative that will be overcome at the end, and if so, how does this speak to his maturation as a character?

Genesis 38 presents an interesting narrative about levirate marriage. What benefit do you see for women under this paradigm? Who is its ultimate beneficiary, the women who are promised offspring and sustenance through marriage to a kinsman redeemer or the men who are ensured progeny and the perpetuation of land ownership? How is this narrative linked to the story of Joseph that surrounds it? Though contemporary interpreters may find the idea of levirate marriage distasteful and a remarkable imposition on both the surviving wife and the brother(s) of the deceased, what conventions for protecting the rights of young widows do we have in our society? Can we learn something from such narratives about the need to establish social systems to attend to the needs of those marginalized in our society?

There is a radical reversal of power dynamics in Genesis 39, as Joseph becomes victim to the sexual predation of Potiphar's wife. Does the presence of two narratives that explore the use of a woman's sexual prowess in the narrative offer a different perspective on the power of women in the ancient world? Are sexuality and sexual power the great equalizer for women in these narratives? How does the presence of such highly charged narratives where sexual manipulation is employed both positively and negatively serve as a challenge to traditional understandings of God's view of sex in our society?

The story of Joseph in Egypt unfolds over the next several chapters. How does Joseph's ascendancy from his nadir attest to the providence of God in his life? Though certainly a crafted narrative, what does the intervention of crises preceding the rise of Joseph say about the nature of the authors'/redactors' view of YHWH's redemptive activity? How might the message about God's providence in the Joseph novella serve as a catalyst for redemption in the lives of the oppressed and disenfranchised in our contexts?

Genesis 42–50 addresses the reconciliation between Joseph and his brothers and the fulfillment of his dream from Genesis 37. Joseph in these narratives becomes an exemplar for forgiveness and reconciliation, as he not only welcomes the brothers who have mistreated him to the sanctuary of Egypt but also assures that their needs are provided. In what way does this narrative serve as a rejoinder to that in Genesis 4 of the conflict between siblings? How could such a narrative address concepts of forgiveness between those whose transgressions have broken relationships in our contexts? What is the theology evident in these accounts of redeemed tragedies? Who is the God we meet in these accounts, and what are this God's attributes?

Perhaps the most disturbing aspect of this narrative is found in Genesis 47. Here the reader learns that as part of his national subsistence strategy for Egypt, Joseph buys the people and enslaves them to the house of Pharaoh. In essence, the narrative attributes the introduction of the corvée, or state-compelled labor, to Joseph. How does that alter our traditional understandings of Egyptian enslavement of the Hebrews? What does it say about the danger of developing oppressive paradigms that disenfranchise "others" in this world and how readily they can be turned against us? What lesson might the authors/editors want us to glean from this matter-of-fact reference to Joseph's fostering of a slavocracy in the precursor to the exodus narratives?

As we end this story, it is important to recognize whence this journey began and where it ends: from the creation of the world and the generality of a universal view of humanity to the land of Egypt and the specificity of a single man's (Israel's) family. It is clear that this focal family is the overarching concern of the authors/editors of these narratives and that these stories are told in a way that enhances their ends. How does this knowledge influence our understanding of the book of Genesis as a basis for the origins of the entire world and its people? What lessons does the reader learn about the nature of God here that can be used to apply to those outside of the purview of this family? How does this story of God's providence continue to prove useful for those in our contexts today?

Lest we forget, Genesis is a story that reaches its glorious conclusion precisely when its focal family is poised to enter slavery! It is a story the ultimate end of which is to lead its focal family to its narratological low point. But it is from this low point that its purpose is fulfilled, for without slavery there would have been no exodus; without tragic circumstances that led Joseph himself to institute systemic slavery in Egypt, his family would never have needed fully to trust YHWH, and they might never have known that their God was faithful to deliver them. As we struggle with the manifold crises that threaten to undo our collective human family, it is important to recognize that even in our darkest hours, God's providence is at work redeeming the world and providing a yet unseen path to a place of promise. This is a necessary message in an uncertain age. This is the message of Genesis.

Works Cited

Bailey, Randall C. 1995. "They're Nothing but Incestuous Bastards: Polemical Use of Sex and Sexuality in Hebrew Canon Narrative." In *Reading from This Place*. Vol. 1, *Social Context and Biblical Interpretation in the United States*, edited by Fernando Segovia and Mary Ann Tolbert, 121–38. Minneapolis: Fortress Press.

Bellis, Alice Ogden. 1994. *Helpmates, Harlots, Heroes: Women's Stories in the Hebrew Bible*. Louisville: Westminster John Knox.

Bellis, Alice Ogden, and Terry L. Hufford. 2002. *Science, Scripture, and Homosexuality*. Cleveland: Pilgrim.

Brueggemann, Walter. 1982. *Genesis*. IBC. Atlanta: John Knox.

Campbell, Antony F., and Mark A. O'Brien. 1993. *Sources of the Pentateuch: Texts, Introductions, Annotations*. Minneapolis: Fortress Press.

Dalley, Stephanie. 1989. *Myths from Mesopotamia: Creation, the Flood, Gilgamesh, and Others*. New York: Oxford University Press.

De La Torre, Miguel. 2011. *Genesis*. Belief: A Theological Commentary on the Bible. Louisville: Westminster John Knox.

Fretheim, Terence E. 1994. "Book of Genesis." In *The New Interpreter's Bible*. Vol. 1, *Genesis–Leviticus*, edited by Leander E. Keck. Nashville: Abingdon.

Gagnon, Robert A. J., 2001. *Bible and Homosexual Practice*. Nashville: Abingdon.

Haynes, Stephen. 2002. *Noah's Curse: The Biblical Justification of American Slavery*. New York: Oxford University Press.

Hiebert, Theodore. 2009. "Genesis." In *Theological Bible Commentary*, edited by Gail R. O'Day and David L. Petersen, 3–25. Louisville: Westminster John Knox.

Hubner, Ulrich. 1992. "Idumea." In *ABD* 3:382–83.

James, Elaine. 2012. "Sarah, Hagar, and Their Interpreters." In *Women's Bible Commentary*, edited by Carol A. Newsome, Sharon H. Ringe, and Jacqueline E. Lapsley, 51–55. 3rd ed. Louisville: Westminster John Knox.

Katzenstein, H. J. 1992. "Philistines." In *ABD* 5:326–28.

King, Martin Luther, Jr. 1986. "A Christmas Sermon on Peace." In *A Testament of Hope: The Essential Writings and Speeches of Martin Luther King, Jr.*, edited by James M. Washington, 253–58. San Francisco: HarperSanFrancisco.

Lemche, Niels Peter. 1992. "Hebrew." In *ABD* 3:95.

Louth, Andrew, ed. 2001. *Genesis 1–11*. Ancient Christian Commentary on Scripture, Old Testament 1. Downers Grove, IL: InterVarsity Press.

McClenney-Sadler, Madeline Gay. 2007. *Recovering the Daughter's Nakedness: A Formal Analysis of Israelite Kinship Terminology and the Internal Logic of Leviticus 18*. New York: T&T Clark.

Meyers, Carol. 1988. *Discovering Eve: Ancient Israelite Women in Context.* Oxford University Press.

Niditch, Susan. 2012. "Genesis." In *Women's Bible Commentary*, edited by Carol A. Newsome, Sharon H. Ringe, and Jacqueline E. Lapsley, 27–45. 3rd ed. Louisville: Westminster John Knox.

Rad, Gerhard von. 1972. *Genesis.* OTL. Rev. ed. Philadelphia: Westminster.

Sadler, Rodney S., Jr. 2005. *Can A Cushite Change His Skin? An Examination of Race, Ethnicity, and Othering in the Hebrew Bible.* New York: T&T Clark.

———. 2006. "Can a Cushite Change His Skin? Cushites, Racial Othering, and the Hebrew Bible." *Int* 60, no. 4:386–403.

———. 2010. "Genesis." In *The Africana Bible: Reading Israel's Scriptures from Africa and the African Diaspora*, edited by Hugh R. Page Jr., 70–79. Minneapolis: Fortress Press.

Sarna, Nahum M. 1989. *Genesis.* JPS Torah Commentary. Philadelphia: Jewish Publication Society.

Scholz, Susanne. 2012. "Judges." In *Women's Bible Commentary*, edited by Carol A. Newsome, Sharon H. Ringe, and Jacqueline E. Lapsley, 113–27. 3rd ed. Louisville: Westminster John Knox.

Seow, Choon-Leong. "Textual Orientation." In *Biblical Ethics and Homosexuality*, edited by Robert L. Brawley, 17–34. Louisville: Westminster John Knox.

Sheridan, Mark, ed. 2002. *Genesis 12–50.* Ancient Christian Commentary on Scripture, Old Testament 2. Downers Grove, IL: InterVarsity Press.

Smith, Mark S. 1990. *The Early History of God: YAHWEH and the Other Deities in Ancient Israel.* San Francisco: HarperSanFrancisco.

Turner, Bishop Henry McNeal. 1998. "Justice or Emigration." In *Lift Every Voice: African American Oratory 1787–1900*, edited by Philip S. Foner and Robert James Branham, 775–90. Tuscaloosa: University of Alabama Press.

Wink, Walter. 2005. *Homosexuality and the Bible.* Nyack, NY: Fellowship Press.

EXODUS

Thomas B. Dozeman

Introduction

Name of the Book and Location in the Canon

Exodus is the second book in the Hebrew Bible. It is one of five books that make up the Torah ("law") or Pentateuch (Greek for "five books"). The title, Exodus, derives from the Greek version of the Hebrew Bible known as the Septuagint (LXX): "Exodus from Egypt." Though the Septuagint title is the more common in English translations, in Jewish tradition, the title consists of the opening words of the book: "And these are the names." The name Exodus emphasizes Israel's departure from Egypt and their salvation from slave labor, the central event in the first half of the book, but it does not adequately describe the content of the entire book, which includes stories of Israel's initial wilderness journey as well as the revelation of the law and the tabernacle sanctuary at Mount Sinai.

The five books of Torah functioned as authoritative revelation for Jews already in the Second Temple period (516 BCE–70 CE). The combination of the five books of Genesis, Exodus, Leviticus, Numbers, and Deuteronomy suggests a close relationship among them. Upon first reading, the narrative sequence in the Torah appears to flow seamlessly. The account of creation and the ancestors (Genesis) brings the family of Jacob to Egypt, setting the stage for the liberation of the Israelites from Egypt (Exodus). The exodus from Egypt launches the nation on a wilderness journey, in which the people encounter God at the divine mountain, receive the law, and construct the sanctuary (Exodus, Leviticus, Numbers). The story concludes with Moses recounting the events from Genesis–Numbers (Deuteronomy), before he dies at the end of the book of Deuteronomy.

Authorship, Date, and Literary History

Exodus is an anthology of liturgy, law, and epic lore from many different periods of Israel's history. The author of Exodus is not explicitly stated, though tradition, including Jewish Hellenistic, rabbinic, and early Christian writings, has assigned the authorship of the book of Exodus and the entire Pentateuch to Moses. Philo, a Hellenistic Jewish author writing in the first century of the Common Era, writes in his commentary on creation, "Moses says . . . 'In the beginning God created the heaven and the earth'" (*Opif.* 26). Josephus also asserts that Moses authored the first five books (*Ag. Ap.* 1.37–40). The rabbis too state, "Moses wrote his own book" (*b. B. Bat.* 14b) and attribute to it divine origins (*b. Sanh.* 99a). Early Christian writers express a similar perspective. The apostle Paul refers to the Pentateuch as the "law of Moses" (1 Cor. 9:9). The author of the Gospel of Luke expresses the same thought, indicating the Pentateuch by simple reference to its author "Moses" (Luke 24:27), later describing it as the "law of Moses" (Luke 24:44).

The historical-critical study of the Pentateuch in the modern era has clarified that neither Moses nor any single author wrote Exodus. The identification of the anonymous authors, the time of their composition, and the method by which the literature was combined into a single narrative have dominated the interpretation of Exodus in the modern period. The central theory in the past century concerning the anonymous authorship of the book of Exodus has been the Documentary Hypothesis. It has provided biblical scholars with a model for identifying three anonymous authors in the composition of Exodus: the Yahwist (J), the Elohist (E), and the Priestly writer (P). The Yahwist and the Elohist composed their work during the monarchical period, while the Priestly author wrote during the exilic or postexilic period. The work of each author is not confined to the book of Exodus, but extends throughout the Tetrateuch (Genesis, Exodus, Leviticus, Numbers). The three authors of Exodus are evident where the same story (repetition) is told from different points of view or with different plot lines (contradiction). Examples include the two names for the mountain of God (Sinai in Exodus 19 and 24; and Horeb in Exodus 33), the two stories of the revelation of the divine name, YHWH (Exodus 3 and 6), several interpretations of the conflict at the Red Sea (Exodus 14–15), divergent law codes (Exodus 20 and Deuteronomy 5), and different accounts of the appropriate sanctuary (the tent of meeting in Exodus 33, and the tabernacle in Exodus 25–31, 35–40). These and many other repetitions confirm the existence of several anonymous authors of Exodus, with divergent views of God, community, and worship. Recent scholars, however, debate whether the Documentary Hypothesis is an adequate model for understanding the book of Exodus, preferring to distinguish simply between Priestly and non-Priestly literature, as compositions from the exilic and postexilic periods.

Historical Context

A central question in the modern interpretation of Exodus is what historical events may have given rise to the elaborate narrative of the book of Exodus. The biblical writers certainly wish to anchor the exodus from Egypt firmly in history. They date the event to the 2666th year (Exod. 12:40-41) from the creation of the world, or year 1 (Gen. 1:26-27). The construction of the tabernacle takes place in the 2667th year (Exod. 40:1-2, 17). Biblical writers state further that the Israelite period of enslavement is 430 years (Exod. 12:40-41), making their arrival in Egypt the 2236th year (Gen. 47:9). Jacob and his family settle in a specific land within Egypt, Goshen (Gen. 46:28; Exod. 8:22; 9:26), also known as the "land of Rameses" (Gen. 47:11). When the Israelites' guest status in Egypt turns into slavery, they are forced to build, according to the MT (the Masoretic text), the cities of Pithom and Rameses (Exod. 1:11; the LXX adds the city of On). During this time, moreover, the Israelite population grows from the original family of Jacob to a nation of 600,000 men (Exod. 12:37), making the total number of those leaving Egypt (including women and children) approximately 2–3 million persons, not counting the mixed multitude that accompanied them upon their leaving (Exod. 12:38).

The specific dates for the exodus, along with the careful numbering of the people, encourage a historical interpretation of the story. But the vague references to geography and the unrealistic number of the group indicate that the book of Exodus is not history. Goshen has not been clearly identified in the delta region of Egypt. Two to three million people in the Sinai desert would have overwhelmed the fragile environment. The internal problems of dating and geography further suggest that the book of Exodus is not history, but legendary literature. Research on the history of an Israelite exodus from Egypt has branched out from the book of Exodus to include the broader study of archaeology and of ancient Near Eastern literature, separating the book even further from a historical interpretation. There is no evidence that the Israelites dwelled in Egypt or that they escaped from slave labor, apart from Egyptian sources that provide information on slave laborers described as *'apiru*—a term some scholars associate with the word "Hebrew" (*Egyptian Papyrus Leiden* 348).

The Israelites are identified in the Egyptian records in the Merneptah Stele, composed during the fifth year of Merneptah's rule (approx. 1208 BCE). In describing his military successes, Merneptah writes: "Canaan has been plundered into every sort of woe; Ashkelon has been overcome; Gezer has been captured. Yano'am was made nonexistent; Israel is laid waste, his seed is not" (*ANET* 378). The Egyptian writing indicates that the middle three references (Ashkelon, Gezer, and Yano'am) are cities, and that the term "Israel" refers to a people, not a city or a particular place. The Merneptah Stele indicates that an "Israelite" people could be identified in some way already in the thirteenth century BCE. But the evidence tends to argue against the exodus from Egypt, since Israel appears to be an indigenous group within Canaan who were the object of Egyptian conquest.

The story of the defeat of Pharaoh and of his army in the Red Sea is a cultic legend that spoke to an ongoing political reality in the life of Israel. Egyptian rule loomed large in Israel's life from her earliest years, and it continued throughout her political history, giving the legend of the exodus from Egypt immediacy and continuing religious significance. The ancient Israelite writers, moreover, were also familiar with Egyptian customs and practices, further underscoring the influence of Egyptian culture and politics on their life in Canaan. Egyptian language influences the book of Exodus in small details and in large events. The name "Moses" (*mosheh*), for example, derives from the Egyptian word *msi*, a common theophoric element in proper names, meaning "son." The word appears on such names as Thut*mose*, "son of Thut," or Ptah*mose*, "son of Ptah." The "bulrush" (*gome*) in which Moses is placed in Exod. 2:3 may derive from the Egyptian word "papyrus" (*g/kmy*). Even the plagues may be polemical actions against Egyptian gods, including Hapi, the god of the Nile, Osiris, the god of the dead, and Re, the sun god.

The influence of Egyptian culture on ancient Israelite writers may reach back to an experience of oppression in Egypt itself, but it need not. The reference to Pithom as one of the cities built by the

Israelites may provide historical background for dating the composition of the story of the Exodus. Donald Redford noted that the name Pithom does not appear in hieroglyphic writing as a specific reference to a town until after 600 BCE. This historical insight would place the author of Exodus in the late exilic period at the earliest (1982, Cols. 1054–58).

Structure and Contents

The book of Exodus probes two central themes concerning YHWH, the God of Israel: the character of divine power and the nature of divine presence in this world. Although the two themes are interwoven throughout the entire book, each takes prominence at different stages in the story, allowing for a loose division in the outline of the book of Exodus. The theme of divine power is explored, for the most part, in the setting of the land of Egypt (Exod. 1:1—15:21). The theme of divine presence is developed in the setting of the wilderness, as Israel journeys with God from Egypt to the promised land of Canaan (Exod. 15:22–40:38).

Exodus 1:1—15:21 narrates the conflict between YHWH and Pharaoh over the fate of Israel. It is an epic battle between kings and gods. The weapons of war are the forces of nature. YHWH summons reptiles, insects, and meteorological elements, including hail and darkness, in an initial assault on Pharaoh (Exodus 7–10). When these elements fail to persuade Pharaoh to release Israel from Egyptian slavery, the personification of death itself, described as "the destroyer," descends on the land of Egypt in the darkness of midnight, slaying all Egyptian firstborn children and animals (Exodus 11–12). Even the plague of death does not dissuade Pharaoh from continuing the conflict. During the night, he musters his army one last time and pursues the fleeing Israelites to the Red Sea (Exodus 13), where YHWH destroys him at dawn, this time using the sea itself as a weapon (Exodus 14). The hymns in Exodus 15 look back over the battlefield and confirm the power of God, praising YHWH as a warrior God who possesses power over Pharaoh and over all the forces of nature.

Exod. 15:22—40:38 describes the ways in which YHWH is able to be present with Israel in this world as they journey toward the promised land. The story is also told on an epic scale. The forces of nature change their role from providing YHWH with weapons of war to signaling the presence of God with Israel. God purifies polluted water for Israel (Exod. 15:22-27). The miracles of water from the rock (Exod. 17:1-7) and manna (Exodus 16) save Israel from starvation. Advice by Jethro, Moses' father-in-law, about worship and government (Exodus 18) provides a transition from the initial wilderness journey to the revelation of the law and the sanctuary on Mount Sinai. Exodus 19–24 describes YHWH's descent on Mount Sinai to reveal covenantal law to the Israelites. Natural forces like thunder, lightning, darkness, and fire signal the nearness of God to Israel and the danger of divine holiness. The need for cultic safeguards results in the revelation of the blueprints for the tabernacle (Exodus 25–31). Construction of the tabernacle holds promise for a divine descent from the mountain into the midst of the Israelite camp. But the process is halted when Israel worships the golden calf (Exodus 32). As a result, the story must begin anew, if it is to continue at all. God forgives Israel (Exod. 34:1-10), issues new laws for covenant renewal (Exod. 34:11-29), and commissions the building of the tabernacle (Exodus 35–40). The book of Exodus ends with YHWH finally descending from Mount Sinai and entering the completed tabernacle on New Year's Day (Exod. 40:1-2, 17), filling the sanctuary with fire and smoke (Exod. 40:34-38).

Reception History

The events in the book of Exodus have been the source of ongoing interpretation from the time of the ancient Israelites to the present. The process of interpretation begins already in the book of Exodus. The Song of Miriam (Exod. 15:21) and the theophany of God on the Mountain (Exod. 19:16-17) are likely early versions of the exodus and the revelation of YHWH on the mountain that were reinterpreted in the formation of the book of Exodus. But reinterpretation is not confined to the book of Exodus. The story of the exodus is also interpreted throughout the Hebrew Bible. The prophet Hosea, for example, interprets the exodus from Egypt as the result of prophetic leadership (Hosea 12:13). The exilic prophet Second Isaiah explores the mythical meaning of salvation from Egypt as a defeat of the sea monster (Isa. 51:9-11), while the prophet Ezekiel views Israel's wilderness journey negatively, as a time of idolatry (Ezekiel 20). The events in the book of Exodus thread their way through the entire Hebrew Bible.

The book of Exodus has also been influential in shaping the broader history of Judaism and Christianity. Jewish writers like Josephus and Philo of Alexandria reinterpreted the exodus and the life of Moses to a Hellenistic culture. Philo describes the tutoring of Moses in arithmetic and geometry by the Greeks (*Life of Moses* 1.21–23). Hecataeus of Abdera interprets the exodus as an expulsion of foreigners from Egypt to Greece, whose leader was Moses. The group founded colonies, one of which was Jerusalem (*Diodorus Siculus* 40.3.1–8.). New Testament writers explore the meaning of Jesus' ministry and passion within the framework of the exodus. Jesus is called out of Egypt (Matt. 2:15), undergoes testing in the wilderness (Luke 4:1-12), and becomes the Paschal Lamb (John 19:36), while Paul identifies the early Christians also with the wilderness generation of Israelites (1 Cor. 10:1-13). The Passover haggadah, or guide to the Passover celebration, continues to propel the events of the exodus through time, interpreting the exodus to new generations of Jewish worshipers.

The exodus also provides a resource for social criticism in contemporary biblical interpretation. Liberation theologians use the exodus as a resource for oppressed people to struggle for liberation from modern tyrants who oppress and repress them as the Pharaoh did the Hebrews. Feminists look to the exodus for models of resistance to power in such female characters as Miriam or the midwives. Postcolonialist interpreters expose the oppressive side of the exodus mythology, in which the promise of land through conquest has provided religious justification for unjust land claims throughout the colonial period to the present time.

Exodus 1:1—2:25: Divine Promise and Human Oppression

Exodus 1–2 describes the process by which the Israelites are enslaved in Egypt, setting the stage for a story of salvation as act of divine liberation. But God is absent as an active force in the life of the Israelites during their enslavement and genocide of infant males at the hands of Pharaoh.

This absence of God in Exodus 1–2 allows the biblical writers to explore the themes of power and oppression from a human perspective. The story moves quickly. Years have transpired since Joseph ruled in the land of Egypt, and the Israelites' guest status has long been forgotten. A series of vignettes provides insight into the growing alienation between the Egyptians and the Israelites, prompting a range of human responses, including fear of Pharaoh and his oppression of the Israelites, the civil disobedience of the midwives against Pharaoh's command for genocide (1:1-21), and the violence of Moses' initial attempt at liberation, when he kills an Egyptian (1:22—2:25).

Exodus 1:1-21: The Midwives and Civil Disobedience

The Text in Its Ancient Context

The section separates into two episodes: the fertility of the Israelites in 1:1-7, which threatens Pharaoh and leads to his oppression in 1:8-21. The first episode, 1:1-7, paints a bleak picture of death and social alienation. Verse 6 recounts the death of Joseph, his brothers, and the entire generation. A similar account occurs in Judg. 2:10, where the death of Joshua's generation signifies the breakdown of tradition and memory, with the result that the generation after Joshua loses all knowledge of their past, including the salvation of God. The same meaning is likely intended in Exodus with the death of Joseph's generation. The Israelites and Pharaoh have forgotten the story of the guest status of the family of Jacob in Egypt and the role of Joseph in saving the Egyptians from starvation. Thus the book of Exodus begins without the memory of the God of the ancestors or the past social hospitality shown between the Egyptians and the Israelites. This loss of memory leads to fear and alienation. A new Pharaoh mistrusts the Israelites, who are "fruitful and prolific" (1:7). The language of fertility ties the opening of Exodus to the account of creation in Genesis 1, signaling the indirect presence of God in the story as the creator of all humans, even though YHWH, the God of Israel, is not active in Exodus 1–2.

In 1:8-21, Pharaoh and the midwives provide conflicting responses to the Israelites' fertility, responses that lead to different ethical actions. Pharaoh reacts with fear over losing power (1:9-10). To safeguard his power over Israel, Pharaoh institutes forced labor (1:11-14). But when slave labor does not curtail the birthrate of the Israelites, he secretly commands the genocide of all male babies (1:15-16). Pharaoh's fear forces him to distinguish between "his people" and "the Israelites" in order to maintain social control. Social alienation spirals out of control, leading to oppression and genocide.

The midwives Shiphrah and Puah resist the abusive power of Pharaoh though civil disobedience. Their conflict with Pharaoh is developed through a play on the motifs "to see" and "to fear," words that often sound similar in Hebrew. Pharaoh secretly instructs the midwives to kill every male Hebrew child that they "see" born on the birthstones (1:16). But the narrator tells the reader that the midwives "fear" God, prompting their civil disobedience; they allow the male babies of the Israelite women to live. The midwives' "fear of the God" is a generic description of the deity not intended to be a statement about formal religious practice but to position conscience against the tyranny of Pharaoh, thus raising the question: Will the midwives conform to the command of Pharaoh and act on what they "see," namely, the birth of Hebrew male babies condemned to death by the state? Or will they follow their conscience and act on their "fear of the God," thus letting the babies live?

The midwives follow their conscience and undertake civil disobedience. They allow the male babies to live (1:17), and they lie to account for their actions (1:18-19). When Pharaoh inquires why his order of genocide is not being executed, the midwives play on his fear, accentuating the difference between the Egyptians and the Israelites that was introduced by Pharaoh. They state: "The Hebrew women are not like the Egyptian women" (v. 19a). Then the midwives play on Pharaoh's more primordial fear, the explosive population growth of the Israelite: "[The Israelite women] are teeming with life, and before the midwife comes to them, they give birth" (author trans., v. 19b).

The Text in the Interpretive Tradition

Interpreters have struggled to discern the identity of the midwives and to evaluate the ethical implications of their civil obedience, which required not only that they oppose the power of Pharaoh but also that they lie. The interpretations vary widely, often reflecting the social and religious context of the community. The Talmud, for example, identifies the midwives as Hebrews, even equating Shiphrah with Moses' mother, Jochebed, and Puah with Miriam (*b. Sotah* 11b). The resistance of the midwives—including their lying to Pharaoh—is heroic, for they risk their lives to save the people of Israel. Writing in the Greco-Roman context, Josephus identifies the midwives as Egyptians, not Hebrews, while still interpreting their actions heroically (*Ant.* 2.206). Nehama Leibowitz underscores the universal application of the story. All humans possess the fear of God, so that even a gentile who does not act on his or her conscience against tyranny and genocide is a traitor to the most elementary obligation of a human being (1:35). But not all agree. John Calvin, for example, condemns the lying of the midwives as sin, which illustrates that all human actions—even those aimed at saving infants—contain mixed motives, requiring divine grace for purification (1950, 34–36).

The Text in Contemporary Discussion

The interpretation of women characters like the midwives in the patriarchal world of biblical literature is an ongoing challenge for contemporary readers. Too often in biblical texts, women are stereotyped in domestic roles, where their status is tied to reproduction, usually of male characters (Fuchs, 311; Steinberg, 174–75). Feminist critics have sought to recover a more prominent role of women in the opening chapters of Exodus by shifting the focus of the identity of the midwives from ethnicity to gender in evaluating their actions. As a result, the midwives model neither the heroic action of Hebrews nor the universal conscience of all humans, but the courage of women to oppose patriarchal oppression represented by Pharaoh. The midwives, whether Hebrew or Egyptian, are tricksters who thwart the evil command of Pharaoh. Had Pharaoh known their cunning, he would have commanded all infant females to be killed (Trible 1973, 34). "Their clever response to Pharaoh is not a lie; they simply do not tell the whole truth . . . a conventional weapon of the powerless, especially women in the Old Testament" (Weems, 29). Not only are they cunning, but the midwives also embody the theme of birth in the book of Exodus. "They are the first to assist in the birth of the Israelite nation" (Setel, 30). In contemporary feminist interpretation, the resistance of the midwives is a window into the heroic role of women throughout the opening chapters of the book of Exodus. The book begins with a focus on women, including the mother and sister of Moses and the daughter of Pharaoh. They defy oppression, give life, and model wisdom. And their actions determine the outcome of events (Exum, 82).

Exodus 1:22—2:25: Identity of Moses and Human Lament

The Text in Its Ancient Context

There is a change in perspective between Exod. 1:1-21 and 1:22—2:25. The fertility of the Israelites is a central but abstract theme in the first episode; the narrative is broad in scope, giving a panoramic perspective on the whole nation of the Israelite people. While the theme of fertility continues in Exod. 1:22—2:25, the lens narrows to a single Levitical Israelite family, telling a more intimate story of the birth of one child, Moses. The liberator of the Israelite people is born during the height of Pharaoh's oppression of the Israelites, in which all the Egyptians are called on publicly to kill the Hebrew male babies. The introduction of Moses includes the account of his birth, rescue from the Nile River, and adoption by the daughter of Pharaoh (Exod. 1:22—2:10) and two stories that probe his identity as a liberator, the act of murder in Egypt (Exod. 2:11-15a) and the rescue of Reuel's daughters in Midian (Exod. 2:15b-22).

The birth and rescue of Moses in Exod. 1:22—2:10 conforms to a common legend in the ancient Near East, in which a hero is abandoned, set adrift in water, and eventually adopted. The most striking parallel to the story of Moses is The Legend of Sargon (*ANET* 119), a Neo-Assyrian account from the eighth or seventh century BCE about the birth of Sargon the Great, who founded the dynasty of Akkad in the late third millennium. In this story, Sargon is the child of a priestess prohibited from conceiving a child. She disobeys, conceives Sargon in secret, and floats the baby on the river in a vessel of reeds. Sargon is rescued from the river and adopted by Akki, the water drawer, who raises him as a gardener, before Sargon becomes king of Akkad. The motifs of abandonment and adoption accentuate the mysterious origin of Sargon, while his humble beginnings are meant to idealize the identity of any king in Mesopotamian tradition. The ideal is that a king does not rise to power through privilege but through heroic deeds. The parallels between The Legend of Sargon and Moses' birth story include anonymous parents from the priestly class, an illegal if not illegitimate birth, a river ordeal, rescue, adoption, the protection of women, and an emphasis on the heroic deeds of Moses to establish his identity. The similarities indicate that the author of Exodus wishes to explore the identity of Moses.

The departure from the heroic pattern in the birth story of Moses provides the point of view for interpreting the theme of Moses' identity as a liberator. The expected pattern of the heroic legend is a rags-to-riches story, in which the hero progresses from the threat of death and anonymity to public leadership. The structure of Moses' birth story is inverted. Moses is indeed exalted into the family of Pharaoh, but only momentarily before he returns to the status of a hunted slave, when Pharaoh seeks his life (2:15). Many interpret the inverted structure against the backdrop of Israelite slavery and the need for Moses to become a liberator of slaves.

The identity of Moses as a liberator is explored further through his actions in the first two stories of his adult life, where acts of liberation lead to the opposite outcomes of murder (2:11-15a) and of the rescue of the oppressed (2:15b-22). The story of Moses in Exod. 2:11-15a is a tale of failed leadership. The story moves quickly. Exodus 2:11-12 narrates Moses' murder of an Egyptian. The scene is told from Moses' point of view, and the narrator identifies him as an Israelite. When venturing out one day, Moses sees the "forced labor of the Israelites (1:11; 2:11), recalling the initial act of slave labor by Pharaoh. After ensuring secrecy, Moses kills the Egyptian and buries the corpse to conceal the secret murder. Although Moses seeks to liberate Hebrews, the violent murder, performed in secret, recalls the private instructions of Pharaoh to the midwives.

Exodus 2:13-14a, told from the point of view of the Hebrews, recounts Moses' initial encounter with Israelites. Moses sees two Hebrews struggling, and he addresses one of the men with the words, "Why do you strike your fellow Hebrew?" The Hebrew questions the authority of Moses, revealing that he knows Moses is no more than a murderer: "Do you mean to kill me as you killed the Egyptian?" Whatever moral authority Moses had hoped to convey as a liberator disappears when the Hebrew slave reveals that Moses is a murderer.

Exodus 2:14b-15a concludes the tale with Moses' realization that his secret act of murder is now public information, which changes his behavior from a moral mediator for others to a fearful fugitive seeking to escape from Pharaoh. Yet, once Moses escapes from Egypt, he acts again as a liberator in the southern desert location of Midian (2:15b-22), when he rescues the daughters of Jethro, the Midianite priest, from their oppressors at the water well, who seek to drive the women away from the source of water.

The two stories of Moses' early adult life highlight different aspects of his innate ability as a liberator. In the first story, Moses sees oppression and initiated liberation by killing an Egyptian. Although intended as justice, the act is described as murder. At the water well in Midian, Moses sees another act of oppression. The words describing Moses' act of liberation in Midian emphasize life, not death. He "saves" the women (2:17). In contrast to the Hebrew man who called Moses a "killer," the daughters describe his action as a "rescue," even though they identify him as an Egyptian, not a Hebrew (2:19).

The Text in the Interpretive Tradition

The killing of the Egyptian has prompted interpreters to discern more carefully the motive of Moses as a liberator, especially in the phrase, "he turned thus and thus." Interpreters debate whether the phrase is meant to idealize Moses as a liberator or to criticize him as a failed leader. The *Mekilta* states that the phrase indicates Moses' complete devotion to the Israelites (*Mekilta Shirata* 1.35–64). In *The Legends of the Jews*, Louis Ginzberg recounts another reading where the phrase "he turned thus and thus" indicates Moses' quest for justice. When none is forthcoming he decides to act himself, but not before consulting the angels. Only then does Moses kill the Egyptian by pronouncing the divine name (2:277–82). For Calvin, the act of "turning thus and thus" indicates hesitation on the part of Moses to risk his security in an act of divinely appointed deliverance. The hesitation is a sign of weak faith, requiring divine mercy (1950, 46–50). Philo stresses Moses' control of his emotions, his tight rein on his passions, and the power of reason guiding his actions. The killing of the Egyptian is a deliberate and just action by Moses. It is a "righteous deed," because "one who lived to destroy men should himself be destroyed" (*Mos.* 1.40–44, Philo 1954). Stephen echoes the same interpretation in Acts 7:23-29. Hebrews 11:23-28 omits the killing altogether, focusing instead on Moses' choice to give up wealth and status in order to take on the suffering of the Israelites. The *Midrash of the Passing of Moses* provides a more critical interpretation, stating that Moses' request not to die is denied him because of his slaying of the Egyptian (Leibowitz, 1:44–46).

The Text in Contemporary Discussion

Contemporary interpreters continue to reflect critically on the ambiguous nature of liberation, whether it is a force to save or to destroy. Writing from a liberationist point of view, George Pixley rightly notes that Exodus 1–2 deals with oppression and liberation. The account of Moses' killing the Egyptian is a story of social class and the coming-to-consciousness of the central character when he sees the mistreatment of a peasant slave. The episode "shows the character of Moses as a man of the upper class who sees, understands, and rejects the suffering of the people of Egypt. He thus proves to be a person whom God can trust to lead his people out of Egypt into freedom" (154–55). Gale Yee counters, however, from a postcolonial perspective, that the story of Moses' act of liberation in killing the Egyptian, and even the larger narrative of the exodus from Egypt as an event of liberation, cannot be read in isolation from the story of Israel's "conquest" of Canaan. In this case, murder as liberation can legitimate a whole range of violent acts of social and political expansion. "This double-sidedness [of liberation] should raise a red flag regarding any reading that enlists the Bible to support its cause" (231).

Exodus 3:1—7:7: The Commission of Moses

The Text in Its Ancient Context

This section of Exodus explores the religious experience of Moses through a series of divine encounters. Twice Moses receives special revelations of his divine commission as a liberator, which repeat many similar themes in two distinct locations: Exod. 3:1—4:17 takes place in the desert at the mountain of God, when Moses stumbles on the burning bush while shepherding his animals; and Exod. 6:1—7:7 occurs in Egypt, after Moses initially fails to free the Israelite people. Exod. 4:17—5:23 links the two stories of divine revelation; it recounts the journey of Moses and his wife Zipporah from Midian to Egypt in order to fulfill the divine commission. This episode, however, contains a third divine encounter that moves in a very different direction from the two commissions. Rather than singling out Moses as the liberator, YHWH tries to kill either Moses or Gershom, his son, in an attack during the night, in which Zipporah, the Midianite, plays the leading role of rescuer. The three divine encounters examine the nature of special revelation and religious experience from distinct perspectives.

The two commissions of Moses single him out as a uniquely chosen liberator, while also highlighting the special status of the Israelites as YHWH's chosen people, who are distinct from all other humans by special divine favor. God reveals the divine name YHWH to Moses (Exod. 3:6; 6:2). God acknowledges a special relationship with Moses as the God of his father (Exod. 3:6), who created a covenant with his ancestors (Exod. 6:4). God promises to be with Moses in a unique and intimate way (Exod. 3:12; 7:1), and clarifies that the commission of Moses as liberator is because YHWH also has a special relationship with Israel (Exod. 3:7-8; 6:5-8). The special revelation separates Moses from Pharaoh as God's chosen messenger (Exod. 3:9; 7:1) and the Israelite people from the Egyptians and all other nations (Exod. 3:8; 6:7-8). The two commissions provide the foundation for the development of Israelite religion in the wilderness. The central themes emphasize the character of YHWH as a compassionate liberator of the Israelites, sharing in the experience of suffering and seeking their welfare by protecting from oppression, rescuing from slavery, and giving them land.

The appearance of YHWH in the attack during the night moves in the opposite direction from the two commissions of Moses. It is not about security, divine compassion, or the ability of God to share in the suffering of the Israelites. Instead, the encounter with YHWH represents the threat of death. The literary context of the divine attack (Exod. 4:24-26) is the journey of Moses, Zipporah, and their son Gershom from the land of Midian to Egypt in order to fulfill the commission of Moses (Exod. 4:18—5:23). The section begins in a positive manner, with Jethro, the father-in-law of Moses, blessing him at the outset of the journey (Exod. 4:18-20) and with YHWH providing instructions to Moses about what he is to do upon reaching Egypt and reaffirming the special status of the Israelites as God's firstborn son (Exod. 4:21-23). But then the story takes a dark turn when the family of Moses rests for the night (Exod. 4:24-26).

The newly proclaimed kinship tie between YHWH and the Israelites as the firstborn son of God (Exod. 4:21-23) is acted out in a negative way in Exod. 4:24-26, when YHWH seeks to kill one of the male family members. It is unclear whom YHWH is attacking during the night, the son or Moses. The attack may represent YHWH's claim on the firstborn, or it may result from the absence of either Moses' or his son's circumcision. In either case, Zipporah stops the attack by circumcising her son and warding off the deity with the bloody foreskin, stating: "Truly you are a bridegroom of blood to me!" (Exod. 4:25). Zipporah likely claims some form of familial relationship with YHWH. Noteworthy in the context of the stories about the special revelation to Moses is that the Midianite Zipporah, and not Moses, performs the proper ritual to appease the deity and to protect her family. The heroic role of the midwives, who feared God more than Pharaoh, already suggested the theme of YHWH's relationship to humanity in general, even though the story of the exodus accentuates the special status of Moses and the Israelites. The story of Zipporah advances the theme beyond the midwives' general fear of God. She possesses special ritual knowledge that saves Moses from the divine attack in the wilderness and allows him to fulfill his divine commission.

The Text in the Interpretive Tradition

Moses' three encounters with God in Exod. 3:1—7:7 have given rise to wide-ranging reflection on the nature of revelation. Interpreters have sought to identify more clearly the divine in the burning bush to provide insight into the nature of revelation within organized religious practice. The rabbis, for example, state that the divine presence in the bush is the Shekinah (*b. Sotah* 5a). Gregory of Nyssa identifies the burning bush with the Virgin Mary, explaining that just as the fire did not consume the bush so also the birth of Jesus did not alter Mary's virginity (2.37–41). Calvin equates the messenger of YHWH with Jesus and the theme of suffering with the persecuted Protestant church (1950, 1:61–62). The burning bush has also been interpreted as a resource for criticizing organized religion, especially in its claim to control revelation and religious experience. Elizabeth Barrett Browning, for example, links the burning bush with the revelation of God through nature (Browning, 265); while James Dickey equates the symbol with poetic inspiration, freed from the confines of organized religion (Dickey, 7–8). The attack of YHWH against Moses is also interpreted to reinforce institutional religious rituals. For the rabbis, the cause for the divine attack is the problem of neglecting circumcision (*b. Nedarim* 31b–32a); while for Augustine the story illustrates the danger of not baptizing infants (4.24–32).

The Text in Contemporary Discussion

The nature of revelation, the relationship of religious experience to organized religion, and the strange role of Zipporah are continuing topics of reflection in contemporary discussion. The burning bush remains the symbol for many branches of the Reformed churches throughout the world (e.g., Reformed Churches of France, Scotland, Canada, Australia, New Zealand), while it also provides a resource for criticizing organized religion as in the Wisconsin-based nonconformist, utopian community the Burning Bush Movement. The divine attack on Moses remains a challenging text about revelation and the nature of the deity in human experience. The author of *Jubilees* already sought to overcome the problem in the earlier period of interpretation by identifying the divine being as Prince Mastema (Satan) rather than YHWH (48:1-8). Rudolf Otto moves in a different direction: he interprets the story as the paradigm of all human encounters with the divine, which he concludes always represent a premoral experience of the numinous. He likens the experience of the numinous to a deeply felt monster (Otto, 60–61). The role of Zipporah continues to demand interpretation, especially in evaluating her role as woman, wife, and a non-Israelite. Elizabeth Cady Stanton voices an early feminist critique, stating that Zipporah represents the role of all women who follow their husband's desires as secondary characters in marriage, taking an active role only when they need to rescue their husbands from danger (75–76). Recent feminist interpreters view the role of Zipporah more heroically, as a non-Israelite ritual expert who saves Moses and her son from the divine attack, thus challenging the exclusive nature of revelation in the two commissions of Moses (e.g., Meyers 2005).

Exodus 7:8—10:20: The Plagues

The Text in Its Ancient Context

This section narrates the many plagues YHWH sends against Pharaoh and the Egyptians. The stage is set for the plagues when Pharaoh rejects Moses' demand that the people be freed to worship

YHWH in the desert (Exod. 5:1-23). Pharaoh's resistance leads to a confrontation with YHWH, not Moses. The plagues are weapons of war against Pharaoh and signs of YHWH's destructive power over the environment of Egypt. The section includes three cycles of plagues, which increase in intensity as they progress through the different elements of nature, from water (7:8—8:15), to land (8:16—9:7), and finally to air (9:8—10:20).

Cycle 1 (7:8—8:15) Nature: Water	**Cycle 2** (8:16—9:7) Nature: Land	**Cycle 3** (9:8—10:20) Nature: Air
Introduction: Aaron sea-dragon (7:8-13)	Introduction: Aaron gnats (8:16-19)	Introduction: Moses boils (9:8-12)
blood (7:14-24)	flies (8:20-32)	hail (9:13-35)
frogs (7:25—8:15)	cattle (9:1-7)	locusts (10:1-20)

In the first cycle, Aaron represents the power of YHWH over the water in the land of Egypt. Pharaoh and his magicians are the opponents. The plague of the sea monster opens the cycle. Its central theme is the transformation of Aaron's staff into the *tannin*, "sea monster." The motif of water associated with the sea monster provides the introduction to two subsequent plagues, the pollution of the Nile River into blood and the infiltration of frogs from the water onto the land. The initial confrontation results in a stalemate between YHWH and Pharaoh, since the Egyptian magicians are able to perform the same acts of power over water as Aaron: they conjure up the sea monster (7:12), turn water into blood (7:22), and bring frogs out of the Nile (8:7). Thus Pharaoh rejects YHWH's claim on the Israelite people and continues to demand their slave labor. Aaron remains the protagonist in the second cycle, where the destructive power of YHWH is redirected from the water to the land of Egypt. Aaron brings forth gnats from the "dust of the earth" (8:17), which surpasses the power of the magicians (8:18), causing them to recognize the power of God (8:19). After the gnats, flies infest the "ground" of the Egyptians, and all the Egyptian livestock of the field die. Yet Pharaoh continues to resist the claims of YHWH. In the third cycle, Moses replaces Aaron as the representative of YHWH. A plague of boils is created on humans and animals from the soot in the air (8:9), a plague so severe that the magicians are not even able to meet him (8:11). Two other airborne plagues follow the boils: a hailstorm ruins the land of Egypt (9:23), and locusts are carried into Egypt on an east wind, destroying whatever survived the hailstorm (10:13).

The description of the divine actions against the water, land, and air of Egypt underscores destructive themes in the narrative. The series of events reinforce the assault of YHWH on Egypt. The ecological disasters are described as plagues (9:3, 14) and strikes (7:27), by which YHWH smites the Egyptian environment (7:17, 7:25; 8:13; 9:15). Yet these same destructive forces are also described as wonders (7:3, 9; 11:9-10) and signs (7:3; 8:23; 10:1-2) that reveal the power and character of YHWH to Pharaoh and the Egyptians (Exod. 7:3; 8:23; 11:9-10), as well as to the Israelites (10:1-2).

The Text in the Interpretive Tradition

The plagues receive surprisingly little interpretation in biblical tradition. They are the subjects of two psalms. Psalm 78 recounts the plagues as actions directed toward the Israelites with the aim of instilling faith in them. Psalm 105 states that the plagues are public displays of power aimed at the Egyptians. Neither psalm follows the form or sequence of the pentateuchal histories, suggesting fluidity in the tradition of the plagues. The plagues are also mentioned in a number of sermons and prayers. Moses refers to the signs performed by YHWH (Deut. 11:3; 26:8), as does Joshua (Josh. 24:5) and Ezra (Neh. 9:10). The book of *Jubilees* interprets the plagues as signs of YHWH's vengeance (48:5-8). Josephus (*Vita* 2.293) and Philo (*Mos.* 1.146), on the other hand, interpret the plagues as occasions for divine protection of the Israelites and for their instruction. In Jewish legend, the plagues parallel the cruel treatment of the Israelites (Ginzberg, 2:345–47). In the New Testament, the sermon of Stephen continues the tradition of Moses, Joshua, and Ezra, referring to the plagues as "wonders" and "signs" (Acts 7:36). The apostle Paul provides a unique midrash on Exod. 9:16 in Rom. 9:17, transforming the motif of Pharaoh's hardened heart to account for the rejection of the Jews to the mission of Jesus. Revelation 16 is more in the tradition of Psalm 105, where the plagues are public, cosmological events performed before the nations, signaling the end of time.

The Text in Contemporary Discussion

The ecological devastation associated with the plagues, in which the destruction of the environment is a divine weapon for saving the Israelite nation, represents a challenge to contemporary ecological theology. In his study of the roots of our contemporary ecological crisis in the Western tradition, Lynn Townsend White argues that Judeo-Christianity represents an anthropocentric religious tradition that is exploitative of the natural world (1203–7). The destruction of the Egyptian environment in the story of the exodus would appear to support his conclusion. The criticism prompted Terence Fretheim to explore anew the relationship of religion, nature, and human action in the story of the plagues. He concludes that the cycle of the plagues, with its emphasis on nature, advances a theology of creation. Central to this theology is the ancient Near Eastern belief that the morality of the king influences the well-being of creation and the fertility of the land (Frankfort, 310–12). As a result, a king who oppresses his subjects risks the ecological ruin of his country. When read from this perspective, the plagues on the land of Egypt do not represent the denigration of nature by God for the salvation of humans. Instead, they are the result of the breakdown in the moral order because of the actions of Pharaoh. Human ethics and ecology become organically related; Pharaoh's oppression not only threatens the well-being of the Israelites but also spills over to pollute the environment of Egypt. The plagues signify the undoing of creation for the Egyptians as a result of Pharaoh's exploitative actions. The breakdown of creation progresses through "every tree," "all the fruit," and "the whole land," until darkness engulfs the land of Egypt.

The intertwining of human morality and the well-being of the land remains a hallmark of the Israelite prophets. Hosea states: "Therefore the land mourns, and all who live in it languish; together with the wild animals, and the birds of the air, even the fish of the sea are perishing," because humans are acting immorally (Hosea 4:3). The prophet Amos also describes drought and even "pestilence after the manner of Egypt" (Amos 4:10) sent by YHWH as a result of immoral action. The prophet Joel too equates an invasion of locusts with divine judgment (Joel 1–2), a motif that will also appear in the plague cycle. The oracles of Hosea, Amos, and Joel indicate that human oppression has ecological consequences. It can undo creation. The same is true for the story of the plagues. The intertwining of human morality and the well-being of the Egyptian environment provides a springboard for evaluating contemporary ecological disasters, such as the Deepwater Horizon oil spill in the Gulf of Mexico or even the increase of violent storms that are tied to global warming, where exploitation goes beyond the oppression of humans to include the undoing of creation itself.

Exodus 10:21—13:16: The Exodus

The Text in Its Ancient Context

Exodus 10:21—13:16 contains the liturgies associated with the exodus from Egypt. The plague of darkness (Exod. 10:21-29) provides the introduction to the death of the Egyptian firstborn during the night of Passover and the Feast of Unleavened Bread (Exod. 11:1—13:16). The story, building on the violent cycle of the plagues in Exod. 7:8—10:20, keeps the power of YHWH at center stage; the divine demand that Pharaoh release the Israelites for worship retains a prominent role in the events of the exodus, while the plagues also continue. The traditional interpretation of darkness and the death of the Egyptian firstborn as plagues in the Passover Haggadah, for example, underscores the continuity between the initial plagues and the events of the exodus.

But there is also intensification from the story of the plagues to the account of Passover. YHWH acts more directly against Pharaoh and the Egyptians, and as a result, the display of YHWH's power is elevated and the intercessory role of Moses recedes somewhat, especially in the death of the Egyptian firstborn. Also, YHWH's power over nature increases beyond water, land, and air to the more primordial forces of light and darkness, and life and death. The plague of darkness sets the stage for the death of the Egyptian firstborn at midnight. The Israelites, too, become active rather than passive participants in the story, as compared to their role in the previous cycle of plagues. Thus they must participate in their redemption through cultic ritual of the Passover, which protects them from YHWH's assault on the Egyptians and the death of the Egyptian firstborn children at midnight. The ritual also provides a means for the Israelites to recall and to reenact the exodus. The central question of the Passover haggadah—Why is this night different from all other nights?—interprets the events of the exodus as a development beyond the previous plague cycle.

The Passover emerges as the central liturgical event in the exodus. The blood of the paschal lamb protects the Israelites from the midnight plague of death, when YHWH strikes down all the firstborn humans in the land of Egypt (Exod. 12:29-30). Thus ritual requirements are carefully outlined, given the need to protect the Israelite firstborn from death (Exod. 12:1-20). Each Israelite family is to slaughter a one-year-old lamb and place the blood on the doorpost to ward off the divine destroyer, who will kill all of the firstborn humans in the land of Egypt during the night. Moses also instructs the elders of the Israelites about the Passover, emphasizing once again that the blood on the doorpost is a protection from the divine attack on the firstborn (Exod. 12: 21-28). And YHWH returns to the topic with further instruction to Moses, outlining who may participate in the Passover (Exod. 12:40-51).

In spite of its central role in the narrative, the Passover was not originally associated with the exodus. It may have originated in seminomadic culture, with the blood of the lamb functioning to protect against the dangers of migration, or perhaps in the monarchical period, as a ritual in the New Year festival. Whatever its origin, the linking of the Passover with the theme of protecting the firstborn from a divine attack is likely ancient, since these themes are already present in the oldest version of the rite in Exod. 12:21-23. The setting of the ritual in the land of Egypt during the events of the exodus, however, likely occurred late in the period of the monarchy, under the rule of Josiah, who is credited with instituting the Passover as a national festival (2 Kgs. 23:21-23). But even here, the Passover is not tied specifically to the exodus. In the present form of story of the exodus from Egypt, the Passover and the death of the firstborn are firmly intertwined. The use of blood to rescue a firstborn child repeats the action of Zipporah, who also used blood to ward off the attack of YHWH in Exod. 4:22-24. Later in the book of Joshua, aspects of the Passover ritual reappear in the story of Rahab, the prostitute in Jericho who rescues the spies (Joshua 2). In this story, the blood of the Passover lamb is symbolized as a red thread in the window to her home, which will protect those inside from the destruction of the city and the genocide of the residents in the Israelite attack. Like the blood of the Passover, the red thread wards off death from the collapse of the walls; it guards the inner space of Rahab's house; and it allows the family members of Rahab who remain in her house to survive the execution of the ban on the city of Jericho. The common theme in the stories of Zipporah, the Passover ritual, and Rahab is the warding off of a divine attack through blood, or in the case of Rahab, a red thread.

The Text in the Interpretive Tradition

The Passover was a central ritual of self-identity in the Second Temple period. Ezra 6 recounts the returning exiles' observance of the Passover in Judah. But unlike the story in Exodus, in Ezra it is the Levites, rather than the individual family members, who administer Passover and slaughter the lamb. The ritual solidifies the identity of the returning exiles. The importance of the festival is further evidenced by a fifth-century-BCE letter from Jews in Elephantine, a colony in Egypt; in the letter, the senders request specific instructions about ritual observance of the Passover (Cowley, *Aramaic Papyri of the Fifth Century B.C.*, 60–65).

The observance of Passover was institutionalized during the Second Temple period into the Seder service, in which participants identify with the story of liberation from Egypt by eating the Passover lamb, unleavened bread, and bitter herbs. This event is central in the Gospel tradition as the Last Supper of Jesus and his disciples (Matthew 26; Mark 14; Luke 22; John 13–17; 19). Hellenistic Jewish authors like Philo reinterpreted the Passover from a meal that celebrates liberation to a spiritual event in which the soul is purified from physical passions (*Spec. Laws* 2.2.29). The author of *Jubilees* concentrates more narrowly on the linking of Passover and the death of the firstborn, noting that proper observance will spare the participant from death (49:15).

The Text in Contemporary Discussion

The Passover continues to represent a ritual of liberation in contemporary interpretation. Göran Larsson, for example, describes the Passover as a celebration of relationship, renewal, and remembrance. The blood on the doorpost symbolizes "the bond between God and Israel and between every member of the people, a bond later sealed through the covenantal blood at Sinai" (82). The ritual, moreover, creates unity through time in the continued observance of the Passover haggadah as an act of remembrance of Israel's liberation from slavery (Larsson, 81–92). Other contemporary interpretations of the Passover explore the ambiguity of the ritual, focusing on the violence of the story. David Mamet's novel *Passover* is a conversation between a woman and her granddaughter while they prepare the Passover meal. The conversation models the need for intergenerational teaching of the exodus that Moses commands in the original participants. The grandmother's story extends beyond the biblical account to include her experience of pogroms, thus highlighting the continued oppression of Jews throughout Western history and the ambiguity of liberation when it is viewed as a singular event in history.

Still other contemporary writers and artists reflect on the ambiguous role of the deity in killing the Egyptian firstborn in an act of liberation for the Israelites. How could such an action on innocent children be good or liberating? William Blake's watercolor *Pestilence: Death of the Firstborn* accentuates the ambiguity of the divine slaughter of the Egyptian firstborn. In the drawing, the agent of death dominates; mothers hover over their dead children while a small angel stands in a doorway seemingly overwhelmed by the agent of death. The scene forces the reader to view the Passover as a complex ritual that gives life but also takes it away. Recent interpreters have also underscored the ambiguous and selective role of remembrance that is central to the Passover, especially as it influences the reader's view of Egypt. Regina Schwartz highlights the fluid, selective, and political role of memories: "They are forged to further some agenda even as they forge agendas" (158). Jan Assmann provides an illustration of Schwartz's general conclusion by focusing on the story of the exodus from Egypt. This story of Israelite liberation takes on a larger role in the history of interpretation, especially in the evaluation of the Egyptians in Western cultural history. Assmann concludes that the historical memory of Egypt in the Bible is reduced in Western culture to the "other," who is rejected, discarded, and abandoned (1–22, 208–12). This is symbolized strikingly in the death of the Egyptian children, who become expendable in the liberation of the Israelites from Egypt.

Exodus 13:17—15:21: Destruction of the Egyptian Army in the Red Sea

The Text in Its Ancient Context

Exodus 13:17—15:21 recounts the Israelite flight from Egypt to the Red Sea (13:17—14:4); the pursuit of Pharaoh and his army (14:5-14); the destruction of Pharaoh and the Egyptian army in the Red Sea (14:15-31); and the celebration of the event in two songs by Moses and Israel

(15:1-18) and by Miriam and the Israelite women (15:19-21). The story of YHWH's control over the Red Sea in defeating Pharaoh and his army is influenced by liturgical motifs from ancient Near Eastern religion, where the sea represents the forces of nature at war with the god of creation. The Canaanite god of fertility, Baal, wars against the chaotic forces of sea and river, the god Yamm-Nahar (Yamm = "sea" and Nahar = "river"; *CTA* 2). The defeat of the sea god Yamm-Nahar signals the victory of order, creation, and fertility in Canaanite religion. The Babylonian god Marduk splits the sea monster Tiamat as the initial act of creation in the mythology *Enuma Elish* (*ANET* 60–99). The ancient Israelite writers know the tradition of the chaotic sea. The sea is often an opponent to God, representing chaotic forces that seek to undo creation. Isaiah 27:1 associates the sea with the sea dragon, the serpent, and Leviathan in celebrating YHWH's punishment of the sea monster. But the mythology of the sea is also historicized in Isa. 5:30 as the army of the enemy, who is compared to "the roaring of the sea." The most prominent blending of the mythological motifs of the sea and the historical enemy is the story of the exodus. Exodus 13:17—14:31 employs the mythology of the chaotic sea to describe the final conflict between YHWH and Pharaoh. YHWH dries up the sea with an east wind, recalling Baal's conflict with Yamm (14:21). At the same time, the sea is split into two walls of water, mirroring the action of Marduk against Tiamat (14:22). In both instances, the sea becomes a weapon of YHWH against Pharaoh, who represents a historicized form of chaos.

The miraculous event of salvation at the sea in Exodus is celebrated in two victory songs, the more extended version of Exod. 15:1b-18 and the shorter account in Exod. 15:21b. Both describe the power of YHWH over the sea in destroying the enemy. There is no indication that the songs were associated with Moses or Miriam in their original composition. Yet both are now thoroughly embedded in the larger narrative context. Each song has an introduction naming the singers as Moses and Miriam. The introductions function much like psalm titles, in which songs become associated with events in the life of a hero. The two songs conclude the story of the conflict between Pharaoh and YHWH: first, Moses and the Israelites sing a song to YHWH in Exod. 15:1-18, the Song of the Sea; and then Miriam and the women sing a song in Exod. 15:19-21, the Song of Miriam.

The Text in the Interpretive Tradition

The power of YHWH to save Israel by controlling the sea remains a central theme in the biblical tradition (e.g., Ps. 77:15-20; Mic. 7:14-17). YHWH remains the primary character in the reuse of the exodus story throughout the Hebrew Bible. Isaiah 52:9-11 refers to the exodus from Egypt as the time when YHWH defeated the sea monster Rahab by drying up the sea. Isaiah 43:16 celebrates the power of God as savior and creator by describing YHWH as the one "who makes a way in the sea, / a path in the mighty waters," suggesting the imagery of the exodus. Isaiah 11:15-16 echoes the same theme, only the sea in this text is described as "the River," recalling the close association of Sea-River (Yamm-Nahar) in Canaanite mythology. In Isaiah 11, the splitting of the River results in seven channels of water (echoing the seven heads of Leviathan), rather than the two walls of water in Exodus 14. Psalm 114 also memorializes God's power over sea and river. The sea flees before the presence of God and the Jordan River turns back.

Hellenistic Jewish authors shift the focus of interpretation to idealize the human characters in the story, especially Moses. Moses is portrayed as a hero by Philo, who accentuates Moses' leadership role (*Mos.* 1.29–32). Josephus, too, underscores the faith of Moses and his courage as a leader in bringing about the exodus (*Ant.* 2.15–16). The idealization of Moses is also evident in the images at Dura-Europos, where Moses is prominent in the representations of the exodus. Gregory of Nyssa wrote the *Life of Moses* to provide the ideal of virtue and perfection in the fourth century CE. Moses is presented as a general in the Old English poem "Exodus" in the medieval Junius Manuscript. Moses continues to be the central figure in the study of the exodus into the modern period, especially in critical-biblical scholarship, which seeks to explore the social, political, and religious environment of the period of the exodus. Hugo Gressmann explored the oral traditions associated with Moses, setting the stage for a series of studies of Moses throughout the modern period (e.g., Buber; Rad; Auerbach).

The Text in Contemporary Discussion

Two topics confront the contemporary reader of the salvation of the Israelites at the Red Sea. The first issue is the problem of violence in the story of the salvation, especially the destruction of the Egyptian army. The text accounts for the divine destruction of the enemy with the motif of the hardening of Pharaoh's heart. This motif is developed throughout the story of the plagues to account for the increased violence on the people and the land of Egypt. The motif comes to a climax at the Red Sea, when Pharaoh leads the Egyptian army into the sea in pursuit of Israel, leading to their destruction. The exercise of divine violence on the Egyptian army, the Egyptian firstborn, or even the indigenous nations of Canaan as part of the salvation of the Israelites presents an ethical problem throughout the story of the exodus. Must the story of liberation for Israel be linked with the death of the "other"?

The second theme is the role of women in the exodus story. Feminist interpreters in the late twentieth century refocused attention on Miriam as the hero of the exodus, as compared to Moses' dominance in the history of interpretation. The central problem of the research is how to recover the tradition of Miriam and to reinterpret the relationship between the Song of the Sea (Exod. 15:1-18) and the Song of Miriam (Exod. 15:19-21). Many solutions emerge. The assumption of one line of feminist research is that patriarchal dominance in the formation of the text and in the history of interpretation has suppressed the role of Miriam in the story of the exodus. The task of feminist interpreters, therefore, is to recover the heroic role of Miriam that threatened patriarchal detractors who "tabooed her to death, seeking to bury her forever in disgrace" (Tribe 1994, 179). Her heroic role is evident in "bits and pieces of story awaiting discovery" (Trible 1994, 183). These stories include her heroic role in the birth story of Moses, where she functions as his savior (Exod. 2:1-10); her prophetic role in interpreting the exodus (Exod. 15:19-21); and the suppression of her voice in the conflict over prophetic authority (Num. 12:2-14). Ursula Rapp concludes that Miriam represents a prophetic group in the Second Temple period that lost authority over time. Some interpreters have reevaluated the literary relationship between the two songs, giving prominence to Miriam's songs in Exodus 15 (van Dijk-Hemmes, 200–206; Janzen, 187–99). Other feminist interpreters have explored anew the role of women and song in ancient Israel, emphasizing the significant role of woman as leaders in musical performance (Meyers 1994, 207–30). Still others emphasize the dynamic role of tradition as midrash, where contemporary feminist interpreters are able to influence tradition by bringing Miriam out of the shadows through imaginative reenactment with the sacred texts (Bach, 243–58).

Exodus 15:22—18:27: The Journey as a Rite of Passage

The Text in Its Ancient Context

The conflict between YHWH and Pharaoh in the land of Egypt (Exod. 7:8—15:18) gives way to the Israelite journey with God in the wilderness (Exod. 15:22—18:27). The central theme shifts from the exercise of divine power against Pharaoh to the presence of YHWH with Israel. The initial stories in the wilderness explore the special relationship between YHWH and Israel made evident through episodes of testing and struggle. The Israelites experience danger immediately in the wilderness in the form of poisoned water (Exod. 15:22-26), absence of food (Exod. 15:27—16:35), and lack of water (Exod. 17:1-7). In each instance, YHWH provides for the people, purifying the poisoned water, providing manna for food, and drawing water from a rock.

After the stories of testing, the narrative broadens in perspective to explore the Israelites' relationship to other nations in two stories. First, the Amalekites are identified as an enemy who attacks Israel on the journey (Exod. 17:8-16); and, second, the Midianites are presented as an ally who provides leadership in worship (Exod. 18:1-12) and in the administration of law (Exod. 18:13-27). The two perspectives toward these foreign nations are recounted in the story of King Saul in 1 Samuel 15. He wages a holy war against the Amalekites, because of their hostility to the Israelites in the wilderness journey, but he spares the Kenites (a.k.a. the Midianites) because of their hospitality. Both nations are difficult to locate in the geography of the ancient Near East, yet each is associated with the southern desert region. Moses first encounters the Midianites in the wilderness when he flees Egypt. The Amalekites are identified as descendants of Esau (Genesis 36).

The war against the Amalekites (Exod. 17:8-16) moves quickly through three scenes: attack (17:8), war (17:9-13), and remembrance for vengeance (17:14-16). The Amalekites attack the Israelites at Rephidim. The motive for the attack is not stated. The location of Amalekites in the southern desert may signify confrontation as the Israelites journey through their territory. Moses responds by calling the people to participate in war for the first time. Throughout the events of the exodus, the Israelites never participate actively in war; in fact, YHWH did not judge the people ready for war (Exod. 13:17). Now, in the wilderness, the people are commanded to wage war, with Joshua as their leader. The battle story, however, focuses on Moses, not Joshua. Moses informs Joshua that he will ascend to the summit of the hill with the staff of God. The war against the Amalekites is regulated at the summit of the hill by the action of Moses with the divine staff. When the hands of Moses and the staff are raised, Joshua prevails. When his hands are lowered, the tide of the battle turns, and the Amalekites gain the upper hand. The circumstances indicate that the power to wage war resides in the staff of God, not in Moses, and certainly not in Joshua or the Israelite warriors. The eventual inability of Moses to raise his arms underscores further that the power in the battle does not reside with him, but with God. Victory is achieved when Aaron and Hur assist Moses, providing a seat of stone and hold his arms up until the setting of the sun. The conclusion of the story is a divine speech to Moses, which turns from the present battle to the future genocide of the Amalekites. YHWH swears vengeance against the Amalekites and predicts the elimination of their memory from under heaven (Exod. 18:14). The genocide of the Amalekites is prophesied again by Balaam (Num. 24:20) and repeated by Moses to the second generation (Deut. 25:19) before YHWH commands Saul to fulfill the oath by exterminating the nation through the execution of the ban (1 Sam. 15:3).

The Text in the Interpretive Tradition

The divine command to exterminate the Amalekites has given rise to a long tradition of interpretation. The rabbis struggled over the problem of divine justice and morality in the command for the extermination of a nation (*b. Yoma* 22b). In the second century CE, Rabbi Judah the Prince underscored Amalek's near fanatical intention to attack the Israelites to account for the divine command, traveling through five nations to achieve the goal (*Mekilta de-Rabbi Ishmael Amalek* 1). The evil intention of the Amalekites continued to be a subject of reflection in the fifteenth century. Abrabanel underscored that there was no reason for the Amalekite attack, thus accounting for their own destruction. Earlier, in the thirteenth century, Nahmanides explained that the Amalekites did not fear God after hearing about the exodus, thus prompting God to seek their destruction.

A more prominent development in the history of interpretation is the identification of the Amalekites with opponents or enemies of one sort or another through time (Feldman). In the *War Scroll* from Qumran Cave 1 (1QM), the Amalekites are identified as the Sons of Darkness, who battle against the Sons of Light (that is, the sons of Levi, Judah, and Benjamin). Philo, however, associates the Amalekites with the Phoenicians (*Mos.* 1.218); Josephus, with the residents of Petra (*Ant.* 3.39–61). The enemy was also spiritualized. The Zohar, for example, states that Amalek is Satan rather than a historical nation.

Yet the practice of identifying the Amalekites with a historical enemy continues. This is perhaps most evident in the tradition in which Haman, the evil protagonist in the book of Esther, is identified as a descendant of Agag, the king of the Amalekites (*b. Sanh.* 96b). The defeat of Jewish enemies, particularly Haman, is celebrated during the festival of Purim. A similar practice is evident in Christian tradition in a letter from Epiphanius to Jerome. Epiphanius encourages Jerome to continue his work of translation while also identifying Origen and his Alexandrian disciples as the Amalekites, who must be destroyed (*Letter 91 from Epiphanius to Jerome*). The process of identifying the enemy with the Amalekites continues throughout Western history. Beginning in the medieval period and continuing into the nineteenth century, some Jewish authorities identified the Armenians as the Amalekites. The Zohar introduces a more symbolic and supernatural interpretation of the struggle between good and evil (3.206–7; Sagi, 330–31). Christians identified Muslims as the Amalekites during the Crusades. In responding to a plea for mercy from Adolf Eichmann's wife, Itzchak Ben Zvi quoted Samuel's words in Sam. 15:33 to King Agag the Amalekite to underscore the inevitability of Eichmann's impending destruction.

The Text in Contemporary Discussion

Alastair Hunter states the problem of the divine curse on Amalek in contemporary discussion: "We ignore at our peril the potential for violence built into the Bible" (92–108). She notes that the Amalekites become the archetypal victims in the Pentateuch, in that the divine instruction to destroy the nation is given on several different occasions, while the circumstances of the war are never clearly stated. In spite of the lack of clarity over the conflict, the presentation of the Amalekites illustrates the rhetorical device of portraying the victim or cursed nation as the aggressor in order to justify their elimination. The result is that the Amalekites exist only to be exterminated. The literary strategy of the Bible to victimize the Amalekites as the cursed enemy has allowed later readers to empty the term of its historical meaning, so that it can be reappropriated in new ways to disenfranchise others. The result is that the word *Amalekite* becomes a cipher for the enemy, whomever it may be. As a consequence, the perpetuation of violence becomes a religious obligation, whether it be the "war on terror" or the "politics of Amalek" waged by West Bank settlers against Palestinians (Masalha, 127–31).

Exodus 19:1-19: Revelation and Covenant

The Text in Its Ancient Context

The wilderness journey halts in Exodus 19 when the Israelites arrive at Mount Sinai to receive the revelation of law and to enter into a covenant relationship with YHWH. The theme of covenant is introduced in the divine proposal (19:1-8), which leads to the initial revelation of law on the Mount Sinai (19:9-19). The research on the meaning of covenant in ancient Israelite religion is extensive. George Mendenhall interprets covenant through comparison to Hittite suzerainty treaties, a form of diplomatic contracts in the ancient Near East between unequal parties. The suzerainty treaty includes (1) the identification of the suzerain or lord, (2) a historical prologue listing the acts of salvation of the suzerain toward the vassal, (3) the treaty stipulations or laws required of the vassal, (4) the provisions for reading the treaty, (5) the witnesses to the treaty, and (6) the curses resulting from disobedience and the blessings arising from obedience (1955, 1–50). By way of its analogy to the political setting in the ancient Near East, the suzerainty treaty provides a framework for interpreting the covenant relationship between YHWH and the Israelites. When the form is applied to Exod. 19:3-6, the call for the Israelites to see a past action of YHWH (19:4) is identified as the historical prologue and the offer of covenant (19:5a) as the legal stipulation. The Israelites accept the divine offer and enter into covenant with YHWH.

"Covenant," according to Steven McKenzie, is the main biblical image for the distinctive relationship between the people of Israel with God (9). It signifies that the Israelites are a "chosen" or "elect" people, meaning they are special to God and thus distinct from all other people in the world. The imagery of being a chosen people emerges from the promise of reward (19:5b-6), which follows the divine offer of covenant (19:5a). If the Israelite people accept the offer of covenant (19:5a), YHWH promises that they will be a "personal possession" of God separated from the other nations.

The translation "personal possession" is from the Hebrew word *segullah*. There is debate over the meaning of this term, however. Some argue that the term conveys inherent value, best translated as "treasured property." In this case, the "chosenness" of the people arises from their distinctive character. Another interpretation, however, is that *segullah* simply describes the quality of the promised relationship between Israel and God, in which case the translation would be "personal possession." Carl Friedrich Keil and Franz Delitzsch represent the first interpretation indicating that *segulla* does "not denote property in general but valuable property" (96). The resulting meaning of the divine promise is that "although all the earth belongs to God," the Israelite people are of more value; hence they are a "treasured possession" (see NIV). Moshe Greenberg favors the second choice, noting that the Akkadian word *sikiltum*, the equivalent of Hebrew *segullah*, is an economic term designating private property regardless of its value (173). The same meaning is evident in two economically oriented texts in the Hebrew Bible, where David (1 Chron. 29:3) and the Preacher (Eccles. 2:8) refer to "private property." The second interpretation emphasizes the relationship between God and the Israelite people as a "treasured possession." In this interpretation, the special relationship between YHWH and Israel forces the people to take on a special role of service to the world as priests. The two interpretations agree that covenant designates the Israelites as a chosen people and hence special in some way from all of humans; they disagree, however, over whether the distinctiveness of the people is based on their character or on their special mission to the world.

The Text in the Interpretive Tradition

The themes of covenant and the chosenness of Israel give rise to a long history of interpretation. In the Second Temple period, the nature of the Israelite's chosen status swings between two poles, one of which emphasizes the special quality of the people, while the other focuses instead on the ethical responsibility that accompanies election and covenant. The book of *Jubilees* describes the special status of Israel as a holy people and a holy seed, which stems from the ancestors, especially Jacob (*Jub.* 2:20, 22; 15:30-31; 16:26; 22:27; 25:18), thus emphasizing the physical descent of the people. The Qumran community followed the same line of interpretation, but they limited the interpretation of being chosen to a remnant represented by their community (1QM 14; CD 3–15). Philo also describes three categories of the "nations of the souls" to explore the nature of election and covenant: the children of the earth (sons of Adam); the offspring of virtue (sons of heaven); and the chosen race of Israel (sons of God) (*Post.* 91–92). Although these categories suggest a qualitative difference between Israel and the nations, he also emphasizes the role of wisdom in defining the different souls of the nations (*Spec. Laws* 4.180–81), thus creating a degree of ambiguity in defining what it means to be chosen of God. In the writing of the apostle Paul, the interpretation of chosenness becomes even more inclusive, since faith becomes the criterion of election (Rom. 10:4, 12-13; Gal. 3:28; 4:22-26). Thus to be chosen, according to Paul, is not tied to the inherent quality or identity of a person or a past promise to the ancestors, but to an ethical action defined as faith. This broad view of divine chosenness is accompanied with a polemic against a narrower view of covenant and election in Second Temple Judaism. Paul forms the argument by contrasting the "old covenant" of Moses, with its narrow view of the chosen people of Israel, to the "new covenant" of Jesus, in which the true Israel is chosen by faith.

The polemical nature of the debate on covenant and chosenness between emergent Christianity and Second Temple Judaism influenced subsequent interpretations in the church fathers and in rabbinic tradition. In the *Dialogue with Trypho*, Justin Martyr builds on the contrast between the old and new covenants and the implications of this distinction for understanding election and the concept of being chosen. The old covenant is the Mosaic covenant of the law, which is surpassed by the new covenant in Christ, suggesting a theology of supersession. The same line of interpretation continues in Irenaeus (*Adversus haereses* 4.5.1; 12.1–5, 13–16), Clement of Alexandria (*Stromata* 4.5.327), and even in Augustine (*Ennarationes in Psalmos* 104.7). Each emphasizes that the new covenant signifies an election based on faith and obedience, which is open to any human. The rabbinic interpretation moves in a different direction. The rabbis state that there are covenants and obligations that influence all humans, but the notion of chosenness in covenant is restricted to Jews and creates its own special sense of obligation (*'Abot* 3:14). Even with this narrower view of chosenness, the emphasis in the rabbinic interpretation remains on obligation, not privilege, although a more biological interpretation is also infrequently suggested (e.g., Judah Ha-Levi, 1086–1145 CE).

The Text in Contemporary Discussion

The theology of covenant and chosenness presents a range of problems in contemporary discussion, where pluralism and interfaith dialogue are important values for religious health. Reuven Firestone explains: "Although God created all humanity in the divine likeness, why is one community of God's loving creatures privileged over all the others? Even with humanity's repeated failures to live up to that likeness without ongoing heavenly intervention, why would a loving God not find a way to allow all of humankind to benefit directly from engagement with the Divine?" (10). In addition to the theological problems noted by Firestone, there are also social challenges. The concept of being divinely chosen as a special people encourages superiority, while also creating the category of the "nonchosen" other, who may in turn also claim the same special, chosen status. Such competing claims create social conflict, violence, and persecution. The challenge of the biblical teaching on covenant, with its confession of being chosen by God, is finding a way to retain the experience of uniqueness that is central to religion while also allowing others to claim their own unique experience of chosenness.

Exodus 19:20—20:20: The Decalogue

The Text in Its Ancient Context

The central content in the revelation of God at Mount Sinai is the Decalogue. Once the Israelites agree to enter into covenant with YHWH (Exod. 19:1-8), the deity descends to the summit of Mount Sinai (Exod. 19:9-19) and reveals the Decalogue to the people (Exod. 20:1-17). The title, Decalogue (also known in English as the Ten Commandments), derives from the Hebrew designation of the law code as the "ten words" used at the close of covenant renewal (Exod. 34:28) and repeated twice in the book of Deuteronomy (4:13; 10:4). The three texts share motifs that underscore the prominence of the law code. The "ten words" derive from God (Deut. 4:13). They form the basis for covenant (Exod. 34:28; Deut. 4:13), and they are written down on two tablets (Exod. 34:28; Deut. 4:13; 10:4), thus forming the core of Scripture. The Decalogue serves as a constitutional law for the Israelites, providing a foundational perspective on God and human relationships.

The authors of the book of Exodus envisioned law as representing the essence of their religion. God promises the Israelites at the outset of the wilderness journey that the revelation of law will be their source of health (Exod. 15:22-27). And the divine origin of the law is made explicit at the divine mountain. God states to Moses in Exod. 24:12: "I will give you the tablets of stone, with the law and the commandment, which I have written for their instruction." Samuel Greengus notes that the anchoring of law in religion may be unique to the legal tradition of Israel in the ancient Near East (4:243–52). The result according to Z. W. Falk is that law and spirituality become merged into one in the formation of the Hebrew Bible. He writes: "The commandments are meant not only as norms of behavior but also as objects of contemplation to lead toward the perception and love of God" (130).

The Text in the Interpretive Tradition

The designation of the Decalogue as "ten words," written on "two tablets," provides clues to its literary structure. Yet the Hebrew Bible neither spells out the specific laws nor their organization into two sections. The ambiguity has given rise to a history of interpretation, especially concerning the number of the laws in Exod. 20:2-6 and in 20:17. In Jewish tradition, the self-revelation of God (20:2) is the first commandment. It is interpreted as a demand for faith in the deity. The prohibition against graven images (20:3-6) is the second law. The distribution of the commands on two tablets is evenly divided between 20:2-12 (five commands: self-revelation, idols, divine name, Sabbath, honor of parents) and 20:13-17 (five commands: murder, adultery, theft, false witness, coveting). The early church read the Decalogue differently. Exodus 20:2 became the prologue to the law code, with the prohibition against images the first command (20:3-6). The Roman church retained the number ten by interpreting the command against coveting (20:17) as two laws. The early church also changed the division of the law code. The first tablet was restricted to three commands (20:3-11), with seven on the second tablet (20:7-17). John Calvin provides yet another interpretation, separating 20:3-6 into two commands: exclusive worship of YHWH (v. 3) and a prohibition on idolatry (vv. 4-6). He retains the number ten by reading the command against coveting (v. 17) as one law as in Jewish tradition (1975, 2.8). Calvin also follows the Jewish division of the Decalogue, separating the law code into two tablets of five laws each (20:3-12 and 20:13-17).

The perspective on human rights in the Decalogue and its demand for singular allegiance to God echoes throughout Scripture and in ongoing Jewish and Christian tradition. The Decalogue is prominent throughout the Pentateuch. In addition to Exod. 20:1-17, the full text also occurs in Deuteronomy 5, with additional references throughout the book (Deuteronomy 4, 9, 10), including the curses for breaking the covenant in Deut. 27:15-26. The Decalogue is also central in the Priestly legislation. The version of the Decalogue in Exodus 20 indicates editing by the Priestly historian, especially in the law of Sabbath observance (Exod. 20:8-11). The result is a P (Exod. 20:1-17) and a D (Deut. 5:6-21) version of the constitutional document. The general character of the laws in the

Decalogue, such as killing, stealing, and lying, makes it difficult to trace a direct influence on other literature. Yet the influence of the Decalogue in Priestly tradition appears to go beyond Exodus 20 and likely includes the laws of holiness in Leviticus 19. The prophets also echo the Decalogue in their preaching. The book of Jeremiah lists ethical commands reminiscent of the Decalogue, warning the Israelite people not to steal, murder, commit adultery, swear falsely, or worship other gods (Jer. 7:9). Hosea includes swearing, lying, murder, stealing, and adultery as unethical actions opposed to the worship of YHWH (Hosea 4:2). The sins of Jerusalem, according to the prophet Ezekiel, include murder; contempt of parents; oppression of the alien, widow, and orphan; slander; adultery; incest; and exploitation of neighbor (Ezek. 22:1-12). The influence of the Decalogue may continue into the Psalms (e.g., Ps. 50:16-20) and perhaps also into the book of Job (Job 24:13-17), where the characterization of the wicked includes many of the laws of the Decalogue.

The influence of the Decalogue continues beyond the Hebrew Bible. It was singled out for daily prayer along with the Shema (Deut. 6:4) in Jewish worship already before the Common Era, and it continues in the liturgy of the Feast of Weeks (*m. Tamid* 4:3; 5:1). Philo of Alexandria reinforced its constitutional character, arguing that the Decalogue contained in essence all the other commands (*Decal.* 154). Direct quotation of the Decalogue is less evident in the teaching of Jesus, although he repeatedly refers to the importance of law, referring to many of the commands from the Decalogue in the Sermon on the Mount (Matthew 5–7). Jesus summarizes the essence of law as love of God above all and love of neighbor as self (e.g., Matt. 19:16-19; 22:39; Mark 10:17-20; 12:28-31). The law takes on a more polemical role in the teaching of the apostle Paul (see Gal. 3:13; 4:24). Yet he too appears to cite the Decalogue in Rom. 13:8–9, listing adultery, murder, stealing, coveting as well as "any other commandment" as actions incompatible with love.

The Text in Contemporary Discussion

The interpretation of the Decalogue as natural law in early Christian tradition placed the law code within the world of Hellenistic ethics, where it played a role in shaping Western culture from the interpretations of Justin Martyr and Thomas Aquinas, through Luther and Calvin. The interpretation of the Decalogue as a legal resource for a just democratic society continues into the present time, as is evident in the research of Walter Harrelson and Paul Lehmann. Both authors argue that the Ten Commandments are more than religious law for believing Christians and Jews; they provide a moral foundation for our common secular society.

The Christian interpretation of the universal truth of the Decalogue for fashioning a just society has created unintended challenges in the contemporary discussion of the law code. Two problems are prominent: the first is the need to separate religion from government in order to ensure that all religions are treated equally under the law; and, second, the secular interpretation of the Decalogue as universal law about human rights threatens to misinterpret the very nature of the Ten Commandments as religious law.

First, the separation of religion and state: Increasingly, religious conservatives are wedding religion and state by arguing that the government should actively promote public morality by advancing specific religious themes and symbols in public life. The public display of the Decalogue in prominent government buildings is at the center of this debate, evident in two legal cases: *Van Orden v. Perry* challenges a large monument of the Ten Commandments in Austin, Texas; and *McCreary County v. ACLU of Kentucky* challenges the display of the Ten Commandments in two county courthouses in Kentucky. The debate is not about the religious significance of the Decalogue for Christians and Jews, but whether a secular democracy should privilege one religious symbol over other religious traditions.

Second, the interpretation of the Decalogue as religious or secular law: The Decalogue has become so central to Western culture, according to Michael Coogan, that we are in danger of blurring its religious and secular role (2). Law in the Hebrew Bible resists simple definition, but it was never intended to function outside of religion. David Daube concludes: it is clear that "the authors of the Bible saw law as part of religion" (1). Law embraces many words and metaphors in the Hebrew Bible, including Torah, judgment, statute, commandment, testimony, and covenant, but none of these of these terms is intended to separate law from religion. The dynamic and religious character of law is conveyed through metaphors of motion and speech. Law is alive, deriving from the voice of God. The words are codified in writing. Bernard Jackson cautions that ancient laws function differently than the modern Western model of law, where the legal judgments of the court are comprehensive and clearly expressed in written language available to participants in advance (70–92). Ancient legal practice was not tied exclusively to written laws, but depended on the context of a situation to resolve dispute. The less specific law or judgment created a roadway through life on which humans were able to walk. The vocabulary indicates the breadth of the subject matter, while the metaphors underscore the dynamic quality of law as a religious resource for change through time. Jewish legal interpretation employs the metaphor of walking, *halakah*, to underscore the dynamic character of religious law in ongoing tradition.

The contemporary debate over the Decalogue and its role in public life is at the center of the larger debate over the separation of all religions from government in modern democratic societies. The separation protects the rights of minority religions, while also ensuring that secular government does not subvert the majority religions by making them the basis of a national civil religion.

Exodus 20:21—23:33: The Book of the Covenant

The Text in Its Ancient Context

The public revelation of the Decalogue (Exod. 20:1-17) is followed by the private revelation of the book of the covenant (Exod. 20:24—23:31). The name for the second law code derives from Exod. 24:7, where Moses is described as writing the law in the "book of the covenant." The laws of the book of the covenant (Exod. 21:1—23:19) are framed by an introduction (Exod. 20:21-26) and a conclusion (Exod. 23:20-33). The laws themselves divide between the *mishpatim*, or casuistic laws (Exod. 21:2—22:17), and the *debarim*, which include a variety of legal statements and divine speeches (22:18-23:1).

Slave laws are central to the book of the covenant. The initial legislation in the law code concerns debt slavery of Hebrew men and women (Exod. 21:2-11), and consists of two slave laws.

Exodus 21:2-6 focuses on the conditions of service and release of Hebrew males from debt slavery; while 21:7-11 outlines the legal rights of a Hebrew female concubine or slave-bride. The difference between the two laws is the absence of release for the female slave as compared to the male. Slave laws for non-Hebrew persons continue throughout the book of the covenant. Laws regulating slaves reappear in three other sections of the book of the covenant: the law protecting a slave from abuse (any slave hurt by an owner is given freedom as compensation for the damage, Exod. 21:26-27), the property rights of a slave master (if a slave is gored by another person's ox, the slave owner must be compensated for the damaged property, Exod. 21:32), and the law of Sabbath rest for slaves (Exod. 23:10-12). The repetition between the Sabbath release of debt slaves (Exod. 21:2-11) and the law of Sabbath rest for slaves is striking (Exod. 23:10-12), suggesting literary design in the composition of the book of the covenant. More recent studies have identified additional structures in the distribution of the slave laws in the book of the covenant (Dohmen, Exodus 19–40, 150). The slave laws organize Exod. 21:2-27: the laws of release (Exod. 21:2-11 and 26-27) form the outer frame, with the law on the assault of slaves (Exod. 21:20-21) at the center. The protection of debt slaves (Exod. 21:2-11) and the protection of the resident alien and poor (Exod. 22:21-25) may also frame the first half of the book of the covenant. The psychological identification with the resident alien from the Israelite experience of slavery in Egypt (Exod. 23:9) certainly reinforces the emphasis on protecting slaves.

The slave laws in the ancient Near East provide a broader vantage point for interpreting the role of the slave laws in the structure of the book of the covenant. The frequent comparison to Mesopotamian law in the exegesis of Exod. 21:2-11 indicates the common culture of the legal tradition regulating slavery in the ancient Near East. In addition to the slave laws from Nuzi, the topic is also included in the Laws of Eshnunna, the Laws of Lipit-Ishtar, the Hittite Laws, the Middle Assyrian Laws, the Neo-Babylonian Laws, and, perhaps most significantly, the Laws of Hammurabi (LH), where the laws regarding male and female slaves are also not confined to any one section but appear throughout the law code under a variety of topics. A central presupposition is that slaves are property requiring a series of laws on property damage (any free person damaging a slave must pay compensation, LH 199, see also 213–214, 231), warranty (an epileptic attack within one month of purchase negates the sale of a slave, LH 278), resale (LH 118–19), insurance against improper health care (a surgeon who kills a slave in operation must repay the owner, LH 219, see also 223), theft (LH 7), and workplace compensation (a slave owner is owed one-third *mina* for any slave gored by an ox, LH 252).

Other laws regulate the behavior of slaves, stating the punishment for aiding a slave in an escape (LH 15–20) or in assisting with the removal of a slave brand (LH 226–27). Still other laws address the circumstances by which a person might move between the different social classes from free to slave (debt slavery, LH 117–19) or from slave to free (the laws of redemption, LH 32, 116–19). The laws regulating marriage also address the change of status between free persons and slaves (LH 144, 146–47, 175–76). The slave laws may also play a role in the structure of the Laws of Hammurabi, similar to the book of the covenant, inaugurating a sequence of themes including slavery, bodily injury, commercial law, and family law.

Muhammad Dandamayev summarizes the prominence of slavery in the ancient Near East: The "institution of slavery had a profound influence on the social structure, ideology, law, social psychology, morals and ethics of the various cultures of the Ancient Near East" (6:61). Ancient society was structured in three levels: independent free persons (landowners and craftsmen), semi-independent serfs (laborers for the palace or temple who might also own property), and slaves (human property or chattel). The slave class, according to Boecker, was an "essential factor in the economy" of the ancient world (77–78).

The Text in the Interpretive Tradition

The interpretation of slave laws in the book of the covenant was central in the nineteenth-century debates over slavery in North America. The Episcopal bishop of Vermont John Henry Hopkins defended slavery based on the clear defense of the practice throughout biblical literature. The slave laws in the book of the covenant played an important role in the debate. Advocates for slavery, like Hopkins, cited Exod. 21:2-11 as evidence for the justification of debt slavery; the laws clarified that slavery is sanctioned by God and incorporated into the national constitution of ancient Israel. Albert Barnes represents nineteenth-century interpreters who opposed slavery. He suggests that the starting point for rejecting the biblical teaching on slavery was to deny the authority of the literal meaning of the laws of slavery, as in Exod. 21:2-11, and to qualify the laws by placing them in an ancient setting. For example, slavery was defined as a form of kidnapping, which is forbidden in Exod. 21:16, thus setting the laws of slavery and kidnapping in opposition. The historical context of the slave laws also allowed for the clarification of the contrast between the ancient practice and the nineteenth century. Barnes, for example, noted that the law of debt slavery in Exod. 21:2-11 is a voluntary action that functions as security against poverty, as opposed to the system of slavery in North America, which was based on chattel slavery for economic profit. The law against striking a slave in Exod. 21:20-21 indicated to some antislavery interpreters that ancient Israelite slavery was actually a benevolent institution aimed at the poor, which has nothing in common with modern chattel slavery. The proslavery advocates responded to these arguments by advocating a literal interpretation of the Bible. The literalist interpretation of slavery in the Bible is illustrated by Governor Hammond, who wrote: "But when I show them (the anti-slavery interpreters) that to hold 'bondmen forever' is ordained by God, they deny the Bible, and set up in its place a law of their own making" (quoted in Swartley, 50).

The Text in Contemporary Discussion

The contemporary discussion of the slave laws in the book of the covenant focuses in particular on the law of the female slave in Exod. 21:7-11. This law describes the sale of a daughter into slavery as a concubine or slave-bride. In this law, the daughter is a commodity, owned by her father. Her economic value is tied to her sexuality. The economic transaction changes the status of the girl from daughter to slave, who becomes the property of the purchaser. The law clarifies further that the master/purchaser may pass his slave-bride on to his son, should he find any fault or displeasure in her.

The emphasis in contemporary discussion of the slave laws is how closely the law of the female slave, as a sexual commodity, mirrors the vast business in human trafficking, where girls are bought and sold in a global marketplace of slavery. Jonathan Tran writes of this practice: "Slavery may be one of the most representative consequences of global capitalism. In the same way that chattel slavery epitomized the period of colonization, so contemporary human trafficking epitomizes the political, economic and social realities of the world in which we find ourselves" (22). As in the biblical law of the slave-bride, the girls in the trafficking business are sexual commodities for males. The United Nations has concluded that the more common form of human trafficking is sexual exploitation (79 percent), followed by forced labor (18 percent). The result is a multimillion dollar industry in which daughters (young virgin girls) are bought in one country for $300 and sold in another for $20,000. In the United States alone, between 100,000 and 300,000 children are yearly being trafficked in the sex industry. The profit in the slave trade of human trafficking is estimated at thirty-two billion dollars, six billion more than the profit of Apple in 2011.

Exodus 24:1—31:18: Sabbath and the Revelation of the Tabernacle

The Text in Its Ancient Context

This section describes the ascent of Moses to the summit of Mount Sinai (Exod. 24:1-18) to receive the architectural plans for the tabernacle (Exod. 25:1—31:11). The revelation of the tabernacle will allow Moses to build a copy of God's heavenly home on earth, so that YHWH might dwell with the Israelites (Exod. 25:8-9). The building of the tabernacle creates a sanctuary, or holy place on earth, which, when coupled with holy time in the law of Sabbath (Exod. 31:12-17), will allow for Israel to commune with God through the experience of rest from work on Sabbath. The sequence of temple building and rest is a common motif in ancient Near Eastern religion. Gods rest after they construct their temples (Hurowitz, 330–31). Nabonidus prays to Shamash, calling Ebabaar the "residence of your rest." Also, Enlil and Ea "dwell on a restful dais in a pure dwelling." The relationship of temple building and the god's rest likely influenced the biblical author, but the focus shifts in the construction of the tabernacle from the rest of the deity to that of the people. The result is the emphasis on Sabbath as a day of human rest from work in the profane world.

The origin of Sabbath observance has been extensively researched without firm conclusions. Sabbath observance may be Babylonian in origin (*sab/pattum*), in which case Sabbath is not a weekly day, but perhaps the day of the full moon. Sabbath does occur in ancient Israel along with reference to the full moon (Isa. 1:10-14; Hosea 2:11-15; Amos 8:4-7). Sabbath is mentioned in the story of the prophet Elisha (2 Kgs. 4:23). King Ahaz of Judah is described as dismantling a Sabbath canopy in the temple in the late eighth century. And the Sabbath command appears in the cultic laws of Exod. 23:10-12. The authorship of each of these texts is debated, yet the distribution suggests the observance of some form of Sabbath in the monarchical period, although its centrality in that period of time is not clear. Sabbath observance takes a more prominent role in the exilic and postexilic prophetic literature. Late Jeremiah tradition (Jer. 17:19-27), the exilic prophet Ezekiel (20:8-26;

46:1-12), and postexilic literature in the book of Isaiah (56:2, 6; 58:13; 66:23) forbid work on the Sabbath. The observance of Sabbath also concludes the postexilic book of Nehemiah (13:15-22).

The observance of Sabbath emerges as a central law in the design of the Priestly literature. The foundation for Sabbath observance is established in creation (Gen. 2:1-3). The ideal rhythm of creation is six days of work punctuated by one day of rest. It is lost with the flood and only reappears gradually in the wilderness journey. Sabbath first appears in the cycle of manna (Exod. 16:22-26); it is established as a law in the Decalogue (Exod. 20:8-11); and the penalty for violating the law is outlined after the construction of the tabernacle (Exod. 21:12-17). The law of Sabbath in the Decalogue is humanitarian; it is a day of rest for all humans, slave and free, as well as animals. The rationale derives from creation, when God rested after the six days of creation (Exod. 20:11). The seventh day of rest would be Saturday, not Sunday. Violation of the humanitarian law, however, carries the death penalty: Exod. 31:12-17 states that Sabbath is an eternal covenant and that the violating of the law would require the execution of the offender.

The Text in the Interpretive Tradition

Sabbath observance is central in Jewish tradition. Sabbath begins at sundown on Friday evening and continues until Saturday evening. Sabbath is observed in the home with a dinner, which begins with the kiddush over wine and blessings over the bread. Sabbath commemorates both creation and the redemption of the Jewish people from Egypt, and it provides a glimpse into the messianic age. It is a time for study and reflection. The Talmud lists thirty-nine activities that are forbidden on Sabbath, including agricultural work, baking, housework, extensive writing, and making fires (*m. Shabbat* 7:2). The prohibitions against work are interpreted in distinct ways. For example, Orthodox Jews refrain from all thirty-nine prohibitions; they may forbid turning on electrical items or driving an automobile, although there may be modifications to the restrictions. Reform Judaism allows for more individual choice with regard to Sabbath practice.

Sabbath observance is equally important in Christian tradition. Jesus observed the Sabbath, even though he argued with Jewish leaders about the appropriate restrictions (Matt. 12:1-12; John 5:1-18). The early disciples also observed the Jewish Sabbath (Luke 23; Acts 3; 5; 13; 18). But eventually, sometime between the second to the fourth centuries CE, Christians began to worship on Sunday rather than Saturday, thus designating the first day of the week as the "Lord's Day." The emperor Constantine made the shift in the Christian "day of rest" official with an edict in 321 CE: "All judges and city people and the craftsmen shall rest upon the venerable day of the sun" (Ayer, 1913, 284–85). The edict also indicates that agricultural work is not forbidden, thus introducing a debate in Christian tradition not only over the proper day for Sabbath, but also about restricted activity. Yet, already in the fourth century CE, the church father Augustine spiritualized the Sabbath commandment, allowing for all types of work. Aquinas, however, interpreted the Sabbath command to be in effect for all Christians because it represented moral law. In the Reformation, Calvin and Luther abolished the religious authority of the Sabbath law, but they followed Aquinas in retaining the law of Sabbath on moral grounds. The Westminster Confession demands the cessation of work on the Sunday as well as all thoughts about work (chap. 21, sections 7–8). The Puritans and other seventeenth-century Calvinists emphasized the strict observance of the Sabbath command even further, introducing a Sunday sabbatarianism. In the nineteenth century CE, Seventh-day Adventists retained the seventh day (Saturday) as the day of rest, marking its duration from sunset to sunset. Seventh-day Adventists forbid work, except in times of need to alleviate suffering.

The Text in Contemporary Discussion

Contemporary discussion of Sabbath has moved in a very different direction from the traditional concerns about the proper day or the approved activities. The most pressing concern in current reflection on Sabbath is the frantic pace of work and cultural lifestyle of modern society, as well as growing economic injustice in the global economy. In 1998, Pope John Paul II addressed the problem of the frantic lifestyle of modern society in the apostolic letter *Dies Domini*. He cautioned Catholics to resist the "weekend" mentality that has come to dominate modern culture by keeping the Lord's Day holy. Other modern authors expand on the same problem of our fast-paced, work-oriented culture. Wayne Muller, for example, bemoans the relentless emphasis on success and productivity, which deprive contemporary humans from any life rhythm or time for reflection (Muller, 1–12). Abraham Heschel deepens the same perspective, arguing that Sabbath is not an interlude between work, but the climax of living (Heschel, 101). The contemporary discussion moves even further away from the past concern about time and orthodox observance by tying Sabbath to the problems of social justice in the global economy. Richard Lowery argues that Sabbath is about recovering proportion, social solidarity, and economic justice in the global marketplace (Lowery, 1–6). The emphasis on economic justice returns to the central theme of Sabbath law in the Decalogue and in the Jubilee laws (Leviticus 25).

Exodus 32–33: The Golden Calf and the Mediation of Moses

The Text in Its Ancient Context

This section describes the construction of the golden calf (Exod. 32:1-6), while Moses is away from the people receiving the tablets of the law at the summit of Mount Sinai. The calf represents the people's request that Aaron make gods for them to replace Moses, because they "do not know what has become of him" (Exod. 32:1). The story moves quickly, recounting the divine rage over the golden calf (Exod. 32:7-14); the destruction of the calf by Moses and the purging of the people by the Levites (Exod. 32:15-29); and the intercession of Moses for the renewed presence of YHWH (Exod. 32:30—33:23).

The construction of the golden calf in Exodus 32 represents Israel's rejection of the covenant, which Moses describes as a "great sin" (Exod. 32:30). But it is difficult to interpret the content of the sin. The golden calf certainly represents the sin of idolatry, since it breaks the second commandment of the Decalogue. The statement of the people, identifying the calf with God, confirms this meaning: "These are your gods, Israel, who brought you out of the land of Egypt" (Exod. 32:4). But the sin of idolatry can be interpreted further. Rabbinic (*m. Abot* 5:18) and New Testament (2 Pet. 2:15) interpreters state that idolatry is more than imaging God in a forbidden manner; it is also a form of human greed—the desire to possess and to control God. This deeper meaning of idolatry is clarified in the parallel account of the golden calf story that takes place during the rise to power of the first northern king, Jeroboam I (1 Kgs. 12:31-32). Jeroboam tries to legitimate his rule by means of religion. To this end, he builds two golden calves and, like Israel in the wilderness, identifies them with God: "Here are your gods, Israel, who brought you up out of the land of Egypt" (1 Kgs. 12:28).

The episode of Israel in the wilderness and that of Jeroboam I are closely related. They provide commentary on each other, clarifying how the golden calf in each story is not only a religious sin but also a political transgression about controlling God through government. The "golden calves" of Jeroboam I represent the apostasy of all monarchs throughout the Deuteronomistic History who sought to justify their rule by anchoring political power in religion. Jeroboam I is guilty of this when he ties his rule with the worship of the golden calves at Bethel and Dan (2 Kgs. 10:29). The biblical authors judge the equation of political power and religion as the sin that leads to the destruction of monarchs (2 Kgs. 17:7-23). The Deuteronomistic History provides a backdrop for interpreting the idolatry of the golden calf in Exodus 32 as a political and religious allegory about the inherent conflict between YHWH and kings. The intrabiblical quotation between Aaron (and the Israelites) and Jeroboam signals that, on one level, the golden calf in the wilderness is the taproot, which will inevitably lead to the political idolatry associated with monarchy in the promised land. In this case, the content of the idolatry is not only imaging God but also worshiping the power of the king over YHWH.

The Text in the Interpretive Tradition

The story of the golden calf is the nearest equivalent to the concept of original sin in postbiblical Jewish literature (Aberbach and Smolar). All subsequent misfortunes that have befallen the Jewish people go back in part to the sin of the calf (*b. Sanh.* 102A). Given the gravity of the sin and its immediacy after the experience of revelation, the rabbis reflected on how the construction of the golden calf was even possible. Solutions include the identification of the guilty party as the "mixed multitude" (Exod. 12:38), who accompanied Israel out of the Egypt, along with the Egyptian magicians Yanos and Yambros (*b. Shab.* 89A). Another possibility was that Moses was late in descending the mountain. The action of Aaron in making the calf also requires explanation; his action may have arisen from fear (pseudo-Philo), perhaps was intensified from the murder of Hur (*Rab. Lev.* 10:3). He may not even have fashioned the calf (*b. Sanh.* 102:2). This is also the conclusion of the Qur'an, where Aaron also does not build the golden calf (sura 20). Instead, a person named Samiri builds the calf, while Aaron warns the people not to worship it.

Early Christian interpreters interpret the golden calf story polemically to illustrate that the Jews had rejected God. The speech of Stephen in Acts employs the story of the golden calf to confirm the Israelite rejection of Moses and God's rejection of Israel (Acts 7:38-43). The idolatry of the golden calf also explained why the Jews lost the covenant (*Epistle of Barnabas* 4.5–9). The polemical reading continues in the church fathers. Ephrem the Syrian interprets Israel's worship of the golden calf as a sign of their permanent impurity (Nat. 14.19).

The Text in Contemporary Discussion

The modern period contains a more political and economic interpretation of the golden calf that is also rooted in the critique of monarchy, which is at the heart of the original story. Benjamin Franklin, for example, identified the anti-Federalists opposing the Constitution to be like the Israelites, who worshiped the golden calf and wished to return to Egypt. The political and economic interpretation of the golden calf has continued into the twentieth century. Dietrich Bonheoffer employed the story of the golden calf in critically evaluating the antisemitic policies of Hitler and the complacency of the German church by contrasting the church of Moses, a church committed to the prophetic word, with the church of Aaron, a worldly church that makes its own gods (Bonhoeffer, 243–48). The political and economic reading of the golden calf is extended in the contemporary social context to signify the decadence of excessive wealth. The golden calf is likened to the Wall Street bull. Donna Schaper, for example, describes carrying a golden calf named "Greed" in the Occupy Wall Street movement as signifying the social and economic decadence in the global economy, which points to a contemporary false god.

Exodus 34: Covenantal Renewal

The Text in Its Ancient Context

After Israel breaks the covenant in the construction and worship of the golden calf (Exodus 32), the successful mediation of Moses (Exodus 33) leads to covenant renewal and the divine promise of land (Exodus 34). Exodus 34 is divided between a new revelation to Moses (34:1-9), which takes place this time in a cave on the divine mountain, and a new law code (34:10-28). The new revelation to Moses emphasizes the quality of divine grace: YHWH is a "God merciful and gracious, slow to anger, and abounding in steadfast love and faithfulness, keeping steadfast love for the thousandth generation" (34:6-7). Divine grace is the basis on which Moses requests forgiveness: "pardon our iniquity and our sin and take us for your inheritance" (34:9). The use of the word "to inherit" introduces the theme of the promised land, since the word is associated with the promise of land throughout the Pentateuch. The Song of the Sea, for example, identifies the inheritance of God with the divine temple in the midst of the land (Exod. 15:17). The epilogue to the book of the covenant also equates inheritance with the land: "Little by little I will drive them out from before you, until you have increased and possess the land (Exod. 23:30). And during the crisis of the golden calf, Moses reminds God of the divine promise to the ancestors: "all this land that I have promised I will give to your descendants, and they shall inherit it forever" (Exod. 32:13).

The divine promise of land requires a violent conquest of indigenous people. YHWH promises to drive out the residents of the land, identified as Canaanites, Perizzites, Hivites, and Jebusites (Exod. 34:11). Once the indigenous people are conquered, the Israelites are also not allowed to interact with them in any way, either through shared worship or through intermarriage (Exod. 34:12-16). The demand for exclusive loyalty to YHWH provides insight into the theological motivation. The identity of the Israelites, as people who are not indigenous to the land of Canaan, fuels the theological demand that the Israelite nation be culturally and religiously separate from other nations in the land of Canaan and from their religious traditions. The exclusive vision of life in the land achieved through invasion is not the only perspective in the Hebrew Bible; it contrasts, for example, to the portrait of the patriarchs in Genesis who are indigenous to the land and make covenant with their neighbors. Sperling characterizes the biblical conquest tradition as a political allegory to support the utopian goal of religious exclusion. The theme of exclusivity arose in the first section of the epilogue to the book of the covenant (Exod. 23:20-26), when God demands that the Israelite people not worship indigenous gods, focusing in particular on the destruction of their cultic objects (Exod. 23:24). In the same context, God also forbids all covenants with foreign gods (Exod. 23:32). The separate commands reinforce the first two commandments of the Decalogue, which also demand that the Israelites serve no other gods than YHWH (Exod. 20:3 = 23:32) and that they refrain from the worship of idols (Exod. 20:4-6 = 23:24-25). Thus the law of covenant renewal reinforces the earlier law codes, which state that faithful obedience to covenant and the realization of the promised land requires the conquest of the indigenous nations.

The Text in the Interpretive Tradition

The themes of the promised land and conquest have undergone a wide range of interpretation. The church fathers turned the themes inward through the method of typology. Origen, for example, interprets the conquest of the indigenous nations as spiritual warfare against the "violent impulses of anger and rage" in Christians, which the believer must expel from the "land of promise" (*Hom. Josh.* 1.5–6). He explains: "Within us are the Canaanites; within us are the Perizzites; here are the Jebusites." The promised land is "the land about which the Lord says, 'Blessed are the meek, who will possess the land as their inheritance" (*Hom. Josh.* 2.2).

In the modern period, most interpreters have rejected the typological hermeneutic of the church fathers, favoring instead a more literal reading of the text. As a consequence, the conquest of the indigenous nations and the realization of the promised land take on political meaning, especially under the influence of nationalism and colonization. The pilgrims identified themselves as the new Israel, a chosen people entering the promised land. Thomas Jefferson employed biblical imagery of the promised land in his second inaugural address, calling for help upon the "Being, in whose hands we are, who led our fathers, as Israel of old, from their native land and planted them in a country flowing with all the necessities and comforts of life" (quoted in Cherry, 65). The influence of the theme of the promised land coupled with a sense of Manifest Destiny in colonization goes beyond North America to include the Afrikaners, who understood themselves as God's chosen people and South Africa as the promised land, and more recently in the rise of the modern state of Israel, with the dispute over land with the indigenous Palestinians (Akenson, 76–77, 319–22).

The Text in Contemporary Discussion

The contemporary discussion centers on the violence of the theme of conquest as a method for achieving the promised land, especially in the postcolonial, multicultural setting of the twenty-first century. Robert Allen Warrior, a member of the Osage Nation of American Indians, argues that liberation is too often narrowly defined from the perspective of Israelites who function as invaders. He counters that any contemporary discussion of achieving a liberated life in the promised land must begin with the Canaanites, not the Israelites. In the story of the exodus, the Canaanites only have status "as the people that Yahweh removes from the land in order to bring the chosen people" (239). The rights of the indigenous people are overlooked. This is a problem not simply of hermeneutics but also of social history. The conquest of the indigenous nations has worked its way into Americans' consciousness and ideology, sanctifying colonialism as Manifest Destiny. Warrior questions whether "Native Americans and other indigenous people dare trust the same god in their struggle for justice" (Warrior, 240). Musa Dube probes the same hermeneutical problem from the perspective of an indigenous African, who stands outside of the Afrikaner myth of being chosen (Dube, 3–7). Writing from a Palestinian perspective, Edward Said judges the use of the exodus-conquest myth in the rise of the modern state of Israel as an instance of blaming the victim (Said, 161–78); the Palestinian priest Naim Ateek declares that the use of the conquest myth in Joshua to accord "the primary claim over the land to Jews" is an abuse of the Bible (Ateek, 227–28). The historical conflicts drive home the conclusion that the themes of the promised land can inspire liberation and legitimate oppression (Yee 2010).

Exodus 35–40: Building the Tabernacle

The Text in Its Ancient Context

The building of the tabernacle concludes the literature in the book of Exodus (chaps. 35–40). The final episode recounts how the heavenly vision of the temple that Moses receives on Mount Sinai becomes an earthly reality, allowing God to dwell on earth in the midst of the people of God (Exod. 40:34-38). The construction separates into four parts: the building materials are presented as a freewill offering by the people (35:4-29); the builders, Bezalel and Oholiab, are identified (35:30—36:7); the construction of the tabernacle sanctuary and its furnishings is completed (36:8—38:20); and there is a census and a tax levy to support the tabernacle cult (38:21-31). Once completed, the deity descends into the sanctuary (40:34-38).

The process of building (Exodus 35–40) repeats the earlier divine revelation to Moses (Exodus 25–31), where the theological signification of the tabernacle is stated in Exod. 25:1-9. God commands Moses in Exod. 25:8 to make a sanctuary (*miqdash*). The word "sanctuary" underscores the quality of the building as holy space, deriving from the root "to be holy" (*qadash*). The conclusion to the Song of the Sea (Exod. 15:17) also describes YHWH's temple as a sanctuary constructed by God, not humans. God further describes the tabernacle and its furnishings in Exod. 25:9 as a "pattern" (*tabnit*) "shown" (*mar'eh*) to Moses on Mount Sinai. The meaning of the text is difficult. The word *tabnit* translates as "form, structure, or shape," while *mar'eh* indicates a "vision" or even the "form" of an object. A *tabnit* describes blueprints for the Jerusalem temple (1 Chron. 28:11), and it may even describe the replica of the temple (1 Chron. 28:19). In Num. 8:4, YHWH shows Moses a form or perhaps a copy (*mar'eh*) of the lampstand. The language suggests that the tabernacle is a copy of the heavenly dwelling of God. The purpose of the revelation is to instruct Moses in the building process, with the goal of allowing God to dwell on earth with Israel in a holy place (Exod. 25:8).

The symbolism of the temple as a copy of God's heavenly home creates a web of related themes from ancient Near Eastern religion, which influence the interpretation of the tabernacle sanctuary. The ability of temples to link heaven and earth is symbolized through the mythology of the cosmic mountain. The cosmic mountain represents the meeting place between heaven and earth, and hence the residency of God within the temple. The Canaanite god Baal, for example, invades the created world by taking up residency in his temple on Mount Zaphon. The same is true with YHWH. The Jerusalem temple is located on Mount Zion, which the psalmist describes as the highest of all mountains, because it is the place where YHWH is enthroned and has "shown himself a sure defense" (Ps. 48:3). The book of Exodus ends with the same mythology of the temple and the cosmic mountain, when YHWH takes up residency in the tabernacle at Mount Sinai, providing a holy place, a sanctuary (*miqdash*), that replicates the heavenly temple, thus allowing God to dwell on earth.

The Text in the Interpretive Tradition

The history of interpretation builds on the understanding of the tabernacle as sacred space. Ancient readers used the details of the tabernacle as a means for symbolic interpretation. The author of *1 Enoch*, for example, describes the details of the sanctuary in a vision (14:1-25). The vision includes not only the house but also a foundation of crystal, a ceiling of stars, cherubim, and a fiery throne. Philo identifies the tabernacle with the universe, in which the building represented the spiritual world, while the courtyard is the material; the colors represent the elements of nature, and so forth (*Mos.* 2.15–26). The author of Hebrews reinterprets the tabernacle to describe Christ as the new high priest, who enters the holy of holies and mediates for humans (Hebrews 8). Origen also interprets the sacred space of the tabernacle to reveal the mystery of Christ and the relationship of Christ to the church. He extends the symbolic interpretation further to correlate the metals in the tabernacle with Christian virtues: gold is faith; silver is the word; and bronze is patience (*Hom. Exod.* 9.3). The English Bede wrote an entire commentary on the tabernacle in the eighth century CE. His interpretation relates the tabernacle to the church, the role of the gospel in the world, the proper interpretation of Scripture, and the role of church leaders (*Commentary on the Tabernacle*). The rabbis moved in a different direction, interpreting the tabernacle in relationship to Torah. The revelation of the tabernacle represents the climax in the revelation of the Torah, which is evident in the central place of the ark (*Exod. Rab.* 34.2).

The modern period shifted the focus from the symbolic meaning of the tabernacle to a literal interpretation within the framework of the history of composition. Julius Wellhausen, for example, concluded that the tabernacle never existed, but was a literary fantasy that sought to reinterpret the temple of Solomon. Other interpreters sought to compare the tabernacle with different tents of worship in the ancient world to provide historical background to the literature. Possible comparative material includes the Bedouin worship tents, or *qubbah*; Persian royal tents that functioned as movable palaces; and Egyptian funeral tents (see Homan).

The Text in Contemporary Discussion

The rise of secularism in contemporary culture challenges the religious meaning of the tabernacle as sacred space. Modernity has not only called into question the role of religion in human experience but also contested the power of sacred space as a resource for channeling the divine presence. As a result, contemporary discussion of the tabernacle is far removed from the ancient symbolic interpretations of the architecture and furnishings, which assumed the power of sacred space. The contemporary questions are whether the sacred is a reality as opposed to profane space and what ritual processes might allow a human to enter the world of the sacred.

Mircea Eliade explores the problem, characterizing the separation between the sacred and the profane as "two modes of being in the world" that give rise to two different qualities of experience. He employs the metaphor of geometry to describe the similarity of experience in the profane or secular world, since geometrical space can be cut and delimited in any direction without qualitative differentiation. Profane experience, like geometry, is "homogeneous space." The sacred, he contends, is a different mode of experience altogether from the homogeneous space of the profane world (Eliade, 14). Arnold van Gennep argues further that the process of leaving the secular world and entering the sacred requires careful rituals of the separation. The rite of passage requires separation from the secular world; the state of transition (or liminality), which opens one to the reality of the sacred; and eventually reincorporation in the profane world, which is now reoriented (15–25).

Works Cited

Ayer, Joseph Cullen. 1913. *A Source Book for Ancient Church History*. New York: Charles Scribner's Sons.

Aberbach, Moshe, and Leivy Smolar. 1968. "The Golden Calf Episode in Postbiblical Literature." *HUCA* 39:91–116.

Akenson, Donald Harman. 1992. *God's Peoples: Covenant and Land in South Africa, Israel, and Ulster*. Ithaca, NY: Cornell University Press.

Assmann, Jan. 1997. *Moses the Egyptian: The Memory of Egypt in Western Monotheism*. Cambridge, MA: Harvard University Press.

Ateek, Naim S. 2006. "A Palestinian Perspective: Biblical Perspectives on the Land." In Sugirtharajah, *Voices from the Margin*, 227–34.

Augustine. 1956. *On Baptism, against the Donatists*. In vol. 4 of *NPNF*[1], *The Anti-Manichean Writings, the Anti-Donatist Writings*. Translated by J. R. King.

Auerbach, Elias. 1975. *Moses*. Detroit: Wayne State University Press.

Bach, Alice. 1994. "With a Song in Her Heart: Listening to Scholars Listening for Miriam." In *A Feminist Companion to Exodus to Deuteronomy*, edited by Athalya Brenner, 243–58. Sheffield: Sheffield Academic Press.

Blake, William. 1805. *Pestilence: Death of the First Born*. Boston: Museum of Fine Arts.

Bloom, Harold, ed. 1987. *Exodus: Modern Critical Interpretations*. New York: Chelsea House.

Boecker, H. J. 1980. *Law and the Administration of Justice in the Old Testament and Ancient East*. Translated by J. Moiser. Minneapolis: Augsburg.

Bonhoeffer, Dietrich. 1965. *No Rusty Swords: Letters, Lectures and Notes, 1928–1936*. Vol. 1. Edited by Edwin H. Robertson. Translated by Edwin H. Robertson and John Bowden. New York: Harper & Row.

Brenner, Athalya. 1994a. "An Afterword: The Decalogue—Am I an Addressee?" In Brenner, *A Feminist Companion to Exodus to Deuteronomy*, 255–58.

———, ed. 1994b. *A Feminist Companion to Exodus to Deuteronomy*. Sheffield: Sheffield Academic Press.

Browning, Elizabeth Barrett. 1996. *Aurora Leigh: Authoritative Text, Backgrounds and Contexts, Criticism*. Edited by M. Reynolds. New York: W. W. Norton.

Buber, Martin. 1946. *Moses*. Oxford: Oxford University Press.

Calvin, John. 1950. *The Four Last Books of Moses Arranged in the Form of a Harmony*. Vol. 1. Translated by C. W. Bingham. Grand Rapids: Eerdmans.

———. 1975. *Institutes of the Christian Religion: 1536 Edition*. Translated by Ford Lewis Battles. Grand Rapids: Eerdmans.

Cherry, Conrad, ed. 1971. *God's New Israel: Religious Interpretation of American Destiny*. Chapel Hill: University of North Carolina Press.

Childs, Brevard S. 1974. *The Book of Exodus: A Critical, Theological Commentary*. OTL. Louisville: Westminster John Knox.

Coogan, Michael D. 1999. "The Ten Commandments on the Wall." *BRev* 15:2.

Cowley, A. 1923. *Aramaic Papyri of the Fifth Century B.C.* Oxford: Oxford University Press.

Dandamayev, Muhammad A. 1992. "Slavery." In *The Anchor Yale Bible Dictionary*, ed. David Noel Freedman, 6:58–65. New Haven: Yale University Press.

Daube, David. 1947. *Studies in Biblical Law*. Cambridge: Cambridge University Press.

Dickey, James. 1968. "The Son, the Cave, and the Burning Bush." In *The Young American Poets: A Big Table Book*, edited by P. Carroll. Chicago: Follett.

Dijk-Hemmes, Fokkelien van. 1994. "Some Recent Views on the Presentation of the Song of Miriam." In Brenner, *A Feminist Companion to Exodus to Deuteronomy*, 200–206.

Dohmen, C. 2004. *Exodus 19-40*. Herders Theologischer Kommentar zum Alten Testament. Freiburg: Herder.

Dozeman, Thomas B. 2010a. *Exodus*. Eerdmans Critical Commentary. Grand Rapids: Eerdmans.

———, ed. 2010b. *Methods for Exodus*. Methods in Biblical Interpretation. Cambridge: Cambridge University Press.

Dube, Musa W. 2000. *Postcolonial Feminist Interpretation of the Bible*. St. Louis: Chalice.

Eliade, M. 1959. *The Sacred and the Profane*. New York: Harper & Row.

Exum, J. Cheryl. 1983. "'You Shall Let Every Daughter Live': A Study of Exodus 1:8—2:10." *Semeia* 28:63–82.

Falk, Z. W. 1990. "Spirituality and Jewish Law." In *Religion and Law: Biblical Judaic and Islamic Perspectives*, edited by E. B. Firmage et al., 127–38. Winona Lake, IN: Eisenbrauns.

Feldman, Louis H. 2004. *"Remember Amalek!" Vengeance, Zealotry and Group Destruction in the Bible According to Philo, Pseudo-Philo, and Josephus*. HUCM. Cincinnati: Hebrew Union Press.

Fernandez, Eleazer S. 2006. "Exodus-toward-Egypt: Filipino-Americans' Struggle to Realize the Promised Land." In Sugirtharajah, *Voices from the Margin*, 242–57.

Firestone, Reuven. 2008. *Who Are the Real Chosen People? The Meaning of Chosenness in Judaism, Christianity and Islam*. Center for Religious Inquiry. Woodstock, VT: Skylight Paths.

Frankfort, H. 1978. *Kingship and the Gods*. Chicago: University of Chicago Press.

Fretheim, Terence. 1991. "The Plagues as Ecological Signs of Historical Disaster." *JBL* 110:385–96.

Fuchs, Esther. 2000. "A Jewish-Feminist Reading of Exodus 1–2." In *Jews, Christians, and The Theology of the Hebrew Scriptures*, edited by A. Ogden Bellis and Joel S. Kaminsky, 307–26. Symposium 8. Atlanta: Society of Biblical Literature.

Gennep, Arnold van. 1909. *The Rites of Passage*. London: Routledge and Kegan Paul.

Ginzberg, Louis. 1909–1938. *The Legends of the Jews*. 7 Vols. Philadelphia: Jewish Publication Society.

Graetz, Naomi. 1994. "Did Miriam Talk Too Much?" In Brenner, *A Feminist Companion to Exodus to Deuteronomy*, 231–42.

Greenberg, Moshe. 1951. "Hebrew *segulla*: Akkadian *sikiltu*." *JAOS* 71:172–74.

Greengus, Samuel. 1992. "Law." In *Anchor Yale Bible Dictionary*, edited by David Noel Freedman, 4:243–52. New Haven: Yale University Press.

Gregory of Nyssa. 1978. *The Life of Moses*. Translated by Abraham J. Malherbe and Everett Ferguson. Classics of Western Spirituality. New York: Paulist Press.

Gressmann, Hugo. 1913. *Mose und seine Zeit: Ein Kommentar zu den Mose-Sagen*. FRLANT 1. Göttingen: Vandenhoeck & Ruprecht.

Harrelson, W. 1980. *The Ten Commandments and Human Rights*. OBT. Philadelphia: Fortress.

Herdner A., editor. 1963. *Corpus des tablettes en cuneiforms alphabétiques découvertes à Ras-Shamra-Ugarit de 1929 à 1939*. Paris: Mission des Ras-Shamra 10.

Heschel, Abraham Joshua. 1951. *The Sabbath*. New York: Farrar, Straus & Giroux.

Homan, Michael M. 2002. *To Your Tents, O Israel! The Terminology, Function, Form, and Symbolism of Tents in the Hebrew Bible and the Ancient Near East*. Culture and History of the Ancient Near East 12. Leiden: Brill.

Hunter, Alastair G. 2003. "(De)nominating Amalek, Racial Stereotyping." In *Sanctified Aggression: Legacies of Biblical and Post Biblical Vocabularies of Violence*, edited by Jonneke Bekkenkamp and Yvonne Sherwood, 92–108. New York: T&T Clark.

Hurowitz, V. 1992. *I Have Built You an Exalted House: Temple Building in the Bible in Light of Mesopotamian and Northwest Semitic Writing*. JSOTSup 115. Sheffield: JSOT Press.

Jackson, Bernard S. 2000. *Studies in the Semiotics of Biblical Law*. JSOTSup 314. Sheffield: Sheffield Academic Press.

Janzen, J. Gerald. 1994. "Song of Moses, Song of Miriam: Who Is Seconding Whom?" In Brenner, *A Feminist Companion to Exodus to Deuteronomy*, 187–99. Sheffield: Sheffield Academic Press.

Keil, C. F., and F. Delitzsch. 1981. *Commentary on the Old Testament*. Vol. 1. Grand Rapids: Eerdmans.

Kirk-Duggan, Cheryl A. 2006. "Let My People Go! Threads of Exodus in African American Narratives." In Sugirtharajah, *Voices from the Margin*, 258–78.

Larsson, Göran. 1999. *Bound for Freedom: The Book of Exodus in Jewish and Christian Traditions*. Peabody, MA: Hendrickson.

Lehmann, Paul L. 1994. *The Decalogue and a Human Future: The Meaning of the Commandments for Making and Keeping Human Life Human*. Grand Rapids: Eerdmans.

Leibowitz, Nehama. 1981. *Studies in Shemot: The Book of Exodus*. Translated by A. Newman. 2 vols. 1976. Reprint, Jerusalem: World Zionist Organization.

Lowery, Richard H. 2000. *Sabbath and Jubilee*. Understanding Biblical Themes. St. Louis: Chalice.

Mamet, David. 1996. *Passover*. New York: St. Martin's.

Masalha, Nur. 2000. *Imperial Israel and the Palestinians: The Politics of Expansion*. London: Pluto.

McKenzie, Steven L. 2000. *Covenant*. Understanding Biblical Themes. St. Louis: Chalice.

Mendenhall, George. E. 1955. *Law and Covenant in Israel and the Ancient Near East*. Pittsburgh: The Biblical Colloquium.

Meyers, Carol. 1994. "Miriam the Musician." In Brenner, *A Feminist Companion to Exodus to Deuteronomy*, 207–30. Sheffield: Sheffield Academic Press.

———. 2005. *Exodus*. New Cambridge Bible Commentary. Cambridge: Cambridge University Press.

Muller, Wayne. 1999. *Sabbath: Finding Rest, Renewal, and Delight in Our Busy Lives*. New York: Bantam.

Origen. 2002. *Homilies on Joshua*, edited by Cynthia White. Translated by Barbara J. Bruce.

The Fathers of the Church. Washington, DC: Catholic University of America Press.

Otto, Rudolf. 1958. *The Idea of the Holy: An Inquiry into the Non-Rational Factor in the Idea of the Divine and its Relation to the Rational*. Translated by J. W. Harvey. 2nd ed. 1923. Reprint, London: Oxford.

Philo. 1929. *On the Creation: Allegorical Interpretation of Genesis 2 and 3*. Translated by F. H. Colson and G. H. Whitaker. Loeb Classical Library. Cambridge, MA: Harvard University Press.

———. 1954. *Moses I. and II.* Translated by F. H. Colson. Loeb Classical Library. Cambridge, MA: Harvard University Press.

Pixley, George V. 1987. *On Exodus: A Liberation Perspective*. Maryknoll, NY: Orbis.

———. 2010. "Liberation Criticism." In Dozeman, *Methods for Exodus*, 131–62.

Pixley, George V., and Clodovis Boff. 2006. "A Latin American Perspective: The Option for the Poor in the Old Testament." In Sugirtharajah, *Voices from the Margin*, 207–16.

Pritchard, J. B., ed. 1969. *Ancient Near Eastern Texts Relating to the Old Testament*. 3rd ed. Princeton: Princeton University Press.

Propp, William. 1999. *Exodus 1–18*. AYB. New Haven: Yale University Press.

———. 2006. *Exodus 19–40*. AYB. New Haven: Yale University Press.

Rad, Gerhard von. 1959. *Moses*. 2nd ed. World Christian Books 32. New York: Association Press.

Rapp, Ursula. 2002. *Mirjam: Eine feministisch-rhetorische Lektüre der Mirjamtexte in der hebräischen Bibel.* Berlin: de Gruyter.

Redford, D. B. 1992. *Egypt, Canaan, and Israel in Ancient Times*. Princeton: Princeton University Press.

———. 1982. "Pithom." In *Lexicon der Ägyptologie*, edited by W. Helck and W. Westerdorf. Wiesbaden: Harrasowitz. Cols. 1054–58.

Sagi, Avi. 1994. "The Punishment of Amalek in Jewish Tradition: Coping with the Moral Problem." *HTR* 87:323–46.

Said, Edward W. 1988. "Michael Walzer's Exodus and Revolution: A Canaanite Reading." In *Blaming the Victims: Spurious Scholarship and the Palestinian Question*, edited by Edward W. Said and Christopher Hitchens, 161–78. London: Verso, 1988.

Schaper, Donna. 2011. "Occupy Wall Street, The Golden Calf and the New Ideology." *Huffington Post*. http://www.huffingtonpost.com/donna-schaper/occupy-wall-street-the-go_b_1004946.html. October 11.

Schwartz, Regina M. 1997. *The Curse of Cain: The Violent Legacy of Monotheism*. Chicago: University of Chicago Press.

Setel, D. O'Donnell. 1992. "Exodus." In *The Women's Bible Commentary*, edited by C. A. Newsom and S. H. Ringe, 26–35. Louisville: Westminster John Knox.

Sperling, S. David. 1998. *The Original Torah: The Political Intention of the Bible's Writers*. New York: New York University Press.

Stanton, Elizabeth Cady. 1993. *The Woman's Bible*. Evanston, IL: Northwestern University Press.

Steinberg, Naomi. 2010. "Feminist Criticism." In Dozeman, *Methods for Exodus*, 163–92.

Sugirtharajah, R. S., ed. *Voices from the Margin: Interpreting the Bible in the Third World.* Maryknoll, NY: Orbis.

Swartley, Willard M. 1983. *Slavery, Sabbath, War, and Women: Case Issues in Biblical Interpretation.* Scottdale, PA: Herald.

Tran, Jonathan. 2007. "Sold into Slavery." *Christian Century* 124, no. 24:22–26.

Trible, Phyllis. 1973. "Depatriarchalizing in Biblical Interpretation." *JAAR* 41:34–45.

———. 1994. "Bringing Miriam out of the Shadows." In Brenner, *A Feminist Companion to Exodus to Deuteronomy*, 166–86.

Warrior, Robert Allen. 2006. "A Native American Perspective: Canaanites, Cowboys, and Indians." In Sugirtharajah, *Voices from the Margin,* 235–41.

Weems, Renita J. 1992. "The Hebrew Women Are Not Like the Egyptian Women: The Ideology of Race, Gender and Sexual Reproduction in Exodus 1." *Semeia* 59:25–34.

Wellhausen, Julius. 1957. *Prolegomena to the History of Ancient Israel.* Translated by J. Sutherland Black and Allan Menzies. 1883. Reprint, New York: Meridian.

White, Lynn Townsend Jr. 1967. "The Historical Roots of Our Ecologic Crisis." *Science* 155:1203–7.

Yee, Gale A. 2010. "Postcolonial Biblical Criticism." In Dozeman, *Methods for Exodus*, 193–233.

LEVITICUS

Robert Kugler

Introduction

A book addressing sacrificial practices, the manner of selecting priests, the relative degrees of purity in animals and humans, and other topics related to ritual practice, Leviticus has come in for more than its fair share of neglect. Compelling narratives like those found in Genesis and Exodus are virtually absent in Leviticus, and its theological significance is difficult to recognize, at least on a casual reading. By comparison with its predecessors in the Torah, Leviticus hardly inspires a reader's rapturous attention.

Worse yet, when Leviticus has received attention, it has often been rather unwelcome. Some early Protestant historical critics used the book's focus on ritual practice to license grossly inappropriate caricatures of Judaism, ancient and contemporary, as lacking in theological depth and reduced to "mere" ritual practice. In more recent years, select passages in the book have also featured prominently in often irrational and emotionally charged debates regarding homosexuality.

Yet for all the obstacles that have been set against Leviticus, it has managed to win a thoughtful readership that has endured for centuries, a readership that points time and again to the considerable theological gravitas the book does in fact possess. From the people of the Dead Sea Scrolls to the great exegetes of rabbinic Judaism, from the earliest Christian communities to the "new evangelicals" of today, from scholars in the school traditions of the ancient world to contemporary cultural anthropologists—Leviticus has elicited a rich history of interpretation and analysis by generations of readers.

The survey of the book's contents that plays a role in the following commentary does confirm, though, that Leviticus is concerned above all with ritual practice. Chapters 1–7 are about sacrifice, chapters 8–10 deal with the priestly selection and ordination, chapters 11–15 are about ensuring the laity's purity for the cult, chapter 16 sets out the annual rite for purifying Israel for the cult, and chapters 17–26 reflect on the consequences of all Israel being made holy given God's presence in the sanctuary. Even chapter 27, an otherwise unrelated appendix, gets in on the act, addressing the redemption of sacred vows made to God. There can be no denying it: Leviticus *is* consumed with rules and regulations governing ritual practice. How, then, can we account for the theological depth generations of interpreters have discovered?

One way to answer that question is to contextualize Leviticus in its larger literary and historical setting, as a key component of the Priestly writer's contribution to the Torah. From the earliest days of the Documentary Hypothesis, Leviticus was assigned to a late exilic or early postexilic Priestly work (abbreviated as P). Many share Martin Noth's early judgment that only Leviticus 8–10 was integral to P as the logical continuation of the narrative that leaves off in Exodus 40, and that the rest of Leviticus, especially the so-called Holiness Code in chapters 17–26, amounted to later additions to this "narrative kernel" of the book (Noth, 13-15; cf. Campbell and O'Brien; Grabbe, 16–19). There is, however, significant dissent from this broad consensus, and this commentary joins that chorus of voices. On this reading, at least Leviticus 1–16 as a whole was integral to P from its inception (e.g., Nihan). As for Leviticus 17–26, the Holiness Code, this commentary joins with those who treat it as an addition to P that aimed to critique P from within (see Milgrom; Knohl).

What date do we assign to P and to Leviticus 1–16, and to the Holiness Code as a later supplement? In spite of valiant attempts by some to place P, Leviticus 1–16, and the Holiness Code in the First Temple period (e.g., Milgrom; Knohl), the weight of the evidence favors a late exilic or early postexilic date for all three (Noth; Nihan), even if some of the specific cultic instructions and priestly ordinances found especially in Leviticus may go back to the First Temple and its practices (see further Grabbe, 13–16).

As for the purpose of P in Second Temple Judea, and of Leviticus in particular, much seems obvious. Constructing a new temple, restarting the cult, establishing a legitimate priesthood, setting purity boundaries for laity vis-à-vis the sacred site—these were sure to be complicated and contested matters among the Judeans who returned to Judea under Persian rule with imperial authorization to do these things; without clear direction, chaotic conflict to control the cult could have reigned supreme. The Priestly work, an account of God's word on these topics to Moses and Aaron in hoary antiquity, settled matters and assured order where there might have been chaos. Leviticus played a key role in achieving this purpose.

Additionally, even though Persia had authorized Judeans to control Judea and manage its temple economy, they faced serious challenges to achieving that purpose. They were just one minority ethnic group in the midst of a veritable hegemonic pluralism of ethnic groups that had taken up residence in the land during the period of Babylonian control. The fields they were to make productive had been sorely abused and neglected in the generations since their forefathers were deported, the temple they were supposed to operate was little more than an open-air altar in the midst of a shambles, and the public infrastructure necessary to support this temple-based economy was nonexistent. Where communal and cosmic order was required to achieve the Persian mandate, there was only chaos; where abundant life was the goal, foreboding death and decay threatened. In response to this, P offered a narrative and ritual-legal prescription for cosmic and communal order and life, and in achieving this purpose, Leviticus also played an important role.

Last, the Priestly tradents were also acutely aware of the fact that not all Judeans were able to live in the land and contribute to its restoration. How should they maintain their Judean identity without that opportunity? This, too, received an answer from the Priestly writers, parts of which appear in Leviticus (esp. chapter 16, the Day of Atonement).

There is little surprise in the general shape of the interpretive tradition that Leviticus engendered, considering the book's focus on ritual, priesthood, and purity, and the character of some of its best-known passages in contemporary thought. The people of the Dead Sea Scrolls, concerned with the Jerusalem temple, its priestly leadership, and its purity or impurity, produced a substantial body of literature that engages with norms laid out in Leviticus. Early rabbinic Judaism, committed in its own way to continued speculation about the temple and priestly matters, was also intensely occupied with Leviticus. The Mishnah, a work dated to around 200 CE, is predicated on the existence of the Jerusalem temple, and as such invokes Leviticus, even if it is often oblique in doing so. *Sifra*, "the Book," is a priest's handbook based on Leviticus, also datable to around 200 CE. And *Leviticus Rabbah*, datable to the fifth century CE and one of the oldest midrashim, is a "homiletical midrash" on Leviticus passages. To be sure, as Christian traditions began to dominate in the production of new interpretive traditions, Leviticus receded a bit from prominence as a focal point for exegetical and hermeneutical interest, but even then it continued to draw interpretive comment and interest, and key passages were often deployed to support and interpret central Christian claims (see, e.g., Rom. 3:25, on Jesus as a "sacrifice of atonement"; cf. Heb. 9:1-14).

To say, however, that Leviticus comes in for a great deal of attention in contemporary discussion apart from the community of scholars devoted to critical study of the Scriptures and/or to tracing Jewish and Christian origins would be disingenuous at best. To be sure, many take great interest in passages thought to legitimate their condemnation of homosexuality (see further on Lev. 18:22; 20:13), but beyond that, vigorous engagement with Leviticus like that which one sees with the well-known stories of Genesis and Exodus is scarce. Perhaps, though, as a result of gaining greater acquaintance with this rich book of the Bible, through this commentary readers will be encouraged to bring it more fully into their own, contemporary imagination and discourse, especially its capacity to address the human experience of chaos and death with such a powerful vision of life and order, authored by God in the words of Moses and Aaron.

Leviticus 1–7

Chapters 1–7, the first large unit of text in Leviticus, can be divided into two subunits: Lev. 1:1—6:7 is a "layperson's manual" for how offerings are to be made, and 6:8—7:38 amounts to a "priest's manual" for making those sacrifices. For the sake of brevity, the corresponding portions of the two subunits are addressed together in the following commentary.

Many commentators observe that Leviticus 1–7 is discordant with the narrative thread that left off at the end of Exodus and that a narrative transition from the latter point to Leviticus 8 is easier to make. That observation supports the theories of compositional disunity described above. Yet coming on the heels of the sanctuary's completion in Exodus 40, instructions for its chief use, in fact, seem to be the natural next step in a larger narrative intended to ground the Second Temple and its operation in the authority of Mosaic instructions received directly from God. Thus skepticism about the place of Leviticus 1–7 in the "first draft" of the Priestly work is unwarranted.

This seems all the more true when we consider the way Leviticus 1–7 functions in P as a whole. Among the concerns of the postexilic Judean community the P tradents surely had to address was how the sacrifices should be offered in the restored temple. We know from a variety of sources (e.g., Ezra, Haggai) that the temple site was in ruins when the people returned from exile; yet they were authorized—indeed, required—by their Persian overlords to rebuild the temple and renew the cult. Haggai, among others, makes it clear that the temple was rebuilt, but we also know from the same prophet and from his contemporary Zechariah that there were disputes about how the new temple was to operate. By whose rules and regulations should the rites be performed in the new temple? Leviticus 1–7, the rubrics for sacrifice in God's sanctuary given by God to Moses in the wilderness, supplied an answer to the question of *what* rules and regulations should prevail. As we shall see, Leviticus 8–10 answered in turn the question of who should administer those rules and regulations.

Leviticus 1:1-17; 6:8-13 (Heb., 6:1-6): A Manual for Sacrifice

The Text in Its Ancient Context

Chapter 1 addresses the burnt or whole offering, which entails immolating the useful parts of the sacrificial animal. Verses 1-17 then address the sacrifice of cattle, goats and sheep, and birds as whole offerings. Leviticus 6:8-13 covers in some detail the manner in which the priests are to do the work of making this sacrifice.

While the purpose of the whole burnt offering in Israel could vary (e.g., dedication of a new altar or sacred site [Exod. 24:5], thanksgiving [Gen. 8:20], penance for sin [Judg. 20:26]; see Budd, 43), from the perspective of this chapter, its chief function is to make a pleasing odor for God (1:9, 13, 17). Thus its meaning is perhaps best understood as an extraordinary gift to God, a *whole* burnt offering (save the hide, which is set aside for the priest; see 7:8) that is meant above all to powerfully draw God's attention to the worshiper.

From the perspective of P as a whole, this offering, the first to be explained, makes it emphatically clear that sacrifice is above all else to ensure a line of communication between God and people, with the altar priest serving as the human mediator in that exchange. Other functions for sacrifice are secondary to this one. This is hardly surprising in postexilic Judea, a time and place fraught with serious challenges to the people's ability to remain faithful to their traditions. Judeans needed a reliable means of remaining tied to their God living under conditions that so threatened to undo their commitment to the Yahwistic tradition they were called to uphold. The whole burnt offering signals the Priestly interest in serving that interest above all others (see Levine, 22–27).

The Text in the Interpretive Tradition

The guidelines for sacrificing a whole burnt offering appear to have been particularly interesting to early Jewish commentators, perhaps because the sacrifice is devoted so completely to the overarching purpose of bringing God's attention to the one making the offering. It is not surprising, then, that among those who disagreed with the ways of the ruling priestly class in the Second Temple, rewriting Leviticus 1 was a popular strategy for doing so. A prime example of this is the revisionist reading of Lev. 1:8-9, 12-13 in 4Q214 2:3-7 (cf. 1Q21 45; 4Q214b 2-3 8), a fragment of *Aramaic Levi*, a third-century-BCE reworking of the life story of Levi that portrays him as the *first* and *most legitimate* recipient of priestly instructions. These are slightly different from those later given to Moses. There can be no mistaking the purpose in such a "rewriting" of Leviticus 1: given to the progenitor of all of Israel's priests, *these* norms for making a whole burnt offering were superior to those of the Aaronites, mere descendants of the original, truest priestly servant of God, Levi.

The Text in Contemporary Discussion

The sacrifice addressed by Leviticus 1 has featured obliquely in modern public discourse about the World War II Nazi murder of Jews. Since the 1960s, the word for the sacrifice detailed in this chapter in the Greek translation of the Jewish Scriptures, *holokautoma*, has been used to refer to the Nazi destruction of the European Jewish communities, the Holocaust. Many find the use of the word in this way troubling, and not just because of the difficulty of associating a sacrifice to God with the Nazi act of genocide. Some within the Jewish community view it as an inappropriate term for the Jewish experience because its original use was to denominate *Greek* sacrificial practices, while others object to its use because they think it *too* Jewish-centric, potentially leading people to overlook the death-dealing violence the Nazis did to non-Jews as well, including people of color, Romani, gay and lesbian people, political opponents, physically disabled persons, and others. A widely used alternative to "Holocaust" used among Jews include *HaShoah*, Hebrew for "the Catastrophe" (on the history of the use of the term, see Petrie).

Leviticus 2:1-16; 6:14-23 (Heb., 6:7-16): Grain Offerings

The Text in Its Ancient Context

According to Lev. 2:1-16, the cereal offering, or grain offering, is an offering of uncooked or cooked "choice flour" (Heb., *sōlet*) mixed with oil and frankincense, from which the priest takes a portion for himself. The offering should contain no leaven, nor should honey be mixed with it, but it must be salted. If you bring a firstfruits offering of grain, it may also serve as a grain offering and should conform to the norms laid out here. The instructions to the priests and the high priest for making their respective cereal offerings are in 6:14-23. A handful of grain is to be offered to God, and the rest of the offering may be eaten by the priests and their male children or the high priest in the courtyard of the tent of meeting, a holy place, as they are holy.

The occasions for making grain offerings are not easy to discern from the wider evidence, let alone from the present chapter. To be sure, though, it is, like so many other offerings, first about getting God's attention and pleasing God in a general sense. It also seems to be an offering that commonly accompanies whole burnt offerings (e.g., Lev. 23:12-13; Num. 8:8; Judg. 13:19), and its natural role in the firstfruits offerings is evident.

The Text in the Interpretive Tradition

In a midrash that typifies the work's interpretive method, *Leviticus Rabbah* 3:1 begins with a quotation of Lev. 2:1-2 and immediately follows that with a quotation of Eccles. 4:6, linking the verses through their shared use of the word "handful." After a typically long and involved exploration of the idea behind the phrase "Better is a handful of quietness" in Eccles. 4:6, the midrashist concludes by saying that the best understanding of the relationship between the two passages associated by catchword is that Qoheleth exalts the handful of grain that a *poor person's offering* amounts to according to Lev. 2:1-2 over the incense of spices brought by the whole community (Lev. 16:12; Neusner, 168–80).

The Text in Contemporary Discussion

A contribution can be made to the emerging subdiscipline of ecological hermeneutics by reading this sacrifice within the larger Priestly tradition. It was the Priestly writer who established the fruit of the earth as God's food gift to humanity according to Gen. 1:29-30. That this Priestly chapter places grain among those fruits that should in turn serve as a food gift to God can be used to suggest a driving logic for giving attention to special care for the earth: the one and the same fruit of the earth that sustains humanity honors its Creator; and as such, human stewardship over creation, granted also by God through the rhetoric of the Priestly writer in Gen. 1:26-28, should be exercised with special reverence.

Leviticus 3:1-17; 7:11-38: The Well-Being Offerings

The Text in Its Ancient Context

Leviticus 3 deals with the well-being offering, addressing in succession the details of making one with cattle, sheep, and goats, and concluding with the prohibition on consuming the blood and fat of the offering. The suet on the entrails, the two kidneys and the suet on them, and the caudate lobe of the liver are to be burned whole as an offering to God, and the rest of the sacrificial animal may be consumed by the offerer. Leviticus 7:11-36 gives the administrative requirements of the well-being offering, a more elaborate declaration against eating fat or blood, and an explanation of the prebends from the well-being offering for the priests. Verses 37-38 serve as the capstone to the entire sacrificial legislation in chapters 1–7.

The purposes of the well-being offering would seem to cluster around familial observances associated with thanksgiving (see Lev. 7:11-18), although public events are also associated with it (e.g., Saul's elevation to king in 1 Sam. 11:15; the restoration of the altar in 2 Chron. 33:16). As for its meaning, the use of the term "peace" in naming it is suggestive, as are the occasions on which it is used; it connotes a restoration of balance between God and those who make the sacrifice, a balance that may have been undone both by negative events (the desecration of an altar) or positive ones (a blessed event happens to a family). This understanding of the sacrifice in light of the larger Priestly prescription for cosmic, communal, and cultic order in the face of the chaos of postexilic Judea is enlightening. Inasmuch as the peace offering provides a cultic avenue to bringing balance and order to situations that have become disordered and imbalanced, it extends the power of sacrifice to meet the existential needs of Judeans living in the difficult conditions of early Persian-period Judea.

The Text in the Interpretive Tradition

A particularly notable aspect of this passage is the stress it places on assigning the offering's blood and fat to God and to God alone. The emphasis features in the interpretive tradition in various ways, but most charmingly in the prayer of R. Sheshet in *b. Ber.* 17a. In the absence of a temple in which to make offerings of blood and fat to God to render oneself acceptable to God, he pleads that the fat and blood he loses by fasting might be counted as such instead (Milgrom 1991, 214)!

On a relatively more mundane level, in 1QapGen 11:17 (*Genesis Apocryphon*) the prohibition against eating blood issued to Noah after the flood (when permission to eat animal flesh was granted) surprisingly echoes more closely Lev. 3:17 than the actual source text for the command, Gen. 9:4.

The Text in Contemporary Discussion

A notable instance of contemporizing this passage was provided by a reflection on the act of giving blood in New York City in the wake of 9/11. Laura Duhan Kaplan entertains the notion that Lev. 3:1-17 is the best analogy in the sacrificial legislation for giving blood after the horror of that day, but opts instead for the sin offering of 4:1—5:13 (to which we will return below), arguing that the celebratory potential of the sacrifice in Lev. 3:1-17 disqualifies it in spite of its emphasis on restoring balance through the gift of blood to God. Kaplan may be right in a specific sense, but her general point—that giving blood for those who need its life-giving qualities is in unrecognized ways analogous to sacrifices that render life force to God—is worth taking note of in regard to the blood-focused legislation for this sacrifice and the disposition of its yield.

Leviticus 4:1—5:13; 6:24-30: The Purification Offerings

The Text in Its Ancient Context

Leviticus 4:1-35 elaborates the purification offering to be made in the event of sanctuary-polluting, unintentional violations of God's prohibitive commandments. It begins with the case of the anointed or high priest who sins unintentionally, and continues with provisions for sacrifice after the unwitting violation of a prohibitive commandment by the whole congregation. In these two cases the offering is to be a bull. In the case of the ruler the offering is to be a male goat, and an ordinary person brings a female goat, although in both cases the goat may also be replaced with a sheep. The chapter concludes with the declaration that making a "sin" offering on the terms laid out in the preceding verses relieves the offerer of guilt. Leviticus 5:1-13 then stipulates some specific instances that require sin offerings. Leviticus 6:24-30 gives the priests instructions for making the offering, providing an unusually significant amount of detail.

Jacob Milgrom argues persuasively that this sacrifice is not about setting a sinner right with God, as one might assume, but repairing the holiness of the sanctuary that was harmed by the sinner's deeds—thus the designation of it as a "purification offering." Citing ancient Near Eastern parallels where the concern is to guard the sanctity of a sanctuary against demonic forces, Milgrom argues that among the Israelites the demonic was replaced by the human actor; the deeds of the Israelites were what endangered the sanctity of the sanctuary and threatened to drive God away from it (Milgrom 2004, 31–33).

Here too the significance of this sacrifice within the framework of the Priestly proposal for postexilic Judea is transparent, especially in light of Milgrom's reading of the offering's significance. With a poignancy mostly overlooked by commentators on the Priestly literature, the sacrifice provides a vital avenue for the people of God to readily acknowledge and ensure the integrity of their dependence on God's presence for them in the restored temple. This must have been a powerful reassurance for them in the challenging world of postexilic Judea.

The Text in the Interpretive Tradition

Leviticus Rabbah 5:1-3 weaves a remarkable discourse together by juxtaposing Lev. 4:3 and Job 34:29-30. The former verse charges the anointed priest with making a purification offering if he sinned unwittingly, and the latter states,

> When he is quiet, who can condemn?
> When he hides his face, who can behold him,
> whether it be a nation or an individual?—
> so that the godless should not reign,
> or those who ensnare the people.

As Jacob Neusner points out in his commentary on the *Rabbah* passage, the long, involved discourse amounts finally to making clear that before God the anointed priest and the lay community are the same in terms of the magnitude of their sin and in the consequences of their sin for purification *and* suffering, such as when God seems hidden from the people. In this the midrashist demonstrates the *Rabbah*'s great virtue—drawing out a theological significance intrinsic to the Leviticus text, but not so easily evident without such illumination (Neusner, 192–98).

The Text in Contemporary Discussion

Jacob Milgrom offers a remarkable contemporizing reading of the purification offering. Reminding readers of his view that the offering is about ensuring that the sanctuary is repaired from the violence done to it by human sin so that God would not flee creation before the magnitude of human immorality, he asks what the priests would see in today's world. He replies to his own question with a litany of the environmental, economic, military, and political injustices and offenses committed by others, which we observe, yet do little to stop and even less to repair the damage they do. To this he imagines the priests would cry out, "How long . . . before God abandon's God's earthly sanctuary?" (Milgrom 2004, 33).

Leviticus 5:14—6:7; 7:1-10: The Reparation Offerings

The Text in Its Ancient Context

This section of text elaborates the sacrifice to be made in reparation for individual unintentional sins that desecrate, that have the impact of "affecting only its committer" (Milgrom 2004, 51). If one has desecrated any of the sanctified things of the Lord, a ram convertible to "silver by the sanctuary shekel" one-fifth of the value of the thing desecrated is due (5:14-16). If one has sinned without knowing it—a possibility that likely occurred to people when they were suddenly experiencing inexplicably difficult life circumstances—a guilt offering of a ram makes the atoning sacrifice (5:17-19). Leviticus 5:20-26 (Heb., 6:1-7) enumerates some specific sins for which a reparation offering may be made (deceiving someone in a deposit or pledge, robbery, fraud, and finding and not reporting a lost object) and prescribes reparation—acknowledging guilt, paying the injured person 120 percent of the value lost, and bringing to the priests a ram for the atoning sacrifice. Leviticus 7:1-10 directs the priest to perform essentially the same ritual for this sacrifice as the one performed for a purification offering.

Given the evidence that reparation for damages done was practiced more widely in the ancient Near Eastern world as a means of placating the gods offended by one's bad act, it seems likely that this particular sacrifice, attested only in P and similarly late texts (e.g., Ezek. 40:39), was a Priestly development that merged the wider practice of reparations to appease the gods with an atoning sacrifice by Israel's priests to set the sinner right with the Lord. Milgrom further argues that the offering process as a whole is the Priestly legist's invention whereby *intentional* sins are converted by acknowledgment and repentance to unintentional sins that can then be atoned for through the sacrifice of the ram (Milgrom 2004). Once more, we see the great concern of the Priestly tradition for the existential needs of the people of Judea.

The Text in the Interpretive Tradition

The document *m. Seqal.* 6.6 answers the interesting question raised by the deposit of monetary reparations by the persons bringing a reparation sacrifice, "What comes of the proceeds of such ritual deposits?" Although the argument is more complex, the Mishnah boils down to a single proof text, 2 Kgs. 12:6, "The money from the guilt offerings and the money from the sin offerings was not brought into the house of the Lord; it belonged to the priests." And how could this be done without unduly enriching the priests? The answer the Mishnah provides is that they used it to purchase whole burnt offerings for the altar, all of which were dedicated to the Lord (save the hide, which was the priests' prebend).

The Text in Contemporary Discussion

The reparation sacrifice offers a fascinating window on the difference between the norms accepted by the ancient legists who lived in the light of their election by the God of Israel and recent historical and contemporary attitudes toward reparations payable to those who have been unjustly wronged by another's sinful act. Taking the case of Japanese Americans interned or relocated during

World War II as a result of Franklin Delano Roosevelt's Executive Order 9066 of February 1942 (which established "exclusion zones" and set in motion a cascade of other public proclamations that facilitated the internment and relocation process), we can see the contrast in stark detail. The Priestly writers treated the act damaging the neighbor as a violation against God that was then in the transgressor's best interest to repent of and repair as speedily as humanly possible, and they prescribed the means for doing so at a level more generous than the damage done. By contrast, getting compensation for the Japanese Americans who lost livelihoods, land, and even families as a result of EO 9066 took nearly five decades to accomplish, and produced a paltry $20,000 in compensation for each internee. Reparations were neither speedy nor generous. One wonders how the process might have gone if much attention had been paid to the example of Leviticus.

Leviticus 8–10

Following the legislation on sacrificial practices, the narrative thread left off in Exodus 40 resumes with the account of the ordination of the sons of Aaron to the altar priesthood (chapters 8–9) and the story of the sin and destruction of two of Aaron's sons, Nadab and Abihu (chapter 10).

As noted above, many assume that since these chapters resume the narrative that was suspended in Exodus 40, Leviticus 1–7 must have been belatedly introduced into a continuous P narrative. However, Christophe Nihan argues that in fact the sacrificial legislation in Leviticus 1–7 is the prerequisite for the priestly inauguration of the cult in chapter 9, which follows the ordination narrative in chapter 8, and thus as a consequence it makes little literary sense to regard chapters 1–7 as a late insertion. Nihan's argument is fortified by the observation that the shift in focus to priests fits what might be a broader pattern of literary structuring employed by the Priestly writer. Exodus 25–31; 35–40 focuses on establishing the space within which priests and laity share in cultic activity; Leviticus 1–7 focuses on the life-sustaining, community-mending cultic activities of the laity in that sanctuary space (aided by the priests); and now the focus shifts to ensuring that the priests who staff the cultic space and carry out the cultic rites for the laity are prepared for their duties. This threefold structure places the lay community and its existential needs at the center, treating the creation of a space for meeting those needs and the personnel required to assist in that as adjuncts to the central concern of the Priestly writer, the good of the Judeans forming community in postexilic Judea.

Leviticus 8:1—9:24: Ordained and Set Apart

The Text in Its Ancient Context

Chapter 8 addresses the ordination of the priests. God commands Moses to take Aaron and his sons the priestly vestments, a bull for a sin offering, two rams, and a basket of unleavened bread to the entrance of the tent of meeting and to assemble the people there. Then Moses cleanses and vests Aaron and his sons, and makes the sin offering of the bull and the ram of the burnt offering. The ordination sacrifice of the second ram follows, a rite that includes touching the blood of the ram to the lobe of each priest's right ear, the thumb of his right hand, and the big toe of his right foot. The chapter then dictates the use of the offerings and prescribes a seven-day waiting period within the entrance of the tent of meeting for Aaron and his sons to complete their ordination. Chapter 9 then inaugurates the cult, with Aaron and his sons performing sacrifices on the eighth day, which include sin and burnt offerings for Aaron and his sons and sin, whole burnt, grain, and well-being offerings for the people. The chapter concludes with a priestly blessing to draw the eighth-day celebration to a close, followed by a theophany whereby the fiery presence of God consumes the whole burnt offering and the fat on the altar.

Relying on the cultural-anthropological notions of liminal states and rites of passage explains how the ordination rite in chapter 8 works in the Priestly agenda. The containment of Aaron and his sons in the sacred space during the ordination rite signals the liminal state between profane and holy status that Aaron and his sons enter into and the transformation they undergo to be set apart for the people's service. Further, smearing the blood of the sacrifice on their body parts intensifies the character of the moment as a rite of passage, joining them in a graphic and dangerous way to the sacrifice as something dedicated completely to God, even unto loss of life, but also for the purpose of giving life to those who make the offering (see by contrast Milgrom 2004, 85–86, who argues that the daubing accomplishes purgation). In this way, the Priestly tradents deploy imagery that signals the lengths and depths to which priests and God will go in partnership together to ensure the integrity of the people's relationship to God. Again, this was a powerful theological message for the people of Judea in the challenging context of the early Persian period.

The Priestly writer underscores this point with the next chapter. Having been set apart for their mediating service between God and people, Aaron and his sons immediately set about doing what they were ordained to do, making the sacrifices that connect God and people. And as if to drive home the point that this is to ensure the presence of God to the people, in 9:4 Moses instructs Aaron to tell the people that in the doing of these sacrifices, "the Lord will appear to you," and God does indeed appear, as fire that consumes the proceeds of the sacrifice (9:24). In the Priestly work, that sort of theophany had taken place once before, as the evidence of God's presence on Sinai (Exod. 24:17). The point is clear: by virtue of the mediating role of the priests, who deliver the people's offerings to God, God is immediate and present to the people in the sanctuary. Here we have yet another assurance from the Priestly tradents for the people living in Persian-period Judea.

The Text in the Interpretive Tradition

Leviticus Rabbah 10:1-4 provides a remarkable reading of Lev. 8:1-3, tackling the problem that Aaron acquiesced to the people's desire to worship an alternative god in Exodus 32. At the beginning of the first unit, the *Rabbah* cites Lev. 8:1-3, with its mention of anointing, and Ps. 45:7, which declares that God has anointed the addressee of the psalm over his fellows because he loves righteousness and hates wickedness. The section in *Lev. Rab.* 10:1-2 then provides a series of proof texts for the notion that those who are anointed are oriented to God's service no matter the circumstances; 10:3 follows by quoting in succession Ps. 45:7 and Exod. 32:1, implicitly posing at last the question the passage has been driving at: How could Aaron, God's anointed, have led the rebellion in Exodus 32? The following pastiche of quotes and an account of a folktale confirm what 10:1-2 established, that God's anointed are tireless in their service to God; and just so, Aaron was tireless in creating the golden calf for the people, "taking upon himself the sin they would have committed had he not made the sacrifice of his own sin." Wonderfully, what one finds at the heart of this exegesis is the evidence of the rabbinic commentators' conscious appreciation of the P tradition's aim of affirming the dedication of the Aaronites in telling the story of the ordination in the first place.

Turning to the offerings made for the people by Aaron and his sons, their reaction in 9:24 to the appearance of the Lord is that they "shouted and fell on their faces." In what could be seen as another example of later exegesis underscoring the joyously awesome nature of this event for the people, the *Temple Scroll* from Qumran gives its own version of that ceremony in column 17, lines 1–5. The interpreter read the ambiguous "shouted and fell on their faces" in Lev. 9:24 as one unequivocal action, rendering it as "the people *rejoiced*."

The Text in Contemporary Discussion

The Priestly writer's notion that ordination is a rite of passage that moves its recipient across a boundary on either side of which are two different ontological states is not common in religion in the contemporary West. The Christian communities that do treat the rite of ordination as sacramental in character (e.g., Roman Catholic, Anglican, Orthodox), struggle to make the rite communicate that significance to their recipients, let alone those who witness the rite. Recognizing the absence of awe in setting apart of a man or woman to the dedicated service of God makes one wonder if this is not testimony to the accuracy of Max Weber's gloomy confidence that Western society is doomed to go ever further down the road of rationalization and disenchantment.

Yet among those Christian communities where a fully developed liturgical rite of ordination is carried out, the eucharistic meal follows, a clear and appropriate echo of the celebration of the sacrifices by Aaron and his sons for all of Israel. In this, at least, the ordination rite in some of its modern, Christian forms does gesture toward the profound significance of assigning to a member of one's larger community the burden and privilege of mediating between God and people.

Leviticus 10:1-20: Aaron's Sons, Nadab and Abihu

The Text in Its Ancient Context

This chapter begins with the tale of Nadab and Abihu offering of "strange" or "unauthorized" fire (incense), their death by fire as a consequence, and the disposal of their bodies. A series of priestly precautions, rights, and duties follows, prohibiting Aaron and his sons from partaking in strong drink before serving in the sanctuary, instructing them to differentiate for the people between the common and the sacred (*ḥōl* and *qōdeš*) and teaching the people of Israel all the statutes given through Moses. Further, their eating of grain offering is restricted to holy space (next to the altar), while the consumption of the "elevation offering" is allowed in any clean place. The chapter closes with Moses' complaint to Aaron and his sons that they acted improperly because they burned the sin offering rather than eating it, and Aaron's reply that it would have been inappropriate for him to consume the most holy sacrifice given the things that "have befallen" him.

This odd story is yet another piece of the picture puzzle the Priestly writer promotes for postexilic Judeans under Persian rule. Some suggest that private offerings of incense may have been seen as low-cost alternatives to sacrifice, a means of making contact with God without the mediation of a priest. Such behavior might have been implied by Nadab and Abihu's actions. If so, this story makes clear that even the priests were subject to the negative consequences of sidestepping the new system of sacrifice and offerings. Maintaining an ordered cult for *all* the people transcended even the rights of the newly ordained priests.

The Text in the Interpretive Tradition

The deaths of Nadab and Abihu have long troubled commentators because they seem so pointless. One sophisticated example of solving that difficulty comes from Philo, who asserts that in fact the brothers were so zealous in their piety that their expression of it transcended the earthly realm and approached the heavenly, and they were thus swept up into heaven as a sacrifice to God through immolation (*Dreams* 2.67). Other interpreters, particularly among early and medieval Christian readers, were more inclined to assume Nadab and Abihu's culpability for some error, using them as examples of the fate that awaits priests who are misdirected in their zeal (Bede, *On the Tabernacle*) or people who abuse the church's sacrament of baptism (Cyprian, *The Baptismal Controversy*; both cited in Lienhard, 175).

The Text in Contemporary Discussion

In a provocative treatment of Leviticus 10:1—11:47, Tamar Kaminkowski picks up Philo's interpretation to argue that he was on the right track in discerning what actually lay behind the story. Indeed, she suggests that the earliest version of the story was a homoerotic account of two men who, having experienced the intensity of the ordination rite, were stirred to seek complete union with the male God into whose service they had been ordained, and so they approached God with zeal to seek deeper intimacy with God. On this reading, God responded *positively* by meeting "them in a passion, taking them in completely." She points to God's declaration in 10:3 that "through those who are near me I will show myself holy" as support for her positive reading of the incident, but she also acknowledges that the remainder of the narrative suppresses the exalted nature of the encounter, placing boundaries around the memory of the encounter, lest all Israel also be so consumed by seeking intimacy with God (Kaminkowski, 135–39).

Leviticus 11–15

These chapters turn attention from the priests to the laity and the sort of purity they must maintain to enjoy the benefits of communion with God made possible by the construction of the sanctuary (Exodus 25–31; 25–40), the pronouncement of the rubrics for making sacrifice (Leviticus 1–7), and the establishment of the altar priesthood (Leviticus 8–9); their purity in contact with the sanctuary is also necessary to prevent them from experiencing the fate that befell Nadab and Abihu (Leviticus 10).

The chapters address what at first seem to be the only loosely related topics of the categories of creatures that are clean and unclean to human beings (chapter 11), the purification for a woman after childbirth (chapter 12), the diagnosis of and purification procedures for skin disease and contaminated garments and buildings (chapters 13–14), and the diagnosis of impurity resulting from genital discharges and modes of purification from them (chapter 15). Yet close reading of this "purity manual" indicates that these chapters expand in significant and sophisticated ways the theological argument the Priestly writer makes throughout Leviticus regarding the sustaining life that God grants to Judea in its postexilic context through the cult, the priesthood, and boundaries for the pure and the impure, the sacred and the profane. Indeed, this textual unit provides something of a hermeneutical key to the rest of Leviticus and the Priestly tradition as a whole: it focuses attention squarely on God's desire that the people of Israel, living in the complex context of Persian-period Judea, have order and life where there might otherwise be chaos and death.

Leviticus 11:1-47: Clean and Unclean Animals and Foods

The Text in Its Ancient Context

A lengthy discourse that classifies animals that are clean and unclean for human consumption—as well as in some cases for mere touch—this chapter is one of the best known in Leviticus. It declares land animals that are divided-hoofed or cleft-footed and also chew the cud clean, but those that are one of these but not the other unclean, and any of the latter group found dead are declared unclean. It designates water creatures that have fins and scales as clean, and all others as unfit for consumption, and unclean to the touch in carcass form. It provides a list of flying creatures that are unclean, declares winged insects to be unclean, except those that also hop, and addresses further kinds of animals encountered in carcass form that make one unclean by contact, including the carcasses of all land animals that go on four paws. It addresses the impurity of eight kinds of creatures that "swarm" upon the earth and ways they can transmit their impurity, and it extends the standard of impurity even to animals that are clean to Israel, but are encountered in carcass form. It returns to concern for swarming creatures, declaring *all* such creatures to be unclean, and justifies the prohibition on the basis of all Israel's holiness before God. It closes with the declaration that all these regulations are *torah*.

The boundless speculations regarding the rationale behind this chapter's seemingly whimsical classification of animals aside, some things are clear regarding Leviticus 11 in the larger Priestly agenda. First, drawing such strong distinctions between clean and unclean animals has the symbolic power to evoke ideas of order and chaos, life and death. Second, one clear rationale in the chapter reinforces the latter point—animals encountered in carcass form, clean or unclean in living form, are unclean—suggesting that the heart of the matter is an opposition between life and death. And third, the purpose in making these distinctions is to ensure that the people of Israel, when they do incur the impurity that contact with loss of life brings on them, do not pollute the sanctuary, the locus of their life-sustaining contact with their God (but see also Milgrom 2004, 104, for the theory that the dietary laws reflect "an ethical guide—a system whereby people will not be brutalized by killing animals for their flesh").

The Text in the Interpretive Tradition

It should not surprise that the challenging nature of Leviticus 11 ensured that broadly allegorical readings would dominate much of its interpretive career. To mention but a few, *Leviticus Rabbah* 13.5 equates the nations that had been hostile to Israel with unclean animals, delivering condemnation by association with the camel, rock badger, hare, and pig to Babylonia, Media, Greece, and Rome (Neusner, 296–305), and among Christians, Clement of Alexandria identifies the clean animals with just persons who look for spiritual nourishment (*Christ the Educator* 3.11.76), and Novatian matches traditional vices with the unclean animals (Novatian, *Jewish Foods* 3.13–23; Lienhard, 176–77).

The Text in Contemporary Discussion

It should come as no surprise that even though the dietary laws in Leviticus 11 were likely symbolic pointers to larger issues, many modern readers find in them practical advice for contemporary dietary practices. Such contemporary appropriations range from thoughtful reflections on food consumption and human health that use the thought world of Leviticus 11 as a departure point, to literalist readings of the text that seek to explain how the rulings might be implemented by "Bible believing Christians," to opportunistic hucksters who use the Bible to legitimate "God's diet" that ensures weight loss! A visit to the "Food and Diet" section of most any bookstore provides abundant evidence of this recurring trend in the "interpretation" of Leviticus 11.

Leviticus 12:1-8: Purity and Childbirth

The Text in Its Ancient Context

Chapter 12 turns to the impact of childbirth on a woman's purity. A woman who gives birth to a male is ceremonially unclean for seven days, and for another thirty-three days of purification, during which she should not come into contact with holy things or the sanctuary; the time of impurity doubles for the birth of a daughter. At the conclusion of the woman's period of purification, sacrifice is required.

The crux in this chapter is the difference in the time of impurity between a male or female child's birth. Although there is much debate and vivid speculation as to why this is so (see, e.g., Whitekettle), that it has to do with the same theme announced in chapter 11—that loss of life, death, is the most impure-making condition possible—seems like the most plausible explanation of the difference. As a woman in childbirth endures the loss of life force, blood, in delivering a child—and is thereby the site of a great contest between life and death, between order and chaos—all the more so is she made impure when she brings a daughter into the world, who will also likely give birth in time. Likewise, she will experience menses as does her mother, another impurity-inducing loss of life force (see Leviticus 15). Thus the doubled time of impurity is unsurprising, especially given the Priestly tradents' intense interest in creating a world where the contaminating threat of death and the loss of life force is kept far removed from the sanctuary.

The Text in the Interpretive Tradition

Jubilees, a Jewish pseudepigraphic work from second-century-BCE Judea, rewrites Genesis 1 to Exodus 14. Among its various purposes was to provide origin stories for legal norms given to Moses at Sinai in the narratives that extend from creation to the escape from Egypt. In doing this, *Jubilees* gets in on the effort to make sense of the double period of purification for a woman who bears a daughter. *Jubilees* 3 explains that God required Adam to wait a week and thirty-three more days before entering Eden, and because she came from Adam, Eve was compelled to wait twice that period before she could enter.

The Text in Contemporary Discussion

Remarkably, there are modern Christian rites that depend on Leviticus 12, although they are now mostly abandoned. One is (or better, was) the practice among Anglicans and Roman Catholics of "churching" (welcoming back into the communion) a postpartum woman at the relevant time. Interestingly, at least in the Anglican Communion, instead of altogether abandoning the outdated and objectionable rite of "churching" prescribed by the 1662 Book of Common Prayer, it has been replaced in the 1979 Book of Common Prayer by the "Thanksgiving for the Birth or Adoption of a Child," a rite that welcomes the newborn and her parents into the community of faith *as soon as the family desires* (for other examples, see further Schearing).

Leviticus 13:1—14:57: Impurity through Skin Eruptions

The Text in Its Ancient Context

This long section deals with what is often referred to as "leprosy," translating the Hebrew word *ṣārāʿat*. But since the word refers to the "disease" in garments and buildings as well, the term is hardly apposite. An alternative approach might be to speak of "consequential eruptions" of the skin inasmuch as the breaking of boundaries that contain human life force seems to be at issue here, as was the case in chapter 12. On this reading, chapter 13 addresses how the priests identify consequential skin eruptions—ones that break the skin and have the potential for loss of blood, life force—and prescribe ways of dealing with them as instances of impurity. The same sort of reasoning about what is a consequential eruption and one that is not seems to be at work in sections that address boils as another form or skin disease, burns, eruptions on the head and in the beard, rashes and blisters, and balding heads. Anyone deemed impure by the priests must live alone, wear torn clothes, cover the upper lip, and cry out in warning to all who encounter him or her, "Unclean! Unclean!" The chapter concludes with a long passage that applies the same rules for determining the significance of eruptions and blemishes in garments.

Chapter 14 lays out the elaborate rite of purification that someone who has suffered from a consequential eruption of their skin must perform, followed by provisions for the poor who cannot afford the offering of the goods normally required for purification. The chapter also addresses the diagnosis and purification of walls in dwellings made impure by "consequential eruptions," probably of mildew.

Understanding this involved treatment of various sorts of "skin" diseases within the framework of the Priestly agenda in postexilic Judea helps one appreciate what might otherwise seem like some of the strangest material in Leviticus. First, recall the concern of the Priestly tradents to assure recipients that the hegemonic pluralism of postexilic Judea would not overwhelm their own communal order with chaos. Next, consider the fact that in many ancient (and contemporary) cultures the human body serves as a metaphor for one's community (Douglas 1966). Then envision how an elaborate system of purity and impurity measures meant to contain and limit instances of skin disease, losses of life force from the human body, might have functioned in the imagination of those postexilic Judeans. On this reading, these chapters were likely intended to inspire the Judeans of Persian-period Judea to share in the responsibility of guarding the boundaries that preserved the integrity of their community, and allusively instructed them on how to do so.

The Text in the Interpretive Tradition

Given the foregoing analysis, it is not surprising that the Dead Sea Scrolls community—a sectarian Judean group that flourished around the turn of the eras—seems to have been particularly adept at deploying some of the legislative norms of Leviticus 13–14 in their own communal organization. For example, according to 1QS 3:5-6, the would-be member of the community who refuses the offer of inclusion in the fellowship is to be shunned and is referred to by the community membership as "Unclean! Unclean!" all the days of his life. The imprecation is a clear use of Lev. 13:45-46, a way of bringing to mind the "scriptural" manual on ensuring that bodily (read: communal) boundaries are observed so as to guard the purity of the body (read: community). This is a remarkable case of using language that mused about bodily boundary disruption as a way of speaking metaphorically of the human community to address directly the disruption of the human community.

The Text in Contemporary Discussion

A survey of homiletical attempts, online and otherwise, to contend with this difficult material is routinely disappointing. On the side of escaping the text's difficulty by occupying oneself with historical observations, discussions of the appropriate terminology for "leprosy" abound; and on the side of reading allegorically or the like are the numerous attempts to make the skin disease discussed in the text a metonym for alienating sin in contemporary human conduct. Neither approach serves much homiletical good, and both show little regard for the text's capacity for depth of meaning. Perhaps a more useful approach would begin by acknowledging how profoundly disturbing this text really is, precisely in the effect the restrictions of the skin-diseased would have had in the ancient Mediterranean world (esp. 13:46). There your identity was constituted by your connections with others; alone, you had no discernible identity. In this light, the insistence that the skin-diseased person afflicted with consequential eruptions remain completely apart—that he or she dwell utterly alone (Heb., *bdd*)—is shocking. A sermon worth listening to would be one that wrestles with this difficulty and asks where in contemporary life and society similar dilemmas appear in our midst—and how we might respond.

Leviticus 15:1-33: Discharge of Life Fluids

The Text in Its Ancient Context

Leviticus 15 concerns genital discharges of various types and degrees of severity. A man with a "flow" from his penis is impure, as is anyone who comes into contact with him or with an object he has polluted. To become pure again, the man with the flow must wait, wash, and make a sacrifice after the flow ceases. The discharge of semen in intercourse is a less severe instance of impurity, requiring only that the man and woman wash and wait until evening to be ritually pure again. Likewise, ordinary menses, though making a woman impure for seven days, is clean again after simply washing and waiting until evening, as is a man who lay with her during menses. By contrast, a woman's abnormal bleeding—presumably menses out of cycle and other conditions that cause vaginal bleeding—requires her to wait the usual seven days, wash and wait until evening on the last day, and like the man with a nonprocreative penile discharge, make an offering to be fully restored to ritual purity. The chapter concludes with the rationale for regulating so closely the variety of potential genital discharges: polluting the tabernacle through one's impurity could be deadly.

Little needs to be said about the role of this chapter in the Priestly agenda—what was already said about the concern to regulate consequential eruptions of the skin applies a fortiori to genital discharges as they are equally losses of life force, if not more so. Any loss of life force is defiling, out of the ordinary losses are most concerning (requiring sacrifice at the end of the purification process), all of them are symbolic of the potential decline of the community itself, and all of them are dangerous to their bearers vis-à-vis the holiness of the sanctuary and potentially damaging to the integrity of the sanctuary as well.

The Text in the Interpretive Tradition

The Qumran community's treatment of Leviticus 15 is an interesting reminder of the surprising diversity we find in the legal writings of that group, which is nonetheless tempered by their shared tendency to intensify the legal norms of Leviticus. For example, the *Temple Scroll*, 4Q274, and 4Q277 address the impurity of a man with a genital discharge; all three extend and intensify the requirements in Leviticus 15, safeguarding him and others from the consequences of his impurity. Yet while 4Q274 and the *Temple Scroll* quarantine the man with the discharge away from the clean and unclean, the concern in 4Q277 that he wash his hands lest the things he touch pollute others who are clean indicates that it does not require quarantine.

The Text in Contemporary Discussion

The late Dame Mary Douglas (1921–2007), one of the twentieth century's most significant anthropologists, shaped a great deal of the contemporary understanding of Leviticus 11–15. Her 1966 book *Purity and Danger* already addressed the dietary laws in Leviticus 11, and suggested that the regulations were not explicable on some hygienic basis, but were symbolic of larger concerns for boundary maintenance (and thus unclean animals were ones that did not fit established categories—they were boundary violators). Even though Douglas later adjusted her argument regarding chapter 11 in particular (suggesting that the aim was rather to map the human body and what it can receive for sustenance to the sacrificial altar; Douglas 2001), this 1966 reading was and remains influential in how people read the purity laws of Leviticus 11–15 as a whole, something evident even in this commentary's approach to this central section of Leviticus.

Leviticus 16:1-34: The Day of Atonement

This chapter is a distinct unit within Leviticus, addressing the procedures for observing the Day of Atonement. Some assume that it originally followed Leviticus 10 because it begins with the announcement that the Lord spoke to Moses after the death of Aaron's two sons, which arguably overlooks everything between the end of chapter 10 and 16. There is also a thematic coherence between the former episode and the rite described in chapter 16, as both relate in some way to ensuring the sanctity of the sanctuary. That said, chapter 16 has its own concerns that transcend the Nadab and Abihu incident, as well as the material that intervenes between that episode and the present chapter: its focus is on the rite by which the high priest ensures all Israel, everywhere, is reconciled to God on an annual basis. In that sense, it can be argued that it was the appropriate conclusion to the trajectory the P tradents constructed beginning with Exodus 25, ensuring as it does that *all* Judeans anywhere in the world would benefit from the temple cult's purpose in connecting them inextricably to their God.

The Text in Its Ancient Context

After recalling the Nadab and Abihu incident, the narrator records God's speech to Moses, warning him that Aaron should not approach the ark of the covenant willy-nilly, lest he die from contact with God's presence. Instead, he should prepare for such an encounter by clothing himself in appropriate garments, and by bringing a young bull for a sin offering and a ram for a burnt offering, as well as two male goats for a sin offering and ram for a burnt offering for the people. The bull is a sin offering for Aaron, and one goat is the people's sin offering, while the other goat is the animal to be sent into the wilderness alive "for Azazel." Aaron confesses the people's iniquity over the goat and sends it into the wilderness by a person designated for the task. Then he washes and changes into his ordinary vestments and makes the burnt offerings of the two rams to atone for himself and Israel, and he turns the fat of the sin offering into smoke on the altar. The one who set the goat for Azazel free washes and returns to the camp, and another person takes the remains of the bull and goat of the sin offerings outside the camp to be burned, after which he washes and returns to the camp. The chapter declares this an annual observance set for the tenth day of the seventh month, a day of fasting and rest from work for all of Israel; the rite should be performed by the high priest as an act of atonement for the tent of meeting, the altar, the priests, and the people altogether.

The Text in the Interpretive Tradition

The interpretive history of Leviticus 16 is understandably rich; the powerful encounter between God and humanity that the Day of Atonement ceremony creates was and is an irresistible topic for Jews and Christians alike. We already see echoes of the rite in the penitential prayers of Ezra 9 and Nehemiah 9 (Bautch). Its observance played a central role in the life of the Qumran community (Gilders), and its abiding significance even after the destruction of the Second Temple is evident in the rich tradition of Jewish and Christian remakings of it for new uses (Stöckl). At the center of this vast interpretive tradition is the goal of invoking and keeping alive the rite's capacity to bring humanity into intense contact with a God who intends to repair all of creation (e.g., Rom. 3:25).

The mysterious character Azazel has also attracted considerable attention in the interpretive history of Leviticus 16 (see, e.g., *1 Enoch* 8:1-3; 10:8, where he is one of the "fallen angels" of Gen. 6:1-4). One of the most important moments in that history came in its earliest stages. The Septuagint (Lev. 16:8 LXX) renders the Hebrew of Azazel with the Greek *apopompaios*, "sent away," so that Aaron casts lots to determine one goat for the Lord and another "to be sent off." The translation of the three further occurrences of the name in 16:10, 26, follow suit, more or less, effectively erasing the existence of Azazel as a separate being, and replacing him with the concept of the "go-away goat," or the "scapegoat," which itself has had a long interpretive afterlife.

The Text in Contemporary Discussion

Surely the Day of Atonement (*Yom Kippur*, the conclusion of the "Days of Awe") competes closely with the feast of Passover for the distinction of being the most widely observed moment in the yearly Jewish liturgical calendar. Apart from the obvious exception of temple sacrifice, all the other requirements of the rite declared in 16:29-34 are kept, and to this have been added other observances related to the day's focus (e.g., *Teshuva*, confession of sins; *Avodah*, recalling the temple sacrifice). Notably, this relatively intense commitment among secular and religious Jews around the world to observing Yom Kippur is in the spirit of the Priestly tradition's likely aim in legislating it. In the Persian period, many Judeans lived in Diaspora, and the ritual acts of the high priest were intended, among other things, to release the sins of all Judeans, everywhere. In its modern form, a sort of democratization of its observance upholds that key focus of the Day of Atonement in Leviticus 16.

Leviticus 17–26

Leviticus 17–26 is commonly called the "Holiness Code" because of the insistence in key passages that the people of Israel be as holy as their God. While the command to be holy appears relatively infrequently (e.g., 19:1-2; 20:7), the title is nonetheless appropriate: the driving interest of these chapters is to address the consequences that come from a different sort of democratization, in this case of the quality of holiness among the people of Israel.

The relationship between the Holiness Code (abbreviated as H) and the rest of the Priestly work, within which it is situated, is a matter of ongoing dispute. Some argue that it was a law code the Priestly tradents knew and appreciated and that they felt comfortable integrating into their larger contribution. Others view it as a friendly amendment to P created by a "priestly" writer interested in bringing Deuteronomic law into alignment with P interests. Still others hold that it is of such a different character, especially in its view of holiness, that it cannot have been embraced by the Priestly tradents but should instead be treated as a critical response to the P material. Among those who take the latter view, there is further division; some treat P and H as First Temple tradents, and others hold to the view that they are Second Temple, postexilic thinkers and writers. (For a full history of scholarship, see Nihan, 4–11.)

This commentary assigns H a post-P, postexilic date, and understands it to have been composed as a literary supplement that offered a critical contrast with the Priestly work. It did this by positing the democratization of holiness and then imagining the consequences for the cult, the priests, and the laity.

Why a thinker might have felt this necessary in Persian-period Judea is easily surmised from the literary evidence that the priests had come to abuse their privileges, and the laity may also have engaged in practices that undercut the justice of the postexilic community. Malachi condemns the priests for replacing pure offerings with blemished beasts from the temple flocks (Mal. 1:7-8) and the laity for bringing similarly unacceptable offerings in the first place (1:13-14). And it is perhaps both groups that Malachi condemns with his withering attack on the infidelity of the people to their God and husbands to their wives, a pairing that may have had to do with the worship of foreign gods and goddesses (perhaps even through cultic intercourse; 2:10-16). And Third Isaiah rails in myriad ways against the priests in particular, but also the economic and power elite for the abuses that inflicted injustice on the nonelite, even calling Israel's "sentinels" and "shepherds" by a most vile name in antiquity, "Dogs!" (Isa. 56:10-11). It is not hard to imagine how these things happened: the priests, enriched by the offerings of the laity, welcomed every opportunity to receive them, and the laity, hoping to benefit from unjust dealings and the occasional worship of other gods, were only too happy to oblige as they sought restoration to God's good graces through sacrificial offerings.

In envisioning a world where the holiness that the Priestly tradition confined to the temple and priests extends to all of Israel—a world where all experience was holy—the Holiness Code offers a powerful thought experiment. What would be the consequences in a world imbued with holiness for the priests and the people if they lived as Malachi and Third Isaiah suggest? As the following commentary suggests, the Holiness Code systematically considers that possibility, and in so doing might well have called the people and their leaders to account for their death-dealing, chaos-engendering abuse of a system meant to give order and life.

Leviticus 17:1-16: Blood Is Life

The Text in Its Ancient Context

Like the other law codes in the Torah, this one begins by addressing sacrifice (cf. Exod. 20:22-26; Deuteronomy 12). But H is truly radical, declaring that any slaughter of a beast must be recognized as a holy act—a sacrifice—through the priest's sacralization of it at the sanctuary's entrance by splashing its blood on the altar placed there and burning some of its fat as a pleasing odor to God; failure to do this results in being "cut off from the people." The chapter further prohibits any human consumption of the blood of the sacrifice and declares that any blood shed in the act of hunting for food must be poured on the ground and covered with earth, and that eating an animal found dead merely makes one unclean, a condition remedied by washing and waiting until evening.

The potential impact of this legislation on priestly prebends is highly suggestive of the Holiness Code's larger agenda. By sacralizing the death of *any* animal, H significantly expanded the opportunities for laypersons to get God's attention through sacrifice and at the same time potentially threatened the supply of prebends to the priests in the temple. The consequence of making all of Israel's experience holy, at least with respect to sacrifice, is to undercut the benefits of the sacrificial system to the priests and increase its capacity to serve the laity. There could hardly have been a better way to suggest the powerful consequences for the priests if holiness, which it was their responsibility to guard and protect, were to escape its boundaries and make all experience holy.

The Text in the Interpretive Tradition

The obvious difficulties of implementing the legislation proposed in Leviticus 17 not only speaks in favor of H having been largely a "thought experiment," a sort of utopian critique of P, but also provoked its share of imaginative reworking by later interpreters who did not see it as such, but as a proposal for actual practice. Column 52 of the *Temple Scroll* from Qumran is an example of this response. It engages in a complex "exegesis" of the chapter that first confirms the ruling in Leviticus 17, but also restricts it by saying that it applies only to those within three days' walk from the temple and that any proceeds from the slaughter-become-sacrifice due the offerer must be consumed at the temple. But then the scroll immediately adds that a *blemished* clean animal may be slaughtered in a profane way and its flesh consumed without the trouble of a trip to the temple at so little a distance as four miles from the sanctuary (52:13-18). Here we encounter a legist who was looking for—and found—a loophole in the Holiness Code law that that would have made it doable, even if still onerous.

Providing a sharp contrast to interpreters of different backgrounds, John Chrysostom ignores the sacrificial impracticalities of Leviticus 17. Instead, he focuses on the heightened concern for the blood of the beast in the chapter to argue that this points to what distinguishes humans from animals—the animal's blood carries its soul (thus the intense concern to treat it with enormous respect), but the human soul is incorporeal and transcends the body (*Homilies on Genesis* 13.10; cited by Lienhard, 186).

The Text in Contemporary Discussion

Interestingly, it was not only in antiquity that the (probably) utopian vision of the H legist was nonetheless treated as a requirement for real practice; at least in one respect, the laws of *kashrut* through the ages reflect respect for the chapter as well. Leviticus 17:10-14 is taken to require that in preparing meat from animals for food, the greatest amount of blood is drained away as possible, something accomplished through soaking meat in water and then salting it and letting it sit before cooking. Today much of that work is done by meat packers so that kosher meat can be purchased, already prepared for the consumer.

Leviticus 18:1—20:27: Being Holy People

The Text in Its Ancient Context

Leviticus 18–20 is perhaps best characterized as a collection of prohibitions and admonitions for laypeople who have been declared holy by their holy God. Leviticus 18 focuses almost exclusively on forbidden sexual relations, declaring that even though the people of Canaan may have indulged in these relations, the people of Israel should not. The prohibitions include sexual relations with women in a man's extended family, with a woman in menstrual uncleanness, with a kinsman's wife, with another male, and between a woman and an animal; additionally, Israelites are forbidden to give their offspring to Molech. The rationale for forbidding these things is that Canaanites did all of them and defiled the land, and if Israel were to follow their example, they would defile the land and be cast out too, and cut off from their people in the bargain.

Chapter 19 follows this set of prohibitions with a more disparate collection of prohibitions and admonitions controlled by the opening declaration, "The Lord spoke to Moses saying: 'Speak to all the congregation of the people of Israel and say to them: You shall be holy, for I the Lord your God am holy.'" An expanded Decalogue of sorts follows, reflecting on the consequences of being declared holy by God, and the chapter concludes with a potpourri of specific regulations dealing with everything from prohibitions on mixing kinds of animals, seeds, and thread types in garments to how a man may trim his beard.

Chapter 20 then recalls many of the offenses already detailed in chapters 18–19 and assigns to them (somewhat vague) penalties, and concludes with general exhortations to keep God's statutes and commandments to be worthy of the land and avoid expulsion from it.

Within the broader agenda of the Holiness Code, this long text unit functions to indict and challenge the laity, just as chapter 17 did the priesthood. It is useful to take the prohibition of various sexual unions in chapter 18 as an example. The range of possibilities as to why such behaviors might have been a concern remains much under discussion, yet some basic options can be surmised: in a male-dominated culture, sexual victimization of weaker parties (women in one's household, men in subservient positions) may have been an ongoing problem, and a practice perpetrators thought they could be "excused" from through the sacrificial system the P tradents offered (see especially the possibility of converting intentional sins into unintentional ones in 5:14—6:7); it is also possible that these were sex acts that could count as worship of fertility gods and goddesses, and could also have been viewed by their perpetrators as remediable under the Priestly system. Assuming something like one of these scenarios (or other possibilities scholarship has conjured to explain this passage), the Holiness tradents offer a stark portrait of the consequences for committing these sins against the weaker members of one's wider community, if all experience were holy: offenders would not be able to make sacrifice and be restored, but would instead be "cut off" from the community, a penalty that may have involved death administered by the community, but was more likely thought to be a consequence that God brought upon the sinner (Milgrom 1991, 457–60)—in any case, it was sin with grave consequences that could not be avoided through the sacrifices prescribed by the P legislation.

The Text in the Interpretive Tradition

The simple declaration in Lev. 18:5 that by keeping and doing God's statutes and ordinances "one shall live" is often missed in the contemporary fascination with the sexual-misconduct legislation in the rest of the chapter; yet it was this verse that had the richer interpretive history in antiquity. One example of that interpretive vein is evident in the *Damascus Document* (CD), a key work from the Qumran community. CD 3.12–20 opens with the declaration that a select group that had kept God's revealed commandments received a further revelation of deeper secrets having to do with calendrical observances and "the testimonies of his righteousness and the truth of his ways, and the desires of his will *which one must do so that he will live by them* (Lev. 18:5)" (3.15–16). The passage continues to make clear that if this select group keeps these norms, they will not just have life, but life eternal. The sectarian author, in short, has claimed the promise of Lev. 18:5 for the special way of life to which his community was committed.

In sharp contrast to this is the way Paul puts Lev. 18:5 in complex tension with other "proof texts" from the Hebrew Bible (including, among others, Hab. 2:4) in Gal. 3:10-14, essentially arguing for the negation of its effect for believers (Martyn 1997, 307–36). Just as the Qumran covenanters thought it a powerful verse for making their claims to superior law keeping, Paul saw it necessary to negate it through complex rhetorical argumentation. There can hardly be better evidence for the degree of influence this one verse in Leviticus exerted over the ancient Jewish and Christian imagination.

The Text in Contemporary Discussion

While Lev. 18:5 fascinated ancient interpreters, the two prohibitions of intercourse between males in Lev. 18:22; 20:13 are what fascinate contemporary audiences, for good or for ill. And no amount of reasoning from a historical-critical perspective that the passages are not about homosexuality, but rather the sexual victimization of a weaker party by a stronger party, seems to call a halt to the vehement use of both verses by parties on all sides of the debate (for one of those sensible historical-critical discussions, see Wright Knust, 147–50). For that reason, perhaps the best way to approach the contemporary debate is through reading reasonable attempts to survey the breadth of actual uses of the passages in Leviticus in discussing homosexuality today (see, e.g., Stahlberg). The result is a dizzying array of readings, many of which speak more to the horizons of the interpreters than of the texts—which may be as much a lesson about interpretation in general as it is about how these simple texts play out in volatile debates.

Leviticus 21:1—22:33: Priestly Holiness and Offerings

The Text in Its Ancient Context

This long section addresses the consequences of holiness for the priesthood and for the offerings of Israel. Leviticus 21 makes (remarkably strong) prescriptions regarding all priests: because they are holy to God and make God's offerings, they should only have limited contact with the dead; they should not mar their bodies or cut away facial or cranial hair unnecessarily; and they should not marry women who are unclean by prostitution, divorce, or other defilement. Laypeople should treat them with the respect owed to the sanctified, and their daughters who profane their line by acts of prostitution should be executed by fire. The chapter further lays out the standards to which the anointed (high) priest is held: he should not make a mess of his hair, tear his garments, have any contact with the dead, or even go outside of the sanctuary lest he defile it, and he can only marry a virgin of his own kin. The rest of the chapter then lists a range of physical blemishes that would disqualify someone of the priestly line from service in the sanctuary, allowing them nonetheless access to the proceeds of the offerings. Leviticus 22 then commands that priests who have somehow incurred any kind of impurity may not approach the sanctified foodstuffs provided to the priests through the people's offerings, and decrees that no layperson may eat of the sacred portions (excepting only those who are of the priest's household by purchase, or by birth and still within the household). Additional detail is added to the general claim that a layperson's animal offering must be without blemish, naming a broad range of circumstances that can render a beast unfit, and there are instructions on how a newly born animal may be offered as a sacrifice. The section closes with another passage remarking on God's holiness as the motivation for keeping the commandments laid out in the preceding section.

Within the framework and agenda of the Holiness Code as a whole, this section seems intended to point out the consequences of intensifying God's holiness in Israel for the priests and the things they deal with. And just as the legislation for the laity in the preceding section makes clear that the chief significance of making all experience holy is to render things possible under the Priestly system impossible—at least without serious consequences coming to bear—the same holds true here. Priests who might have qualified for service and all of its benefits in the Priestly world—and certainly did, if we are to believe the level of corruption that Malachi and Third Isaiah identified—would be summarily dismissed from contact with the sacred offerings and precincts under the Holiness Code's stipulations. Similarly, the rules on how prebends might be handled were more limiting, as were the norms for everything from whom a priest might marry to how he might groom himself. On the reading of the Holiness Code promoted in this commentary, at least, this section is thus a wily indictment of the priestly abuses which might have been allowed by the Priestly perspective achieved precisely by taking with utmost seriousness the P tradition's own view that the priests, the sanctified offerings of Israel, and the space they worked in were the locus of God's holiness.

The Text in the Interpretive Tradition

Because of the Qumran community's intense interest in the purity (or better, impurity) of the priesthood and temple practice in Jerusalem and in creating their own alternatives to those, portions of this passage in Leviticus were frequently commented on by the Essene tradents. Two examples from 4QMMT, a legal document that lays out a number of the group's (early?) legal positions, demonstrate this.

The first instance involves a reading of Lev. 22:28, which prohibits slaughtering an offspring with its parent on the same day. 4QMMT B 36–38 seems to rely on an expansive reading of that rule in answering the question of what one does if an animal brought for sacrifice proves to be pregnant: the text seems to read the "slaughter" of Leviticus as "sacrifice" and "parent" and "offspring" as "mother" and "fetus" to decree that both may not be counted as an offering to God. The second instance is 4QMMT B 75–82, a much-discussed passage, that in any case agrees with and seems to intensify the sharp limitations on who might be acceptable as a wife for a priest (Lev. 21:7, 14).

Interestingly, the Essene use of this section of Leviticus grows out of the same sort of concerns this commentary assumes provoked the author(s) of the Holiness Code to create their utopian, corrective, critical vision of what the Priestly work wrought. The Essenes, however, distinguished themselves sharply from the Holiness school, using H's extension of holiness to all Israel and all of its experience not merely as a utopian corrective but also as a guide for rules they wanted to be implemented in real time, in the real world.

The Text in Contemporary Discussion

In a somewhat embarrassing contemporary use of the same regulations regarding priests and marriage in Leviticus 21, one does not have to search far on the Internet to discover American right-wing fundamentalist readers of the Bible who cite Lev. 21:13 (in a selective and decidedly nonliteralist way!) to argue that the prohibition on married clergy in the Roman Catholic communion is antibiblical. And searching just a little further turns up those among the latter group who will go so far as to suggest, ignorantly, that the sex abuse scandals that plagued Catholicism in recent decades would have been avoided if only marriage had been permitted. That it is difficult to find much from this portion of Leviticus in contemporary discussion may say more about the sensible allergy to getting caught up in such nonsense than about the availability of this section of text for thoughtful reflections on contemporary pastoral and priestly leadership across Christian and Jewish denominations.

Leviticus 23:1-44: Feasts and Sacred Observances

The Text in Its Ancient Context

Alongside Num. 28:1—29:40, this chapter offers P's calendar of feasts and sacred observances. After an introductory passage in verses 1-2, verse 3 declares the Sabbath. Then verse 4 gives a typical Holiness Code title to all that remains: "These are the appointed festivals of the Lord, the *holy* convocations, which you shall celebrate at the time appointed for them." Passover is addressed in verses 5-8, verses 9-14 address the offering of the firstfruits, verses 15-22 the Feast of Weeks, verses 23-25 the Feast of Trumpets, verses 26-32 the Day of Atonement, and verses 33-44 the Feast of Booths (Sukkoth; see below). Here too a recurring feature is reference to holiness as a feature of the feasts and/or a motivation for them. And by now, the role of a text like this within the Holiness Code's larger agenda should be relatively predictable. In this case, the concern is to extend the imagined world as imbued with holiness to the concept of time itself.

The Text in the Interpretive Tradition

It almost goes without saying that the calendar laws articulated in this chapter, in spite of featuring in a work that was likely utopian in its original vision, had great impact on later Jewish and

Christian liturgical calendars, both in terms of the timing of major observances and on the way in which observances were carried out.

More interesting, though, were the ways in which some interpreters sought to spiritualize or moralize the temporal legislation in chapter 23. A parade example comes from Augustine, who instructed his congregants in a sermon on the true meaning of the admonition in Lev. 23:3 not to perform any "servile work" on the Sabbath. He argued that observing the Sabbath in that sense is to resist sin, as sin is servile work (*Homily* 270; cited in Lienhard, 193–94).

The Text in Contemporary Discussion

The calendar of major observances laid out in Leviticus 23 continues to shape modern Jewish practice, and in a time when many religionists in America are working to revive their traditions, various of the customs in Leviticus 23 that may have gone by the wayside in the past are being observed with renewed vigor in contemporary Jewish life. One visible example on many college campuses across America every fall is the observance of Sukkoth by Hillel groups, who construct in a public, open space and use according to rabbinic teaching a *sukkah* ("booth").

Leviticus 24:1-23: Temple Observances and Blasphemy Punishment

The Text in Its Ancient Context

This chapter, seemingly out of context, addresses two vaguely related "temple" topics, the maintenance of an eternally burning lamp inside the sanctuary and the provision of the "sanctuary bread" consumed on a regular basis by the Aaronites as their "perpetual due," and the tale of a blasphemer that forms an inclusio around a list of communal crimes and their punishments. The chapter closes with the declaration that Israel should have a common law for the alien and the citizen.

The Text in the Interpretive Tradition

Early Christian interpreters were understandably drawn to the twelve loaves stipulated in Lev. 24:5-9, evoking so easily thoughts of the dozen apostles and the Eucharist. In the (rather unwelcome) spirit of supersessionism, Cyril of Jerusalem argues that the bread and cup of the Eucharist bring the "Old Covenant" reflected in this passage to an absolute end and replace it with the "New Covenant" (*Catechetical Lecture* 4.5; cited in Lienhard, 196). More imaginative is Bede's suggestion that this foretells the twelve baskets of bread fragments the twelve apostles gather from the five loaves they distributed to the hungry, and that this story refers to the "sacraments of the Scriptures," which the multitudes could not receive, but which the "apostles" and "apostolic men" (read: ecclesiastical elites) could take in (*On the Tabernacle* 1.7; cited in Lienhard, 196).

The Text in Contemporary Discussion

"Diaspora studies" is a vibrant new field in the academy. Leviticus 24:22 surely has something to contribute to those who study populations in diaspora, seeking to make their way in legal systems that are alien to them along with just about everything else they experience. What would it mean to take seriously the verse's admonition that there be *one law* for the alien and the citizen? In its

Holiness Code context, it seems certain to have been a stipulation meant to critique a system in which that was not the case, and presumably the alien was experiencing injustice as a consequence. In a globalized world, does this same, implicit critique hold true? Or have circumstances become such that a country's legal systems need to become more pluralistic, more flexible to take into account the norms and customs of guest people? This is surely the issue in several European countries and America today as judicial systems and legislation seek to be responsive to the needs of guest peoples, and in some instances seek the opposite, to require guest populations to conform to local law and custom. Applying Lev. 24:22 to today's context, in fact, presents interesting questions of justice, though far removed perhaps from those the text originally might have sought to address.

Leviticus 25:1-55: Sabbatical and Jubilee Years

The Text in Its Ancient Context

In this long chapter, the Holiness Code gives the rules for observing the Sabbatical and Jubilee Years, the rationale for their observance, and the specifics of implementing the general guidelines for both observances. Every seventh year is a Sabbatical Year, a year of rest for the land; and every fiftieth year is a Jubilee Year, in which land sold to others reverts to the original owners, and Israelites in servitude to others are freed to return to their own homes and families. The chapter offers further instruction on how to execute redemption of property in the Jubilee and how Israel should treat its own poor and impoverished resident aliens, particularly when their poverty leads to indentured servitude (which can be resolved by redemption).

This chapter surely originally followed Leviticus 23 and as such continued the utopian legislation to sanctify all of Israel's experience, including its time. And it is this chapter in particular that suggests the utopian nature of the Holiness Code. As lofty as the ideal is of giving the land and indentured servants rest from their respective labors and of returning land purchased to sellers at regular intervals in time, these were very likely stipulations few if any observed, and may even not have been intended as such by the H tradent. It was perhaps enough for this writer to make clear again the consequences of taking seriously God's intentions for Israel and its resources; if God's holiness were extended to *all* of Israel's time, *all things* would be required to experience their rest in ways no one could have otherwise ever imagined.

The Text in the Interpretive Tradition

The Jewish interpretive tradition that builds on this chapter's Sabbatical and Jubilee legislation is enormously rich. Elements of the *Enoch* traditions hearken to it, its echoes are present in the Jesus traditions, and of course, the Jewish pseudepigraphon *Jubilees* relies on its basic principles. It is remarkable, then, that the Dead Sea Scrolls were actually able to enrich our database in this regard. 4Q226, a document that looks to have been a Hebrew text resembling *Jubilees* (thus its moniker, 4QPseudo-Jubilees) seems to recall the exodus much as it is narrated in *Jubilees* 48. However, this fragment echoes the otherwise singular instance of marking a Jubilee as "holy" in Lev. 25:12. The author of the *Jubilees* narrative, it seems, sought to "out-holy" the Holiness Code, designating the Jubilee related to the exodus as transcending even the "ordinary holiness" of an ordinary Jubilee.

The Text in Contemporary Discussion

While the "Jubilee Year" is not recognized in modern Judaism, since 1300 CE the Christian church has marked its passage and the tradition survives in modern Roman Catholicism. The last observance of it was from Christmas Eve 1999 to Epiphany (January 6) 2001, under the leadership of John Paul II. Echoing the merciful aspects of the biblical Jubilee, the pope marked the beginning of the year by opening the *porta sancta*, the "holy door," to St. Peter's Basilica, which is unsealed only in the Jubilee Year to signal the opening of the portals of grace to the whole church.

Leviticus 26:1—27:34: Blessing and Curse, Vow and Offering

The Text in Its Ancient Context

Chapter 26 completes the Holiness Code, and as such performs a typical purpose, offering blessing and curses on those who keep or do not keep the statutes and ordinances contained in the rest of the code. Roughly the first third of the chapter describes the blessings that flow from obedience to the triple commandment to avoid idolatry, to keep the Sabbath, and to honor the sanctuary. Nearly the remaining two-thirds rehearse the deepening crisis God would bring on Israel in the land if it were not to obey, culminating in the people's expulsion from the land and the land's Sabbath rest from their affliction of it. The chapter draws to a close by offering the possibility that even if Israel is driven from the land by its own sin, if Israel calls on the Lord again from its exile, God will not spurn them but will remember them and the covenant with their ancestors.

This is surely the closing chapter of the Holiness Code. As such, it admirably achieves the purpose of drawing to a resounding conclusion the argument for a utopian vision makes vis-à-vis the reality it critiques. It states clearly the consequences of living *as though* God's holiness filled every aspect of Israel's experience—what this utopian visionary commends to his audience as the remedy for the abuses of the Priestly system—and it paints a picture of the fulfillment of Israel's destiny as God's people prosperous and at peace in the land God promised. With equal clarity, it lays out the consequences of living *as though* God's holiness could be disregarded at every turn—the loss of the promise, of peace, of prosperity, and of the land itself.

Clearly an appendix to Leviticus as a whole, chapter 27 gives guidelines for redeeming vows of persons (vv. 1-8), animals (vv. 9-13), buildings (vv. 14-15), land (vv. 16-25), firstlings (vv. 26-27), other things devoted to the Lord (vv. 28-29), and tithes (vv. 30-33); verse 34 indicates that the preceding regulations were given to Moses by God for the people of Israel on Sinai.

The Text in the Interpretive Tradition

The last word in the interpretation of Leviticus goes to Augustine, who in alluding to Lev. 26:12, "I will be your God," writes: "God will be the source of every satisfaction, more than any heart can rightly crave, more than life and health, food and wealth, glory and honor, peace and good—so that God, as St. Paul said, 'may be all in all' (1 Cor. 15:28). He will be the consummation of all our desiring—the object of our unending vision, of our unlessening love, of our eternal praise. And in this gift of vision, this response of love, this paean of praise, all alike will share, as all will share in everlasting life" (*City of God* 22.30; cited in Lienhard, 204).

The Text in Contemporary Discussion

Just so, in contemporary reflection on Leviticus, it is chapter 26 that most evokes soaring theological sentiments, and for good reason. Beginning with blessings for the covenant keepers and continuing with curses for those who fail by the covenant's standards, the chapter nonetheless returns to the theme of God's blessing for those who seek a connection with God, even from the circumstances of sin and rebellion. As John Goldingay remarks in a discussion of "Old Testament answers" to "key questions for Christians," Lev. 26:42, 44-45 makes clear that God is not constrained by the covenant from "taking action on the people's behalf" even "in the context of their wrongdoing"; indeed, it is God's being "mindful of the covenant" (123) that ensures such graciousness even for a wayward creation.

Works Cited

Bautch, Richard. 2012. "The Formulary of Atonement (Lev 16:12) in Penitential Prayers in the Second Temple Period." In *The Day of Atonement: Its Interpretation in Early Jewish and Christian Interpretations*, edited by Thomas Hieke and Tobias Nicklas, 33–45. Leiden: Brill.

Budd, Philip. 1996. *Leviticus: Based on the New Revised Standard Version*. NCB. Grand Rapids: Eerdmans.

Campbell, Antony, and Mark O'Brien. 1993. *Sources of the Pentateuch*. Minneapolis: Fortress Press.

Douglas, Mary. 1966. *Purity and Danger*. Oxford: Routledge and Kegan Paul.

———. 2001. *Leviticus as Literature*. Oxford: Oxford University Press.

Gilders, William. 2012. "The Day of Atonement in the Dead Sea Scrolls." In *The Day of Atonement: Its Interpretation in Early Jewish and Christian Interpretations*, edited by Thomas Hieke and Tobias Nicklas, 63–73. Leiden: Brill.

Goldingay, John. 2010. *Key Questions about Christian Faith: Old Testament Answers*. Grand Rapids: Baker Academic.

Grabbe, Lester. 1997. *Leviticus*. OTG. Sheffield: Sheffield Academic.

Kaminkowski, Tamar. 2009. "Nadav and Avihu and Dietary Laws: A Case of Action and Reaction *Parashat Shemini* (Leviticus 9:1–11:47)." In *Torah Queeries: Weekly Commentaries on the Hebrew Bible*, edited by Gregg Drinkwater, Joshua Lesser, David Shneer, and Judith Plaskow, 135–39. New York: New York University Press.

Kaplan, Laura Duhan. 2001. "The Blood of Life: Priestly Sacrifice and September 11." *The Maqom Journal for Studies in Rabbinic Literature* 2, n.p. http://www.maqom.com/journal/paper3.pdf.

Knohl, Israel. 1995. *The Sanctuary of Silence: The Priestly Torah and the Holiness School.* Minneapolis: Fortress Press.

Levine, Baruch 1974. *In the Presence of the Lord: A Study of Cult and Some Cultic Terms in Ancient Israel.* Leiden: Brill.

Lienhard, Joseph T., ed. 2001. *Exodus, Leviticus, Numbers, Deuteronomy*. Ancient Christian Commentary on Scripture, Old Testament 3. Downers Grove, IL: InterVarsity Press.

Martyn, J. Louis. 1997. *Galatians: A New Translation with Introduction and Commentary*. AB. New York: Doubleday.

Milgrom, Jacob. 1991. *Leviticus 1–16: A New Translation with Introduction and Commentary*. AB. New York: Doubleday.

———. 2000. *Leviticus 17–22: A New Translation with Introduction and Commentary*. AB. New York: Doubleday.

———. 2004. *Leviticus*. CC. Minneapolis: Fortress Press.

Neusner, Jacob, trans. and ed. 1986. *Judaism and Scripture: The Evidence of Leviticus Rabbah*. Chicago: University of Chicago Press.

Nihan, Christophe. 2007. *From Priestly Torah to Pentateuch: A Study in the Composition of the Book of Leviticus*. Tübingen: Mohr Siebeck.

Noth, Martin. 1965. *Leviticus: A Commentary*. OTL. Louisville: Westminster John Knox.

Petrie, Jon. 2000. "The Secular Word HOLOCAUST: Scholarly Myths, History and 20th Century Meanings." *Journal of Genocide Research* 2:31–63.

Schearing, Linda. 2003. "Double Time . . . Double Trouble? Gender, Sin, and Leviticus 12." In *The Book of Leviticus: Composition and Reception*, edited by Robert Kugler and Rolf Rendtorff, with the assistance of Sarah Smith Bartel, 429–50. Leiden: Brill.

Stahlberg, Lesleigh Cushing. 2008. "Modern Day Moabites: The Bible and the Debate About Same-Sex Marriage." *BibInt* 16:442–75.

Stöckl Ben Ezra, D. 2003. *The Impact of Yom Kippur on Early Christianity*. Tübingen: Mohr Siebeck.

Weber, Max. 1976. *The Protestant Ethic and the Spirit of Capitalism*. 2nd ed. Sydney: George Allen & Unwin.

Whitekettle, Richard. 1996. "Levitical Thought and the Female Reproductive Cycle: Wombs, Wellsprings, and the Primeval World." *VT* 46:376–91.

Wright Knust, Jennifer. 2011. *Unprotected Texts: The Bible's Surprising Contradictions about Sex and Desire*. San Francisco: HarperOne.

Yang Murray, Alice. 2008. *Historical Memories of the Japanese American Internment and Struggles for Redress*. Stanford: Stanford University Press.

Numbers

Karl N. Jacobson

Introduction

"Numbers," or "In the Wilderness" as it is called in the Hebrew Bible, is the story of the nation of Israel from its first encounter with God at Mount Sinai (see Lev. 27:34), to the final instructions given by God to Moses on the plains of Moab at the banks of the Jordan opposite Jericho: the "beachhead" of Israel's entry into the promised land (see Joshua 2). "Numbers" is an appropriate title for the work in the sense that Israel is counted in its entirety (both the eleven lay tribes and the Levites) not only once, but twice. "In the Wilderness" is equally fitting—and perhaps more so—in that the bulk of the book's material takes place in this particular physical landscape. What's more, "in the wilderness" serves as a "spiritual geography" (Olson 1996, 2), and so the book is and has been readily accessible to successive generations of readers.

There is in Numbers great variety of literary genre; there is prose (Numbers 11) and poetry (6:24-26), narrative (20), law (29), censuses (1–3; 26), and itineraries (33:1-49). In addition, there are various markers or transition points in the story. These markers are chronological (1:1, "on the first day of the second month, in the second year"; 10:11, "in the second year, in the second month, on the twentieth day"; 33:38, "in the fortieth year . . . on the first day of the fifth month"); geographical (1:1 "after they had come out of the land of Egypt"; 12:1, "While they were at Hazeroth"; 13:3, "So Moses sent them from the wilderness of Paran"; 21:11, "They set out from Oboth, and camped at Iye-abarim, in the wilderness bordering Moab"); and generational (14:22; 26:24; 32:11; 33:1). Such literary diversity, and the attendant difficulties of identifying a clear flow to the book, has resulted in no clear consensus as to how best to understand the order or structure of the material, as well as a range of disciplinary approaches to understanding the book (Childs, 195; Olson 1997, 2–3; Milgrom, xiii). A great deal of intertextual interpretation takes place in conversation with Numbers, both in the Hebrew Bible and the New Testament. Numbers shows literary connectedness (both influence and dependence) with Exodus, Leviticus, Deuteronomy, and Joshua (Milgrom, xxi), as well as Chronicles and Psalms (Dozeman, 214). The question of the "direction" of influence is muddy at best, as Milgrom notes: "the pericopes of Numbers are not, in the main, unitary compositions but are composites of or contain insertions from other sources. Some of these sources are old poems, narratives in Exodus, and cultic material from Leviticus. Conversely, Numbers material can be shown to have influenced the composition of Exodus and Deuteronomy" (xxi). In the New Testament, there are several examples of reinterpretation of Numbers: In Matthew (5:33-37), Jesus alludes to Numbers 30, rejecting outright the laws on making vows; in John (3:14-15), the story of the bronze serpent is reinterpreted as a sign for Jesus, who saves not from the immediate threat of physical death, but brings life through death; and Paul (1 Cor. 10:11) refers to this same incident as an example for the believer, to keep from evil and complaint.

This intertextuality is characteristic of the book of Numbers itself as well. As will be shown below, the book of Numbers is structured (however imperfectly) around parallel panels of material. The stories and census lists, as well as patterns of legal and votive materials, once established are revisited within the book. Numbers 32:6-15 is a response to two tribes asking for their allotment of territory to be outside of the promised land. Numbers 32 recalls a story from Num. 13:25—14:25 to make response, exhorting the Reubenites and the Gadites to remain faithful, and to continue to follow after the Lord. This distinctive intertextuality *within* the book is central to how Numbers functions literarily.

For the purposes of this essay, both in terms of the layout of the following commentary, and in an attempt to navigate the literary function of the material, the work of Dennis Olson will be used (Olson 1996, 5–6). The structure and flow of Numbers is best seen as a series of parallel episodes or panels that centers the experience of a people wandering in the wilderness, a wilderness both literal and figurative. In this commentary, these parallel episodes will be treated in tandem. There are four major parallel sections in the book of Numbers, and one stand-alone section. The format of these parallels is as follows:

1. The Numbering of Israel: Tribes and Levites (1–4 / 26)
2. Women, Vows, Offerings, and Passover (5–9 / 27–30)
3. Complaint, Jealousy, and Restoration (10–21 / 32–35)
4. A. The Balaam Cycle (22–24)
5. War against Midian (25 / 31)

The reader of Numbers is called to join in the transition from the generation that complained, doubted, and died to the generation born out of the wilderness, trusted in their God, and was settled in the promised land, to live.

Finally, let us return to the title of the book, as it is critical to understanding the theological significance of the work as a whole: In the Wilderness (*bĕmidbar*). Order in, through, and out of chaos is an important lens through which to view the varied literature of Numbers, the various interpretations it has enjoyed, and the applications it may find. The operative theological and religious modus operandi of the book is, in keeping with the first book of the Pentateuch, one of creation. In the locale of "the wilderness," and thus in the book of Numbers, the nation of Israel, its religious and social structure, its worship and laws, are created by God. It is out of the wilderness of wandering that the nation of Israel is made. Commenting on the story of the bronze serpent, Martin Luther noted that this is the creative, life-giving power that is attested to in Numbers.

> The serpent which Moses raised up in the desert (Num. 21:9) did not make alive through its inherent character (for it was made of bronze, just as we could form a serpent from bronze now); but the Word which was added to that brazen serpent was life-giving because God commanded the serpent to be set up, and added the Word (Num. 21:8): "Whoever looks at it will be healed." This Word you do not have if you form a serpent from bronze today. Moreover, the reason for the healing lay not in looking at it but in the command from God that they should look at the serpent and in the promise of deliverance. (*LW* 1:227)

The book of Numbers is, at its core, a theological argument; an argument for life ordered by God, among a people marshaled by God, in a land (read: Land) created for this people by the promise of God.

Numbers 1:1—4:49; 26:1-65: The Numbering of Israel, Tribes, and Levites

The Text in Its Ancient Context

The book of Numbers opens with four chapters dedicated to a "census of the whole congregation of Israelites" (1:2a). The census of Israel is literally a "counting of the heads" (*śĕ'û 'et-rōš*). The recurring verb in Numbers 1 is *pāqad*, "to number, allocate, or muster"; *muster*, as in a military ordering, a point to which we return below. *Pāqad* is used twenty-one times in the first chapter of Numbers, in the introduction to the census (1:1-19), in the "enrolling" of each of the tribes (including the two "tribes" of Joseph's sons Ephraim and Manasseh; 1:20-43) in the census, and in the summary of the census (1:44-54). The Levites alone are not to be counted (1:49-50), until they are counted in a different kind of census that is not martial but clerical.

In addition to the Levites, it must be noted that this census is not of the whole congregation; rather, it is of all the men of the eleven tribes of Israel (excluding the twelfth tribe, the tribe of Levi) who are of fighting age: "in their clans, by ancestral houses, according to the number of names, every male individually; from twenty years old and upward, everyone in Israel able to go to war" (1:2b-3). In the lists of each of the tribes, the enlistment age is twenty (cf. 2 Chron. 25:5 and the census taken by Amaziah). As each of the tribes is enrolled, the phrase "everyone able to go to war" (*kōl yōṣē' ṣābā'*) occurs; fourteen times total. The phrase *yōṣē' ṣābā'* literally means "to go forth as a host." This phrase is striking in that it connects the tribes of Israel to one of the central epithets of the God of ancient Israel, *'ădōnāy ṣĕbā'ōt*, "YHWH of Hosts." While the title never occurs in the book of Numbers (or anywhere in the Pentateuch), through this phrase YHWH is understood as the divine King who goes into battle before the hosts not just of heaven but also of the people of Israel (cf. Ps. 24:10); and the people of Israel are to be understood as God's host.

As the "able-bodied" men of the eleven tribes are counted ("enrolled," NRSV), they are in fact being enlisted and mustered. While there may be some discomfiture for certain modern readers with the military language employed here in Numbers, and the emphasis it places on the conquest model of the settlement of the promised land, it cannot be denied. The repeated phrase (always bridging the end of one verse and the beginning of another) is *kōl yōṣēʾ ṣābāʾ pĕqūdêhem* (see, e.g., 1:20-21, 22-23, 24-25, 26-27, 28-29, 30-31, 32-33), and is perhaps best translated "all those able to go to war, those mustered." Thus the census list here in the book of Numbers is not a numbering of the people of Israel; it is the marshaling of Israel in the wilderness in preparation for the conquest of the promised land.

The transition from the census of the fighting men of Israel to the prelude to the appointment of the Levites to service in the tabernacle (1:48-51, anticipating 3:14-39) is marked by a confluence of identical terminology. The language of marshaling and census is used both to prohibit the Levitical census and to define their appointment in successive verses. Numbers 1:49 declares: "Only the tribe of Levi you shall not enroll [*tipqōd*], and you shall not take a census [*wĕʾet-rōʾšām lōʾ tiśśāʾ*] of them with the other Israelites." Linguistically, it may be that there is a distinction here, as Milgrom finds (10), between the numbering of individuals and sum totals, but this does nothing to explain why the same terms are employed both in prescription and prohibition. In Num. 1:50, the central term for the enrollment of Israel is employed again, this time in an affirmative sense for the appointment of the Levites to serve in the tabernacle, "Rather, you shall appoint [*hapqēd*] the Levites over the tabernacle of the covenant." Textually, there is rather abrupt movement—using the same terminology—from the prohibition of counting the Levites, to the appointment of the Levites to a particular role in the religious—and military—life of Israel.

The prohibiting language parallels the prescriptive language in Num. 1:2-3, "Take a census [*śĕʾû ʾet-rōš*] of the whole congregation of Israelites. . . . You and Aaron shall enroll [*tipqĕdû*] them." From a literary perspective, the function of the balancing of directive and prohibition may be inclusion, setting the marshaling of Israel—by Israel's prophet and priest—within the context of Israel's religious identity. Later in Numbers (31:6) it is the high priest who leads the hosts of Israel to war, preceded not by the instruments of war, but the "holy instruments" (Niditch, 52). The ordering of the encampment, with the tabernacle in the center and the hosts of Israel encamped around it, facing the tent of meeting (2:1-34), which follows the military census, matches the inclusio nicely.

The census of the Levites that follows in two parts (3:14-39 and 4:34-49) is carried out "according to the word of the Lord"—*ʿal-pî yhwh*, 3:16, 29, 51; 4:37, 41, 45, 49. The emphasis in this particular census is that it is the Lord who does the counting (Milgrom, 19).

At the end of chapter 4, following the enrollment of the subclans of the tribe of Levi, the Kohathites, the Gershonites, and the Merarites, there is an abrupt shift in the narrative flow, in the genre of the text, to legal material. This shift not only marks a break in the sense units of the book but also highlights the impetus of the census lists in chapters 1–4, which orders the people of Israel, gives them vocational and spiritual direction. Chapters 5 and following move to ordering the relational life of the newly ordered community, to which we will turn below.

The parallel panel in 26:1-65 relates the second census in Numbers, the census of the new generation that will succeed in the conquest of the promised land, where the former generation failed. As in the first census, the second is a census of "everyone in Israel able to go to war" (*kōl-yōṣēʾ ṣābāʾ bĕyiśrāʾēl*). This, again, is the military enlisting of the people. This second account is terse compared to the first, and the emphasis is on the transition to the new generation. Numbers 26:64 sets up the enrollment of the new generation in contrast with the fate of the old: "Among those there was not one of those enrolled by Moses and Aaron the priest, who had enrolled the Israelites in the wilderness of Sinai" (cf. Numbers 1; 14; 26). Milgrom characterizes Num. 26:63-65 as a "postscript" (227), while Olson sees these verses as sounding "the theme of the whole book. . . . This text provides a programmatic summary of the structure of Numbers. The second census list is both a sign of completed judgment on the first generation and a sign of God's promise for a new generation" (1996, 163).

The Text in the Interpretive Tradition

One of the thornier issues raised by the censuses, specifically in the second census in Numbers 26, is in the allotment of tribal territory. As Jewish commentators from Rashi, to Ramban (Rabbi Moshe ben Nahman), to Abravanel have wrestled with (for a detailed discussion, see Milgrom, 227–28, and Excursus 62), there seem to be two competing means of deciding on the allotment of land to the tribes. The first is according to tribal size (26:54); the second, by lot (26:56). Solutions to the problem of which means was preeminent are legion. Milgrom rightly points out that the simplest solution is based on "the basic principle of apportioning the land according to tribal clan size (26:53-54, with Ramban), qualified by the secondary principle that, initially, the location of the tribal and clan territory should be determined by lot (26:55-56, with Abravanel)" (Milgrom, 482). Rashi, however, concluded that God saw to it that the lot fell a certain way, so that the drawn lots were in accordance with tribal sizes and needs. Thus the use of lots was understood as a means of gauging the divine will. As is seen subsequently in Numbers (34:13; 36:2-3) and elsewhere in the Bible (Josh. 14:1-2; 18:1-10), the lot was the primary means of allocating tribal inheritances.

Regardless of the motivation behind the pairing of lot and need-based allocation, this, once again, seems to be a matter of ordering the people. The divine goal, it would appear, is to afford a balance between need and fairness. God's ordering is, therefore, along both lines.

The Text in Contemporary Discussion

The census lists of Numbers 1–4; 26, serve to emphasize a dialectic of wrath and promise. The intent is to order the people, to marshal them so that they might occupy the promised land. The intervening narrative reports that this ordering of the people was disordered by their lack of trust in God's work (see the story of the spies and their report in 13:17—14:25). For the present reader of Numbers, this is the tension to which the book speaks. In recent generations, the move to allegorical interpretation has often been either deemphasized, or rejected outright. There is, however, a sense in which the wilderness allegory is a central one: not merely because it makes sense to the present-day reader of Numbers but also because this is how Numbers is most clearly employed in the Scriptures themselves.

It was noted above that census lists of Numbers 1–4 are meant to order, organize, galvanize, and motivate the people. And in Numbers 26, the second census sees the intention realized; Israel is reordered, reorganized, regalvanized, and this time to full effect.

Exploring the tale of Israel between the wildernesses of Sinai and Moab may well resonate with any number of similar tensions today. In the midst of the "wildernesses" of our time—the wildernesses of loss, of mistrust, of human-on-human crime, of religious pluralism, of searching for genuine, life-changing faith in an increasingly complicated and wild world—the story of Israel "in the wilderness" is potentially meaningful. The struggles that believing people face, in their daily living as individuals and in their lives as a part of community, can be made sense of "in the wilderness."

And therefore the vocations of believing people—of people who not only trust God's ordering of their world but who also see themselves as a part of God's chosen people—may be fruitfully explored and informed through an interaction with Numbers. To what is God mustering us, as parents and children, spouses and siblings—in the communities of our families, faced with brokenness and loss; as employees and bosses, as citizens of our home nations and of the world—when we are faced with the ethical and moral ambiguities of our decisions; as members of religious communities adrift in a world of rich diversity and competing truth-claims? We are, all of us, very much "in the wilderness," as we live and move and have our being. To what is God calling us who read Numbers and seek to answer God's mustering-call? The answers may well be different—perhaps markedly so—depending on who and where we are.

The census lists of Numbers 1–4 and 26—at first blush either uninteresting or confusing, much like the genealogies that begin the Gospel of Matthew—offer the setting through which the rest of the book is understandable. It is believed by many that God speaks order into human community, and that this ordering is trustworthy. Those who are unable or unwilling to trust it, according to Numbers, will not see the promises of God come to fruition; perhaps their children will.

Numbers 5:1—9:23; 27:1—30:16: Women, Vows, Offerings, and Passover

The Text in Its Ancient Context

Numbers 5 marks the first major shift in terms of genre in the book. Following the ordering of the tribes into martial units, the text moves abruptly not to the march, or to battle, but to legal questions of purity, fidelity, and worship. This shift may strike the reader as disjointed, but what is happening in the narrative flow—which if understood correctly is actually quite smooth—is the ordering of daily life in the encampment, the next step in the forming up of Israel.

Numbers 5 is made up of three sections addressing, respectively, different challenges to the community. First, Num. 5:1-3 addresses unclean persons, whether through disease or contact with the dead. Any person who is unclean, and therefore a danger to the wider community, is to be put outside the encampment. This expulsion is not, however, to be taken as permanent. Providing the unclean have been cleansed, they can be restored to the community (cf. Leviticus 13–14 regarding leprosy, and Num. 19:11-22 regarding those who have touched the dead).

Second, Num. 5:4-10 is about broken vows, which are characterized as "breaking faith with the Lord" (*lim'ōl ma'al byhwh*, 5:6). This brief passage acknowledges that human community is threatened by transgression whenever "a man or a woman wrongs another." Here transgressions against one's fellow human beings are equated with breaking faith with God (a not uncommon move in Leviticus; see 5:15, 21), which is reminiscent of the exhortation in Genesis 9 against murder.

Whoever sheds the blood of a human,
    by a human shall that person's blood be shed;
for in his own image
    God made humankind. (Gen. 9:6)

Because human beings are made in God's image, to wrong another is to wrong God, and therefore to jeopardize the community. Here again there is hope, or means provided by which the community can be restored even after such wrongdoing, through restitution not only to the individual wronged (5:7) but also to the community in his or her stead, either the next of kin in the case of death, or the community as a whole (5:8-11).

Finally, in the longest section, 5:11-31, the dangers of adultery are addressed. The case law concerning suspected adultery includes a ritualistic trial by water to ascertain guilt or innocence in the case of a woman accused of unfaithfulness.

What is striking is that in each case these legal matters address both men and women, a remarkably egalitarian stance within the larger biblical corpus (see 5:3, 5, 29-30; cf. Exod. 21:28-29; Lev. 13:29, 38; Deut. 17:2-7). At stake is "disruption of human relationships" (Olson 1996, 39), and this includes every human being, both male and female.

Following legal matters, the narrative moves on to matters of vows and offerings, enumerating key elements of the nation's relationship with God. Olson, addressing the second of the parallel panels (Numbers 28–29), notes that the pattern of offerings leading up to the celebration of the Passover, which orders the Israelite people and their relationship with God, is wrought through "a systematic program of offerings and sacrifices that mark important boundaries of time" (Olson 1997, 237). As with the clerical numbering of the Levites, the vow of the Nazirite and the series of offerings by the leaders of the people (7:1-83) are set up, and apart, for a purpose: "The structure of time and temporal boundaries that stands behind these offerings and sacrifices regularly reminds the Israelites of their status as God's holy people and sustains the order of the community's social and religious life against the forces of chaos" (Olson 1997, 237). Through law, ritual setting apart, and ritual observance, the young nation is stabilized.

The parallel panel of Num. 27:1—30:16 includes, again, a treatment on vows, offerings, and the celebration of Passover. It also includes a striking passage on the place of women, this time having to do with inheritance. The case of the daughters of Zelophehad, a member of the tribe of Manasseh who died without a male heir, sets a precedent for female inheritance in Israel. The case is remarkable as a whole, as it includes women speaking in the assembly in the Tent of Meeting, that they argue for women's inheritance, and that each of these women is named—Mahlah, Noah, Hoglah, Milcah, and Tirzah (Nowell, 115). As is the case with the laws concerning levirate marriage (see Deuteronomy 25), the inheritance practices endorsed here—which do not go unchallenged (Numbers 36) but which do stand—serve as a protection and provision for the women of Israel. While it may not seem obvious even to the critical eye, this case law precedence regarding inheritance parallels the case law and trial by ordeal of 5:11-31. In both cases, provision is made so that a woman cannot be excluded from the community, in terms of either her place as a daughter or her rights in relationship to her spouse. Numbers 5:1—9:23; 27:1—30:16 is, in largest part, aimed at the ordering of Israel's internal relationships in terms of its relationship with God. This matter is about order in, and the preservation of, God's chosen people.

The Text in the Interpretive Tradition

Much in these parallel passages has been the cause of interpretive and applicative struggle. There is, perhaps, no more difficult text in the book of Numbers than the case of suspected adultery. Olson articulates accurately the tension this story raises. On the one hand, the woman, when accused, has no choice but to undergo the ordeal, drinking bitter water made dangerous by dust taken from the sanctuary floor and the infusion of an inky curse to see whether she is in fact guilty. The history of interpretation of this text—or, if Olson is correct, the history of attempted "softer interpretation," that is, of making the text palatable—is rich (see his survey in Olson 1996, 36–39). What seems often to be overlooked is the conditional nature of the ordeal. Irene Nowell (29) suggests that the accused woman must respond to a curse that presumes her guilt (see Num. 5:21-22) with "Amen, amen!" Olson seems to prioritize the assumption of guilt, while allowing for some potential for innocence: "Much of the legal case seems to assume the woman's guilt, although the possibility of her innocence is acknowledged in 5:14 and 5:30" (36).

Olson further represents a significant majority of interpreters of this text when he states that it is "highly disturbing," reflecting "cultural mores that most readers would find unacceptable today," and that it "seems extremely repulsive and degrading to women." These criticisms of the text cannot be dismissed out of hand, for they are correct insofar as modern culture would demand far more equality than this text is able to engender. However, the modern reader ought to be careful not to react so strongly that the conditional nature of trial, and therefore the protection that it is—to some degree at least—affording the accused woman, is overlooked. In 5:19-20, conditional clauses clearly differentiate the two possibilities: if the woman is innocent, she will be immune; and if she is guilty, she will succumb to the holy water. The conditional nature of the ordeal is, at the very least, an attempt to protect the woman from an unfounded accusation. She cannot simply be put aside without proof or trial. While it must be made clear that this standard falls short of what we would practice today (one hopes)—and indeed, there seems to be no fallout for the man who has accused his wife falsely—it was an attempt, a beginning of sorts, at protecting the women of Israel. And as Geoffrey Hartman notes, "We are often returned by the Jewish Bible to a realistic transaction that indicates how human rights are not a given, but are established by grant and negotiation" (41). Numbers 5:11-31 can be helpfully read through the lens of an early attempt, or early evidence of a community of people, shaped by their relationship with God, creating space for a trial mediated by a vow to their God.

Similarly, the matter of the order of inheritance raised in Numbers was taken up in the early Jewish practice. In *Baba Batra* 8:1-3 (376–77), the question of inheritance was applied critically:

> This is the order of inheritance: *If a man die and have no son, then ye shall cause his inheritance to pass unto his daughter* (Num. 27:8)—the son precedes the daughter, and all the son's offspring precede the daughter; the daughter precedes the brothers (of the deceased) and the daughter's offspring precede the brothers. (367)

And again,

> The daughters of Zelophehad took three portions of the inheritance: the portion of their father who was of them that came out of Egypt, and his portion among his brethren from the property of Hepher, who also, in that he was the firstborn, received a double share. The son and the daughter are alike concerning inheritance. (367–77)

Each of these cases, that of the daughters of Zelophehad and the trial by ordeal of the suspected adulteress, have been critical but sensitive matters that readers and interpreters of the book of Numbers have taken up.

The Text in Contemporary Discussion

No modern reader with any sensitivity to the treatment of women can be comfortable with simply accepting and applying Num. 5:11-31. This intricate case law concerning the dangers both of adultery and of jealousy is not the kind of casuistic text that we should appropriate as our own and apply. However, if the modern reader can explore this text's implications without merely applying it simplistically, then Num. 5:11-31 may still have something to teach us. Following closely the admonition that to wrong another is to transgress against God (5:6), this text explores the real dangers posed by broken faithfulness in human relationship. Numbers 5:11-31 takes these dangers seriously and works, in at least a limited fashion, to allow for a testing of faithfulness against jealousy. If, with Genesis, we hold that both men and women bear the divine image, then the intent of this text appears to be to hold the relationship between man and woman—between wife and husband—in close care. Such a text, difficult as it may be, which works to establish safer grounds for the evaluation of guilt or innocence, should be honored for what it is, limits and all.

Our modern world is no less troubled by the dangers inherent in adultery, in divorce, and in the harm to and even destruction of families, than was wilderness-bound Israel. In fact, considering divorce rates, and the expanding understanding of what marriage is and for whom it is available, the intersection of faithfulness, jealousy, and human brokenness is all the more dangerous and dear. While modern communities will not apply Numbers 5 directly, we do well to be mindful of the power that human love and human relationships have in—and on—human communities, and to consider the admonition that closes out the chapter, that all such relationships should be "set before the Lord" (5:30).

One final note. The first panel of this sense unit in our parallel, intertextual reading of Numbers is anchored by the first of several poetic fragments that stand out in Numbers. In 6:22-27, we find the priestly blessing, in which the people of Israel is claimed and blessed by God:

> The Lord bless you and keep you;
> the Lord make his face to shine upon you, and be gracious to you;
> the Lord lift up his countenance upon you, and give you peace.

This blessing is described as a sort of "nameplating" of Israel, for by the blessing, "they shall put my [the Lord's] name on the Israelites" (6:27). This is, in a basic and fundamental sense, an invocation, the calling on the name of God, a claiming of the divine name that serves to establish and shape the identity of the people in all they do. In terms of the internal relationships of the people, this blessing and naming of Israel as God's hearkens back to the closing verses of Numbers 4, in which the Levites are enrolled (marshaled) "according to the commandment of the Lord" (4:37, 41, 45, 49). For the present reader of Numbers, for communities of believers, this blessing, naming, and claiming is not only an anchor for communal living but also a lens through which to view the world—the wilderness world in which we live, and the promised world toward which we move.

Numbers 10:1—21:35; 32:1—35:34: Complaint, Jealousy, and Restoration

The Text in Its Ancient Context

At the end of the last sense unit (9:15-23), the narrative of Numbers brings its version of Israel's travelogue even with the ending of the book of Exodus (40:34-38). Although the details and terminology clearly show divergence, reflecting differing literary traditions, Num. 9:15-23 appears to be an extension or extrapolation of Exodus, enumerating the same stages of travel, and a similar pattern to Israel's sojourning:

1. The glory of the Lord was on the tent of meeting (*'ōhel mô'ēd*, Exod. 40:34), and/or tabernacle (*hammiškān*, Exod. 40:34; Num. 9:15), or tent of the covenant (*'ōhel hā'ēdūt*, Num. 9:15).
2. When the glory of the Lord, a cloud by day and fire by night (Exod. 40:38; Num. 9:15, 16), lifted, the people would set out on the next stage (Exod. 40:36; Num. 9:17).
3. At times the cloud/fire would remain over the tabernacle, and the people would remain encamped (Exod. 40:37; Num. 9:18-23).

Exodus relates this pattern in a scant five verses, while Numbers does so in almost twice that; this is because Numbers is more concerned with the length of time that Israel might stay encamped, allowing for a time variance of "two days, or a month, or longer" (9:22).

Having arrived at the same relative point in the story of Israel's journey from Egypt, Numbers then departs drastically from the Exodus tradition. In Exodus, the people complain, asking for water and food, prior to their arrival at Sinai (Exodus 17). In Numbers, the complaining begins after the people have departed Sinai (Numbers 11). This marked difference—shifting the complaining vis-à-vis the locus of Sinai—serves to highlight a key difference in the Numbers complaint account. As Olson (1996, 61) has noted, the complaints of Israel are, in the book of Exodus, "treated as legitimate needs: the people need water (Exod. 15:22-26), the people need food (Exodus 16), and the people again need water (Exod. 17:1-7). In each case God takes the complaints seriously and fulfills the needs of the Israelites." But in Numbers, the complaints are portrayed as signs of Israel's lack of trust, a prelude of sorts to the episode of the spies sent into the promised land, which follows shortly (13:25—14:12). The initial response of God to the complaining of the Israelites is not provision, but pyrotechnics, "Then the fire of the Lord burned against them, and consumed some outlying part of the camp" (11:2).

Over the course of Numbers 11–21 we find several parallel complaints, often different in articulation, but representative of a single fundamental issue: mistrust of God and God's chosen leaders. At key points in the recurring pattern of mistrust or jealousy, God responds to the people's complaining in varied ways. The litany of complaints is as follows:

Numbers	11	complaint about manna and meat; a question of trust
	12	complaint about Moses' leadership; Aaron and Miriam's jealousy
	13–14	complaint about the promised land; a question of trust
	16	complaint about Moses' leadership; Korah's rebellion
	20	complaint about water; a question of trust
	21	complaint about food and water; summary of Israel's lack of trust

The first complaint is to and against Moses because the people are hungry. They complain about the manna (11:4-6). But the people want meat. God's response is to "come down and talk," first to talk to Moses (11:17) and again to empower the elders appointed to help Moses manage this "rabble" (11:25). When God comes down to speak to Moses, Moses is told to tell the Israelites that they will have more meat than they can handle, so much that it will "come out of your nostrils and become loathsome to you" (11:20). Israel's ungracious complaining is met with provision that becomes punishment: as Num. 11:33 puts it, "while the meat was still between their teeth, before it was consumed, the anger of the LORD was kindled against the people, and the LORD struck the people with a very great plague." Unlike in Exodus, God's provision is tinged with threat, danger.

Aaron and Miriam also raise a complaint against Moses, angered (supposedly) by their brother's Cushite wife (12:1). It is unclear what is meant by the phrase *ha'iššâ hakkūšît*. The only wife of Moses of whom the Bible otherwise speaks is Zipporah, who is a Midianite, not Cushite. Milgrom (93) suggests correctly that settling the question is irrelevant, because the real reason for the complaint is that Aaron and Miriam are feeling marginalized: "Has the LORD spoken only through Moses? Has he not spoken through us also?" (12:2). As Micah 6:4 relates, the tradition maintains to some degree the shared leadership of Moses and his siblings. But here their complaint suggests that their influence—among the people? with Moses?—is flagging. As with the complaint about food, "the LORD came down . . . and called" out to Aaron and Miriam, putting them in their place:

> And he said, "Hear my words:
>
> When there are prophets among you,
> I the LORD make myself known to them in visions [*bammar'â*];
> I speak to them in dreams [*baḥălôm*].
> Not so with my servant Moses;
> he is entrusted with all my house.
> With him I speak face to face—clearly, not in riddles;
> and he beholds the form of the LORD." (Num. 12:6-8)

Moses is the prophet extraordinaire, no mere dreamer (*ḥălōmôt*) or seer (*rōʼeh*), but the prophet to whom God comes down to speak with directly.

These complaints—against Moses because of the food and because of his pride of place in leadership—serve in part as a prelude to the response of the people to the report of the spies who are sent into Canaan. Representatives of each tribe are sent, under the direction of Joshua, to survey the promised land (13:1-24). The report is that the land is good, flowing with "milk and honey" (13:27), but that it is occupied by the Nephilim (13:33), the "heroes that were of old, warriors of renown" (see Gen. 6:4). The conclusion of the people is that they cannot possibly take the promised land (13:32). They have, it seems, forgotten what their God did both in Egypt and in their own encampment. And so again, and for a third time, the Israelites complain. In response to this renewed complaint, God concludes that this people, faithless again, are unworthy to bear the name of God and to be so blessed; Moses—and his offspring—will take their place. For this third complaint, the people will receive the ultimate punishment, the withdrawal of God's promise.

But Moses intercedes for them. And what is striking about his intercession is that he remembers, and reminds God, of what the Israelites have apparently forgotten, what God did in Egypt (see 14:14, 16) and the promise that ought to be Israel's because of who God is; as God said,

> The LORD is slow to anger,
> and abounding in steadfast love,
> forgiving iniquity and transgression,
> but by no means clearing the guilty,
> visiting the iniquity of the parents
> upon the children
> to the third and the fourth generation. (14:18; cf. Exod. 34:6-7)

And it is here that one of the core statements of Deuteronomy (5:1-3) in comparison is, on the surface, observably false. YHWH, reminded of the divine character, does forgive, but does not clear the guilt of this faithless generation, almost none of whom will see the promised land (14:20-25). This generation, which fails in its attempt to enter the promised land (14:26-45), will be effaced by the generation to come, which follows more closely, trusts more fully, and is rewarded with the inheritance of Canaan and the Transjordan (32:1—34:20).

Following Moses' intercession, the narrative once again shifts quite drastically, returning to two matters of ritual practice. First, offerings are again prescribed and outlined. These offerings pertain primarily to the promised land, and do seem somewhat out of place, although there are numerous connections to the preceding chapters (11–14) as Olson has outlined (1996, 97–99). Those connections notwithstanding, it seems clear the movement to ritual action and—more importantly—dress serves the purpose in the narrative of turning the people's attention away from their complaining and back to God. The movement forces the Israelites, and the reader, to remember what God has done.

In Numbers 16 there is, again, a challenge to the leadership of Moses, this time by Korah, Dathan, and Abiram. Korah accuses Moses of going too far, of elevating himself above the people, all of whom are holy (16:3). The complaints of Dathan and Abiram echo the complaints of the manna incident indicting Moses as a failure: "it is clear that you have not brought us into a land flowing with milk and honey" (16:13-14). And once again, God answers, the earth opening up and swallowing the households of Korah, Dathan, and Abiram, and fire consuming 250 others. What follows, in Numbers 17–19, is the elevation of the Aaronic priesthood and the reestablishment of the order God put in place in Numbers 1–4; 26.

The final episodes of complaint, in chapters 20–21, serve to summarize Israel's lack of trust in God's provision. In these successive episodes, the people complain about water, then about food and water: "The people spoke against God and against Moses, 'Why have you brought us up out of Egypt to die in the wilderness? For there is no food and no water, and we detest this miserable food'" (21:5). God's response this last time is to send "fiery serpents," poisonous snakes, into the camp; the people are bitten and die. Only when Moses makes a serpent of bronze (*nĕḥaš nĕḥōšet*)—a play on words in Hebrew similar to assonance, in which the two words sound very much alike—and the peoples' eyes are drawn to it are they then drawn back to God; seeing it they remember and live.

The pattern of complaint, punishment (or struggle, see Num. 14:26-45; 20:14-21), and restoration that shapes this largest portion of Numbers is a familiar motif in the Hebrew Bible (cf., e.g., the pattern in Judges). The back-and-forth movement in these chapters sets the table for the cleansing of Israel, for the new generation to be born and begin to grow in faith and trust even as the old generation wanes. The end of this section (10–21) sounds the first positive note in Israel's attempt to conquer the promised land, with the victories over the Amorites (21:21-32) and Bashan (21:33-35). These notes echo resoundingly in Numbers 32–35, in which Israel's conquests become decisive, and they at last reach the end of their journey.

The Text in the Interpretive Tradition

The book of Numbers itself—interpreting the tradition within the tradition—picks up this transition, and in chapters 32–35 revisits and summarizes the journey from Egypt (in chapter 33)—a journey that is martial in nature, the people going out "in military formation" (*lĕṣib'ōtām*), that is, as a host to war—then next charts the boundaries of the land (34), and lays out the cities in which the Levites will live. The end of chapter 35 (vv. 16-34) returns once more to case law. This is, yet again, an apparently strange transition in the narrative, but takes seriously the strains and perhaps the proclivities of a people schooled in war, trying to live in peace.

The incident of the bronze serpent is taken up in the biblical text in a couple of places. It reappears first in the story of Hezekiah's reforms (2 Kings 18), when the king destroys the *nĕḥuštān*, the "bronzed thing," because it had become an object of worship for Israel. In the New Testament, the serpent in the wilderness becomes an allegory for the crucifixion of Jesus who, like the serpent in the wilderness, will be lifted up (John 3:11-15). In the case of Jesus, it is not simply seeing the crucified Christ that brings life, but believing in him. The parallel is striking, that life out of death—whether deliverance in this life or eternal life after death—comes from turning away from complaining (or in the case of Nicodemus, questioning and doubting) and being reoriented to God.

These incidents of complaining are taken up in the New Testament as well, in 1 Cor. 10:1-21, in which Paul draws on Israel's story to exhort his listeners to avoid the dangers of idolatry. The purpose, according to Paul, of retelling Israel's story—a relatively common move in Acts in particular, see Acts 2:14-36; 7:1-53; 13:16-43—is to "serve as an example, and they were written down to instruct us" (1 Cor. 10:11).

One of the most striking features of this sense unit is found in the complaint Moses makes to God. In Num. 10:15, Moses employs the extended metaphor of motherhood. He argues with God, asking, "Did I conceive this people? Did I give birth to them that you should say to me, 'Carry them in your bosom, as a nurse carries a sucking child,' to the land that you promised on oath to their ancestors?" (Num. 11:12).

The feminine metaphor, which *Targum Onqelos* 11:12 rejects, altering the expression "Did I give birth to them" to "Am I the father of," is fitting, according to Ramban, because "it is the mother who suffers the pains of rearing children" (Milgrom, 85). But the maternal metaphor Moses uses for himself and his leadership of the people is, in verse 15, taken a step further still. When Moses turns his accusation directly and aggressively to God, he says, "If this is the way you are going to treat me, put me to death at once." What is striking is that the pronoun Moses uses when addressing God in this verse is feminine (*'at*). Moses addresses God literally as Israel's mother. As Nowell puts it, "Moses points out that he is not their mother; God is! God conceived them and gave them birth, so why does Moses have to nurse them?" (Nowell, 50).

As Nowell observes, it may be shocking to some readers to imagine God as mother rather than father—to others it may be refreshing!—but the address fits the metaphor perfectly. Moses is tired of playing wet nurse to a whining Israel, and wants the people's Mother to get back into the picture.

The Text in Contemporary Discussion

While there are a number of elements of this major section that will have implications for the modern reader or community—from jealousy and sinful challenging of leadership, to the dangers of idolatry in personal and ritual religious practice, to the dangers of lives shaped both overtly and subtly by violence—there are two particular aspects of Numbers 10–21 and 32–35 that are particularly ripe for contemporary discussion and interpretation.

The complaint accounts of Numbers show a sharp departure not just from the comparative account in Exodus but also from a broad biblical tradition that takes complaint seriously. While this probably reflects the predominant pattern in many Christian religious communities—where music is for praising, prayers are for thanking, and crying out bitterly to God is frowned on—for many readers this may be the most difficult aspect of the book as a whole. The complaint that is so central to the prayers for help or lament in the Psalms, and the complaint of Job, which God calls true and faithful speech (Job 40:7), seems to be stifled in Numbers. This is problematic. As Hartman concludes, the situation in which Israel finds itself—wandering in the wilderness, lost between the relative "bounty" of Egypt, "the cucumbers, the melons, the leeks, the onions, and the garlic" (Num. 11:5), and the promise of Canaan, of "milk and honey . . . an inheritance of fields and vineyards" (Num. 16:14)—does not allow much room for Israel to trust; complaint may be the only outlet. "Starvation does not breed trust. It is a reasonable cry that is heard, of men afraid not only for themselves but also for their families. They recall the Promise made to them and, instead of its realization, see the opposite: decimation or even destruction, rather than increased numbers in a land of their own" (Hartman, 47). But is their complaint truly legitimate? One may well wonder if what Numbers is doing is outlining the kind of complaining that is neither true nor faithful.

The tension in these stories of complaint is critical: the people have been freed from slavery, met by God, ordered, mustered, and led to the promised land. And in the face of all of this, they are not satisfied, and will not trust. The modern reader does well at this point to follow Paul's lead and take from these stories of complaint a warning, and a lead. What is enough for us? Enough education, enough wealth, influence, family, and health? What challenge, be it professional, familial, political, is so great that the God "who brought you out of the land of Egypt, to be your God: I am the LORD your God" (Num. 15:41) cannot be your God even now? The kind of baseless, faithless complaining that the Israelites do—at least according to Numbers—is to be resisted, and these stories are best read with an eye to learning from them; they may be, for any reader, metaphorical fringes on the corners of our garments, so that when one reads it, "when you see it, you will remember all the commandments of the LORD and do them, and not follow the lust of your own heart and your own eyes" (Num. 15:39).

And perhaps most importantly—as has already been noted—Numbers reveals what may seem a surprisingly progressive stance toward women and an equally surprisingly flexible theological imagination. The Bible is by no means replete with feminine imagery for God. It is, however, much more comfortable with that kind of imagery than the religious communities have been in the generations since these stories were written. There are other examples of such imagination employed in theological construction, from Isaiah's depiction of God's love for Israel in terms of a mother's love (Isa. 49:15), to the psalmist comparing herself to a weaned child to God's weaning mother (Ps. 131:2), to Jesus longing to gather the people to himself like a mother hen gathers her brood (Matt. 23:37; Luke 13:34). Moses' use of the feminine metaphor, paired as it is with a feminine pronoun used in direct discourse to God, is remarkable in several ways.

Neither metaphor nor pronoun is used ironically, or negatively, but they serve to deftly illustrate both the nature of God's relationship to and care for the people of Israel, as well as to illustrate the nature of the leadership role. In a world in which theological imagination has, for a long time, been predominantly masculine, Moses' use of feminine imagery is refreshing and freeing. This ancient text can empower the theology of a new generation in both directions, in thinking about the nature of the divine and in reflecting on the struggles of believing leaders—in both religious and secular settings.

Numbers 22:1—24:25: The Balaam Cycle

THE TEXT IN ITS ANCIENT CONTEXT

One of the few stories from Numbers that is more or less well known, the story of the prophet Balaam, is the only stand-alone narrative within the book. After Israel's victory over the Amorites (Num. 21:21-32), their neighbors, the Moabites, are in fear of Israel, this horde that "has come out of Egypt" (Num. 22:5). Balak, king of Moab, sends to the prophet Balaam, asking him to curse Israel on Moab's behalf.

Three times Balak asks for a curse, and six times Balaam responds in a telling manner. Balaam emphasizes, at every turn, that as a prophet of the LORD he can speak only the words the LORD gives him to speak.

22:8 "I will bring back word to you, just as the LORD speaks to me."
22:18 "Although Balak were to give me his house full of silver and gold, I could not go beyond the command of the LORD my God, to do less or more."
23:3 "Perhaps the LORD will come to meet me. Whatever he shows me I will tell you."
23:12 "Must I not take care to say what the LORD puts into my mouth?"
23:26 Balaam answered Balak, "Did I not tell you, 'Whatever the LORD says, that is what I must do?'"

Finally, at the close of the exchanges between Balak and Balaam, in response to Balak's desperate anger, Balaam replies to Balak, "Did I not tell your messengers whom you sent to me, 'If Balak should give me his house full of silver and gold, I would not be able to go beyond the word of the LORD, to do either good or bad of my own will; what the LORD says, that is what I will say'?" (24:12-13).

The emphasis here is both on the LORD's control of the situation—the bellwether theme of the trust-faithlessness dialectic of Numbers—and on Balaam as a true prophet. Balaam's insistence that he can say only what God gives him to say is in keeping with the standard by which later prophets will be evaluated, according to the Deuteronomic principle:

> I will raise up for them a prophet like you from among their own people; I will put my words in the mouth of the prophet, who shall speak to them everything that I command. Anyone who does not heed the words that the prophet shall speak in my name, I myself will hold accountable. But any prophet who speaks in the name of other gods, or who presumes to speak in my name a word that I have not commanded the prophet to speak—that prophet shall die. (Deut. 18:18-20)

It is interesting that we find in Balaam a non-Israelite Yahwist—not unlike Jethro the Midianite (or Hebob in Num. 10:29; Exodus 18)—who is portrayed in this story in an entirely positive light. And it is beyond question that Balaam is, in fact, a prophet of YHWH, as he says for himself in 22:18, "I could not go beyond the command of the LORD my God, to do less or more."

As Michael Barre notes, "In Numbers 22–24 he never wavers from his resolve to report only what God has communicate to him, whether for good or ill, and whether it pleases the king or not. Balaam is portrayed as a man of integrity, a seer completely open to the divine message, whatever it might be" (Barre, 259).

In the broadest terms, this story fits into the larger narrative of Numbers perfectly, serving to demonstrate both to Israel—in the face of its doubt, lack of confidence, and forgetfulness—and to Israel's new neighbors that it is God who is in control. Even down to the prophetic voice of an ass.

The Text in the Interpretive Tradition

As has already been seen, the book of Numbers frequently reengages the tradition, repeating, reiterating, and reinterpreting stories it has already told. This appears to be true of the Balaam cycle in two ways.

First, Numbers portrays Balaam as a prophet of YHWH (the LORD), and it does so methodically. And then, rather strangely, the book returns to the Balaam cycle in chapter 31, altering what is an otherwise positive portrayal of this non-Israelite Yahwist, connecting him explicitly to the apostasy of Israel and its sin in the matter of the Baal of Peor (see Numbers 25; 31:16). According to Num. 31:8, 16, Balaam is killed—slain by the Israelites during the Midian campaign—presumably because he influenced a number of Midianite women to make "the Israelites act treacherously against the LORD in the affair of Peor" (31:16). The shift in the portrayal is difficult to follow, from staunch Yahwist to idolater. It should be noted that almost every other reference to Balaam in the Bible, Hebrew and New Testaments alike, is negative. In Josh. 24:9-10, God is made to say of Balaam, "I would not listen" to him, and the same again in Deut. 23:4-7, while in 2 Pet. 2:15 the "way of Balaam" is described as loving gain and speaking in God's name to get it, for which he is punished; finally, in Rev. 2:14, "the Balaam stories in Numbers 22–24 and the Baal Peor incident in Numbers 25 are combined in such a way that it is Balaam who induces Balak to harm Israel by enticing them to partake of pagan practices" (Barre, 255). It seems likely that the shift in the way Balaam is portrayed in Numbers 31 reflects the wider biblical tradition (of the Hebrew Bible that is), while incorporating the Balaam cycle—its own discrete narrative—into its narrative largely as is.

The second example of intratextual influence in the story of Balaam and his mule is a strange one, and creates an odd disjunction within the narrative. Prior to the first oracle and after the second invitation, Balaam first tells the king no, and then, having heard from God in a dream, "Balaam got up in the morning, saddled his donkey, and went with the officials of Moab" (22:21). It is likely that this was, at one point, an intermediate ending to the story. Another Balaam tradition (perhaps from the early stages of the reimagination of the prophet's character and identity) then picks up in 22:22, where we find God suddenly angry with Balaam that he is going to Moab, even though God told Balaam to do so. The incongruity is marked.

What follows is the best-known part of Balaam's story, where God speaks to the prophet through his donkey. Traditional interpretation has echoed with the ironic humor of the exchange.

Martin Luther loved the story of Balaam and his mule so much that he used the image several times in his writing:

> If God spoke then through an ass against a prophet, why should he not be able even now to speak through a righteous man against the pope? (*LW* 44:136)
>
> God once spoke through the mouth of an ass [Num. 22:28]; therefore, no man is to be despised, however humble he may be. (*LW* 45:121)
>
> In ancient times God actually spoke through an ass against the prophet who was riding it [Num. 22:28]. Would to God that we were worthy to have such doctors given to us. (*LW* 44:205)

The Text in Contemporary Discussion

Who speaks for God? And when God is spoken for, what is at stake? The stories of Balaam and his oracles provide an important framework for thinking about addressing social, political, and personal issues in theological terms. The prophet—and so the preacher, the disciple, churchgoer—speaks only what God gives her to speak. So what are the implications of speaking theologically, of speaking in the wildernesses in which the reader of Numbers wanders, in God's terms?

First, Balaam's stories suggest caution in this regard. God's word is God's and not ours in a fundamental sense. A modern Balaam should be as careful as the early Balaam to listen to what God says—through Scripture, prayer, and the mouths of others, and be careful not to speak words that are simply pleasing either to the listener or the speaker. God's word, whether curse or blessing, whether encouragement or challenge, is not for sale or for manipulation to our own ends.

Second, it is important to note that Balaam is, in certain very important ways, an outsider; he is not an Israelite, and he is not one who came out of Egypt. Yet God speaks with him, appears to him, and uses him. If we think of ourselves as the insiders, then we ought to be mindful that God can work and speak through others who are not like us, living in the same place or way as we do, with the same struggles, and that through others such as these God can bless God's people.

Finally, following Luther's laughing takeaway from the story, the modern reader might dare to be bold. If God will speak through an outsider, and yes even through an ass, then God can speak through anyone. While Balaam did not add to or determine what God's word would be, he spoke that word boldly, both in his responses to a king and in his blessing of God's people. Balaam withstood the ire of a king, holding to the power and importance of God's will. And Balaam, seeing that it pleased the Lord to bless Israel, did not look for omens or visions or signs, but "set his face toward the wilderness," and spoke God's blessing. If Balaam's story holds any truth, it lies in this: God's word does not return empty, but accomplishes its purpose (Isa. 55:11). Numbers echoes this basic biblical claim, exerting it on any who would read it.

Numbers 25:1-18; 31:1-34: War against Midian

The Text in Its Ancient Context

The story of Israel's apostasy at Peor is the wilderness generation's final failure. It is paired here with the victory over the Midianites, the final step in securing the promised land. The narrative is relatively sparse, stating only that the people "yoked itself" (*yiṣṣāmed*) to the Baal (a word that in this case simply means "lord" or local god) of Peor. This was done when Israel intermarried with the people of Moab and Midian and defiled themselves not through their sexual relations or intermarrying but through the attendant religious mingling. The people attended sacrifices and ate from the offerings made to another God.

As has been frequently observed (see Olson 1996, 153–54; Grossman, 59–61), Israel's apostasy with the Baal of Peor is likened to the incident of the golden calf in Exodus 32. There are numerous parallels, but the most striking aspect of a comparison of Numbers 25 with Exodus 32 is the sense that the practices described—at least in their original settings—are not what are objectionable; rather, it is the object of devotion that is a problem. In Exodus 32, it is not the nature of Israel's worship that is problematic but that they have made an idol—a false image of the true God. The transgression in Numbers 25 is more serious and, if it builds to some degree on Exodus 32, amplifies Israel's guilt; again, not because their worship practices are wicked in and of themselves, but because they worship an idol—an image of a false god. There is no sense whatsoever in the original narrative that eating, drinking, and rising up to revel are a problem, nor that their worship is explicitly sexual in nature (contra Grossman, 59; see Nowell, 105). What is stunning in Numbers 25 is that Israel, moving far beyond complaint and mistrust of YHWH, has turned for the first time, and fully, to the worship of another god. And once again, God punishes Israel, this time sending a plague that fulfills the judgment pronounced in Num. 14:23.

This is the final failing of the untrusting generation that will not enter the promised land. As Olson notes, "The story of Israel's worship of an alien god in Numbers 25 brings to an end the life of the first generation of Israelites who came out of Egypt. The twenty-four thousand Israelites who died in the plague of 25:9 are presumably the last remnants of the old generation. They have left the stage to make room for a new generation who will again stand on the edge of the promised land" (1996, 156).

One of the difficulties in Numbers 25 is that there appears again to be a conjoining of two different narratives. Verses 1-5 report the difficulties caused by Moabite women. This vignette could stand alone, but to it has been added the incident of a Midianite woman being "brought home to meet the parents" in 25:6-9. What this blending of stories serves to do is point to the war against Midian in Numbers 31, providing the reason and the motivation for the extermination of the Midianites, on whom the Israelites are seeking vengeance. The implications of the cultural and religious intermingling, brought about through marriage, are presented as fraught with danger; and in the case of the Baal of Peor incident, with disaster and mass death. Only through the intercession of Phineas does the plague—God's judgment on Israel—stop short of spilling over from one generation to the next.

The Text in the Interpretive Tradition

The incident of the Baal of Peor has a lasting effect in the biblical text. In the historical Psalm 106, which was likely used as a form of liturgical remembrance and instruction, this part of the story is recalled graphically,

> Then they attached themselves to the Baal of Peor,
> and ate sacrifices offered to the dead. (Ps. 106:28)

Meat offered to idols is the danger. In Joshua (22:10-20), the incident is recalled as a part of a conflict after the tribes that had settled in the Transjordan build an altar; the tribes that have settled in Canaan, with worship "centralized" at Shiloh, fear that the altar will be a place of false worship again. This may also reflect a later tradition, centered on the temple in Jerusalem, and be reading back into earlier narrative tradition a distinctively Jerusalemite concern. Finally, in Deut. 4:1-4, Peor is an illustration of what happens when anything is added or taken away from the commandments of God.

As Susan Niditch has observed, there are serious questions and concerns raised by the just war themes brought together in Numbers 25 and 31, not least of which is the role the women play first as "sensuous and evil enticers, embodiments of the wrong way" (45), but also as booty. "Their presence marks the passage into war and the exodus from it; they are marginal, border figures, central in the events around them, and yet they are usually nameless, voiceless items of exchange and symbols of transition" (44). On the one hand, these foreign women are seen as dangerous. On the other, they are the spoils of war, and central to new life in Canaan.

The connection between these two chapters, bringing together the motivations for Israel's holy war of conquest and the danger of intermarriage, of idolatry, syncretism, and more, serve as a sort of prelude to the issues that will define the rest of the biblical narrative that follows in the so-called historical books. Israel's life in the promised land will be marked by this same tension.

The Text in Contemporary Discussion

These two chapters present—in a rather stark and pressing way—a reality that not only remains a part of global reality, but is also, if anything, greatly intensified and far more pressing today than it was in the days described in Numbers: the reality of pluralism. Racial, social, and religious intermingling brings many advantages, including opportunities for growth and learning; but pluralism also can bring struggle and tension. This was the promised-land reality for the people of Israel, and it is the reality of life in a shrinking global community as well.

In the aftermath of dealing with false worship and idolatry in the face of interracial marriage and shared life—the aftermath of slaughter and destruction—the officers of Israel bring an offering to God saying, "we have brought the Lord's offering, what each of us found, articles of gold, armlets and bracelets, signet rings, earrings, and pendants, to make atonement for ourselves before the Lord" (Num. 31:50). The key phrase here is "to make atonement for ourselves," but for what are they making atonement? Niditch has captured the struggle revealed in this move beautifully.

> In Numbers 31, as in the ban texts, war on some level is ritual, and yet war in Numbers 31 is not cleansing or whole-making in the spirit of extirpation of wayward Israelite cities in Deuteronomy 13 or the ban texts demanding erasure of the idolaters from the land. Doubts have crept in about the whole enterprise, for in killing one becomes part of the abomination, the enemy one seeks to eliminate. . . . Is it in recognition of this ambivalence that the commanders are pictured to offer up what each has found among the personal effects of the dead enemies . . . , "to make atonement for ourselves before the Lord"? For what do they atone? Is it for sins in general, is it finally to close the matter of Baal Peor (Olson, 88), or is it to atone for the defilement of bringing death to human beings (Wenham: 212; de Vaulz: 359)?

These are the questions, the tensions, the realities of life in the wilderness, both the wilderness of Sinai and Moab, and the wilderness of human sin—on interpersonal and intercontinental levels.

Numbers raises a series of questions: questions of trust in God, questions of fidelity and true worship, questions of life and death; questions that are meant, in the end, to reorient the reader, to remind her or him both of what God has done in this people's past and to declare that God and God's Word will have the final say.

Works Cited

Barre, Michael L. 1997. "The Portrait of Balaam in Numbers 22–24." *Int* 51, no. 3:254–66.

Childs, Brevard S. 1979. *Introduction to the Old Testament as Scripture*. Minneapolis: Fortress Press.

Danby, Herbert. 1933. *The Mishnah*. Oxford: Oxford University Press.
Dozeman, T. B. 1999. "Numbers." In *Dictionary of Biblical Interpretation*, edited by John H. Hayes, 2:214–18. Nashville: Abingdon.
Grossman, Jonathan. 2007. "Divine Command and Human Initiative: A Literary View on Numbers 25-31." *Biblical Interpretation*, no. 15:54-79.
Hartman, Geoffrey H. 1987. "Numbers: The Realism of Numbers, the Magic of Numbers." In *Congregation: Contemporary Writers Read the Jewish Bible*, edited by David Rosenberg, 39–50. New York: Harcourt Brace Jovanovich.
Levine, Baruch A. 2000. *Numbers 21–36*. AYB. New Haven: Yale University Press.
Milgrom, Jacob. 1989. *Numbers*. JPS Commentary. New York: Jewish Publication Society.
Niditch, Susan. 1993. "War, Women, and Defilement in Numbers 31." *Semeia* 61, no. 1:39–57.
Nowell, Irene. 2010. *Numbers*. New Collegeville Bible Commentary. Collegeville, MN: Liturgical Press.
Olson, Dennis T. 1996. *Numbers*. IBC. Louisville: John Knox.
———. 1997. "Negotiating Boundaries: The Old and New Generations and the Theology of Numbers." *Int* 51, no. 3:229–40.

Deuteronomy

Harold V. Bennett

Introduction

Deuteronomy, traditionally known as the fifth book of Moses, occupies a very important place in current discussions about the life and faith of ancient Israel. The title of the book comes from the Greek *Deuteronomion*, meaning "the second law." The title of the book in Hebrew is *'elleh haddebarim* ("These are the words") or, more simply, *debarim* ("words"; see 1:1) which comes from the opening words of the manuscript. Those who explore the book of Deuteronomy may get the impression that it is a single, unified speech of Moses, which he delivered to Israel as they prepared to enter the promised land and receive the fulfillment of YHWH's promises to Abraham, the theological progenitor of those who comprised biblical Israel.

While Deuteronomy appears as a single oration delivered in one instance, four pieces of evidence justify raising questions about whether that is true: (1) Multiple superscriptions are present, for example, Deut. 1:1-5; 4:44–49; 29:1; and 33:1; (2) accounts in which Moses appear are written in the third-person singular—as though someone were talking to us about Moses; (3) duplications and inconsistencies are present in the laws in Deuteronomy 12–26; and (4) a report about the death of Moses appears at the end of the book (Deut. 34:1-8). Critical scholarship argues that a movement composed of scribes, priests, and prophets collected and brought together the individual speeches, cultic traditions, legislation, and narratives that constitute Deuteronomy, and that this movement, which began its work in the South in the latter part of the seventh century BCE, completed its project during the sixth century BCE (A. D. H. Mayes 1991, 34–55; Alexander Rofé 2002, 4–9; Moshe Weinfeld 1992, 1–9; and Richard Nelson 2002, 6–9).

Points of contact are present between the present structure of Deuteronomy and treaties between suzerains and vassals in the ancient Near East. Moreover, the book of Deuteronomy employs a distinctive language and phraseology. It also advocates for a particular ideology. This point of view serves as the basis for the distinct historiography that appears in Joshua, Judges, 1–2 Samuel, and 1–2 Kings. What is more, the theological and moral ideas that appear in Deuteronomy serve as the backdrop for action against ethnic groups, social classes, and religious communities. Moreover, political and religious leadership gets prescribed, proscribed, and appraised. This essay focuses on Deuteronomy as a whole, the Deuteronomic program in biblical Israel, and the distinct ways the book has been understood. It also calls attention to the significance of Deuteronomy for theological, philosophical, social, and ethical conversations today. Unless otherwise noted, the translations of Deuteronomy, which appear in the following article, are those of the author.

Deuteronomy 1:6—4:43: Setting the Stage for the Covenant

The Text in Its Ancient Context

Deuteronomy 1:6–4:43 gives an account of Israel's journey from Horeb to Moab, and important differences appear in its narrative. Horeb, not Sinai, is the name for the site from which the journey commenced and the name of the mountain where Moses received the revelation from YHWH. This section contains the account of Moses' appointing officials to help with governance in the Israelite community. The version of this event in Exodus 18 introduces Moses' father-in-law into this event, and it suggests that Moses himself identified the men who would serve as leaders among the people. Deuteronomy 1:6—4:43 neither mentions Moses' father-in-law nor places the onus for identifying the men that will act as judges on the shoulders of Moses. In the account of Deuteronomy, the people choose these officials.

Deuteronomy 2:26—3:17 introduces the theme of sacred war (*herem*), namely, the practice of slaughtering opponents in combat, destroying their property and livestock, and razing their cities. The concept of holy war describes the way the redactor viewed the conflict with Sihon king of Heshbon and Og king of Bashan. The redactor of Deuteronomy will introduce this campaign throughout the narrative, for the traditions about the destruction of Sihon and Og play a major role in the moral thought of the Deuteronomic program. Key motifs and metaphors in Deut. 1:6—4:43 are also present in Judges, 1–2 Kings, Hosea, Jeremiah, and in the literature of early Christianity. The key motifs and metaphors are as follows: The charge to exterminate entire groups of people (Deut. 2:26—3:11); the demand to embrace the worship of YHWH (Deut. 4:1-14); the command to abjure idolatry (Deut. 4:15-20); the metaphor that YHWH is a consuming fire (Deut. 4:21-24); and the indication that banishment from the land will be the punishment for apostasy (Deut. 4:25-31).

The Text in the Interpretive Tradition

Several key thinkers in the history of Christianity adopted the idea that YHWH is a consuming fire. Origen (184–253 CE) contends that this metaphor best explains God's dealings with sins and human imperfections. According to Origen, the presence of God as fire cleanses the believer for the sake of purity. Ambrose (340–397 CE) proffers that just as illumination is a feature of fire, so God is a consuming fire (Lienhard 2001, 278). Spinoza uses the language of God as fire to argue for the use of allegorical hermeneutics in interpreting the Hebrew Bible (Spinoza 2001, 86–104).

The Text in Contemporary Discussion

How should one speak about God? Which metaphors are apropos? What evidence should inform our beliefs about the nature of God? Which metaphors do Deut. 1:6—4:43 support? Undoubtedly, the battle reports in Deut. 1:6—4:43 call attention to beliefs about the moral fiber of God (Craigie 1978, 9–19; Niditch 1993, 3–27; Copan 2011, 158–97; Seibert 2009, 24–26). Deuteronomy 2:26—3:11 recounts the killing of women, children, and other noncombatants, and it places the onus for this act of violence on the shoulders of Sihon. Yet one cannot help but be bothered by this story. At the center of this troubling report is Deut. 2:30, which reads: "YHWH, your God hardened [*qāšâ*] his spirit and toughened [*'āmēṣ*] his heart." Thus YHWH instilled obstinacy in Sihon, and this stubbornness led to his death and to the massacre of a large segment of human beings. If one allows this text to inform the attributes and designations he or she uses for the Holy, then Deut. 2:30 elicits questions about the character of God, for it invites discussion about how the moral agent on the present scene should speak about the moral attributes of the deity. As it was mentioned above, Paul Copan 2011 and Eric Seibert 2012 help to describe the backdrop against which to discuss this issue. Copan frames the discussion by asking: "Is God a moral monster?" Seibert also contends that disconcerting notions about God are in the Hebrew Bible. Both thinkers draw attention to the brutality and hawkish nature believed to comprise the deity in the Deuteronomic traditions; therefore, investigations into beliefs about the moral attributes of God receive treatment in popular literature as well as in standard discussions in the philosophy of religion (Peterson et al. 2013, 135–56).

Deuteronomy 5:1—6:19: Faithfulness to YHWH

The Text in Its Ancient Context

Deuteronomy 5:1-5 narrates the specific obligations of the covenant between YHWH and Israel. Since the group of liberated slaves with whom YHWH cut a covenant at Horeb/Sinai was not present as Israel *entered* the promised land, the redactors of Deut. 5:1-5 inserted Deut. 5:3 into the record. It says: "YHWH our God did not cut this covenant with our fathers, but with all of us who are here today." By adding the aforementioned statement, Deut. 5:1-5 suggests that the group standing in the plains of Moab, preparing to enter the land, consists of the ones with whom YHWH cut this particular covenant (Weinfeld 1991, 237–38). Moreover, Deut. 5:1—6:19 indicates that the people saw "fire" on the mountain and that YHWH spoke to them from the midst of the fire, but that Moses translated the voice of YHWH to them.

Deuteronomy 5:1—6:19 contains two important texts for understanding orthodox Yahwism in biblical Israel. The Decalogue, on the one hand, appears in Deut. 5:7-21. Walter Harrelson points out that various ways for numbering the commandments in Deut. 5:6-21 are present (Harrelson 1985, 45–48). At the center of this problem is whether to list the verse that contains the self-introduction of YHWH and the deliverance from Egypt as a commandment as well as whether to combine into a single commandment the prohibitions against worshiping other deities and idolatry. It is noteworthy that its treatment of the commandment to observe the Sabbath, or day of rest, possesses a noticeable difference from the commandments to observe the Sabbath in Exod. 20:8. The commandment to observe the Sabbath in Deut. 5:12-15 contends that persons should observe the day of rest *because they were no longer slaves in Egypt*, but the legislation to observe the Sabbath in Exod. 20:8 instructs the moral agent to respect the Sabbath *because the deity completed creation in six days and rested on the seventh day*. The commandment in Deuteronomy has a ring of justice, focusing on using the Sabbath to treat even slaves with compassion (since the Israelites were once slaves themselves), while the Exodus version focuses on establishing the Sabbath as day when work and other activities cease.

The Shema, on the other hand, appears in Deut. 6:4-19. It reads: "Hear, Israel, YHWH our God: YHWH is one." The Shema acquires its name from the Hebrew term *šĕma'*, which means "hear" or "listen." The Shema articulates sole monotheism, a tenet that is critical for understanding the theological precommitments of the group that was responsible for codifying the traditions that appear in Deuteronomy. One can argue that prior to the Babylonian period, monolatry or henotheism was the ascendant religious ideal in Israel. During the Babylonian period but before the Persian period, monotheism and the notion of exclusive loyalty to YHWH became the ascendant religious ideology in the decimated community of Israel.

The Text in the Interpretive Tradition

The sentences that comprise the Ten Commandments have been understood in a variety of ways. For the sake of manageability, the following section will cast light on the commandment to observe the Sabbath. In short, this legislation has often been interpreted to mean avoiding or not performing physical labor on the seventh day. Rabbinic exegesis cites thirty-nine categories of work that are forbidden on the Sabbath (*m. Ñabb.* 7:1-4). Jesus, however, permits work on the Sabbath day (Matt. 12:1-8; Mark 2:23-28; and Luke 6:1-5). It is noteworthy that the Qur'an, on the one hand, advocates for observing the Sabbath, but it is silent on how to observe it (Qur'an 4:154). In short, it does not command Muslims to abstain from work on the seventh day. What is more, the Qur'an does not advocate that the deity needs rest from work (Qur'an 2:255). Augustine (354–430 CE) interpreted the biblical commandment to rest on the Sabbath to mean that people should regularly involve themselves in moments of tranquility. For him, the commandment to observe the Sabbath is an invitation for the spirit of a person to take a break and to rest in God (Lienhard 2001, 104).

The Text in Contemporary Discussion

Deuteronomy 5:1—6:19 contains the Ten Commandments, a set of sentences that are perhaps the most well-known norms for decision making in the West. These regulations claim to have their origin in YHWH. The belief that the deity bequeathed these moral principles to humankind opens the door for an exciting conversation in metaethics. That is to say, as one attempts to delineate those issues, conditions, or phenomena that must be present for a meaningful morality to exist, he or she must account for the origin of morality. Deuteronomy 5:1—6:19 assumes the existence of God, and that ethical truth proceeds from God. This way of talking about the source of moral truth has it benefits. The reality, however, is that we live in a postmodern world. Concomitant with postmodernity is the skeptical point of view that truth does not exist, or if it does, is unknowable. This line of thinking leaves the door ajar for arguing whether the existence of

God is a necessary condition for the presence of systems for good decision making (Nielsen 1990, 70–112). The Ten Commandments invite the present-day believer in God to formulate a theory about morality that accounts for the origin and presence of justifiable moral ideas about the good life, happiness, moral responsibility, and meaningful human existence against the backdrop of a postmodern worldview.

Deuteronomy 6:20-25: Passing on the Sacred Traditions

The Text in Its Ancient Context

Deuteronomy 6:20-25 envisions parents, male and female, educating their children about the significance of the distinct stipulations that define the agreement between YHWH and the group that stands on the brink of possessing the land. Salient among the terms in this passage is the word "testimonies" (*'ēdōt*). This term also appears in Deut. 4:45 and 6:17, and it receives frequent usage in Psalm 119. One expects this term to denote a statement or account that a witness gives about his or her personal experience regarding a specific event. Nelson and Mayes support this understanding of *'ēdōt*, but they advocate for a report that accentuates the tradition about the law-giving at Horeb. These scholars maintain that the phrase "testimonies, statutes, and judgments" is a direct reference to the Ten Commandments, and that the placement of these terms into a single literary formula is characteristic of the Deuteronomic narratival tradition (Nelson 2002, 72; Mayes 1991, 159–60). What is more, the storyteller uses language and concepts, for example, "great and evil wonders," to compel the children to appreciate that YHWH acted on their behalf, and that YHWH perpetrated a series of "amazing and extraordinary deeds" against Pharaoh and Egypt. Thus the tradition about the rescue from bondage in Egypt is a major piece in the catechizing of Israelite children.

The Text in the Interpretive Tradition

The tradition about the deliverance of the Hebrew slaves from bondage in Egypt contains symbols and motifs that are central to liberation theology, ethics, and biblical exegesis and hermeneutics. These themes and their symbols are the following: (1) a source of power, domination, and exploitation in a social order (Pharaoh); (2) a milieu saturated with injustice and dehumanization (the presence and variety of slavery in Egypt); (3) an oppressed social class (Hebrew slaves); (4) a liberator deity who sides with the weakest in society (YHWH and the plague stories); and (5) an ongoing desire and struggle for freedom from dehumanization (the Sea of Reeds and wilderness wanderings stories). Persons of African descent, in the African Diaspora, and persons from other groups that exist on the periphery of the socioeconomic and political structures in the West find parallels between their plight and struggle for freedom and the plight and existential situation of Israel prior to its emancipation from subjugation in Egypt. Liberation theologians, ethicists, and biblical scholars take the tradition about the exodus from Egypt to mean that YHWH identifies with the weak and most defenseless in society, and that YHWH acts in ways that seek to ameliorate the conditions of the poor and those who suffer exploitation at the hands of the powerful (Gutiérrez 1999, 29–46; Hopkins 1999, 42–43).

The Text in Contemporary Discussion

The exodus from Egypt is an important event in the lore of ancient Israel. Chief among the sequence of events that freed the Hebrew slaves from captivity was the death of the firstborn of the Egyptians; therefore, the death of human beings who might have had nothing to do with the cruelty toward the Hebrews was one of the great and evil wonders of YHWH, and the Deuteronomic narratival tradition demands that Israelites pass on this story to their children; but it proceeds without any attempt to appreciate the very important and problematic implications of this claim.

The present reader is compelled, therefore, to assess the philosophy of education implied in Deuteronomy 6:20-25. The research of Paulo Freire helps to cast light on this issue. In his classic book *The Pedagogy of the Oppressed*, Freire contends that human beings should strive for the humanization of all peoples, and that the recognition of the inherent dignity of all human beings entails that one denounce social conventions, ideas, structures, and other phenomena that exploit and degrade people. Education is a critical element in this process. Thus one goal of the education of children on the current scene should be to enable them to analyze and evaluate in a dispassionate manner traditions and other cultural phenomena they have received from their ancestors (Freire 2005, 43–87).

Deuteronomy 7:1-26: Conquest and Election

The Text in Its Ancient Context

Deuteronomy 7:1-26 casts light on the notion of election, a fundamental issue in Deuteronomic legislation. The notion and language of election finds its clearest expression in Deut. 7:6, for this verse says that YHWH chose (*bāḥar*) Israel to be a *sĕgullâ* (a collection of prized jewels). Deuteronomy 7:7 seeks to limit any pride or arrogance that might arise in the community regarding its being chosen by YHWH, by pointing out that it was simply the deity's love (*'ahăbâ*) and the deity's loyalty to the promise made to the ancestors of Israel that accounts for its being selected by YHWH to be in this exclusive relationship. It was a favor that a superior showed to an inferior.

Deuteronomy 7:1-26 tells Israel that because it is in a special relationship with YHWH, there are obligations that accompany this arrangement. Salient among these responsibilities are the following: (1) Israel is to annihilate the inhabitants of the land that lived there prior to their entry (Deut. 7:2, 16, 24); (2) Israel is to eradicate the cults of these people (Deut. 7:5); (3) Israel is not to practice exogamy (i.e., marriage outside their own people) (Deut. 7:3); and (4) Israel is to obey YHWH (Deut. 7:12). The instructions to massacre and expunge the cultures of the Hittites, Girgashites, Amorites, Canaanites, Perizzites, Hivites, and Jebusites from the promised land receive reiteration throughout this chapter. Obviously, the biblical community did not carry out the total destruction of these peoples when they entered the promised land because the Jebusites were around in the time of David. Rather, the narrative introduces the claim that the Israelites are to destroy seven nations. Mayes and Nelson suggest that the usage of the number seven is a rhetorical and ideological device to indicate completeness or total destruction of these social groups (Mayes 1991, 182–83; Nelson 2002, 99). One cannot help but to notice that Deut. 7:1-26 is replete with terms that denote horrific acts of violence to entire groups of people, and protecting and reverencing the YHWH cult is the justification offered for these types of behaviors by the Israelites.

The Text in the Interpretive Tradition

This notion of Israel's election appears throughout the classical prophets. Amos 3:1-2 contends that the deity has chosen Israel, and that discipline at the hand of the deity is concomitant with this status. Hosea 11:1 links deliverance from bondage in Egypt to being elected by the deity. Isaiah 42:5-9 implies that because the deity chose Israel, it is to serve as a witness to the nations elsewhere in the world about the power of YHWH. These schools of thought agree that YHWH has chosen Israel, namely, the sociopolitical entity that traces its ancestry back to Abraham through Isaac.

The tradition about YHWH choosing Israel received treatment in the theological program of Paul. In Romans 9–11, Paul contends that Israel is not a biological, genetic classification; it is a religious category. Israel and those whom the deity has chosen are those persons who accept salvation as offered through Jesus. The writer of Ephesians contends that the elect were the believers in Christ whom the deity handpicked before the foundation of the world (Eph. 1:3-14). Camps in Christendom, therefore, advocate for the position that descent from Abraham through Isaac is unnecessary for inclusion in Israel, the elect of God.

The Text in Contemporary Discussion

Deuteronomy 7:1-26 raises two important issues for consideration. One issue is whether peaceful strategies should be the method for addressing religious diversity on the local or international scenes. Given the supposed humanitarianism of Deuteronomy, it is odd that Deut. 7:1-26 prescribes the complete separation from or annihilation of entire groups of people who ascribe to faith traditions that are different from Israel's faith tradition. Perhaps Deut. 7:1-26 is inviting the theological agent to reject the approach that Israel utilized and to frame a paradigm that respects religious, philosophical, and cultural difference, while at the same time permitting people to inhabit a common spatiality and realize the beloved community.

While the text contends that YHWH "handpicked" Israel, debate is widespread about how one appropriates this theme of election. For the sake of manageability, the following comments cite three of these difficulties: (1) Who is Israel? That is to say, is "Israel" a social, political, or theological designation? Does this designation refer to a group of people that descended from "Jacob"? It is noteworthy that the notion of "Israel" as a political entity changed during the history of Israel. (2) Is Israel in these regulations synonymous with the sociopolitical entity called Israel, that country, which is located in the Middle East, on the southeastern coast of the Mediterranean Sea? (3) Does election mean that Israel receives a set of special favors, or does it mean that as a community it has been assigned a group of distinctive humanitarian responsibilities?

Deuteronomy 8:1—9:6: Not on Your Own

The Text in Its Ancient Context

Deuteronomy 8:1—9:6 reiterates the theme of the undeserved goodness of YHWH. This motif appeared in Deut. 6:10-15, citing the provision of food, clothes, and good health as Israel made its trek to the promised land. Deuteronomy 8:1—9:6 mentions the fruitfulness of the bovine herds that Israel owns, and the fecundity of the land in which the Israelite people will live. It also contends that abundance and fertility are signs of the unearned compassion of the deity toward Israel. Deuteronomy 8:1—9:6, however, introduces one caveat: Israel must bear in mind that when it begins to enjoy the bounty of the land, it should remember that it was the generosity of YHWH that made this "good life" possible.

The Text in the Interpretive Tradition

In the tradition about the temptation of Jesus, the Synoptic Gospels report that Jesus drew on Deut. 8:1—9:6 and took it to mean that there are other items that give human life its vitality and importance, namely, possessing faith in God and ensuring that one's innermost being is in right standing with God (Matt. 4:4; Luke 4:4). Clement of Alexandria (150–215 CE) casts a different light on Deut. 8:1—9:6, by talking about this story against the backdrop of the virtuous person. His reading of this passage brings into play the view that the truly righteous person, that is, the moral agent who is in right relationship with God, will never be in a permanent condition of involuntary physical neediness. Ambrose introduces into the marketplace of ideas an alternative reading of Deut. 8:1—9:6, saying that this passage teaches against self-sufficiency. Ambrose argues that this speech warns against confiding totally in one's strength, and he directs individuals not to overestimate their own ability to provide for themselves. According to Ambrose, accepting that God is the source of sustenance undermines pride and other vices that ground themselves in hubris (Lienhard 2001, 289).

The Text in Contemporary Discussion

Deuteronomy 8:1—9:6 invites the community to recognize the source of life and success. This passage states that YHWH ensured the safety and well-being of Israel, and that the community should remain aware that YHWH is the staple of life. Israel must not forget YHWH. The question naturally arises: How do persons on the current scene forget about God? While several answers to this question vie for our attention, the response that receives the most support, in light of Deut. 8:1—9:6, is ingratitude. The text encourages people to demonstrate gratefulness daily to God for life, health, and strength. In doing so, people can face life with a degree of optimism regardless of their circumstances.

Deuteronomy 9:7—10:22: Rebellion against YHWH

The Text in Its Ancient Context

Deuteronomy 9:7—10:22 recounts three episodes in the plight of Israel. It retells the story of Moses ascending Horeb to receive the commandments from YHWH. It rehearses the incident involving the making of the golden image, and describes Moses' breaking of the tablets, which contained the "Ten Words." While elements in the narrative about Moses' ascending the mountain, the making of the idol, and his shattering of the tablets correspond with parts in the accounts about these same events that appear elsewhere in the Pentateuch, noticeable inconsistencies are present. While *Horeb* in Deuteronomy refers to the name of the mountain where Moses received the law, *Sinai* denotes this site in the account in Exod. 24:12-18. Moreover, the version in Deuteronomy mentions that Moses fasted forty days and forty nights; however, Exod. 24:12-18 says nothing about Moses fasting while he was on the mount. Deuteronomy 9:7—10:22 suggests that Moses made the trek to the mountain by himself, but Exod. 24:12-18 indicates that Joshua accompanied Moses on his trek to the mountain. The narrative in Deuteronomy also omits the account, included in Exodus 32, of the Levites killing thousands of Israelites and the use of this incident to justify the Levites being set apart for the service of YHWH.

The Text in the Interpretive Tradition

The wilderness-period motif played a key role in the prophecies of Jeremiah, Hosea, and Ezekiel. Jeremiah and Hosea, however, interpret the wilderness-period motif differently from its articulation in Deut. 9:7—10:22. Jeremiah and Hosea take the wilderness period to indicate that moment in Israel's history when it was loyal and faithful to YHWH (Jer. 2:2; Hosea 2:14). Yet, Ezekiel agrees with the Deuteronomic program and contends that the wilderness period was when Israel showed her obstinacy toward YHWH (see Ezek. 20:13). The author of Hebrews understands the wilderness experience typologically; it is to be thought of as a *method for understanding an event* in the history of Israel. Hebrews 3 takes the wilderness motif to represent obduracy and the way a person can respond to the voice of the deity. The theology in Hebrews urges the audience not to repeat the wilderness experience in regard to its response to God. The audience is told to accept, not to resist, God's invitations for fellowship.

The Text in Contemporary Discussion

Resisting the will of the Holy and frequently rebelling against God are common themes in the Deuteronomic literature, and the notion of this resisting the deity is a commonplace in the religious traditions of the world commonly referred to as Western religions: Christianity, Judaism, and Islam. Each believes in different ways that this issue is a fundamental feature of the human condition, and each offers strategies for managing and perhaps ultimately correcting this problem. Christianity emphasizes the notion of sin, and in some ways maintains that rebellion against God is one of the ways that this problem perennially demonstrates itself. Christianity therefore advocates for its adherents to perform ongoing self-inventories to guard against standing in mutiny against God.

Deuteronomy 11:1-32: YHWH Delivers

The Text in Its Ancient Context

Deuteronomy 11:1-32 admonishes the people to love and remember the deeds of YHWH, and to honor the statutes and regulations of YHWH. In citing some of the deeds of YHWH, this passage introduces the account of the Israelite deliverance and escape through the sea. It also mentions the incident when YHWH opened the ground, and it swallowed Dathan and Abiram. Numbers 16 gives the reader another account of this story. In fact, the version in Numbers 16 provides more detail, in that it identifies the principals in the story and some of the issues that spawned the event. Deuteronomy 11:1-32 closes out this section of the book by contending that a nexus exists between obedience and prosperity, and that a correlation is present between disobedience and misfortune. In classic Deuteronomic fashion, Deut. 11:1-32 invites the Israelite community to understand that because YHWH delivered them from servitude in Egypt, it owes its allegiance to YHWH. Thus, once they cross the Jordan, they are commanded to call down the blessings from Mt. Gerizim and to invoke the curses from Mt. Ebal.

The Text in the Interpretive Tradition

It is noteworthy that the motif of the deliverance at the sea resurfaces in different hermeneutical traditions. The Hebrew text of Deut. 11:4 uses the term *yam-sûph* ("sea of reeds") to denote this body of water, while the translators of the Septuagint use the term "Red Sea" (*thalassēs tēs erythras*). A Negro spiritual says in the chorus, "Moses don't you weep, and Martha don't you mourn. Pharaoh's army drowned at the Red Sea, so Moses don't you weep, and Martha don't you mourn." Different terms for the body of water through which the people escaped appear in the lore of ancient Israel. Regardless of the terms used, the theme persists: YHWH delivers.

While Deut. 11:1-32 talks about liberation, it cites Dathan and Abiram, men who played critical roles in a mutiny in the wilderness; it excludes Korah from its rendition of its account of this episode. Jeffrey Tigay contends that two rebellions occurred. Dathan and Abiram were the principal actors in one revolt, and Korah was the leading figure in another, separate rebellion. He then argues that the account in Deut. 11:1-32 reports the uprising led by Dathan and Abiram, and represents a stage in the interpretive history of the story prior to the combination of the accounts (Tigay 1996, 111).

The Text in Contemporary Discussion

The theme of deliverance is central to the narrative in Deut. 11:1-32. This idea appears frequently in Pentecostal and charismatic pneumatologies. While Deut. 11:1-32 implies that deliverance is liberation from a socioeconomic and political predicament, these religious groups link deliverance to freedom from personal moral bankruptcies such as lying, drinking, illicit sexual activities, stealing, and other private vices. In other words, private morality and individual psychological phobias are the backdrop against which Pentecostals and Charismatics discuss deliverance. Thus they also take deliverance to mean freedom from fear, uncertainty, hopelessness, despair, faithlessness, and other psychological phenomena.

Deuteronomy 12:1-32: Only One Place to Worship YHWH

The Text in Its Ancient Context

Deuteronomy 12:1-32 directs the Israelite colonizers to destroy the cults of the inhabitants of the promised land. One cannot help but contrast these injunctions with the codes in Deut. 7:1-26.

Conspicuous, however, are some inconsistencies between Deut. 7:1-26 and Deut. 12:1-32. While Deut. 12:1-32 uses the term *gôyîm* to refer to the residents of Canaan, Deut. 7:1-26 specifies that Hittites, Girgashites, Amorites, Perizzites, Hivites, Jebusites, and Canaanites are the occupants of the land. Given the difficulties one encounters when attempting to account for the presence of these groups in Syria-Palestine at the end of the Late Bronze Age, the placement of these peoples in a single list is likely a stylistic device and theological maneuver of the redactor (see the section above on Deut. 6:20-25).

Deuteronomy 12:4-14, 26-28 builds a framework for understanding the proper altar for sacrifice in the Deuteronomic program. It is important to note that the placement of regulations having to do with altars appears at the start of the Covenant and Holiness Codes. It has been argued that this placement at the start of the Deuteronomic Code is consistent with the practice of beginning law codes with stipulations regarding the altar (see Nelson 2002, 146). Deuteronomy 12:4-14, 26-28, instructs the people of Israel to present their offerings at a single site. This ideology emerges from the chosen place theology and its concomitant phrase "the place that YHWH your God will choose," which are widespread in the Deuteronomic program (see Weinfeld 1992, 324–26). While it is probable that the origins of this philosophy lie in the North, the Deuteronomic redactor applied this ideology to sites in the South. The Jerusalem temple became the legitimate site for celebrating festivals, worshiping YHWH, fulfilling vows, presenting tithes, and encountering the power of YHWH (e.g., Deut. 12:17-19; 14:22-27; 16:1-17; 26:1-11).

Deuteronomy 12:15-16, 20-25, provides guidelines for the slaughter of animals for food and directions for the disposal of their blood. Members of Israel were allowed to kill and consume these animals in their local villages. This regulation may have been the Deuteronomic response to the demand that if the killing of animals for food was in fact sacrifice, and that this cultic act could occur only at the Jerusalem temple; traveling to this site to kill animals for food might have been too impracticable (Mayes 1991, 225–27; Nelson 2002, 146–47). The only stipulation is that the blood is to be poured out (*šāpak*) on the ground. Points of contact are present between Deut. 12:15-16, 20-25, and Deut. 15:19-23. Both regulations deal with the slaughter and consumption of animals. It is noteworthy, however, that Deut. 15:19-23 indicates that the Israelite community is to protect firstlings, which are to be offered at the central sanctuary. These animals are not to be involved in the plowing of fields or in the carrying of cargo. The firstlings of the sheep are not to be sheared. Animals that possess a flaw are not to be sacrificed to YHWH; these animals are to be slaughtered and consumed in the local villages. Consistent with Deut. 12:16 and, because the blood is the sole possession of YHWH, the blood of the slaughtered animals must be disposed of properly.

The Text in the Interpretive Tradition

Deuteronomy 12:4-14, 26-28 instructs the people of Israel to present their offerings at an authorized site. These regulations limit the sites where persons in the community may perform their cultic activities. The people are told that there is one place where they are authorized to worship. Perhaps this regulation alludes to a single corporate sanctuary in each of the tribal areas, or to just one shrine for the entire community. The ambiguity of this regulation clears space for arguing for the existence of as many shrines dedicated to YHWH as there were "tribes" in the Israelite community, or it allows one to contend that there was one and only one shrine for members of the YHWH cult to worship and carry out their religious duties and activities.

Single-sanctuary language appears in Deuteronomy 12, and one cannot help but conclude that this law had serious effects in Israel. Josephus links the requirement for a single sanctuary in Israel to monotheism. He argues that the presence of many sites for worship supported the claim that many deities were present in Israel. Maimonides argued that Deuteronomy 12 is to be understood as an attempt by YHWH to limit the role of sacrifice in worship and to maximize the role of prayer in religiosity. Abravanel, a fifteenth-century Jewish scholar, understood Deuteronomy 12 as an attempt to prevent Israelites from killing animals in the wilderness and offering sacrifices to demons (Tigay 1996, 460–64).

The Text in Contemporary Discussion

Deuteronomy 12:1-32 demands that only the YHWH-alone cult was to be permitted to exist in the promised land. According to the Deuteronomic agenda, if these cults were allowed to remain, their presence would jeopardize the existence of the YHWH-alone cult. What is the reader on the present scene to make of the Deuteronomic proclivity for religious intolerance? Through the Internet, Facebook, and other forms of social media, persons have access to a plethora of information about religions and competing faith traditions. The Deuteronomic agenda, then, invites people for whom religion is a key force in life to frame a paradigm for how they should respond to the presence of different, conflicting faith communities and various belief systems on the global landscape.

Several options for addressing the issue of religious tolerance vie for our attention. Persons can opt for pluralism, the belief that multiple religions contain equal soteriological and ethical truth; exclusivism, the position that one and only one faith tradition is acceptable and efficacious; or inclusivism, the view that while a degree of truth and soteriological efficaciousness is present in many religions, one religious tradition is supreme. In light of globalization and the presence of competing diverse faith traditions in a common socio-spatiality, the moral and theological behavior in Deut. 12:1-32 puts the issue of religious tolerance into play.

Deuteronomy 13:1-18: Backsliding

The Text in Its Ancient Context

Deuteronomy 13:1-18 identifies four possible sources with whom the temptation to abandon the worship of YHWH could originate. This literary unit suggests that prophets (Deut. 13:1-5), family members and close friends (Deut. 13:6-11), and anonymous wicked persons in the general population of a city (Deut. 13:12-18) are possible initiators of infidelity to YHWH. According to Deut. 13:1-5, the enticement by the prophet to serve deities other than YHWH is the indication that YHWH has not endorsed this person: this individual is a false prophet. Since the predictions of false prophets can happen, this makes the false prophets credible. The speaker in this passage tells the people not to be swayed by the signs and wonders that the prophet or dreamer of dreams performs. The effort to persuade people to abandon the worship of YHWH is treason, and Deut. 13:1-5 prescribes the death penalty for the false prophet.

Deuteronomy 13:6-11 draws attention to family members, friends, and other close relationships that might instigate serving deities other than YHWH. This literary unit, therefore, warns that each member of the biblical community should be on guard for covert invitations from their closest relatives to abandon the worship of YHWH. It is noteworthy that these types of enticements come from persons who might have tremendous emotional influence in the lives of their loved ones, and that the attempt to lure an Israelite away from devotion to YHWH is a capital offense. One also cannot help but notice that Deut. 13:10 prescribes death by stoning as punishment for this crime. One cannot help but to notice that points of contact are present between the scene depicted in this case and that of a public lynching. Weinfeld and Mayes argues against the "public lynching scenario" by claiming that the text calls for a trial, and that if the alleged provocateur is found guilty, the Israelite who witnessed the crime should throw the first stone and the entire community is to join in after him in the stoning of the instigator; consequently, the entire community participates in administering the death penalty. Mayes is careful to point out that Deut. 13:10 is one of the few passages in the Hebrew Bible that prescribe death by stoning for certain offenses in the biblical community (Weinfeld 1992, 95; Mayes 1991 234–35).

Deuteronomy 13:12-18 deals with the fate of entire cities or social groups that have succumbed to the temptation to embrace the worship of deities other than YHWH. Deuteronomy 13:13 suggests that "men, the sons of Belial," instigated the infidelity. Peter Craigie attempts to cast light on the meaning or identity of these "men, the sons of Belial," by translating this phrase as "wicked men" (Craigie 1976, 226). Mayes translates this phrase as "base fellows" (Mayes 1991, 236). While the term "Belial" is not widespread in the Hebrew Bible, Craigie (1976) and Mayes (1991) link this phrase to the notion of moral and theological corruption. Thus, when "Belial" appears in this appositional phrase in Deut. 13:13, it seems fair to claim that the phrase denotes immoral and apostate individuals who lured an entire city into infidelity to YHWH. After the suspicion of treason against YHWH has been verified by some judicial proceeding, the inhabitants of the city are to be killed, the livestock in the city are to be slaughtered, and the city is to be destroyed by fire and never rebuilt.

The Text in the Interpretive Tradition

Vincent of Lérins suggested that from time to time, teachers who stray from the truth arise. He argued, however, that these are moments when the Christian should invoke principles and concepts in Deuteronomy 13 to demonstrate his or her commitment to the deity. Chief among these ideas are that the believer should love God with all of his or her heart and soul (Deut. 13:3); cleave to God (Deut. 13:5); and obey the voice of God (Deut. 13:18). The Deuteronomic program instructs Israel to withstand the temptation to abandon YHWH. YHWH alone is God. YHWH is to be worshiped. Vincent, therefore, builds on this theological legacy by contending that the true Catholic loves God with all of his or her being (see Lienhard 2001, 296).

The Text in Contemporary Discussion

Death, as the punishment for instigators of apostasy, was a major feature of the Deuteronomic program. Deuteronomy 13:12-18 does not consider a response that would position the people to reexamine their decisions and decide the truth of the competing religious claim that confronts them. If a faith community on the present scene senses that unbelief is gaining ground in its ranks or that something is awry with the theological or philosophical views of one of its member communities, then taking actions that seek to correct those perspectives, while simultaneously humanizing the constituents, may be the appropriate choice. Creating an environment for groups in the community to explore the veracity of faith claims to which they are supposed to adhere, not a climate that demands the execution of the alleged nonconformist group or a milieu that mandates blind obedience to religious doctrine from collections of conscious individuals, should be the prescribed strategy for dealing with people who seek to adjudicate the various sides of a theological issue. In *When Religion Becomes Evil*, Charles Kimball cites features of dangerous religiosity and invites the reader to consider problems that arise when faith communities use force to coerce people into accepting a specific religious ideology. To avoid many of the crises that Kimball articulates, a critical assessment of the handling of apostasy in Deuteronomic theology and moral philosophy is essential for individuals for whom the Hebrew Bible is normative for faith and praxis.

Deuteronomy 14:1-21: Mourning Rites and the Diet of a Holy People

The Text in Its Ancient Context

Deuteronomy 14:1-21 contains two subgroups of moral injunctions. Regulations treating mourning rites, on the one hand, appear in Deut. 14:1-2. An injunction of this type also appears in Lev. 19:28. Juxtaposing these regulations reveals the following similarities and differences: (1) Both Deut. 14:1-2 and Lev. 19:28 ban two and only two moral actions; (2) both laws indicate that making incisions in one's flesh for the dead is unacceptable; (3) Lev. 19:28 forbids placing writings or marks on the body for the dead; and (4) Deut. 14:1-2 disallows removing part of one's eyebrows for the dead. The common denominator between these laws is the ban on lacerating one's body in response to the death of another person, and the difference between them is that one bans tattooing the body for the dead while the other law prohibits shaving off part of one's eyebrow for the deceased. While Lev. 19:28 limits its prohibitions against participation in certain mourning rites to priests, Deut. 14:1-2 extends this prohibition to include the laity.

Archaeological finds from Ras Shamra have bequeathed to us a body of texts that contributes to our understanding of the Canaanite pantheon. The mythological texts that come to us from this city cite a plethora of deities, for example, El, Baal, Dagon, Yamm, Mot, and Anat, and these texts suggest that these mythological figures played key roles in the lore of subgroups who inhabited Canaan during the Late Bronze Age. Moreover, many of these peoples believed they existed in a special covenantal relationship with their deity (Craigie 1983, 62–66; Miller 2000, 1–45). Therefore, it comes as no surprise that the individual or school that determined the Deuteronomic agenda sought to impress on the people of Israel that they belonged to YHWH, that they were a *sĕgullâ*, and that this privileged relationship with YHWH should exhibit itself in ways that differentiated the Israelites from their neighbors.

Placing deep cuts in one's flesh and cutting bald spots in one's hair for the deceased were practices associated with the cults of other gods; therefore, Nelson (2002) suggests that Deut. 14:1-2 could refer to demonstrating grief for the death of a person or to expressing extreme sorrow in the cults of other deities (Nelson 2002, 179). He, therefore, leaves the door ajar for claiming that this ritual bans mourning practices in cults for people who have died or for mourning the death of a deity. Mayes (1991) steps into this gap by interpreting "dead" in this passage to refer to humans or a god; consequently, he suggests that this regulation is a response to mourning practices in the Baal cult. Thus he interprets this regulation to identify another type of apostasy, namely, that involvement in mourning rituals linked to any other deity counts as abandoning the YHWH cult (Mayes 1991, 238–39).

The Text in the Interpretive Tradition

Regulations treating diet, on the other hand, appear in Deut. 14:3-21. The codes in Deut. 14:3-21 deal with the consumption of land animals (Deut. 14:4-8), water creatures (Deut. 14:9-10), fowl (Deut. 14:11-19), and insects (Deut. 14:20), and these laws place no restrictions on those vegetables, plants, and fruits that the people of Israel may eat. The Deuteronomic program adopts the principles of clean (*ṭāhôr*) and unclean (*ṭāmēʾ*) to classify animals; animals that are categorized as "clean" are fit for consumption, and fauna that are classified as "unclean" are unfit for consumption. A competing set of codes regulating the consumption of animals appears in Lev. 11:2-23, and a significant difference between these codes is present. While the regulations in Lev. 11:2-23 give detailed attention to citing those animals that Israel may not eat, Deut. 14:4-8 cites those animals that the people are permitted to consume.

While the dietary ordinance in Deut. 14:3-21 instructs the people to eat clean animals, one cannot help but notice that this law does not articulate the criteria that inform its ideas about "cleanliness and uncleanliness." Considerable difference of opinion is present among scholars over why animals are classified as either clean or unclean and about how the reader should interpret these regulations on fauna in the biblical legal corpora. Critical scholarship on the HB identifies four organizing principles or frameworks for classifying the fauna and for understanding the arrangement of the dietary stipulations in Deut. 14:3-21. The gist of the positions is as follows: (1) The hygienic construct proffers that in the worldview of biblical Israel, the flesh of certain fauna was unhealthy and carried disease and thus it was unfit to eat; (2) the cultic framework contends that those animals that are cited as unclean were fauna that were linked to the cults of the people who inhabited Syria-Palestine with biblical Israel; (3) the subjective construct proffers that YHWH decided the issue and that is the end of it; and (4) the ethical/representational framework argues that these regulations are symbolic of a higher moral principle, namely, the belief that Israelites must respect life as they seek to satisfy their appetite for protein (Ross 2002, 251–52; Milgrom 2004, 102–15; Houston 2003, 142–61).

The Text in Contemporary Discussion

A model for interpreting biblical law that is informed by critical legal studies clears space for arguing that those codes regarding edible fauna in the Hebrew Bible worked to the disadvantage of certain social divisions in ancient Israelite society (Bennett 2002, 12–21; Knight 2011, 1–86). Two issues naturally arise: which social subdivision in the biblical community was affected adversely by these codes, and how did they affect this social class? A plausible response to the question might be the following: While the goal of Deut. 14:3-21 might have been to place limits on the diet of members in Israel, these codes placed hardships on "the have-nots," that is, the largest and most diverse social class in the community. Mark Sneed (1991) offers a collection of essays that point out that biblical scholars have used a plethora of terms and systems for arranging and discussing the demographics of Israelite society subsequent to the appearance of the monarchy. He contends that while a plethora of terms are present for delineating the social subdivisions in Israel, the consensus of social-scientific research on ancient Israel contends that at least two major socioeconomic classes were perennial features of ancient Israelite society during the Late Iron Age I and Iron Age II. One subdivision possessed wealth and political power (the haves), and the other subdivision was without wealth and political power (the have-nots). Slaves, widows, free peasants, orphans, sharecroppers, and perhaps other vulnerable groups constituted the have-nots (Sneed 1991, 54). This social class daily eked out their existence and lived at the mercy of urban elites, priests, and creditors. Absent from this social class were the concomitants of wealth, that is, a wide choice of food options and the means to obtain whatever they wanted to consume. It therefore stands to reason that while the have-nots might have viewed certain fauna as clean or unclean, it is highly improbable that the groups comprising this category had the luxury of refusing to eat certain meats to the degree that was present among the haves. Hungry stomachs know no morality when it comes to food; while the have-nots in Israel might have demonstrated some allegiance to religious codes, it stands to reason that these people would be more concerned with putting an end to their daily hunger problems than they would be concerned with being ethical and theologically correct or even nutritious when it comes to diet. They just wanted their children to be fed and the pain in their empty stomachs to subside. Chances are that the have-nots, the majority of Israelites, were compelled more often to consider eating "unclean animals," however reluctantly, in order to survive.

Consequently, Deut. 14:3-21 invites the reader to consider the role that this legislation played in a fundamental issue of social justice, namely, whether laws in the Hebrew Bible contributed to the problem of hunger in Israel. When read through a lens shaped by current sociological studies of law and the conversation on demographics in ancient Israel, Deut. 14:3-21 appears to provoke circumstances that those who lived at the mercy of urban elites, priests, and creditors might not have been able to navigate.

Deuteronomy 14:22-29: Tithes

The Text in Its Ancient Context

Deuteronomy 14:22-29 deals with tithes in the biblical communities. According to these legal traditions, the tithe (*ma'ăśēr*) is one-tenth of grains, wine, oil, cattle, and sheep. Genesis 14:18-20, on the one hand, cites Abram and links him to this practice of paying tithes, for Abram gives tithes to Melchizedek. While Gen. 28:18-22 and 35:1-14, on the other hand, link the practice of tithing in ancient Israel to Jacob, these traditions in which he appears never provide the textual basis for concluding that Jacob fulfilled his vow to give tithes to the deity. First Samuel 8:10-18 also casts light on tithing in ancient Israel. This narrative recounts Samuel's speech to those elites who request transitioning from a loose, acephalous configuration of tribes to a single, political entity headed by a monarch. In his response to them, Samuel tells these leaders that the crown will exact one-tenth of their produce and flocks, and that it will use them to fund its operation. This passage, therefore, provides a basis for arguing that tithes were a major element in the fiscal system that supported the royal bureaucracy in ancient Israel.

H. Jagersma (1981) and Marty Stevens (2006) situate the conversation about tithes in ancient Israel in the larger discussion on tithes in the ancient Near East. The former cites textual data from Mesopotamia and indicates that the custom of paying tithes was present in the third dynasty of Ur. The latter cites data from Mesopotamia and Egypt and points out that tithes and taxes were key elements in systems for the upkeep of the temple and for funding the programs of the crown. According to Stevens, the term *eśrû*, a term that denotes a tenth of one's income, appears in the Mesopotamian data. Stevens also calls attention to data from the Old Babylonian period and shows that people were obligated to give one-tenth of their crops and orchards to the cult and royal administration. He points out that the term *miksu* appears in the data from the Old Babylonian period, and that this term denoted income received by the state and temple. The data also suggest that the payment of tithes was one element in the exacting of revenue from crops and herds from the general population in ancient Southwest Asia. This income was for temples and for the king. The custom of paying tithes appears in Israelite society, but how it made its way there may be forever lost to us.

The Text in the Interpretive Tradition

Two traditions about tithes appear in Deut. 14:22-29, and these regulations stand in stark contrast to the law on tithes in Deut. 12:2-7. The ordinances governing tithes in Deut. 12:2-7 are silent on how frequently the tithes should be brought to the site that YHWH chooses. Deuteronomy 14:22 opens with the command "you will set aside tithe of all the increase of your seed that the field brings forth each year." What is more, Deut. 14:23 directs Israel to present the tithes in the place where YHWH's name is present, that is, "in the place where YHWH has put YHWH's name." This centralization formula forbids the consumption of these tithes in local villages. It is worth noting that Deut. 14:22-27 makes a concession: if the person who desires to present tithes resides a great distance from the central sanctuary, the regulation allows for the presenter to exchange for money produce, animals, or other items, and make the trek to the place where the name of YHWH is present. Once he or she arrives at the central shrine, he or she is to purchase food and drink and consume it there. Thus the annual tithe is the focus of Deut. 14:22-27.

Deuteronomy 14:28-29 directs the biblical community to offer tithes "every three years," but this piece of legislation instructs the biblical community to store the tithes "in their villages." Deuteronomy 14:28-29 reminds the biblical community to share their tithes with the widow (*'almānâ*), stranger (*gēr*), fatherless (*yātôm*), and Levites. It is argued that the widow, stranger, and orphan appear together in a single literary formula because they share minimally two social features: (1) The individuals in this social group are bereft of a masculine protector; and (2) the persons in this social group are vulnerable and are at the mercy of priests, urban elites, land owners, creditors, and other exploiters in Israel (Bennett 2002, 55–56). Thus the regulations on tithes instruct the community to share tithes with these people on a regular basis.

These regulations on tithes in Deut. 14:22-29 are very different from the regulations governing tithes in Lev. 27:30-33 and Num. 18:21-32. Leviticus 27:30-33, on the one hand, contends that the tithes are holy to YHWH, meaning that these items belong to the priests. The passage indicates that if one fails to present the complete 10 percent of the tithes to the priest, he is penalized, and must increase the amount of his tithes by 20 percent the next time he presents them. Numbers 18:21-32, on the other hand, stipulates that the tithes are for the support of the Levites and their households in lieu of their not having any inheritance in Israel. This passage, however, adds an additional element to the regulation on tithes: the Levites are instructed to share 10 percent of their tithes with the priests.

Deuteronomy 14:22-29 suggests that the payment of tithes was an important feature of the religious and economic milieu in biblical Israel. The evidence on tithes in the Deuteronomic program and on tithes in the program advanced by priests suggests that there were, minimally, three traditions about obligatory tithing in Israel: (1) There was the annual tithe that was to be presented and eaten at the central sanctuary by the presenter, his family, and the cultic official; (2) there was the annual tithe that was to be presented at the cultic site and was the sole property of the Levites; and (3) there was the triennial tithe that was stored in the local village and was to be shared with the vulnerable in Israelite society. Moreover, 1 Samuel 8 supports the claim that tithes were one element in the material endowment of the monarchy.

The Text in Contemporary Discussion

Deuteronomy 14:22-27 identifies those items that are subject to tithes, and this regulation provides guidelines on the consumption and distribution of these items in Israel. Deuteronomy 14:22-27 regulates the annual tithe, and Deut. 14:28-29 regulates the collection and distribution of the triennial tithes. What gives these codes relevance for today is the ethic that informs them. In short, these codes are of significance for the current conversation on social justice. Deuteronomy 14:22-29 provides at a minimum temporary economic relief to vulnerable groups. That is to say, these regulations provided these persons with food and other items that they needed to live. Providing temporary, immediate aid to the vulnerable is one of those actions that Islam, Judaism, and Christianity find praiseworthy.

Deuteronomy 15:1-18: Indebtedness and Slavery between Israelites

The Text in Its Ancient Context

Deuteronomy 15:1-18 contains two distinct regulations. The common denominator between these legal injunctions is a response to socioeconomic conditions and problems, which proceeded from poverty and debt. Deuteronomy 15:1-11, on the one hand, demands the forgiveness of loans; Deut. 15:12-18, on the other hand, regulates behavior towards persons who have become slaves as a result of personal debt or as a consequence of the loans or debt of someone else. Both pieces of legislation command creditors and enslavers to extend mercy, and these legal injunctions specify that every seven years debts should be canceled and slaves should be given their freedom.

Jeffries Hamilton (1992) aids in delineating a cross-cultural backdrop against which to discuss the regulations on forgiveness of debt and the manumission of slaves that appear in Deut. 15:1-18. Hamilton also cites data from the third dynasty of Ur and from other cultures in Mesopotamia. According to him, *mīšarum* decrees demanded clemency in the form of the forgiveness of individual debts and the forgiveness of selected taxes owed by individuals to the state, and some *mīšarum* decrees demanded the release of slaves. He further indicates that monarchs issued these proclamations, and that these legislations were frequently concomitant with the ascendency of a new king. Hamilton notes that the Mesopotamian evidence attests also to the *andurārum* proclamations. However, he points out, there is considerable difficulty in interpreting the texts where the *andurārum* edicts are present. They provide inconclusive evidence about the direct object of the *andurārum*; therefore, whether the *andurārum* act refers to the release of slaves or to the freeing of someone from some other debtor obligation remains open to debate. Thus, while the cross-cultural parallels in the ancient world are sometimes ambiguous, the larger discussion on social justice in the ancient world nevertheless provides a helpful context for considering the individual stipulations in Deut. 15:1-18.

The Text in the Interpretive Tradition

The legal injunction in Deut. 15:1-11 instructs creditors in Israelite society to discontinue attempts to collect monies owed to them by their debtors. The translation "remission of debts" appears in English translations of Deut. 15:1-11. The term in biblical Hebrew is *šĕmiṭṭâ* (the act of letting something drop) and the LXX uses the Greek term *aphesis* (the act of discharging something). The general sense of this piece of legislation, then, is to "drop from the books" or "to give a debtor a zero balance for arrears incurred over the past seven years." Mayes contends that the law of release that appears in Deut. 15:1-11 circulated first as a legal sanction governing the use of the land, and that the Deuteronomic program reappropriates a legal injunction that demanded that farmers allow the land to rest by reapplying this code to the forgiveness of loans (Mayes 1991, 246–49). Craigie (1976) argues that *šĕmiṭṭâ* codes call for a suspension of any attempts to collect debts in the seventh year (Craigie 1976, 236–37). Mayes, then, disagrees with Craigie by rejecting the notion that Deut. 15:1-11 calls for only temporary relief or for only a brief suspension of attempts to collect monies owed by the poor. In doing so, Mayes contends that Deut. 15:1-11 calls for the permanent forgiveness of arrearage by creditors. Because of its demand to show kindness to remit debts, Deut. 15:1-11 often appears among those regulations that attest to the humanitarian ethos in the book of Deuteronomy.

Points of contact are present between the legal injunction in Deut. 15:12-18 and the regulations in Exod. 21:2-6 and Lev. 25:39-46. These traditions deal with the release of slaves who are Hebrew. It has been a commonplace in Hebrew Bible studies to contend that the collection of laws in Deuteronomy 12–26 is a redaction of the legal traditions in Exodus 21–23. Bernard Levinson, however, invites us to consider the implications of this presupposition. Central to his argument is the claim that the ideology in the laws in Deuteronomy 12–26 neither depends entirely on the ethos of legislations in Exodus 21–23. He therefore leaves the door ajar for arguing that another social, political, and theological agenda sculpted those legal injunctions, which are present in Deuteronomy 12–26 (Levinson 1997, 1–22).

Juxtaposing Exod. 21:2-6 and Deut. 15:12-18, therefore, is a fruitful enterprise. The law on the manumission of Hebrew slaves in Deut. 15:12-18 contains several innovations. (1) This piece of legislation includes treatment of the Hebrew female slave with the treatment of the Hebrew male slave (Deut. 15:12); (2) this law demands that the enslaver give the slave provisions and other commodities when he liberates the slave (Deut. 15:13-14); (3) this legal injunction contains no directions about what to do if the Hebrew male slave marries; (4) this code is silent about the fate of any children born to the Hebrew male slave while he is enslaved; and (5) this regulation adds a motive clause to this revised law on the liberation of slaves in Israel (Deut. 15:15). The inconsistencies in this piece of legislation compared with the Exodus laws fit with innovations that appear elsewhere in the Deuteronomic collection of laws that deal with the vulnerable in Israelite society by instructing the reader to develop sensitivities to the plight of the less fortunate.

The Text in Contemporary Discussion

Deuteronomy 15:1-18 invites the community to explore ways to improve the economic conditions of persons who exist on the margins. This subgroup of legislation advocates for the forgiveness of debts and for the manumission of Hebrew slaves. The question arises, however, whether these regulations are in support of all persons who exist on the fringes of society or support primarily the improvement of conditions for the Hebrew poor. Be mindful that these laws advocate the forgiveness of the debts for Israelite kinsmen and for the release of Hebrew/Israelite slaves only after seven years.

Deuteronomy 15:1-18, therefore, sanctions retaining the debts of the non-Israelite poor, and institutionalizes the ownership of human beings in society. By formulating laws that indicate that the enslavement of certain groups by Israelites is acceptable, this code provides a basis for arguing that enslavement of certain races is just. Deuteronomy 15:1-18 ensures that a subgroup of human beings who may be in need of financial support or economic relief might not receive it.

Deuteronomy 15:1-18 foreshadows the socioeconomic and political theology and policies that informed notions about the enslavement of Africans in the antebellum South. It is unfortunate that Deuteronomy uses religion to shape social conventions that legitimize the perpetual exploitation of certain ethnic groups.

Deuteronomy 16:1-16: Major Cultic Celebrations

The Text in Its Ancient Context

Deuteronomy 16:1-16 delineates three cultic celebrations. These festivals are Passover (Deut. 16:1-8), the Feast of Weeks (Deut. 16:9-12), and the Festival of Booths (Deut. 16:13-16). Deuteronomy 16:17 lists the required festivals in a single independent clause; and Exod. 23:14-19 also lists these festivals together. Competing passages that treat festivals appear elsewhere in the legal corpora in the Hebrew Bible. These passages are Exod. 34:18-26; Leviticus 23; and Num. 9:1-14; 28:1—29:40. It is important to note that the previously mentioned texts are not the only regulations that deal with major cultic celebrations in the ancient biblical communities.

Inconsistencies are present among the regulations that govern the festival calendar in Deut. 16:1-17 and those found elsewhere in the Hebrew Bible. It has been argued that the code governing the Feast of Passover in Deut. 16:1-8 combines two independent cultic celebrations, namely, the Festival of Unleavened Bread (*maṣâ*) and Passover (*pesaḥ*) (Mayes 1991, 254–55). Duane Christensen (2001) cites three salient positions present in scholarship, which seek to adjudicate this literary feature of Deut. 16:1-8. These theories are the following: (1) The tradition concerning the Feast of Unleavened Bread was added to an extant tradition on the Festival of Passover; (2) a tradition concerning the Festival of Passover was added to an extant tradition dealing with the Feast of Unleavened Bread; (3) the Feasts of Unleavened Bread and Passover existed concurrently without referencing each other (Christensen 2001, 331). When one juxtaposes Deut. 16:1-8 with Exod. 12:21-28, one notices that the regulation governing *pesaḥ* in Deut. 16:1-8 removes the Passover celebration from the home of families and mandates that households celebrate the Passover at a central location in Israel, namely, the site YHWH chooses. This difference casts light on the Deuteronomic agenda of removing the celebration of major cultic festivals from local homes and relocating them to the central site, which placed control of key resources there and created opportunities for the YHWH-alone cult to promulgate its key tenets to persons in Israelite society.

The Text in the Interpretive Tradition

Scholarship that proceeds from the Jewish tradition on Deut. 16:1-8 contends that it is better to translate *pesaḥ* as the "protective sacrifice." Tigay (1996) contends that this naming of the sacrifice commemorates the fact that YHWH spared the eldest children of the Israelite households (Tigay 1996, 153). He also draws attention to the fact that the regulation on *pesaḥ* in Exod. 12:21-28 limits sacrifices to sheep and goats, while Deut. 16:1-8 includes bovine animals among those items that can be consumed in the festival that recollects the protective sacrifice in Egypt. Jesus, in the Synoptic tradition (Luke 22:14-23), expresses an eagerness to consume the Passover meal, or protective sacrifice, with his disciples. Jesus takes this ritual to mean that the moment for a second act of deliverance is imminent. In fact, the author of Luke links the tradition about the protective meal in Egypt with the tradition of the death of Jesus and the shedding of his blood to establish a new covenant and deliver those persons who were held captive by the power of Satan and evil.

The Text in Contemporary Discussion

The tradition about the Passover, or the protective meal, receives wide currency in Christian theology. As mentioned above, it becomes the backdrop against which many discuss and interpret the death of Jesus. In fact, this ancient tradition provides the symbolism for linking the two Testaments in the Christian canon. That is to say, the blood of the Passover sacrifice in the First Testament was seen as that which protected and delivered Israel from the death angel in Egypt. The blood of Jesus in the Second Testament was seen as that which delivers people from their sin and positions the faithful to triumph over the powers of evil (Rev. 12:11). What is more, the tradition about the protective meal informs Easter, which is a central time of the year for Christians worldwide.

Deuteronomy 16:18—17:20: Ethical Leadership

The Text in Its Ancient Context

Ensuring that ethical leadership is present in the Israelite community is the focus of Deut. 16:18—17:20. To this end, this section prescribes behavior for persons in the judiciary who are responsible for settling disputes among Israelites, and it prescribes what counts as acceptable conduct for the monarch. Deuteronomy 16:18—17:13, therefore, deals minimally with four items: (1) It identifies the group on whom the onus rests for selecting the persons who will carry out justice (*mišpāṭ*); (2) it points out who had the specific responsibility of administering *mišpāṭ*; (3) it identifies the site for the administration of *mišpāṭ*; and (4) it indicates the principle that should govern the resolution of controversies. Deuteronomy 17:14-20 provides insight into what is expected of the king, and it treats this issue by delineating primarily an assortment of actions that he should avoid.

In reference to the pursuit of *mišpāṭ*, Deut. 16:18a directs Israel to abet the pursuit of justice. It instructs them to appoint persons from their communities to assume responsibility for settling disagreements. While the text is silent on the process of selection, it is noteworthy that the people, not a prophet, priest, or monarch, are to select these persons.

Judges (*šōpĕṭîm*) and officers (*šōṭĕrîm*) are to be appointed, and they are charged with responsibility for solving disputes in the community. While Deut. 1:15-18 indicates that the leaders of tribes were judges, Deut. 16:18a does not specify the social group from which the *šōpĕṭîm* and *šōṭĕrîm* come; perhaps these judges and officers were heads of tribes, persons of affluence, priests, prophets, or aged persons. Scholarship on these legislations proposes that villages selected chiefs from amongst the prominent elders, and that these village chiefs became judges (Tigay 1996, 160;

Christensen 2001, 363). Perhaps, there might have been a special class of persons trained in adjudication in ancient Israelite society.

Deuteronomy 16:18 directs Israel to appoint *šōpĕṭîm* and *šōṭĕrîm* in their "gates." This text casts light on the location in the local village where *šōpĕṭîm* and *šōṭĕrîm* heard cases, namely, at the local "gate." The local city gate was the site for the administration of justice. It contained compartments, and these spaces were often the site for small gatherings, official public activities, the transaction of business deals, and that from time to time, the gate was the location where prophets sought to bring the word of YHWH to Israel (Drinkard 2007, 523; Ruth 4:1-11; Amos 5:10-17).

The phrase *mišpāṭ-ṣedeq* appears in Deut. 16:18b. In English translations, one can render it "righteous judgment." Deuteronomy 16:20a contains the wording *ṣedeq ṣedeq tirdōp* ("righteousness and righteousness only you shall pursue"). The admonition to do what is right, honest, and fair implies that *šōpĕṭîm* and *šōṭĕrîm* were responsible for providing a neutral, impartial conflict-resolution process in Israelite society. The *šōpĕṭîm* and *šōṭĕrîm* were to avoid favoritism: they were to assess facts, resolving disputes based on a careful weighing of the evidence, not on friendship, relationship, or the promise of personal gain. In the words of Deut. 16:20a: righteousness and righteousness alone you shall pursue!

Deuteronomy 17:2-7 discusses the role of adequate, dependable evidence in the pursuit of *mišpāṭ*. The passage brings into play the possibility that gossip is spreading through the community, and the report is that a man and his wife have been engaged in the worship of foreign deities. Deuteronomy 17:4 directs the judge or the officer to investigate the case. As he hears the report, the judge or the officer is to ensure that sufficient evidence is present for a conviction, because Deut. 17:6 indicates that the judge or officer cannot base his decision on the testimony or evidence presented by one and only one witness. A verdict of guilty has to be based on reliable, sound evidence. This type of judicial process positions judges and officers to be objective adjudicators of issues in the biblical communities.

Deuteronomy 17:8-13 attempts to ensure justice in Israel by providing guidelines for adjudicating a series of issues that might be too hard to be resolved in the local tribunal. Deuteronomy 17:8 contains the following terms: *dām* ("blood"), *dîn* ("a disagreement requiring resolution"), and *nega'* ("wound"). Christensen (2001) contends that these terms pertain, respectively, to issues of homicide, civil offenses, and disputes involving physical injury (Christensen 2001, 374–75). Perhaps the evidence is inconclusive or insufficient. Yet the litigants are instructed to carry the matter to the central sanctuary and allow the priest (*kōhēn*) or judge (*šōpēṭ*) who is present at that site to adjudicate the issue. Deuteronomy 17:12 indicates that verdicts issued at the central sanctuary are irrevocable, and that the death penalty can be applied to the individual or group who decides to disobey these rulings.

In reference to the king, Deut. 17:14-20 permits the community to move from a decentralized, acephalous society to a form of sociopolitical organization that is centralized and has a figure over it. Deuteronomy 17:15 allows the community to appoint a king (*melek*) over it; however, the king must be one whom YHWH chooses and approves. The rest of the passage specifies a legitimate king, and it identifies those actions the king must avoid and embrace. The legitimate king must not be a foreigner (*nokrî*); he must be from one of the tribes that constitute Israel. Chief among the actions the king must avoid is the amassing of horses for himself (Deut. 17:16). Perhaps assembling such a large number of horses was for military usage or for prestige. The king is told not to form a harem (Deut. 17:17). It is probable that this code prohibited entering marriages with foreign women. These marriages were concomitant with political alliances; therefore, the prohibition on entering marriages with many foreign women was an attempt to keep the Israelite monarch from entering polity coalitions with many of the nations in the ancient Near East. The king is also banned from the stockpiling of silver and gold for himself. He is to avoid greed and must not become an object of worship in Israel. Deuteronomy 17:18-20 instructs the king to keep a copy of this code, and to read it frequently to remind himself of the duties of a legitimate king.

The Text in the Interpretive Tradition

Deuteronomy 16:18—17:13 develops the circumstance that received treatment in Deut. 1:13-17, namely, the conversation about judiciary decorum in ancient Israel (Tigay 1996, 160). While the judicial system established in Deut. 1:13-17 worked while the people were en route to the promised land, this system for the administration of justice became problematic. Thus Deut. 16:18—17:13 adjusts to the need for justice in the promised land by instructing the people to select magistrates. The Israelite community, then, might have assigned village chiefs to the position of judges and included cultic officials in this group, which was responsible for the adjudication of conflicts among members and social groups in Israel. Yet the persons responsible for solving disagreements in the community were instructed not to take bribes and to ensure that righteous decision making prevailed in regard to settling disputes.

Caesarius of Arles casts light on the passages treating judges and the pursuit of *mišpāṭ* in the legal codes in Deuteronomy. He takes these regulations to teach that in the acceptance of bribes, the judge or priest may have obtained some profit or income. The income, however, cost them something of far greater value—their conscience. Caesarius of Arles, then, takes these codes to mean that the inner voice of right is that to which one should adhere, regardless of the financial profit he or she might receive (Lienhard 2001, 301–2).

What is more, the position on monarchy in Deut. 17:14-20 contrasts with the tradition about monarchy in subgroups of texts in the Deuteronomistic History (DtrH). That is to say, evidence is present in DtrH that subgroups in Israel were hostile to the notion of a centralized government headed by a king. These texts are the following: (1) 1 Sam. 8:1-22; (2) 1 Sam. 10:17-27; and (3) 1 Sam. 12:1-15. In the Deuteronomy passage, YHWH supports the establishment of a monarchy, but in the 1 Samuel passages, YHWH does not.

The Text in Contemporary Discussion

Deuteronomy 16:18—17:20 provokes us to ensure that ethical leadership is in our judiciary, government, and religious communities. This conversation invites the critic to identify those principles that inform decision making and legal judgments by individuals and groups in key legal, political, and religious offices in our communities. This conversation also necessitates exploring the possibilities that particular agendas are in play regarding the rendering of judicial decisions, the formation of policies, and the sculpting of theological claims. Recent cases dealing with racial profiling; clergy sexual misconduct; and the misuse of religion to acquire money, status, and property invite modern-day thinkers to practice what critical theorists call a *hermeneutic of suspicion* when it comes to viewing magistrates and other persons in leadership positions.

Deuteronomy 18:1-8: Payment of Priests

The Text in Its Ancient Context

Deuteronomy 18:1-8 deals with the remuneration of cultic officials in the community. Notably, this code presents a different point of view about who can preside over the sacrifices and sacred rituals and direct matters in the cultus. Deuteronomy 18:1 uses asyndeton: it omits the use of conjunctions from a series of clauses that are in sequence; therefore it reads: "the priests, the Levites, the entire tribe of Levi." This syntactic maneuver suggests that all the personnel in the Israelite cultus were of equal rank. According to Deut. 18:1, all males from the tribe of Levi are priests and have no inheritance in Israel. The Priestly tradition, for example, Num. 3:5-10, avers that a tiered system governing responsibilities and personal remuneration constituted the Israelite cultus. According to the Priestly tradition, the priests were the sons of Aaron, and they presided over the sacrifices, officiated at the sacred rituals, and adjudicated matters of ceremonial cleanliness. Numbers 3:5-10 relegates other men who constituted the tribe of Levi to positions of servitude to the priests, the sons of Aaron. What is more, Num. 18:25-32 directs the Levites to give the priests a portion of the compensation they received from working in the cult. Deuteronomy 18:2-8, however, permits all Levites to serve at the central shrine, and it prescribes that they should receive economic support from the rituals and sacrifices over which they preside. Deuteronomy 18:1-8 does not direct the Levites to share their income with any other personnel in the Israelite cultus.

The Text in the Interpretive Tradition

The notion about the support of Levites in the Israelite cultus informs notions about the remuneration of clergy in the early church. Paul, however, writes: "Do you not know that those who are employed in the temple service get their food from the temple, and those who serve at the altar share in what is sacrificed on the altar? In the same way, the Lord commanded that those who proclaim the gospel should get their living by the gospel" (1 Cor. 9:13-14 NRSV). Paul takes the tradition about the method for the support of personnel in the Israelite cult to mean that ministers in the early Jesus movement are entitled to the resources of a subgroup in the community because congregations should support those clergy from whom they received services.

First Timothy links the notion of the remuneration of cultic officials in Deuteronomy to the material endowment of ministers in the early church. While 1 Timothy does not cite Deut. 18:1-8, the author establishes a line of thought and connects it with the economic philosophy expressed in Deut. 18:1-8. The author writes: "for the scripture says: 'You shall not muzzle an ox while it is treading out the grain,' and, 'The laborer deserves to be paid'" (1 Tim. 5:18 NRSV). The person responsible for this epistle cites Deut. 25:4 and uses it to advocate for clergy receiving compensation for the work they performed in the promulgation of the gospel. Key persons in the history of early Christianity grounded notions about the payment of clergy in notions about the compensation of cultic officials in Deut. 18:1-8.

The Text in Contemporary Discussion

Deuteronomy 18:1-8 indicates that the material support of priests should come from the services they provide at the central sanctuary. This system for compensating priests raises the current question about the remuneration of clergy, and, as it is to be expected, considerable difference of opinion about compensation and benefits for clergy is present today. Several items receive treatment in this conversation. Chief among these issues are the following: the method for arriving at equitable compensation; the amount of compensation the minister will receive; services for which the minister will receive compensation; and the particular system the institution will use to pay the minister. Some congregations adhere to a specific set of salary guidelines that have been determined and approved by a larger authority, while some congregations are autonomous and decide for themselves the compensation they are going to provide to clergy who serve them. The implication of Deut. 18:1-8, however, is that economic support should come from the services ministers provide to congregations and to the community.

Deuteronomy 18:9-22: The Prophet Like Moses

The Text in Its Ancient Context

Deuteronomy 18:9-22 contends that YHWH uses a human to communicate with the people. The text calls this individual a prophet (*nābîʾ*); this code emphasizes that this person will emerge from within Israel, and Deut. 18:15 points out that he will resemble Moses. Chief among this point of contact between Moses and this envisaged person is that of being the mediator between the deity and the people, and that of being the spokesperson on behalf of the deity to the people. The fact that the prophet, not the priest, is the intermediary between YHWH and the people is a significant feature of the Deuteronomic program. Elsewhere, in other parts of the Hebrew Bible that reflect the ideology in the Deuteronomic code, the prophet carries messages from YHWH to the king and to other individuals in the community. Deuteronomy 18:9-22, therefore, orders the people to obey this prophet, and not to engage diviners, soothsayers, witches, or other types of persons who play key roles in the cultic practices of those non-Israelite nations that inhabit Syria-Palestine with biblical Israel.

The Text in the Interpretive Tradition

The Hebrew Bible identifies people and events that are important for understanding Judaism, Christianity, and Islam. While it is possible to mention quite a few individuals and circumstances, no one in these literary traditions is as important as Moses. What is more, Judaism, Christianity, and Islam contain different ways of reading, discussing, and appropriating texts where Moses is present. These religious traditions apply different hermeneutical lenses to Deut. 18:9-22, and especially to the words of Moses in Deut. 18:15: "YHWH will raise a prophet, from your brothers, who is like me." Camps in Judaism contend that Elijah is that prophet about whom Deut. 18:15 speaks. Instances of this hermeneutical move are found in Mal. 4:4-6 [3:22-24 MT] and Sir. 48:1-11. Camps in the early Christian community saw Jesus as this new Moses, and this connection becomes the backdrop against which to discuss the Gospel according to Matthew. What is more, Muslim communities took the claim that the deity would raise a prophet *like Moses* from among the brothers in the community to refer to the prophet Mohammad (Phipps 1996, 102).

The Text in Contemporary Discussion

"A prophet like me" is a significant phrase in Deut. 18:9-22. This expression leaves open the possibility that a person who has a link to the divine will appear, and that this person will resemble Moses in some form or fashion. The fact that competing interpretations of this person are present in Judaism, Christianity, and Islam brings into play the crux of the problem, namely, delineating those criteria that must be satisfied for a person to be "a prophet like Moses." Since Deut. 18:15 is silent about these measurements, this has left the door ajar for believing that a person may arise in the modern world and, in the custom of the *nābî'*, deliver a message that speaks in a redemptive way to the theological, ethical, and socioeconomic predicaments of people. Marcus Garvey (1887–1940) immediately comes to mind as an example (see Erskine 2005, 116–68).

Deuteronomy 19:1-14: Manslaughter

The Text in Its Ancient Context

Deuteronomy 19:1-14 prescribes the response to inadvertent homicide in the Israelite community by identifying six additional places of safety to which one who is guilty of a fortuitous homicide of another Israelite (*rēʿēhû*). This legislation introduces the avenger of blood (*gōʾēl haddām*). Scholars have competing views about the identity of this person: the avenger of blood was the male next of kin who bears the moral responsibility of retaliating against the perpetrator for the killing of his family member (Tigay 1996, 181). The avenger of blood was thought to be an appointed official, whose assignment it was to retrieve the perpetrator from the city of refuge and to administer the death penalty (Mayes 1991, 286–87). Regardless of the identity of this person, Deut. 19:6 attempts to prevent the avenger of blood from acting out of pure emotion; this code seeks to undermine decision making about culpability without getting the facts about the homicide. If neither malice nor premeditation played a part in the homicide, then the perpetrator is without blame. The asylum is for the innocent party, not for the guilty party.

Thematic points of contact exist between Deut. 19:1-14 and other regulations in the Hebrew Bible that deal with the unintentional killing of another Israelite. Deuteronomy 19:1-14 is similar to Exod. 21:12-14. Both codes deal with the loss of life. While Exod. 21:12-14 legislates behavior in the case of inadvertent homicide, it does not mention the setting aside of cities for protection of the supposed killer until the situation is resolved; rather, it indicates that a single place is set aside for asylum for the perpetrator. Similar to Deut. 19:1-14, Deut. 4:41-43 lists cities to which persons guilty of an unplanned homicide may escape. DtrH designates a place of safety for supposed criminals. This site is the altar in the sanctuary, for the fugitive is allowed to grab hold of the horns of the altar, and while he is holding to the horns of the altar, the supposed criminal is granted mercy (see 1 Kgs. 1:49-53). The fact that 1 Kgs. 1:49-53 predates the construction of the Jerusalem temple raises questions about the role that these cities, that is, places of safety, played in the case of a chance homicide. In its handling of the case, Deut. 19:1-14 attempts to avert the intentional killing of an innocent Israelite by the *gōʾēl haddām*. Seen through this lens, Deut. 19:1-14 seeks to protect the lives of Israelites, not simply to exculpate one who is responsible for the death of another Israelite. Protecting the lives of innocent Israelites is also a major feature of Num. 35:6-34 and Josh. 20:1-9, for these texts identify asylums for Israelites accused of manslaughter.

The Text in the Interpretive Tradition

Gregory the Great (540–604 CE) takes an interesting hermeneutical approach to Deut. 19:1-14. He views this passage through the lens of counseling, that is, through ensuring self-discipline while caring for the souls of human beings. He therefore likens the forest in Deut. 19:1-14 to the shortcomings of human beings. He associates the cutting of wood with making an effort to address the shortcomings of other humans. He connects the ax head to the notion of chastising someone. Gregory then contends that the ax head slips off the handle when moral and spiritual correction contravenes appropriate boundaries. Thus "an accidental killing" occurs when a person abandons or loses self-control when she or he is rebuking another person and delivers a form of correction that is extremely brutal and insensitive, which brings about the emotional and psychological devastation of another human being. He therefore urges people to practice self-control when seeking to correct other moral agents (Lienhard 2001, 305).

The Text in Contemporary Discussion

While Deut. 19:1-14 deals with the murder-versus-manslaughter distinction in homicide cases, it invites us to ensure that persons accused of crimes are given opportunity to defend themselves. This becomes a very important issue given the fact that emotion, relationships, and assumed moral obligation inform decision making and conclusions about culpability. The person or entity who is responsible for the administration of justice should practice self-control and strive to demonstrate conclusively, in an unbiased way, that a crime has been committed.

Deuteronomy 19:15-21: Suspect Evidence in Tribunals

The Text in Its Ancient Context

While Deut. 16:18—17:13 mandates multiple attestation for capital cases only, Deut. 19:15-21 requires accurate evidence to sustain a conviction in any matter that warrants adjudication. In its attempt to ensure *mišpāṭ*, Deut. 19:15-21 requires the presence of three items: (1) reliable evidence

(Deut. 19:15-16, 18b-19); (2) responsible leadership (Deut. 19:17); and (3) good judgment on the part of the magistrates (19:18a). Deuteronomy 19:17-18a indicates that the judges (*haššōpetîm*) and priests (*hakkōhănîm*) are responsible for supervising the administration of justice. Deuteronomy 19:18a instructs these persons to undertake a painstaking, meticulous investigation (*hêṭēb*). If it is discovered that a witness presents misleading information, then the magistrates are directed to impose on the false witness the punishment that would have befallen the accused. In its attempt to impose the penalty on the false witness, Deut. 19:21 specifies that the judge apply the *lex talionis*, the law of retaliation in ancient Israel. Exodus 21:22-25 and Lev. 24:17-21 provide additional attestation of the *lex talionis*. In each of the passages that cite this custom, the goal is to control the impulse to get revenge by placing limitations on punishment or compensation for wrongdoing; thus the reprisal or penalty for the false witness in Deut. 19:21 should be specific and should be in proportion to the crime.

The Text in the Interpretive Tradition

Flavius Josephus takes this code to mean that a minimum of two good witnesses is required for a conviction in any legitimate tribunal. According to Josephus, a reputable witness is male and is of virtuous character. He expands this legal tradition to include prohibitions against the testimonies of women and slaves being admissible in a court proceeding. At the heart of Josephus's problem with women is the belief that women are frivolous. He believes that slaves cannot provide good testimony because of their shameful, immoral being. What is more, Josephus works with the assumption that the prospect of freedom or punishment might influence the testimony of servants (*Ant.* 4:15).

The Text in Contemporary Discussion

Deuteronomy 19:15-21 advocates for truth-telling when reporting or reconstructing an event: it demands faithful witnesses. This code even requires punishment for the person who misrepresents an event or issue. This code, then, brings into play the importance of getting the story right. This type of thing is very much a concern not only in legal disputes but also in the business of reporting the news, and in reconstructions of history, for one can examine books about the history of the United States and notice that the story of blacks and other minorities fails to appear. Critical theorizing about history-writing invites us to raise the question about *whose story is being told.* We must raise the question: Is history-writing propaganda, or is it a trustworthy attempt to reconstruct a previous event or period? What is more, this business of accurate reporting is a real issue, given the ability to spread misinformation quickly through modern technology, particularly social media. With just a few keystrokes, someone can misrepresent a situation, and in seconds, this lie can be all over the world, doing enormous damage to a person's reputation. Truth-telling, the gist of Deut. 19:15-21, is critical.

Deuteronomy 20:1-20: The Conduct of War

The Text in Its Ancient Context

Two subgroups of regulations appear in Deut. 20:1-20. Verses 2-9 deals with gearing up for combat. In this regulation, the priests exhort the men not to fear the enemy, regardless of the size and strength of the enemy's infantry and cavalry, because YHWH is fighting this battle for Israel and will effect victory (*lĕhôšîaʿ*) on their behalf (Deut. 20:1-4). What is more, the officers (*šōṭĕrîm*) are told to strengthen the quality of the force in combat by weeding out the weak links; therefore, they identify three categories of men who are exempt from combat. Men who have planted a vineyard but have not eaten from it; men who have built a house but have not inhabited it; and men who have recently got engaged but have not consummated the marriage are excused from military service (Deut. 20:5-9). What is more, men who are scared to death are simply told to go home to avoid spreading timidity to the rest of the men who are preparing to attack a city and engage the enemy in combat.

Deuteronomy 20:10-20 details the method of warfare. The code assumes that Israel is on the offensive, for it says, "when you draw near" (*kî-tiqrab*). Deuteronomy 20:11-15 sets out policies for dealing with cities that are not within the borders of the Israelite community. This piece of legislation instructs Israel first to see if the people are unwilling to fight and are willing to surrender the city. If so, then Israel is to enslave the inhabitants of the city (*yihyû lĕkā lāmas*). If the inhabitants of the city decide to fight for their lives and defend their property, then Israel must attack and kill all the adult males of the city. While Israel may pillage the city, they are told to spare the women, infants, and the large cattle. Deuteronomy 20:16-20 sets out the policy for dealing with non-Israelite cities that are within the borders of Israel's land. In short, Israel is instructed to annihilate them. The Girgashites are missing from this list of peoples (see Deut. 7:1). This piece of legislation, however, tells Israel that while she is waging war she is not to kill the trees that bear fruit.

The Text in the Interpretive Tradition

Deuteronomy 20:1-20 has received considerable discussion among different groups. In Excursus 18, Tigay (1996) provides insight into Jewish views about this law on warfare. Citing M. Greenberg, he contends that the rabbis recognized the harshness of this code and, aligning themselves with a humanitarian ethic at odds with the moral ideas about the treatment of the Canaanites expressed in this regulation, rejected it. According to Tigay, Maimonides argued that this code represents an offer of surrender to all groups, not just to the Canaanites (Tigay 1996, 470–72).

Clement of Alexandria also reads this piece of legislation from a humanitarian perspective. He argues that it is merciful in that it exempts unfocused men from combat. For Clement, the fact that men who would be unenthusiastic about fighting in a war are to be excused from combat is a good example of compassion in the Deuteronomic regulations (Lienhard 2001, 307).

The Text in Contemporary Discussion

Deuteronomy 20:1-20 provides a divine sanction for the annihilation of the Canaanites. This bifurcation provides the theological basis for seeing one group as the people of God and all other people as not being the people of God. God is on one side and fighting against the other. This type of thinking provides theological justification for crusades, jihads, and other types of religious wars. What is more, seeing one group as good and another group as evil creates an ideology that spawns all types of atrocities toward other human beings. In light of the conversation surrounding terrorism and Christian-Muslim relations on the modern scene, the theological and moral ideology promulgated by Deut. 20:1-20 warrants sustained conversation.

Deuteronomy 21:1-9: Unsolved Homicide

The Text in Its Ancient Context

Deuteronomy 21:1-9 casts light on the handling of an unsolved homicide. The Hebrew term that appears as "body" in English translations of Deut. 21:1a is *ḥālāl.* The usage of this term suggests that some type of puncture wound contributed to the death of the person. A thematic similarity is present between this regulation and a law governing the commission of a homicide during a robbery in the Code of Hammurabi. In both instances, the notion of corporate culpability is in question. The law in the Code of Hammurabi calls for the city in which a homicide during a robbery occurred to incur the responsibility for the death of the person (Roth 1997, 85). Deuteronomy 21:1-9 links guilt for the homicide to the nearest city where the corpse was discovered. Whereas the Code of Hammurabi directs the city and its political leader to pay a fine, Deut. 21:1-9 requires the elders of the city nearest to the site where the body was discovered to bring a cow down to a place of flowing water, break her neck (*ʿōrep*), wash their hands over the cow, declare the noncomplicity of the city in the homicide, and ask YHWH not to hold the city responsible for the death of a fellow Israelite.

The Text in the Interpretive Tradition

Deuteronomy 21:1-9 deals with bloodguilt. This regulation contains an array of perplexing actions associated with breaking the neck of a heifer. Tigay (1997) indicates that rabbinic exegesis grouped this command with the goat sent to Azazel and the regulation on the red heifer, and that the rabbis contended that these three regulations are simply hard to understand. What is more, Tigay contends that due to the widespread, conspicuous practice of homicide, rabbis put an end to the carrying out of this ritual in the first century CE (Tigay 1997, 473).

The Text in Contemporary Discussion

Deuteronomy 21:1-9 invites leaders to consider the importance of ensuring that they are not complicit in wrongdoing. This regulation seeks to hold someone accountable for the loss of life, and it suggests that persons in leadership should be the first ones to affirm their innocence in the matter. Political leaders should work to guarantee that their policies do not victimize people. Religious leaders make sure the theologies, moral theories, and social programs they advance neither prevent individuals from actualizing the human potential nor contribute to the dehumanization of particular religious, ethnic, economic, or religious groups. Remember, the regulation on bloodguilt demands that leaders set the moral example of not taking part in criminal behavior and of respecting life.

Deuteronomy 21:10—25:19: Laws on Marriage, Family, and Miscellaneous Subjects

The Text in Its Ancient Context

Deuteronomy 21:10—25:19 governs a host of unconnected subjects. Deuteronomy 21:10-14 treats the duty of Israelite men to women they have captured in combat and subsequently married. While Deut. 21:10-14 permits exogamy, Deut. 7:3 prohibits it. This regulation instructs Israelite men to allow these women to mourn for one month. Once the month passes, he may have sex with the woman. If for some reason the male is not pleased with the woman (*'im-lō' ḥāpaṣtā*), he has the option of allowing her to leave. He, however, cannot sell her for money or into slavery. Deuteronomy 21:10-14 is the first of three codes on marriage in Deuteronomy 12–26. These other codes are 22:13-30 and 24:1-4. The fact that three codes governing marriage appear at different places in the Deuteronomic code supports claims that Deuteronomy 12–26 is a collection of legislations that come from different periods and sociopolitical conditions in the history of Israel.

Deuteronomy 21:15-17 provides guidelines on duties owed to the son of the hated wife (*haššĕnû'â*). The text specifies that if a man has two wives, the firstborn male child of the father receives the majority of the possessions of his father regardless of how his father felt about his mother. This law privileges the firstborn of the union between Israelite men and mainly Israelite women, not the firstborn of any woman that an Israelite man might marry, for a woman could have had children from a previous relationship, for example, women taken captive in war. This regulation works to ensure that property remains in the Israelite community.

Deuteronomy 21:18-21 specifies a procedure for the treatment of an unruly child. This regulation says that if a man has an insolent child (*bēn sôrēr*), he and his wife are to grab the child (*tāpśû bô*) and take him to the elders of the city and declare openly that the child is unruly. Deuteronomy 21:21 authorizes the men of the city to execute the child. By doing this, the men of the city send a message that disrespect for parents will not be tolerated. Parents, therefore, had to watch the village elders kill their son. It stands to reason that this incident casts an extremely negative shadow on the parents, for one cannot help but wonder what in the upbringing of the child could have culminated in this disrespectful behavior.

Deuteronomy 21:22—22:12 is another group of various regulations. This assortment of laws deals with the treatment of a corpse that has been hung (*tālâ*) on a tree (Deut. 21:22-23); the duty of one Israelite to another Israelite in regard to wandering livestock (Deut. 21:1-4); the practice of cross-dressing (Deut. 22:5); the extinction of animal species (Deut. 22:6-7); the avoidance of culpability for homicide (Deut. 22:8); and the promotion of harmony in society (Deut. 22:9-12).. While the codes on the promotion of harmony in society argue against mixing certain practices or items (e.g., different kinds of seed, animals of unequal strength, and different fabrics), there appears to be no logical or thematic points of contacts between these legislations, which treat animals that have wandered off, transvestitism, and bloodguilt in Israel.

Deuteronomy 22:13-30 deals with sex and marriage in ancient Israel. (1) Deuteronomy 22:13-21 indicates that a man has the option of imposing the death penalty on a young girl (*hanna'ar*) whom he has married and suspects has had intercourse with another man prior to their marriage. The parents of the young girl have the responsibility of refuting the charges, by presenting evidence of the young girl's virginity (*bĕtûlê hanna'ar*). Tikva Frymer-Kensky argues that the tokens of virginity were the blood-stained cloths from the bride's last menstrual cycle, thus proving that the bride was not pregnant (Frymer-Kensky 1992, 57). If the charge of unchastity is unsubstantiated, the complainant shall pay the father one hundred pieces of silver, and the accuser forfeits the right to divorce her. (2) Deuteronomy 22:22 prescribes the death penalty for a married woman who has sex with a man who is not her husband. It may be inferred from this piece of legislation that adultery is a voluntary sexual relationship of a married or engaged woman with a man to whom she is neither engaged nor married. (3) Deuteronomy 22:23-29 prescribes the death penalty for both the man and the woman in the case of a young girl who is a virgin and engaged, and who has been raped in the city. This regulation implies that the girl did not seek to prevent the rape. If the rape happens in the field, only the man shall be executed, for it is implied that the girl attempted to prevent the rape. According to Deut. 22:28-29, if a young girl, who is a virgin but is not engaged is raped, the rapist has to pay the victim's father fifty shekels of silver and marry the victim. He can never divorce her. (4) Deuteronomy 22:30 prohibits a woman from having sex with her son-in-law. No penalty is prescribed for this action.

Deuteronomy 23:1-8 denies the following people membership in the congregation of YHWH (*qāhāl yhwh*), that gathering of fully enfranchised Israelite males who are members of the YHWH-alone cult: (1) men with damaged sexual organs (23:1) and (2) the *mamzēr*, or bastard (23:2). There has been considerable discussion regarding the identity of the *mamzēr*; several options vie for our attention. Rabbi Akiba says a *mamzēr* is a person who is the offspring of a sexual relationship between near relatives that Israelite law prohibits. Rabbi Joshua says that a *mamzēr* is the offspring of any sexual relationship that was punishable by death in Israelite law. Thus the offspring of incest, an adulterous relationship, or a liaison with a person who is one of those ethnic groups with whom Israelites are forbidden to intermarry would be considered a *mamzēr* (*m. Yebam.* 4:13). Be mindful that a *mamzēr* is not simply a child who is born out of wedlock.

Deuteronomy 23:1-8 also denies the Ammonite or Moabite membership in the *qāhāl yhwh*, a cultic term for the assembly of fully enfranchised Israelite male citizens, which served as a pool from which men were taken for military service in the community. This gathering of adult males met to conduct large-scale political transactions, such as inaugurating a new monarch (Tigay 1996, 209–10; Mayes 1991, 315). Since the *qāhāl yhwh* is a religio-political designation, those persons who are excluded from membership in it are individuals who are deemed unacceptable by those principles that were consistent with the YHWH-alone cult and its political program.

Deuteronomy 23:9-14 regulates cleanliness in the army camp (*mahăneh*), that is, a gathering of Israelite men in the field and preparing for battle. This regulation prescribes purity on the part of the individual and the group. Reaching this level of hygiene requires that the soldiers in the camp expel for a short period men who have ejaculated during a dream, and that they readmit these individuals to the camp once they have cleansed themselves. Deuteronomy 23:9-14 also prescribes the designation of a site outside of the camp for the members to relieve themselves of human waste. Deuteronomy 23:14 requires the military camp to maintain a strict level of sanitation because

YHWH is walking around in the midst of the camp (*mithalēk bĕqereb maḥăneka*). If the military camp is polluted, it might provoke YHWH to abandon it, and the absence of YHWH from the camp guarantees Israel's defeat in combat. It is argued that these rules for cleanliness governed the gatherings of Israelite men during sacred pilgrimages, when the community reenacted its beliefs about YHWH and holy war (Christensen 2002, 543–44).

Deuteronomy 23:15-25 is another collection of miscellaneous legal traditions. These laws deal with slavery (Deut. 23:15-16), prostitution (Deut. 23:17-18), exacting interest on loans (Deut. 23:19-20), fulfilling vows (Deut. 23:21-23), and handling hunger while traveling (Deut. 23:24-25). Regulations on several of these subjects appear earlier in the Deuteronomic code. Both Deut. 23:15-16 and Deut. 15:12-17 deal with slavery. Deuteronomy 15:12-17 places no limits on the length of time an Israelite may enslave a non-Israelite, and Deut. 23:15-16 instructs Israel to become a safe haven for runaway slaves. The Code of Hammurabi prescribes the death penalty for providing asylum from capture to fugitive slaves (Roth 1997, 84). Since the general term for slave (*'ebed*) is in Deut. 23:15-17 and, since Deut. 15:12-17 required Israelites to release Hebrew slaves every seven years, it is probable that this code refers to persons who were Hebrews. Deuteronomy 23:17-18 prohibits Israelites from becoming temple prostitutes or from engaging in prostitution in general. The terms in Hebrew, which are at the center of this controversy, are *qādeš* ("male prostitute") and *qĕdešâ* ("female prostitute"). It has been argued that these terms, on the one hand, denote prostitution associated with festivals, rituals, vows, and other religious activities (Craigie 1976, 301–2), and that these terms, on the other hand, refer to prostitution in general (Tigay 1996, 215–16). What is more, this code leaves unanswered whether these prostitutes engaged in heterosexual or homosexual activity. What is clear, however, is that this law forbids accepting money for the payment of vows that comes from prostitution, regardless of the gender of the prostitute, for terms that denote both genders are in Deut. 23:19 (*zônâ*, a female prostitute, and *keleb*, a male prostitute).

Deuteronomy 23:19-20 regulates interest on loans to Israelites. The code states its position firmly by using the absolute negative particle "never" (*lō'*). This piece of legislation says never, ever charge your brother (*'āḥîkā*) interest on anything you give him. In the tradition of the Deuteronomic program, the Israelite is allowed to lend to the foreigner (*nokrî*), and he may assess as much interest to the food, money, and anything else loaned to this type of person as he desires. Clearly, membership in the community has its obligations, namely, to assist any brother who is in need and not to exacerbate his situation.

Deuteronomy 23:21-25 deals with the making of vows and travelers obtaining sustenance while they are en route to their destination. Deuteronomy 23:21-23 advises against making promises recklessly to YHWH. It encourages the moral agent to think about what is at stake when pledging to do something for YHWH and then failing to carry out the agreement. Deuteronomy 23:21-23 indicates that it is better for a person not to make a promise than it is to make one and then fail to do what one has said. No verse on the making of vows appears in the Covenant Code, and the fact that theological and philosophical points of contact are present between Eccles. 5:4-6 and Deut. 23:21-23 might be an instance of the influence of the wisdom traditions on the Deuteronomic school of thought (Mayes 1991, 321; Christensen 2002, 218).

Deuteronomy 23:24-25 regulates the amount of food one Israelite can consume from his neighbor's field while he is traveling. Traveling Israelites can eat as much as they want, but they are not allowed to package any of the food and take it with them. The traveler must recognize the property rights of the owner of the field (Craigie 1976, 321; Tigay 1996, 219).

Deuteronomy 24:1-4 deals with the issue of whether remarriage to a previous spouse after divorce from a former spouse is permissible. This regulation specifies that once a woman has been sent out of the house of her first husband and remarries and her second husband dies or hates her and sends her out of his house, the first husband is not permitted to remarry her. It is possible that this proscription prevents the first husband from gaining control of any property his former wife might have acquired from a previous remarriage (Frymer-Kensky 1992, 60). The law cites "not finding grace in the eyes of her husband" (*'im-lō' timṣa'-ḥēn*) and the presence of a "flaw" (*'erwat dābār*) as grounds for divorce, and the meaning of these phrases remained at the center of considerable controversy in ancient Israelite moral philosophizing. In Deuteronomy, divorce is the prerogative of the husband. In the Code of Hammurabi, a woman is permitted to leave her husband (Roth 1997, 107–8).

Deuteronomy 24:5—25:19 is another large block of laws that treats different subjects. Deuteronomy 24:5 exempts a newly married man from combat or from any duty linked to military service. This regulation contrasts with Deut. 20:7, which exempts a man that is engaged and has not consummated the marriage from combat or from any duty linked to military service.

Deuteronomy 24:6 sets limits on what can serve as collateral for loans by prohibiting lenders from taking possession of those essential items that borrowers would need to survive. The creditor is banned from seizing the millstones (*rēḥîm*) or the upper millstone (*rekeb*) from a borrower. These items were used to crush or grind grain so that it could become flour and be used in the making of bread. Without these items, the debtor might not have the ability to produce the main element in his or her daily diet (Christensen 2002, 572–73). Perhaps taking millstones or at least one of them from debtors was a commonplace in Israel, and Deut. 24:6 attempted to end this practice.

Deuteronomy 24:7 bans the kidnapping and selling of Israelites into slavery. This regulation says nothing about stealing or selling non-Israelites into slavery. Moreover, Deut. 24:7 conflicts with Deut. 15:12-18, for Deut. 15:12-18 permits the enslavement of Israelites. Deuteronomy 24:7, however, shares a socio-ethical point with Deut. 15:12-18, for as it has been noted, neither piece of legislation offers protection to all types of human beings. Note should be taken that Deut. 15:12-18 permits the perpetual enslavement of persons who are not Israelites, and that Deut. 24:7 assigns neither a penalty nor a consequence to either stealing or enslaving a person who is not an Israelite.

Deuteronomy 24:8-9 directs people in the community to pay attention to any possible skin infection. This code uses the term *ṣāra'at*, which is widely translated in most English versions as leprosy. The Hebrew term *ṣāra'at*, however, could denote a spectrum of skin diseases. The Israelites are admonished to deal immediately with any intimation that *ṣāra'at* is present by consulting the priests and following the treatment they prescribe.

Deuteronomy 24:10-15 defends the dignity of the poor. Deuteronomy 24:10-13 reminds creditors to practice self-control by not going into the house of a debtor to seize collateral for a loan. If a garment is used to guarantee the loan, the creditor is required to remain outside the debtor's house and allow the debtor to exit the house and surrender his garment. The creditor is reminded to return the garment before sunset so that the debtor will have covering for warmth at night. Deuteronomy 24:14-15 requires employers to pay the poor and economically vulnerable by the end of the day for the work they have provided. Payment should be made to both the Israelite worker and to the stranger (*gēr*) who works. This code cites fear of retribution from YHWH as the reason employers should pay these types of people before sunset.

Deuteronomy 24:16 deals with personal accountability. It specifies that parents should not be penalized for the behavior of their children, and that children should not be punished for the actions of their parents. At the center of this regulation is the assumption that a moral agent should be punished for his or her own actions. Points of contact are present between this legislation and the speech on personal accountability in Ezek. 18:1-32. One cannot help but notice that this notion of personal accountability does not apply to Ammonites, Moabites, or Amalekites, for the descendants of these groups are punished for the actions of their ancestors (Deut. 23:3-6).

Deuteronomy 24:17-21 prescribes social justice for the stranger (*gēr*), the fatherless (*yātôm*), and the widow (*'almānâ*). These types of persons appear in lists throughout Deuteronomy (Deut.14:22-29; 16:9-12, 13-15; 24:17-18, 19-22; and 26:12-15). According to these regulations, the stranger and the fatherless person should receive fair treatment in trials. The stranger, fatherless, and widow are entitled to gleanings in the field, and the prohibition is present against seizing the garment of a widow as collateral for a loan. This piece of legislation reminds one of Deut. 24:10-13.

Deuteronomy 25:1-3 places limitations on the number of lashes a judge may prescribe as punishment for a specific offense. This code argues that the magistrate may rule that the guilty party receives no more than forty lashes, because applying forty-one lashes to a human being is abusive and undermines the dignity of a human being. This seems quite odd in light of the fact that Deut. 25:1-3 demands that the guilty party receives a beating in public.

Deuteronomy 25:5-10 casts light on the institution of the *yābām*, that is, the responsibility of the brother-in-law. This custom requires that if a man dies without a male heir, the eldest living brother of the deceased has a moral obligation to marry the wife of the deceased and to impregnate her. According to Jewish tradition, a widow had to wait three months before she could enter a marriage with the eldest brother of her deceased husband (*m. Yebam.* 4:10). Deuteronomy 25:7 specifies the procedure to follow if the brother-in-law refuses to carry out the institution of the *yābām*. This institution is the backdrop against which to understand the Ruth-Boaz account in Ruth 4. Perhaps the goal of the codes in Deut. 25:5-10 was not to ensure male heirs as much as it was to ensure that property remained in the family (Mayes 1991, 328).

Deuteronomy 25:11-12 also seeks to ensure that families do not become extinct. It indicates that if two men are fighting, and the wife of one of the men in the altercation grabs the penis of the man with whom her husband is fighting, the magistrate is to amputate the hand of the woman. By demanding the maiming of the woman who grabs the sexual organ of the male, perhaps the goal of this regulation is to protect the ability of men to procreate so that sons can be born.

Deuteronomy 25:13-17 prescribes economic justice in Israel. It directs persons to use fair and equal standards in issues of commerce. Merchants are required to use the same type of weights when selling, buying, and exchanging goods. In other words, merchants are not to use one unit of measurement when they are selling goods and another unit for weight when buying goods. Fraudulent activity in commerce is to be avoided. Deuteronomy 25:16 contends that dishonest merchants are an abomination to YHWH.

The Text in the Interpretive Tradition

Subgroups of distinct legislations are present in Deut. 21:10—25:19. Present amongst these codes are laws on divorce. Due to the relevance of this issue, this section will discuss the laws on divorce. Codes on divorce in Deut. 21:10—25:19 (i.e., Deut. 21:10-14; 22:13-21, 28-29; 24:1-4) have an extensive history of conversation. Matthew 19:3-9 and Mark 10:2-12 suggest that divorce was at the center of considerable debate in Judaism during the time of Jesus. In both accounts, the Pharisees raise different issues about this subject. In Mark 10:2-12, the Pharisees ask about the legality of divorce. In Matt. 19:3-9, the issue is the reason a husband divorces his wife. Matthew 19:3-9 brings Deut. 24:1-4 into play, for it permits a husband to end the marriage if he dislikes or finds some flaw in his wife. According to the account in Matthew, Jesus declares that only sexual immorality (*porneia*) on the part of the woman is grounds for divorce.

Rabbinical schools often differed over the meaning of the "not finding favor" clause in Deut. 24:1. The school of Rabbi Shammai interpreted this clause to refer to sexual immorality on the part of the wife. The school of Rabbi Hillel argued that the "not finding favor" clause in Deut. 24:1 permits the ruining of a meal by a wife to suffice for divorce. Rabbi Akiba contends that the "not finding favor" clause in Deut. 24:1 means that finding a wife more beautiful than one's current wife is grounds for divorce (*m. Git.* 9:10). According to the account in Matthew, Jesus sides with the school of Rabbi Shammai on the meaning of the "not finding favor" clause in Deut. 24:1.

Augustine takes Deut. 24:1-4 to mean that husbands ought not be too quick to end their marriages. He contends that this is the reason Deut. 24:1-4 requires the husband to draft a bill of divorce. By drafting this document, the husband will have time to consider the situation. Thus, this piece of legislation is a tool designed to curb eagerness to dissolve the union and to provoke introspection on behalf of the husband regarding his marriage (Lienhard 2001, 315–16).

The Text in Contemporary Discussion

Marriage is a key institution in our society. Current reports suggest that between 40 and 50 percent of first-time marriages will end in divorce. This statistic is important because it is highly probable that divorce works to the detriment of children, and that ending marriages contributes to socioeconomic problems for society. Deuteronomy 24:1-4, then, invites us to explore the role husbands can play in reducing the divorce rate. At the center of this claim is the fact that Deut. 24:1 places the onus for initiating divorce on the husband, for it states that if he notices a "fault" in his wife, he has grounds for terminating the marriage. It is virtually impossible to imagine a wife (or a husband) who has no shortcomings. Husbands can adopt an ethos that promotes compassion and forgiveness toward their wives and thus strengthen marriage.

Deuteronomy 26:1-19: Two Liturgies, One Site

The Text in Its Ancient Context

Deuteronomy 26:1-15 contains guidelines for two ceremonies. Verses 1-11 delineate the procedure for offering the firstfruit (*rēʾšît*, Deut. 26:1-11). The code directs the presenter to place these items in a basket and to carry the basket to the central sanctuary. Once there, the basket will be given to the priest and placed in front of the altar. Included in this ritual is a declaration that reviews key events in the history of Israel. According to this speech, Jacob was a wandering or perishing Aramean (*ʾărammî ʾōbēd*) who went down into Egypt and whose people increased numerically and experienced oppression at the hand of Pharaoh and deliverance by YHWH (Deut. 26:5-9). Gerhard von Rad argues that this recitation is a very old declaration of faith from the lore of ancient Israel. G. E. Wright refers to the contents of this credo as the "mighty acts of God" (Christensen 2002, 632). This celebration closes by the presenter declaring that he brought the firstfruits from the land the deity gave to him (*hāʾădāmâ ʾăšer-nātattâ lî*).

Deuteronomy 26:12-15 regulates the triennial tithes, and Deut. 26:16-19 contains an admonition to remain faithful to YHWH. Deuteronomy 26:12-15 reminds Israel to share these tithes with the widow, stranger, fatherless, and Levites. Deuteronomy 26:12b specifies that the local villages are to be the venues for the distribution and consumption of the triennial tithes. Similar to the ritual for the presentation of the firstfruits, a declaration accompanies the presentation of the triennial tithes. It is conspicuous that no declaration accompanies the presentation of the triennial tithes in Deut. 14:28-29. Perhaps the addition of a speech to the presentation of the triennial tithe in Deut. 26:12-15 occurred at a later stage in the formation of the book of Deuteronomy (Merendino 1969, 371–72).

The Text in the Interpretive Tradition

The rabbis reflected on the meaning of Deut. 26:12-15, and attention to their musings reveals the following tenets: (1) Portions of the seven kinds, namely, wheat, barley, grapes, fig trees, pomegranates, olive trees, and honey, constituted the firstfruit offering; (2) there are people who can present firstfruits and make the public declaration; (3) there are people who can present firstfruits and not make the public declaration; (4) there are people who can neither present firstfruits nor make the public declaration; (5) firstfruits should be brought to the central sanctuary between Pentecost and the Festival of Booths, which is between late spring/early summer and early fall (*m. Bik.* 1:1-10). Deut. 26:13 directs the presenter to perform this ritual *in the presence of the deity*, and elsewhere in Deuteronomy, where this phrase appears, it denotes the official sanctuary. While depositing and allocating the poor-tithe occurred in the local villages, it is probable that the Jerusalem temple is the site for the ritual accompanying the poor-tithe, that is, the tithe in the third year (Mayes 1991, 336).

The Text in Contemporary Discussion

Deuteronomy 26:12-15 points out that a class of oppressed social groups constituted Israelite society. While this piece of legislation identifies members of this socioeconomic category, the reader must keep in mind that others in ancient Israelite society constituted this class. Once the poor-tithe had been allocated and consumed, these types of persons returned to eking out their existence with virtually no one to help them. This circumstance, then, placed them at the mercy of creditors and other nefarious types of persons in ancient Israel.

Deuteronomy 26:12-15, then, invites the present reader to make the following claim: the onus rests on someone or some entity to work to improve permanently the circumstance of the vulnerable in society. Oppression works against the chances of human beings developing self-respect and becoming self-determining moral subjects. This passage invites social institutions, namely religious organizations, to do more than provide temporary relief to the oppressed: it invites them to formulate strategies and adopt legislations that seek to remove the causes of oppression in society. Thus these texts challenge those religious communities for whom the Hebrew Bible is normative for faith and praxis to take seriously its duty to effect social justice among some of the most distressed individuals in our communities.

Deuteronomy 27:1—28:68: Blessings and Cursings

The Text in Its Ancient Context

Form criticism suggests that Deuteronomy contains the following elements: (1) Historical introduction(s) (Deut. 1:1—11:32); (2) stipulations of the agreement (Deut. 12:1—26:19); (3) citation of blessings and punishments for keeping or violating the covenant (Deut. 27:1—28:68); and (4) miscellaneous materials (Deut. 29:1—34:12). The following are major features of Hittite treaties: (1) The self-identification of the suzerain; (2) the historical recapitulation, in which the suzerain cites mercies shown to the vassal; (3) the stipulations of the agreement; (4) reiteration of the need for frequent rehearsal or review of the covenant; and (5) a curse and blessing for either violating or keeping the covenant. Although fragmentary, the data suggest Assyrian treaties contained the following elements: (1) Lists of witnesses; (2) the stipulations of the agreement; and (3) curses for violating the covenant (Mayes 1991, 32). Therefore, it is widely accepted that treaty traditions in the ancient Near East are the backdrop against which to discuss the present structure of Deuteronomy (Weinfeld 1992, 146–57).

Hittite and Assyrian treaties contain concluding sections that cite curses for violating the agreement. Deuteronomy 27:1—28:68 contains a series of curses and blessings. It appears to have been appended to Deuteronomy 12–26 by the redactor, for this narrative connects with the account that ended abruptly in Deut. 11:29-32. The presence of these series of curses and blessings ensures that the pattern of the final form of Deuteronomy more closely resembles that of treaty traditions in the ancient Near East.

The Text in the Interpretive Tradition

Moses and the elders instruct the people to erect stones, cover them with plaster, and write this teaching (*hattôrâ hazzôʾt*) on them (Deut. 27:1-8). While the text is silent on the specifics of "this teaching," contemporary Jewish scholarship on this verse suggests that "this teaching" denotes the regulations in Deuteronomy 12–26 (Tigay 1996, 248). What is more, rabbinic exegesis of this passage claims that the Israelite community wrote the contents of "this teaching" in seventy languages on the stones (*m. Sotah* 7:5).

Deuteronomy 27:4-5 instructs the community to construct an altar on Mt. Ebal, where the Levites, with six of the tribes that composed Israel, cite twelve morally and theologically reprehensible behaviors. The Levites also declare a malediction (*'ārar*), a divinely established, permanent condition of disaster, trouble, suffering, and pain in the lives of those who perpetrate them (Deut. 27:15-26; 28:16-68). Deut. 27:15-26 refers to twelve actions that are surreptitious but known by YHWH; consequently, YHWH will punish those who commit these offenses (Tigay 1996, 251–57). The text indicates that YHWH will use a nation from afar (*gôy mērāḥôq*) to punish Israel. The identity of the nation from afar (*gôy mērāḥôq*) spoken of in Deut. 28:47-68 that will subjugate Israel is unknown. In light of the calamities that befell Israel in 722 BCE and 586 BCE, Assyria and Babylon are often cited as this nation from afar (Tigay 1996, 269).

Deuteronomy 27:12 and 28:1-14 indicate that six of the other larger kinship subgroups that constitute Israel should stand on Mt. Gerizim and invoke a blessing (*bārak*), a divinely established, permanent condition of favor, happiness, health, fecundity, and peace in the lives of those who obey the contents of this teaching. Basil the Great (329–379 CE), one of the three Cappadocians fathers, applies an allegorical reading to this text by associating the basket in Deut. 28:5 with the soul, and argues that if the soul gets developed, it can be prosperous, that is, filled with good things. According to Basil, it must be nurtured and refreshed by heavenly waters (Lienhard 2001, 321). Current Pentecostal biblical scholarship would argue that growth of the soul comes from allowing the Spirit of God to nurture one's soul (Warrington 2008, 46–48).

The Text in Contemporary Discussion

Deuteronomy 27:15-26 lists twelve evil curses. These maledictions condemn seedy actions that are perpetrated in secret or without an audience. Since these deeds are carried out in private, it is easy for one to think that these actions are less dangerous than those moral actions that are noticeable by all and are easily detectable. Deuteronomic moral thought invites us to consider that furtive wicked deeds are a detriment to the community. Thematic similarities are present between key assumptions about the moral agent that inform Deut. 27:15-26 and the account about the Ring of Gyges in book 2 of Plato's *Republic*. Both of these accounts bring into play the tenet that clandestine actions reveal the true character and real moral qualities of a moral agent. Actions done in secret neither hide our character nor obfuscate those values that underlie them: they reveal them.

Deuteronomy 29:1—30:20: Moses Speaks

The Text in Its Ancient Context

Deuteronomy 29–30 contains another sermon by Moses. In these chapters, Israel is standing on the brink of entering the promised land, and Moses once again rehearses the deeds of YHWH in the life of Israel. The most conspicuous of these actions is the tradition of YHWH's rescuing an oppressed group of slaves from bondage in Egypt, the nucleus of biblical Israel, and of YHWH's entering a formal relationship with this group at Horeb. Moses admonishes Israel to abide by this covenant. He cites Sodom, Gomorrah, Admah, and Zeboiim, and contends that the fate of these cities is what lies on the horizon if Israel violates the agreement YHWH has made with them. These chapters, therefore, continue that type of thinking that is widespread in Deuteronomic thought by making obedience to the law a necessary condition for well-being, fecundity, peace, and good fortune. Speeches of Moses introduce and are appended to the large block of law and curses and blessings in Deuteronomy 12–28. These orations "bookend" the nucleus of the book.

The Text in the Interpretive Tradition

Deuteronomy 29–30 reviews the journey of the Israelites from Horeb to Moab. What is more, this account revels in the defeat of Sihon and Og, two monarchs whom the Israelites engaged in combat on their way to the promised land. These chapters mention both Horeb and Moab, indicating that YHWH made covenants with Israel in both of these locations. The speech concludes with Moses admonishing the people to be faithful to YHWH by choosing life over death. It is argued that Deuteronomy 29–30 contains the concluding charge of the book (Craigie 1976, 356).

Deut. 29:14 contains a very interesting phrase. It says that the covenant was with those who are not here with us today (*'ăšer 'ênennû pōh 'immānû*). This wording attracts attention, because elsewhere in Deuteronomy the narrator says that covenants were made at Horeb (Deut. 1:6) and at Moab (Deut. 1:5; 29:1). Since the people with whom YHWH cut a covenant at Horeb died in the wilderness, Deut. 5:2 implies that YHWH was cutting a covenant with those who were present at Moab. Now, Deut. 29:14 talks about YHWH cutting a covenant *with those who are not present*. About whom is the text speaking? Rabbinic exegesis contends that those "not present" in Deut. 29:14 refers to the souls of future generations of Jews. YHWH is cutting a covenant with those who are present at Moab as well as with those Jews who are forthcoming (Tigay 1996, 278).

The notion of YHWH cutting a covenant with Jews was a source of discussion in the early Christian community. The author of the epistle to the Hebrews says: "In speaking of 'a new covenant,' he has made the first one obsolete" (Heb. 8:13 NRSV). He also introduces Jer. 31:31-34 into the discussion of soteriology and Christology, arguing that the work of Jesus has brought into play a new, different mechanism for people to maintain a relationship with God. This covenant is not tied to the ongoing offering of animal sacrifices for atonement, but is linked to the act of accepting by faith the salvific atoning work of Jesus. For the writer of Hebrews, the first covenant, the one that was instituted at Horeb/Sinai and Moab, has been superseded by the covenant through Jesus.

The Text in Contemporary Discussion

The "prosperity gospel" is present in many religious communities. This type of theology argues that good health, money, power, cars, and temporal success are how a right relationship with God is measured. In fact, it has become quite fashionable in many Christian circles to claim that obtaining possessions, capital, affluence, power, physical well-being, and good fortune is the entitlement of a person who is in good standing with God, via Jesus. At the center of this phenomenon is a type of preaching, teaching, and exposition of the Bible that reads the text through the lens of prosperity, perhaps through the lens of Deut. 30:15. This trend in theologizing brings into play a host of interpretive and theological issues, chief of which is an approach to biblical hermeneutics that embraces one, single idea or principle as the key criterion for understanding the Bible. In the case at hand, enjoying great wealth, success, and good fortune in this world is the theme that unites all of Scripture. While portions of the Bible speak about prosperity, a close look at prophecies in Amos, Jeremiah, and Micah reveals that a host of other principles are also present. Perhaps the reader should be wary of all forms of hermeneutical monism and embrace a framework for reading the Bible that affirms the texts' diversity of thought surrounding the moral life.

Deuteronomy 31:1—34:12: Concluding Matters

The Text in Its Ancient Context

Deuteronomy 31–34 casts light on several important speeches, deeds, and events in the final days of Moses: (1) The transfer of leadership to Joshua (Deut. 31:7-8, 14-15, 23; 34:9). Traditions that anticipate this event appear in Deut. 1:38 and 3:28. Moreover, Num. 27:12-23 contains an alternative account of Joshua's appointment as the next leader of Israel. (2) The command to read the law every seven years during the Festival of Booths/Tabernacles (Deut. 31:9-13). (3) The construction of a poem, the Song of Moses, which speaks about Israel's inclination toward apostasy and the proclivity of YHWH to punish Israel for her unfaithfulness (Deut. 32:1-43). A poem by this title appears in Exod. 15:1-21, but it celebrates the deliverance of Israel from slavery in Egypt. (4) Moses' blessing of the tribes of Israel (Deut. 33:1-29). Genesis 49:1-28 preserves the traditions that Jacob uttered when he blessed those twelve tribes that afterward would constitute Israel. (5) The death and eulogy of Moses (Deut. 34:1-12). Deuteronomy 31–34 reflects the essence of the Deuteronomic program, namely, that observing the laws of YHWH and commitment to the exclusive worship of YHWH bring prosperity.

The Text in the Interpretive Tradition

Because the Song of Moses (Deut. 32:1-43) contains several individual literary units that imply moral and theological ideas, it has been the object of considerable reflection among the early church fathers. John Cassian (360–435 CE) took Deut. 32:7 to mean that individuals should take advantage of the wisdom of the elders and, when possible, they should confer with church leaders when unsure about decisions regarding ethical and theological matters. John Chrysostom (347–407 CE) took Deut. 32:15 to mean that the moral agent should guard against the dangers of abundance, for according to Deut. 32:15, bounty often leads to ungratefulness and to a set of other behaviors that cause one to ignore his or her need for God (Lienhard 2001, 332–34).

The Text in Contemporary Discussion

Israel was in transition: it was on the brink of entering the promised land, and Moses had taken them as far as he could take them. However, he understands that if the community does reach the promised land, they will not reach it under his leadership. The Song of Moses provides a paradigm for transitioning leadership in religious organizations. It invites leaders to appreciate several items: (1) Leaders need to recognize that their time for supervising and providing leadership to a community will expire; (2) leaders can be gracious to individuals in the organization when they depart; (3) leaders can depart and pass on some insight into what they foresee will be challenges for the success of the organization; and (4) leaders can find public ways to support their successors before they depart. Leaders can finish strong.

Works Cited

Bennett, Harold. 2002. *Injustice Made Legal.* Grand Rapids: Eerdmans.

Christensen, Duane L. 2001. *Deuteronomy 1:1—21:9.* Nashville: Thomas Nelson.

———. 2002. *Deuteronomy 21:10—34:12.* Nashville: Thomas Nelson.

Copan, Paul. 2011. *Is God a Moral Monster? Making Sense of the Old Testament God.* Grand Rapids: Baker Books.

Craigie, Peter C. 1976. *Deuteronomy.* Grand Rapids: Eerdmans.

———. 1983. *Ugarit and the Old Testament.* Grand Rapids: Eerdmans.

Danby, Herbert, trans. 2011. *The Mishnah: Translated from the Hebrew with Introduction and Brief Explanatory Notes.* Peabody, MA: Hendrickson.

Drinkard, Joel, E. 2007. "Gates in the Old Testament." In *The New Interpreters' Dictionary of the Bible.* Volume 2. Edited by Katherine Doob Sakenfeld. Nashville: Abingdon Press.

Erskine, Noel Leo. 2005. *From Garvey to Marley: Rastafari Theology.* Gainesville: University of Florida Press.

Freire, Paulo. 2005. *Pedagogy of the Oppressed.* Translated by Myra Bergman Ramos. New York: Continuum.

Frymer-Kensky, Tikva. 1992. "Deuteronomy." In *The Women's Bible Commentary.* Edited by Carol A. Newsom and Sharon H. Ringe. Louisville: Westminster John Knox.

Gutiérrez, Gustavo. 1999. *A Theology of Liberation.* Translated and Edited by Sister Caridad Inda and John Eagleson. Maryknoll, NY: Orbis.

Hamilton, Jeffries M. 1992. *Social Justice and Deuteronomy: The Case of Deuteronomy 15.* Atlanta: Scholars Press.

Harrelson. Walter J. 1985. *The Ten Commandments and Human Rights.* Philadelphia: Fortress Press.

Hopkins, Dwight N. 1999. *Introducing Black Theology of Liberation.* Maryknoll, NY: Orbis.

Houston, Walter J. 2003. "Towards an Integrated Reading of the Dietary Laws of Leviticus." In *The Book of Leviticus.* Edited by Rolf Rendtorff and Robert A. Kugler. Atlanta: Society of Biblical Literature.

Josephus, Flavius. 1985. "The Antiquities of the Jews." In *Josephus: Complete Works.* Translated by William Whiston. Grand Rapids: Kregel.

Kimball, Charles. 2008. *When Religion Becomes Evil.* San Francisco: HarperOne.

Knight, Douglas A. 2011. *Law, Power, and Justice in Ancient Israel.* Louisville: Westminster John Knox.

Levinson, Bernard M. 1997. *Deuteronomy and the Hermeneutics of Legal Innovation.* New York: Oxford University Press.

Lienhard, Joseph T., ed. 2001. *Exodus, Leviticus, Numbers, Deuteronomy.* Ancient Christian Commentary on Scripture, Old Testament 3. Downers Grove, IL: InterVarsity Press.

Mayes, A. D. H. 1991. *Deuteronomy.* NCB. Grand Rapids: Eerdmans.

Merendino, Rosario P. 1969. *Das Deuteronomische Gesetz.* Bonn: Peter Hanstein.

Milgrom, Jacob. 2004. *Leviticus.* CC. Minneapolis: Fortress Press.

Miller, Patrick D. 2000. *The Religion of Ancient Israel.* Louisville: Westminster John Knox.

Nelson, Richard. 2002. *Deuteronomy.* OTL. Louisville: Westminster John Knox.

Niditch, Susan. 1993. *War in the Hebrew Bible: A Study in the Ethics of Violence.* New York: Oxford University Press.

Nielsen, Kai. 1990. *Ethics without God.* Amherst, NY: Prometheus.

Peterson, Michael, William Hasker, Bruce Reichenbach, and David Basinger. 2012. *Reason and Religious Belief: An Introduction to the Philosophy of Religion.* New York: Oxford University Press.

Phipps, William E. 1996. *Muhammad and Jesus: A Comparison of the Prophets and Their Teachings.* New York: Continuum.

Rofé, Alexander. 2002. *Deuteronomy: Issues and Interpretation.* OTS. London: T&T Clark.

Ross, Allen. 2002. *Holiness to the Lord.* Grand Rapids: Baker Academic.

Roth, Martha T. 1997. *Law Collections from Mesopotamia and Asia Minor.* Atlanta: Scholars Press.

Seibert, Eric A. 2009. *Disturbing Divine Behavior: Troubling Old Testament Images of God.* Minneapolis: Fortress Press.

Sneed, Mark. 1999. *Concepts of Class in Ancient Israel.* Atlanta: Scholars Press.

Spinoza, Baruch. 2001. *Theological Political Treatise.* Translated by Samuel Shirley. Indianapolis: Hackett.

Stevens, Marty. 2006. *Temples, Tithes, and Taxes: The Temple and the Economic Life of Ancient Israel.* Peabody, MA: Hendrickson.

Tigay, Jeffrey H. 1996. *Deuteronomy.* Philadelphia: Jewish Publication Society.

Warrington, Keith. 2008. *Pentecostal Theology: A Theology of Encounter.* London: T&T Clark.

Weinfeld, Moshe. 1991. *Deuteronomy 1-11.* AB. New York: Doubleday.

———. 1992. *Deuteronomy and the Deuteronomic School.* Winona Lake, IN: Eisenbrauns.